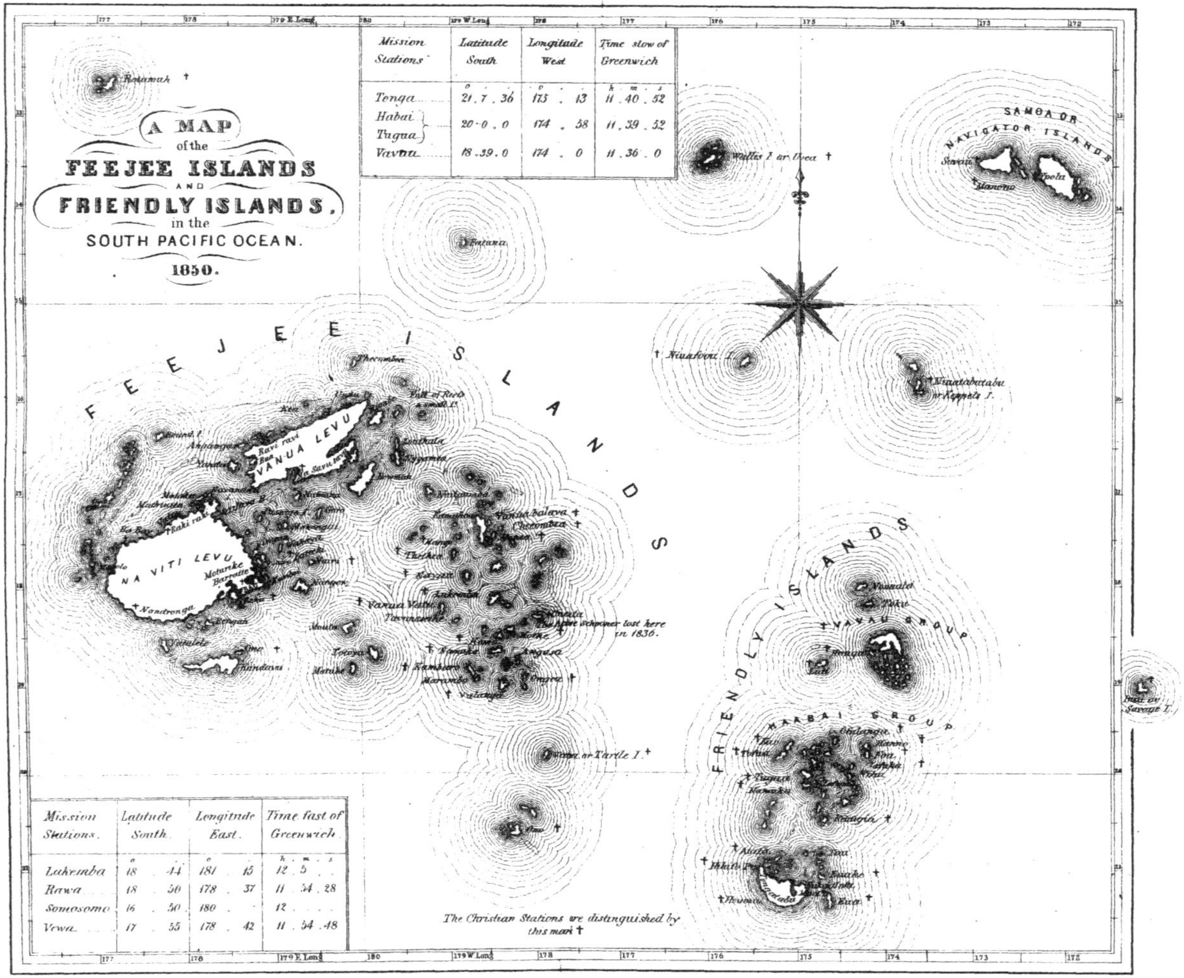

A MAP of the FEEJEE ISLANDS AND FRIENDLY ISLANDS, in the SOUTH PACIFIC OCEAN.

1850.

Mission Stations	Latitude South	Longitude West	Time slow of Greenwich
	° ′ ″	° ′	h. m. s
Tonga	21 . 7 . 36	175 . 13	11 . 40 . 52
Habai, Tugua	20 · 0 . 0	174 . 58	11 . 39 . 52
Vavau	18 . 39 . 0	174 . 0	11 . 36 . 0

FEEJEE ISLANDS

NA VITI LEVU

VANUA LEVU

FRIENDLY ISLANDS

HAABAI GROUP

VAVAU GROUP

SAMOA OR NAVIGATOR ISLANDS

Rotumah

Wallis I. or Uea

Niuafoou I.

Ono or Turtle I.

A schooner lost here in 1836.

Mission Stations.	Latitude South.	Longitude East.	Time fast of Greenwich
	° ′	° ′	h. m. s
Lakemba	18 . 44	181 . 15	12 . 5 . .
Rewa	18 . 50	178 . 37	11 . 54 . 28
Somosomo	16 . 50	180 . .	12 . . .
Vewa	17 . 55	178 . 42	11 . 54 . 48

The Christian Stations are distinguished by this mark ✝

Lith. of Sarony & Major 117 Fulton St. N.Y.

MISSIONS

IN THE

TONGA AND FEEJEE ISLANDS,

AS DESCRIBED IN THE JOURNALS OF

Rev. Walter Lawry.

REVISED BY DANIEL P. KIDDER.

New-York:
PUBLISHED BY LANE & SCOTT,
FOR THE SUNDAY-SCHOOL UNION OF THE METHODIST EPISCOPAL CHURCH,
200 Mulberry-street.
JOSEPH LONGKING, PRINTER.
1852.

PREFACE

OF THE AMERICAN EDITOR.

THE present volume contains all the journals of the Rev. Mr. Lawry, relating to the Tonga and Feejee Islands, that have been published up to the present time.

This matter was originally published in the "Notices" of the Wesleyan Missionary Society, and subsequently in two volumes, entitled "First and Second Missionary Visits," &c.

The two volumes having been published two years apart did not correspond in type and style of execution; the second being greatly superior in its appearance to the first, gave evident proof of the unexpected interest with which the former journals had been read, and of the high rank to which their merits entitled them.

The two volumes are now combined in one, and presented in an appropriate and uniform style of typography. They are also illustrated with additional engravings. For a clear statement of the character of Mr. Lawry, and the circumstances in which his voyages were made, the reader is referred to the prefaces of the English editor, the Rev. Mr. Hoole, one of the General Secretaries of the Wesleyan Missionary Society.

Seldom, if ever, has there been placed upon record a more interesting narrative of the progress and power of the gospel than the present. It will be read with unfeigned delight by all who love the Saviour, and will be handed down to posterity as a proof of what moral triumphs the gospel is capable of achieving over the most degraded heathen and the fiercest cannibals.

NEW-YORK, *February*, 1852.

PREFACE.

The Rev. Walter Lawry is the General Superintendent of the Wesleyan Society's Missions in New-Zealand, and Visitor of the Missions in the Friendly Islands and Feejee Islands.

This missionary, now truly venerable by age and services, proceeded to New South Wales in the year 1817, with the hopes of communicating religious instruction to the settlers and convicts, and to the native inhabitants of that country. In 1820 he was appointed to commence a mission in the Friendly Islands; he found an opportunity of proceeding to Tonga, or, as it is often called, Tonga-Tabu, in June, 1822; and he remained on the island, exposed to many privations, and to dangers and anxieties innumerable, until November, 1823, when he returned to New South Wales.

After an absence of nearly twenty-five years, he has again had an opportunity of visiting the Friendly Islands, now no longer idolatrous and uncivilized, but converted to the faith of Christ; and the interest of the Journal, now first published separate and entire, is greatly heightened by the remarkable contrast he witnessed in the character and state of the people when compared with their savage and Pagan condition. It is almost superfluous to commend to the reader's attention Mr. Lawry's graphic descriptions of all he witnessed. He has had the advantage of old acquaintance with the scenes he visited; he writes under the liveliest emotions of grateful joy; and his naturally lucid style is rendered more effective by the warmth of the feelings by which he was animated.

If one portion of Mr. Lawry's Journal may claim a pre-eminence of interest, it is that which relates to the Feejee Islands. Of this large and populous group of islands, there was no accurate detailed information, until lately, except by means of missionary publications. And what a picture of fallen human nature, and of bold and successful missionary enterprise, is here presented to us! The Feejeean exhibits no deficiency of intellectual capacity, no deterioration of outward form; he inhabits some of the most lovely and fertile spots upon the globe, supplying the necessaries and luxuries of life in return for a very small amount of labour; and yet he is the most habitual and ferocious cannibal that has yet been discovered. For the missionary to find him in this state, and to aim at his conversion and salvation, was simultaneous. The object was philanthropic; the experiment was most hazardous; the success has been complete. No undertaking could have appeared more hopeless than the conversion of these savages; and nothing can be more wonderful than the glorious success which the missionaries have witnessed. The doctrines of revelation alone enable us to fathom the depravity of the heathen, to estimate the motives of those who seek their salvation, and to account for the powerful and divine results of their labors.

Great pains have been taken in this volume to present a complete view of the present state of this part of Polynesia. The map is the most perfect one which has yet been published, having been corrected by Captain Buck. He has added the results of his own observations to the valuable information furnished by Commodore Wilkes, who surveyed the islands for the government of the United States of America.

The wood-cuts relate chiefly to the Feejee Islands, and are illustrative of the manners and appearance of those remote localities, of which they are a correct representation. A few views of the Friendly Islands, sent by the Rev. Charles Tucker, were received too late to be rendered available.

A history of the missions in New-Zealand, and in the Friendly and Feejee Islands, would be a most welcome addition to our ecclesiastical records; as it would detail some of the most remarkable triumphs of Christianity over Paganism, and idolatry, and savage life, which have ever been witnessed since the days of the apostles. Until this desirable task shall be accomplished, the journals, and letters, and separate narratives of the missionaries will continue to be read as a valuable mine of information. We refer particularly to the Memoir of the Rev. William Cross, by the late Rev. John Hunt; the Memoir of Mrs. Cargill, by her husband; the Journals of the lamented Rev. John Waterhouse, as published in the Missionary Notices for May, 1841, and February and March, 1844; and the letters and journals of the missionaries, as they have appeared in the Missionary

Notices, for the last thirty years. It may be safely conjectured that an attentive perusal of Mr. Lawry's Journal will give an interest to the older documents now referred to, even surpassing that which they justly claimed on their first appearance.

Meantime it is hoped that the account of the Friendly Islands, and of the Feejee Islands, appended to this volume, embracing many particulars of history, description, and statistics, not comprised in the Journal of the Missionary Visit, will be found worthy of perusal and reference.

The very extraordinary change which has been effected by Christian teaching within the life of one generation in these distant islands of the sea, is just cause of thankfulness and joy; but it should be remembered, that it has been effected at the cost of much physical and mental suffering on the part of the missionaries and their families, who have been "separated from their brethren" for the accomplishment of this great work,—many valuable lives have been sacrificed; many widows and orphans are left to the charity of the churches; the laborers now in the field are in circumstances which demand our kindest sympathy, and our most earnest prayers in their behalf.

The missions themselves are not in any considerable degree self-supporting; they require costly supplies of food and clothing, and goods for barter, which have to be conveyed over half the world.

The missionary ship was never more useful than at the present, and never more indispensable to the maintenance of the missions.

The creation of a literature for a people entirely

ignorant of letters, is, in itself, a work of great magnitude. The reduction of the languages to grammatical rule and order; the compilation of vocabularies; the translation of the Holy Scriptures, and of works of religious and general information; the toils of printing and book-binding, and the right distribution of books as they issue from the press,—are all in the hands of the missionaries; and the cost of furnishing materials for the publications, and support for the labourers, is easy to be imagined.

The Missionary Committee undertake the arrangement and dispatch of the required supplies; but they depend on the society at large, and on the Christian public, for the means by which the good work is to be sustained.

Many groups of "isles" in the South Pacific Ocean, still "wait for the law" of Jehovah: they will probably receive it from those islands which are already Christian; but, in order to this desirable result, the ground now won must be maintained, and the ranks of the missionary army must be speedily and largely recruited.

It is hoped that the readers of this volume will permit themselves to be moved to a devout and practical sympathy with this important undertaking. Missionaries are "the messengers of the churches:" they are comparatively few in number, but they do the work assigned to the churches by their Lord and Master; and in the discharge of their representaive duties they have a just claim on our prayers and kindest sympathies, and on our free and liberal support. They who come to behold Christ's glory in his kingdom "bring their silver and their gold with them."

It is worthy of remark, that the missions to the Feejee and Friendly Islands were commenced without any political motive, and without any protection or patronage, or help from the government. In this respect they are similar to the missions in New-Zealand, which, thirty years ago, were commenced by men whose sole desire was to reclaim the savage natives to the knowledge of God, and the blessings of Christianity. The voluntary efforts of religious philanthropy have sustained these missions from their beginning, and will no doubt continue to do so. Small spots of earth, and small communities of men, of whom governments cannot afford to take the cognizance and protection, are specially devolved on the care of the Church of Christ. New-Zealand would have been converted without treaties or colonization; and however much the inhabitants may be ultimately benefited by the influx of Europeans, the missionaries and their converts had no reference to any such results. So, also, the Friendly Islands and the Feejees receive the law of Jehovah without any prospect of improving their political condition or relations. Christ's "kingdom is not of this world," and his kingdom will come whether the world wills it or not; but our nation has already won its brightest honors from the labors of its missionary sons, and is deriving from their results some of its most solid advantages.

Nevertheless, it cannot be too distinctly set forth, that the object of the missions described in this volume, is the propagation of Christianity, the pure and peaceful religion of the Holy Scriptures. The men who are appointed to the duty of conveying the gospel to the Pagan islanders have been chosen for their employment in consequence of their personal knowledge of religion, and their ability to teach it. Their high and spiritual aim is, at the first, not at all understood by the dark and debased tribes of men whom they seek to convert. But the savages soon discover the purity and truth of the missionary character; and listen with attention and respect to their instructions. It does not surprise the missionaries when they witness very striking effects produced by their teaching on the minds of their disciples. In every country, and in society the most enlightened and civilized, fallen man is not saved from the guilt and dominion of sin without "sorrow after a godly sort," and the exercise of penitential prayer, and faith, "repentance toward God, and faith in our Lord Jesus Christ;" and every Christian has known the transition, more or less sudden, from the "darkness" of spiritual ignorance and guilt, to the "light" of divine knowledge and peace, "and from the power of Satan unto God." The same process is experienced by the South-Sea islander, when the word of God comes to him "in power and in the Holy Ghost;" and in the following narrative many such are allowed to describe the feelings of their hearts, and their progress and advancement in the knowledge of divine truth. We may learn from these examples, that "the same Lord over all is rich unto all them that call upon him."

The missionaries take with them the manners and arts of civilized life, and become the patterns of their flocks, whose desire it is to copy their example. Thus the gospel is the pioneer of civilization; the untutored children of nature become acquainted with the decencies and amenities of Christian society; the fear of God becomes the beginning of wisdom; the rudiments of education are received with gratitude; books are compiled and translated; the printing-press multiplies copies of them; information is diffused; the advantages of commerce are appreciated; and whole communities, which a short time ago were savage in their nature, and barbarous and repulsive in their manners, now greet with welcome the intercourse of men of intelligence, and vie with their European visitors in Christian courtesy and politeness.

In every respect, missions are charities of the highest kind. Fallen and sinful men are converted from the error of their ways; barbarous tribes, which had ceased almost to be regarded as human, are restored to a place of honor in the family of man; philanthropic exertion has the high reward of complete success; the merciful purposes of our Saviour Christ are accomplished; and God is glorified. Who will not exclaim, "Let Christian missions be perpetuated, and let them be extended throughout the widest continents, and to the remotest islands of the sea?"

WESLEYAN MISSION-HOUSE,
BISHOPSGATE-STREET-WITHIN, LONDON.
March 11th, 1850.

CONTENTS.

CHAPTER I.

VISIT TO THE FRIENDLY ISLANDS.

CHAPTER II.

VISIT TO THE FEEJEE ISLANDS.

CHAPTER III.

MISSIONARY CRUISE AMONG THE FEEJEE ISLANDS.

CHAPTER IV.

REVIEW AND RETURN.

APPENDIX.

ILLUSTRATIONS.

DEPARTURE OF THE "JOHN WESLEY" FROM SOUTHAMPTON.

MISSIONS

IN THE

FRIENDLY AND FEEJEE ISLANDS.

CHAPTER I.

VISIT TO THE FRIENDLY ISLANDS.

AUCKLAND, NEW-ZEALAND, *May 29th*, 1847.—We left Auckland in the missionary brig,* "John Wesley," on her first voyage to the Friendly and Feejee Islands, with Mr. and Mrs. Ford, and two children, Mr. and Mrs. Malvern, and one child, Mr. and Mrs. Daniel, Mr. and Mrs. Amos, and Mr. and Mrs. Davis.

June 3d. After several days' fair wind and smooth water, we were met by a gale right ahead. The sea wrought, and was very boisterous; the rain poured in heavy torrents; the lightning glared, and the thunder

* The "John Wesley" missionary ship sailed from Southampton on her first voyage, November 21st, 1846. This beautiful vessel was built by Messrs. White & Sons, of West Cowes, and is admirably adapted for missionary service among the reef-girt islands of the South Pacific Ocean. The missionary party who sailed in her from England, were Mr. and Mrs. Harris and child, and a female attendant, for Sydney; Mr. and Mrs. Adams, for the Friendly Islands, who also remained at Sydney for a season; Mr. Kirk, who proceeded to New-Zealand. The remainder were the five missionaries and their families who are mentioned above, and whom Mr. Lawry accompanied to their respective stations in the Friendly Islands, and in the Feejee Islands.—EDIT.

pealed in awful grandeur. With slight intervals, this distressing weather continued four days. I have never before witnessed anything so terrific. We had a drenched crew from day to day, and all the alternations of distressing weather; but we had a good ship under us, and Captain Buck seemed formed for such scenes. The men behaved well; and our mission-band gave themselves to prayer, both men and women; and these disciples in a storm *did pray*, while God was speaking to us all from the secret place of thunder. At one of our regular evening services, while the elements were in mighty conflict, and the glare of forked lightning was quickly followed by peals and torrents, there were all our company singing sweetly,—

"When, passing through the watery deep,
I ask in faith his promised aid,
The waves an awful distance keep,
And shrink from my devoted head:
Fearless, their violence I dare;
They cannot harm, for God is there!"

We have on board the "John Wesley" our larboard and starboard classes of sailors; and these comprehend most of the seamen in the ship. And they are not mere professors in name, but so far they give evidence of having the "root of the matter." One of them, Robinson, said to-night in the class, "I have just been up taking in reefs, while the rain poured in torrents: the time was when I should have been uttering the most wicked curses; but now my soul has been so happy while on the yard-arm, that I felt as though I could have flown away towards heaven."

12*th*. We came to anchor at Tonga, after a rough and stormy passage of a fortnight, which in most vessels would have been at least three weeks; but the "John Wesley" does wonders, and is a first-rate vessel in all respects.

The sight of these most lovely isles has filled my whole soul with associations, emotions, and feelings of the most touching kind. Here I landed twenty-four years ago. The people then were all Pagan: most of them are gone to their account; but the seed has been sown, even the pure word of God, and now I find a rich harvest of Christian fruit. The Rev. John Thomas, an honored servant of the great Master, came on board, and we soon followed him ashore, where everything teemed with luxuriance and beauty.

The missionaries and their wives had not language to express their delight. We visited the king and queen after their return from the Saturday evening prayer-meeting. Their dwelling is simple, but lovely; and they were engaged in reading the Scriptures by two lamps. They said, with animation, "We are glad to see you, and praise the Lord for sending you." Filled with grateful emotion, I returned with Captain Buck to the ship, leaving the mission-families under the roof of good Mr. and Mrs. Thomas.

Sunday, 13*th*. I went ashore and breakfasted at seven A. M. During our repast, an earthquake shook the coffee in the cups; and we afterwards learned that it extended over the whole island: for myself, I did not know what it was, but supposed that the motion of the ship had not ceased to affect me, as I generally feel rocked for several days after landing from a stormy voyage; but Captain Buck and Mrs. Thomas looked gravely on all present, and said, simultaneously, "Do you not feel the earthquake?"

At nine o'clock the native service began. The large chapel was filled with devout hearers. Mr. Thomas preached, and the king prayed after the sermon; so energetic and touching was his prayer, that tears and sobs became general throughout the congregation. Both sailors and passengers retired from the place deeply affected; and each asked the other, if he had ever before witnessed a scene half so delightful as this.

In the usual order, the English service commenced at eleven o'clock, when I preached to about twenty-seven Europeans, and one American lady. I believe we all felt that God was in the midst of us.

At half-past two, Mr. Thomas and I administered the Lord's supper to the mission-families and the crew of the brig, and to about five hundred natives, among whom were the king and queen of Tonga. All was order, solemnity, and devotion.

The English service in the evening was conducted by Mr. Amos with great acceptance; and those of us who slept on board returned to the brig highly delighted. As we passed down through the grove which lies between the mission-premises and the sea, there was scarcely a house in which the inmates were not engaged in family devotion, by singing, reading the Scriptures, and prayer.

19*th*. I went to the Mua, the place where I resided twenty-four years ago. Most of my old friends were dead, or removed; but a few remained, who were glad to see me. The son of the old chief lives there, who was an infant at the period above mentioned. I lectured to them, in the house which stood on the spot which I formerly occupied. They heard with the most solemn attention, and seemed very grateful for our services. I then visited a chief of great distinction, called Tui-Tonga, who nominally ranks above George, and who does not *lotu*.* By his side sat a Popish priest; but the Tui has not yet received Popery. I told him there was but one way for all sinners, and only "one Mediator between God and men;" with much more to the same purpose. All was well received; and I hope again to visit this place, which appears very familiar to me, though by no means improved.

Mr. Miller and Captain Buck accompanied Mr. Thomas and myself in the ship's boat. The contrast between the *lotu* and heathen villages is too obvious to be mistaken. I am full of hope, with Mr. Thomas, that great good will follow our visit to this ancient and sacred fortress.

Sunday, 20th. I preached in the large chapel at Nukualofa in the morning, Mr. Thomas interpreting. This is rather a feeble way of imparting truth; but novelty came in with her aid; and the people listened with devout solemnity, while I explained to them the day of final account.

In the afternoon the king preached in the same pulpit. The attention of his audience was riveted while he expounded the words of our Lord, "I am come that ye might have life." The king is a tall and graceful person; in the pulpit he was dressed in

* By the word *lotu* is meant prayer, or worship, particularly Christian worship; it is of frequent use in the letters of the missionaries from the Friendly or Tonga Islands, and is used to mark the difference between Christian converts and those who remain in heathenism.—Edit.

a black coat, and his manner was solemn and earnest. He held in his hand a small bound manuscript book, but seldom looked at it. I believe, however, that his sermon was written in it. His action was dignified and proper; his delivery fluent, graceful, and not without majesty. He evidently engaged the attention of his hearers, who hung upon his lips with earnest and increasing interest. I perceived that much of what he said was put forth interrogatively; a mode of address which is very acceptable among the Tongans.

It was affecting to see this dignified man stretching out his hands over his people, with one of his little fingers formerly cut off, as an offering to a heathen god; a usage among this people before they became Christians. But while he bore this mark of Pagan origin, he clearly showed that to him was grace given to preach among the Gentiles the unsearchable riches of Christ.

About eighteen years ago, when George first embraced Christianity, and lived at Lifuka, and before he had been renewed in the spirit of his mind, he showed his naturally bold and earnest disposition by some pranks which he played upon one of the *toulas*, or "inspired" women. Accompanied by several young fellows like-minded with himself, he put on sackcloth, and went to the spirit-house, presenting some *cava* to the female Atua. She quickly became "inspired," and soon gave him to understand that she had "a rod in pickle" for him and his associates. This was fully anticipated by the old woman's visitors, who instantly rose, and George drew his *palalafa* (stem of a cocoanut leaf) from concealment, and giving her a heavy blow under the ear, sent her flying towards the *taka-pou*, where she lay quiet enough for these zealous chiefs to paint her as black as they chose. Her terrified attendants fled in consternation; and it does not appear that any of the idolaters had courage to avenge this indignity put upon their sacred person and their religious faith. One of the *Towla Egi*, or "chief-priests," told George, that, now he had abandoned their gods, there was none to defend him, and that one day the sharks would eat him, if he ventured into the sea; a thing which he knew George was very fond of doing. Instantly George challenged this priest to swim in the open ocean, which was accepted: the result was that George came in after a long swim in perfect safety, and the other was so torn by the shark's teeth that he soon died.

21*st.* We weighed anchor, and soon sailed for Vavau. The whole day was occupied in threading our way between the reefs which lie in the passage out. Light winds from the point we wished to sail for, lengthened our passage; but a very violent thunder-storm, with forked lightning and torrents of rain, varied the scene, and sent us all to our Master's feet in prayer. This little passage, usually performed in two days, cost us eight; for we were delayed by calms and light airs. Vavau is a beautiful harbor; only the water is so deep that it is not easy to find convenient anchorage.

Sunday, June 27th. I was pleased to find that, while working our way to the harbor among the numerous islets, not a single canoe came off to us; we saw only a few carrying the local preachers to their respective places for the day; while, more than once, as we neared the shore in tacking, the beautiful groves were vocal with the congregations singing in their usual places of worship. This was the Sabbath morning, and only one fire was seen. On my former visit to these isles, fleets of canoes would have surrounded us, clamorous to barter; but the pure word of God has come to the people, and they are changed from Pagans to Christians.

We landed in the afternoon, and were cordially received by Mrs. Turner and Mrs. West; but their husbands were both at out-places, and the head station, Neiafu, was left to a local preacher. Our reception by the natives was very cordial; so much so, that Mr. and Mrs. Davis, who are to remain here, were very greatly delighted. And well they might be; such salutations and shaking of hands could not fail to cheer us all. At sundown I held a short service with our crew, and the few English, and one American, who heard the word with deep seriousness. At the close of the day, I returned to the brig, leaving Mr. and Mrs. Davis at their new home, to pursue their work in a new tongue, and to acquire new habits, in this fertile tropical isle. Mrs. Turner is very ill; and we fear her disease is chronic. Mr. and Mrs. West, and their infant boy, were in good health, and greatly cheered by the arrival of the brethren, and by the receipt of letters from "home, sweet home." Mr. West preaches with considerable fluency and acceptance in the native language, having been here just one year.

30th.—We are busy in landing the stores and baggage. I am not a little mortified to see the idle natives, with very few exceptions, standing on the beach, and looking on, while the sailors and passengers are all landing their goods; and they utterly refuse to assist without payment, and that upon a high scale. In vain did we urge that here were men who had given their lives to the Church for their benefit, and that they owed their all to the gospel which we were sent to publish. These natives have plenty of love in their mouths; but they are sadly deficient in practical proofs of it. I am sorry to add, that, with few exceptions, this state of things exists generally in these islands. If English domestics could be procured, I apprehend few of the natives would be employed by our missionaries. This state of things may be attributed very much to the heat of the climate, and to the ease with which the natives procure what they need. They can be supplied with no motive sufficiently powerful to induce them to engage in hard labor. In this respect the New-Zealander stands on advantageous ground: he is not enervated by the climate, nor above working from sunrise to sunset, for better food and better clothes than could be obtained by him without such labor.

This morning I attended the school, and was deeply affected while there. Could you have witnessed that sight, your tears would have flowed as fast as mine. About sixty boys and girls were there, clean, intelligent, and well-instructed in useful knowledge. They sat in four rows, in the centre of a large house. A local preacher and his wife were at the head, and six other grave natives were assisting. All was silent order and well-disciplined attention. They showed good knowledge of the Scriptures; and some of the children are decidedly pious. Of such schools we have about sixty in the Vavau Circuit. Here is the groundwork of civil and moral elevation for this lovely race of Friendly-Islanders. These schools are a credit to the excellent ministers under whose fostering care they have grown up. The Rev. Peter Turner is of this number.

Since I began writing the above sentence, the house where I write has been well shaken by an earthquake.

This afternoon I attended the weekly meeting of the local preachers, of whom there are two hundred and four on the Vavau plan. They seem to be an excellent body of grave and zealous men, of godly lives, and trained in wholesome discipline.

I measured the chapel. It is a hundred feet by forty-five.

The scenery at Vavau is fine, and the harbor very good. There are about eleven smaller islands, at short distances from, and connected with, Vavau, which is moderately elevated, and in some places tolerably fertile: and though the soil is not so rich as that of Tonga, the same trees, fruits, and shrubs are found on both islands. Twelve islands are inhabited, and one hundred and forty others are mere islets. Here are the majestic *ovava*, the cocoa-nut, the bread-fruit, the banana, the yam, the pine-apple, with fruits, shrubs and flowers, elegant, delicious, and almost numberless.

The mission-premises in both islands are adorned with large orange, citron, and lime-trees, which are seldom without blossom and fruit. Besides these, I find the custard-apple, with its grateful fruit, and the melon and pumpkin in great abundance, in one place creeping on the ground, and in another running over the branches of stately and spreading trees. These are of excellent flavor in this tropical climate; and yet they are in such small repute among the natives, that I purchased yesterday eight pumpkins, weighing in all about ninety pounds, for two empty bottles. The grape-vine has been introduced; but though it grows, it does not thrive.

This is eminently the land for indigenous tropical fruits; while New-Zealand, failing in this distinction, bears away the palm for exotics from the temperate zone. The apple, pear, and plum of England, with the fruits of France and Spain, enrich the horticulture of New-Zealand, where the loaded grape-vine is seen growing beside the forest oak.

Vavau is in the neighborhood of four large burning mountains, or islands, all now in action. They are very noisy, and send forth a vivid glare, with sometimes a strong smell of sulphur. One of them has lately been divided asunder, in an extra volcanic convulsion.

July 3d.—I examined three fine native local preachers, who are candidates for the work as assistant native missionaries; namely, Benjamin Latuselu, Jone Latu, and Jone Faubula. They gave a clear account of their conversion from heathen darkness to Christian light and life.

The following is a minute of the Christian experience and call of Benjamin Latuselu, Jone Latu, and Jone Faubula, who were examined at Neiafu, Vavau, July, 1847:—

BENJAMIN LATUSELU related his experience as follows:—"There were two things by which I was brought to know the Lord. The first was, the death of King Zephaniah. Then my mind was made to attend to religion, and to seek the Lord; and in a sermon preached by the Rev. Peter Turner, these feelings were greatly increased. I greatly repented of my sins, and, looking by faith to Jesus Christ, I believed upon him with trust in the very root of my mind, and found peace and joy, and ever since have felt the influences of, and been guided by, the Holy Spirit." In relation to his call to teach and preach, he said, "I know and believe it is the will of God that I should be employed in his work, because, first, his missionaries have given me work to do; and, secondly, while in Samoa, I received a baptism of the Holy Spirit, by which I felt moved to work for Christ, to save some spirits from sin and death; and I have seen fruit of my work in the turning of sinners to the faith of the Lord Jesus Christ."

JONE LATU stated his experience as follows:—"From the time I heard of the Lord from the missionaries, the Lord has worked in my mind, and I was made very sorrowful for my sins, and, having believed in Jesus Christ, received the forgiveness of them. I have known the Lord for a long, long time. But since the time I attended the school of Mr. Francis Wilson, my love has been increased and strengthened. I first received the knowledge of my sins forgiven, in the great revival in Vavau, in 1834. Then I knew the love of God, and since then I have stood in that love. I believe the Lord has called me to teach and preach the gospel. I have seen fruit of my work in Niua Foou, and also here in Vavau."

JONE FAUBULA stated:—"I resided in my own land, Feejee, and heard the missionaries there. There went to Feejee Mr. Cross and Mr. Cargill. They came to the place where I was. They told our people to 'repent and believe the gospel;' and we did become religious, and we begged for teachers. After this, others came from Tonga, and told me to *lotu.* I did become religious, but did not know its meaning. My mind was not yet changed; it was still dark. I heard the missionaries preach, and then I knew the light from God. I knew I was a sinner. In my repentance, I knew great grief of mind because of my sins. Then a canoe came from Vavau to Lakemba, and about that time I received the forgiveness of my sins. But my relations tempted me again to become a heathen; and this was the cause or reason of my leaving my own land to come and dwell in Tonga. I came here that I might still love and serve the Lord Jesus Christ. Whilst yet in Feejee, the missionaries allowed me to preach a little; and, when coming to Tonga, I called at Niua Foou. There my preaching was made a blessing; and, since I first arrived here till now, God has moved my mind to preach the gospel. This I know from the call of the Spirit in my heart."

Benjamin is one of the finest and brightest specimens of primitive Christianity with which I have conversed in these islands. His talents are far above the usual standard among the Tongans. His spirit is excellent, and his attainments superior to those of his brethren. He speaks the three dialects of Tonga, Feejee, and the Navigators' Islands. The other two are very rich in promise; and such as I can most cordially approve as men fit to be separated to the work of teaching among the out-islands, which cannot be visited by a missionary more than once a year.

Their wives are devoted women, willing to go any where with their husbands in the name of the Lord.

Monday, July 5th. I left Vavau, with Messrs. Turner and West, for the district-meeting at Tonga, calling at Hapai. The wind was high, and the sea rough, and all the passengers were very sick. These little voyages cause much suffering to those of us whom nothing can preserve from sickness at sea.

On Tuesday morning we anchored at Lifuga, but did not recover all day from the misery we endured while "lying to" the previous night. Mr. Rabone came off in his canoe, with Joel, the king, on board, who was one of my domestic lads twenty-four years ago at Tonga, but who is now a fine-looking man, a wise magistrate, and a good local preacher. We were glad to meet again. Mr. Rabone is a great man here; a good sample of the fine old English gentleman. We landed, and found his wife cheerful and blooming, and a fine family of six children around her. All countenances were lighted up. The boxes came ashore; presents from uncle, cousins, grandmother, and many friends. These things occur but once a year, and are therefore times of deep interest and much excitement. The mission here is healthy, and steadily progressing. The Lifuga chapel measures one hundred and twelve feet long by fifty wide. The whole island is about fifteen miles in length, and not generally more than a mile in width. The number of members in this island is about five hundred. The total population is about one thousand, and the number of local preachers, thirty. A large proportion of the youth, and many adults, attend the schools. The group of Hapai has two thousand members on its various and scattered islets. One of the missionaries resides at Tungua, forty miles from Lifuga.

8th. I visited the *Tamaha* at Tungua. She remembers, not only my residence here, but the visit of Captain Cook. Her age is about eighty-five, and her sight gone; but she is ripe for eternity, having been a steady Christian for many years. On our leaving her palace, (for she ranks first among all the chiefs of Tonga,) we were presented with a large hog, and about half a ton of yams. Mr. and Mrs. Webb live here, happy, diligent, and useful. Mr. Webb and Mr. West were upset in a native canoe, and were overboard in the open sea, about one hour, in the dark night. Their faithful natives, however, kept them up, and, having righted the canoe, repaired its outrigger, and paddled them home in safety. Mr. Webb had been on board the brig, and was taking with him letters, papers, and parcels, which were swallowed up in the great deep. On visiting them to-day we heard not a murmur for the loss of these things, but all were thankful to God, that he had spared the valuable lives of his servants.

9th. Being detained by contrary winds, we lay at anchor at the isle of Haafeva. In the morning we landed, and found that almost all the people were members of our society, and living in peace and plenty. In the centre of this little isle, about three miles round, stands a fine old *ovava*-tree. We measured it, and found its girth forty-five feet round its trunk; its width, from the extremes of opposite branches, one hundred and ninety feet; its height, far more than one hundred feet. Four houses stood beneath its shade; one belonged to each of the four parts into which this sea-girt empire was formerly divided. This noble tree throws down many suckers to the earth, which grow and become props to its far-extended lateral branches, similar to the banian-tree, to which family it probably belongs.

10*th*. As we lay at anchor on account of contrary winds, the island of Tofua, which is about ten miles in circumference, was clear in sight, and occasionally sent up a sudden flame from its smoking crater. There are about one hundred people living there, one half of whom are members of our society. A native teacher conducts the school, and nearly all the children attend. This island is under the care of the Rev. William Webb, who told me that about two years ago the natives of Tofua were warned of an approaching eruption, as they usually are, by the trembling of the whole island, and by a rumbling noise. This sign was the signal of flight to a cave in a very distant part of the island, as was the practice of their fathers in all similar cases. But on this occasion they failed in their attempt to reach the cave, on account of the shower of stones falling around from the volcanic eruption. While, however, the awful process of this terrific phenomenon was raging in its grandeur, these trembling people were screened in another place, where they awaited the termination of the convulsion. They afterwards proceeded to view the cave, which they had endeavored to reach, and where their forefathers were accustomed to find shelter; and, to their amazement, they found it filled with burning lava. In this deliverance they saw and acknowledged the hand of the Lord; and to this hour they speak of it with gratitude and admiration.

Tofua has a basin in its centre, and at the bottom, nearly on a level with the sea, is a pool of clear fresh water, about three miles across. The mouth of the volcano is about half-way up this basin. A few miles distant from Tofua, which is about three-quarters of a mile high, is a lofty conical island, just one mile high, with a volcano in action. The smoke has been pouring forth in clouds ever since we have been here. Its name is Kao. "Great and marvelous are thy works, Lord God Almighty: just and true are thy ways, thou King of saints."

Sunday, July 11*th*. The wind is still contrary. Several of the brethren who were on board have sallied forth from the ship to preach among the various isles to-day; while others conduct the services on board the brig. Our patience is tried on our way to the district-meeting; but the winds are under the absolute control of Him who is our Master and Lord.

13*th*. We reached Tonga with difficulty, and landed in a torrent of rain. The next morning we commenced our district-meeting, and we concluded the business in six days. Many important matters were agreed upon; and among them the immediate revision of the New Testament, and the translation of the Old, with the view of printing the entire Scriptures as correctly and with as little delay as possible. The final revision and bringing out of all the books which are agreed upon to be printed, is committed to the Rev. Stephen Rabone, in whom the district-meeting has full confidence that he will not delay to place the word of God in the hands of the Tongans. This work has very urgent claims upon us, and those claims have existed for several years: but there is no sufficient reason why they have not been met long ago. I here record the opinion of most of the Tonga missionaries.

Another important step taken by this meeting is the admission of a native of Tonga into the sacred office of assistant missionary. Benjamin Latuselu is a chief of high rank, well and long tried as a local preacher, a man of deep piety, clear understanding, and thoroughly imbedded in the affections of our people. He is sent forth to take charge of Keppel's Island, where we have a flock of several hundreds without an authorized shepherd. He is the first of his nation admitted into the Christian ministry on probation by the laying on of hands; but we may hope that by such an agency the wants of these infant churches will be much more generally and efficiently met than they could be only by ministers sent out and supported from home. I earnestly pray the Lord of the harvest to multiply such laborers.

A third matter of great consequence was the education of this people. For the more efficient working of our educational operations in the Friendly Islands, the parent committee has sent out Mr. Amos, who has studied the training system at Glasgow, and will forthwith start his training-school at Nukualofa, composed of three divisions; namely, 1. Children; 2. Catechists; and, 3. The most hopeful of our young men, who are likely to become teachers of their countrymen, and in some cases, it may be hoped, rise to the rank of native assistant missionaries.

The native institution, which had declined after the death of Mr. Francis Wilson, is again revived; and from it I shall fully expect to see the same beneficial effects as we witness in New-Zealand from the institution there. Upon the whole, I shall be ever grateful for this meeting with my Christian brethren, who have gone forth for a long period, sowing precious seed; and now they see the ripe sheaf and golden harvest bowing before them in all directions; a sight which many righteous men desired to see, but they did not witness this happy and holy gathering, around the Saviour's mediatorial throne, of those who sow and those who reap rejoicing together.

At the close of our sittings the meeting presented me with the following paper:—

"*Resolved,* That this meeting cordially expresses its thanks to the Rev. Walter Lawry, for his visit to the Friendly Islands, the scene of his early labors; and also its deep sense of the kind, judicious, and Christian manner in which its business has been examined and conducted; and begs to assure him that any future visit will be hailed with pleasure.

(Signed,) "John Thomas,
"Peter Turner,
"Stephen Rabone,
"Matthew Wilson,
"William Webb,
"George R. H. Miller,
"Thomas West."

Wednesday, July 21st. We weighed anchor at Tonga, early in the morning, and reached Hapai in the evening, close hauled all the way. The following day the wind was right a-head; but we were snugly anchored and landing the stores of Mr. Webb at Tungua, (thanks, under God, to our fast vessel!) or we should now have been at sea beating about among reefs and islets. It would be difficult to say how much we owe to this admirably well-constructed brig, both in point of safety and comfort. The "John Wesley" is every way a very fine vessel—so clean and wholesome, and so well fitted for the service to which she is appointed, that I have seen nothing yet to be compared to her. She has not and could not have a poop-deck, but she has very lofty 'tween-decks, and is therefore airy and pleasant in warm climates, such as she has to navigate. She sails well at all points, and under all circumstances: generally, she is a very fast vessel, and remarkably easy.

Tuesday, August 3d. Neiafu.—Having made our voyage to Lifuga, in the Hapai group, and back again to Vavau, removing the brethren Turner and Rabone with their almost endless luggage and lumber, I have had an opportunity of observing the operation of these removals in these parts of the Lord's vineyard. I doubt if they do much good to the natives, who, I believe, would be less restless and unsettled if one pastor were stationed permanently among them. In New-Zealand the natives will not permit their father, as they call their first missionary, to leave them. If these islanders are more fickle, it may be traced to their different training. The mission premises suffer greatly in these changes. The gardens lie waste, and improvements are looked for in vain: the tenant is soon moving away to another station. The ship has hereby not only a great increase of work, extra voyages among the reefs, and the loading and unloading of luggage, but she will soon be filled with vermin, as the "Triton" (a former missionary brig) was. By these, almost everything is destroyed, all on board are subject to perpetual annoyance, and in course of time the vessel herself will be frittered and injured.

This is my birth-day, and, by God's mercy, health, strength, and peace are vouchsafed to me, with an increase of pleasure in my Master's work, at the end of fifty-four years. The day has been signalized by the various schools assembling at this place, Neiafu, and each section, whether of children or adults, presenting their offering of love to us at their examination. Some brought a yam, a piece of cloth, a shell, an egg, a fowl, and others a basket, or a mat. Each section was headed by its teacher and chief. They sang a hymn as they approached, and as they retired from, the mission-house; and all were beautifully dressed and oiled. The queen was among those who approached, with her thank-offering,—a fine bleached and ornamented mat. I was struck with the change which I now witnessed in this people. At my first visit I saw these offerings brought and laid at the shrine of their false gods, and connected with much that was immoral and cruel. They have now changed their object of worship, and their mode of conducting this ancient practice. The missionaries have done wisely to control, but not to destroy, the thank-offerings of the people. I observed that many aged persons, who were very poor, laid down their shell, or an egg, with all the majesty and air of self-complacency peculiar to these singular people. These *mea ofa* have little value, only that they are intended to express the obligation of the people to God, and to his Church and ministers.

The same ceremony was gone through at Hapai, where the schools also appeared in excellent order, full of interest and efficiency. The result at this place was a *mea ofa* (or "thank-offering") of a ton and a half of yams, and forty fowls and turkeys, which were sent on board the "John Wesley" to be used on the voyage.

Wednesday, August 4th. A wedding took place today in the large chapel here, between Naphtali (the son of the late king, and grandson of Feenow, the celebrated warrior mentioned by Mr. Mariner) and Virginia, a chief of high rank, and each about seventeen years old. At midnight there was a cry made, which continued till daybreak, to this effect: "Lift this food to the house of the bride." In all directions Vavau was vocal with the song of the multitudes who were bearing, or drawing on slides, ponderous burdens of food, consisting of pork, turtle, fish, and fowl, and yams without number. The bales of native cloth and mats were piled aloft in ample plenitude. Presents passed freely from chief to chief. The dresses of this gracefully-formed people were ample, flowing, and *rich*, as the Tongans count riches. Their heads and faces were profusely anointed with sweet-scented cocoa-nut oil; while rosettes, and odorous strings of flowers, were the ornaments of their necks and shoulders.

The ceremony was performed with all proper solemnity by the Rev. Peter Turner, in the midst of an overflowing congregation. The feasting lasted three days. In the afternoon we met a selection of the various adult and children's schools in the same very large chapel; but such was the crowd on this high day that the walls of cane were removed, and the multitude under the roof and in the lawn could now *see* as well as *hear* the organized masses performing their recitals, drawn up in rows, about fifty in a row, the males facing the females, and all rehearsing portions of the New Testament, a lesson in numerals, and the Conference Catechisms; closing with a native hymn, which they sang with zest and unity, producing a very powerful thrill. As I sat in the large pew which surrounds the pulpit, and looked at the regular columns of scholars, with their numerous teachers bearing each his staff of office; then extending the view to the great multitude beyond, who were joying and beholding their order; and then still further to the gorgeous foliage of natural scenery beyond the lawn, formed of the cocoa-nut, bread-fruit, and banana trees, with many others still more lofty and wide-spreading, all waving in native grandeur and luxuriance, I could not help wishing that some landscape-artist had been there, and that loveliness so exquisite, combined with objects so deep in interest, might be conveyed to my friends at home. These schools are co-extended with our missions in the South Seas, and will most assuredly exert an influence upon the rising generation of these lands such as New-Testament truths only can beget, and the fruits of which it is cheering to contemplate.

Thursday, August 5th. We sailed from Neiafu, in Vavau, for Hapai, with Mr. and Mrs. Turner, having landed at Vavau Mr. and Mrs. Rabone and family in their place. We had on board, for the out-islands, one assistant missionary and three native teachers. The parting of these from their friends, especially of

Jehoshaphat, was very touching. Those who were going were *melted*, but not *shaken;* while their friends, some afloat, and others on the beach, set up such a cry as pierced our hearts, and echoed from shore to shore among the islanders in the harbor. "Our love is too great,—we cannot let you go: have you not been our teacher, and are not our hearts cleaving unto you? are not our breasts full of sharp pain, and will you leave us behind as orphans to pine in sorrow until our day goes down? Full of anguish are we! O why will you leave us weeping till we have no tears?" Such were the expostulations of these children of the wood.

These, however, were not the only sounds audible to us on the deck of our vessel. In the evening, from the time the light died away till eleven o'clock, we could distinctly hear the children of the respective schools repeating their Scripture-lessons, and singing, as their manner is, what amount of knowledge they possessed of figures. These sounds reached us from this small islet, and from that large valley. It was heard again as early as three in the morning, and then followed their morning devotion,—singing, reading the Scriptures, and prayer. This is the island of Vavau.

Tuesday, August 17th.—We are at sea, on our way to the islands of Niua. The wind was high, and the sea tossing so boisterously, that all of us, who were prostrated by sea-sickness, agreed not to call this the Pacific Ocean. In the morning we passed close under the lee of the *remains* of that very extraordinary island, Funua-lai. Although suffering severely in my berth below, I resolved at all risks to go on deck, and see this great sight.

Funua-lai presented the most awful and terrific appearance in the form of a natural phenomenon, that it had hitherto fallen to my lot to witness. It was a circular and rather high volcanic island, about ten miles round, until of late, when it became so frightfully convulsed, that it was turned inside out, and split into two parts! God had sent such clear warnings by the heavy earthquakes which preceded this eruption, that the people had left the place, and had gone to Vavau, where they are now living. To us on our ship's deck it presented an appearance of desolation, which filled us with awe, and caused a sigh to escape from every beholder. The sailor, the native teacher, the missionary, all exclaimed, "Come, see the desolations which the Lord hath made!" The idea it impressed upon our minds was that of a *ruined world.* It smelled very strongly of sulphur, and exhibited rents, and piles of burnt sand and vitrified matter, as if the bowels of the earth had been turned outside. Volumes of smoke were pouring forth at twenty places, sometimes closing here and opening there. The openings of crater after crater were seen in all directions, and the sea, for a great distance, was discolored by the floods of lava poured forth. The light of the flame caused quite an illumination at Vavau, distant thirty-five miles; and the noise of this fiery disgorge was distinctly heard for three successive days at Niua Foou, distant one hundred and thirty miles! The dust and vitrified matter were discharged from this deep volcano to such a height, that we saw much of it and its withering effects, thirty-five miles off, at Vavau, where the damage was very considerable, both to the trees and to the crops generally. Persons who were passing about the time of the phenomenon have recorded the following particulars:—

"Captain Samson, on his way from Tonga to Vavau, entered a shower of ashes. At the time it was a double-reefed-topsail breeze from the north-east; but it was a beautiful, clear, starlight night. As he approached, it appeared like a squall; and as soon as he entered, the eyes of the men on watch began to be covered with fine dust. Captain Samson put the ship about; but being persuaded that there was no land near, he continued his course. So soon as the sun arose, the dust appeared of a dark red color, rolling over like great volumes of smoke, presenting an awful appearance. At eight o'clock it was so dark, that candles had to be lighted in the cabin. At eleven, A. M., it began to clear a little, the sun appearing occasionally. By noon they had got out of it, being then in 170* 45′ west, and 11* 2′ south, having sailed across the shower at least forty miles. Captain Cash, of the ship 'Massachusetts,' got into the shower about the same time, though at least sixty miles to the east of Captain Samson, and not far from Savage Island. The ashes penetrated every crevice of the ship, and fell in such quantities, that Captain Samson believes that tons fell on the deck, which had to be cleared from time to time. The question is, How could such a shower be carried so far, right in the teeth of the prevailing winds? It can only be explained, I think, by supposing that the ashes had been thrown at once with great force to a very great height, into an upper current of air, and, after being borne several degrees to the east, had then fallen into the under-stratum, and so been carried back again towards the island whence they came. The dust is of a dark-gray slaty color, of specific gravity 1.076, containing a large proportion of sulphur, and so much of free sulphuric acid as to give it a sharp taste. It also contained a small proportion of iron. No doubt a minute analysis would give the usual combinations of silica, and several of the sulphates usually found in volcanic dust."

For many weeks before, as well as at the time of this disruption, the earthquakes for a space of fifty miles around, and especially at Vavau, were truly terrific, and, even now, they seldom miss a shaking every moon. About a year since, this oceanic mountain was covered with verdure, and abounded with fruit-trees; but, behold, it has now become a barren mass of lava and burnt sand, reduced from a fine cone to a divided and ghastly heap of scoria and black powder, without a leaf or a blade of grass of any kind, and all things living are destroyed! Such at present is Funua-lai, a monument of God's power to create and to destroy.

Thursday, August 19th.—We reached Niua Tobu Tabu, or Keppel's Island, and succeeded in landing Benjamin Latuselu and two native teachers there. This island is small, and there is neither harbor nor anchorage in any part. The wind blew strong; and no sooner had we landed our men, than we were blown off to sea, unable to effect a landing ourselves, much to our disappointment. The presence of Benjamin and his fellow-helpers went far to meet the necessity of the case; but Mr. Wilson and myself were sadly cast down at the thought of having come so far, at so much inconvenience, without even putting our feet on shore. We learned that all was peace, but that a heavy calamity had lately befallen this people in the form of a hurricane, which had greatly diminished their food, and blown down their fruit-trees. They sigh for a missionary, and greatly rejoice that Benjamin has come among them. Having obtained this information, we submitted to our circumstances, and were hurried away upon the foaming billows to the other Niua, praying that the Lord would stand by and bless his word and ordinances in the hands of our excellent friend and brother Benjamin.

Friday, 20th.—We sighted Niua Foou this morning, having run above one hundred miles in the night, the wind and waves hurrying along with us. This remarkable island, composed for the most part of blocks of lava, is far from being rich or fertile, about fifteen miles in circumference, and has the singular feature of being hollow in the middle. It resembles the brim of a hat, the centre being no doubt the crater of a volcano. A sheet of brackish water covers this immense cavity, which, I am informed, has never been fathomed, though the attempt has been often made. It stretches about three miles across, and seems to have no communication with the sea. This unruffled lake, with three small islets covered with trees, forms a beautiful contrast to the troubled sea, whose roaring billows continually lash the vitrified iron-bound coast of the outer rim, or circle on which the people live. There are no fishes of any kind in this lake. The probability is, that this cavity has been formed by successive eruptions blowing the centre of the island into the ocean. Upon the whole of the circle now left, there is scarcely a drop of fresh water, except what falls from the clouds, which the natives secure in trees scooped out for the purpose. This is the first land I have yet visited where little or no water is; and yet about eight hundred people live here, and refuse to remove to any other part of the Friendly Islands, where there is plenty of land, with a cordial welcome: but they prefer a land vitrified and comparatively sterile, without water, and having no harbor or landing-place, and where the sea is generally very turbulent, because, they say, their fathers lived there before them, and there they are buried. This little oceanic nation contains no less than two kings. One is *Tui*, (King,) and the other *Tui Niua*, (King of Niua.) They are reported as pious men; but I saw them not, as they were making a visit to other lands. As a natural curiosity, this island has the first place among all the islands hitherto seen by me. The view of the internal lake studded with islets, as seen from an elevation of some thousands of feet; the peep, through the ravines of the ring, out upon the surging ocean; and then a landscape of woods, fruit-trees, and plantations, interspersed with melted blocks of scoria, as if fresh from the mouth of a furnace,—constitute scenery not familiar even to a well-traveled observer.

The climate is intensely hot, being in latitude 15* south. The tropical fruits, shrubs, and flowers, usual in these islands, are found here, but of inferior growth, and the timber indicates a soil not such as we find in Tonga or Vavau. The people are in all respects Friendly Islanders, speaking the same language, and observing the same customs and usages: only, being far removed, and seldom visited by vessels, they are simple and unsophisticated above all that we have seen.

Saturday, August 21st.—Having landed on a rock to leeward, we had to travel six miles to reach the metropolis. The burning sun and high hills made this a formidable matter to me; but I was soon relieved by the natives carrying me on their shoulders on a *hamo,* a kind of hand-barrow. Away they tripped over the craggy steeps, shouting as they ran. Mr. Wilson chose to walk behind, unwilling to give so much trouble; but with me the case was one of necessity.

As we went along there was a general rising. The extraordinary shouts of these children of the wood passed thrillingly from glen to glen, and, like a snowball, our company became larger and larger as we went on, until it was manifest that the whole community was up and in motion. From the royal city we were met by troops at every turn, every eye flashing fire, and ecstasy beaming in each uplifted countenance. To shake hands with me was the first object, and to get the shoulder under the *hamo,* the next. Our pace was that of a full run; and as we passed along, the piercingly shrill shouts of the natives announced to the dwellers in the wood and in the dale the progress of our cavalcade. "Thanks to the Lord Jesus for his servants! thanks for their coming, and for their safety on the sea!" were uttered and echoed in all directions. The Spirit that animated Isaiah had foreseen this sort of procession: "Sing unto the Lord a new song, and his praise from the end of the earth, ye that go down to the sea, and all that is therein; the isles and the inhabitants thereof. Let the wilderness and the cities thereof lift up their voice, the villages that Kedar doth inhabit: let the inhabitants of the rock sing, let them shout from the top of the mountains. Let them declare his praise in the islands." Many of the teachers were there, distinguished by their staff, and a book under their arms. We were bearing a large supply of books to them from our press at Vavau: and their delight at receiving so many good things admitted of no expression, but in the most thrilling vociferations I ever witnessed. My own feelings will never be uttered; but at different times they alternated greatly. At one time the grateful tear flowed freely down; in a few seconds an extra gush of feeling would find vent in a shout; and a keen sense of the ludicrous would not permit the suppression of a smile once and again. The manner in which the children would dash from the road-side by which we passed, in simple amazement, together with the capering of old women with only a few rags on them, called up to the imagination the fool of Horace kicking the clouds. The dogs fled to the heights, and barked amain, and even the pigs, with their tails tucked in close, with one ear up and the other down, would sheer off askance, almost seeming to say, "The strange people are come!" Certain I am that had my ride across this island been seen by a few old English peasants, I could not have stood it, but must have left my *hamo* and run away. But here all is simplicity; and what to me seemed *outré* was to them gravely earnest, and religiously sober.

Having arrived at the government-house, which was politely surrendered for our use, the bearers gracefully handed me to a large elbow-chair, and then awaited the arrival of Mr. Wilson, who very soon came steaming up to the house. Two bedsteads in the form of sofas were placed in a bed-room for our use; and now we proceeded to plan the services for the next day, which was the Sabbath.

Sunday, August 22d. At seven in the morning the beautiful large chapel was crowded with a deeply-impressed congregation, who worshiped reverently, and with much emotion, before the mercy-seat. At nine we registered ninety-four children and one adult; at ten we baptized them with water "in the name of the Father, and of the Son, and of the Holy Ghost." At eleven we administered the sacrament of the Lord's supper to the whole society, (the sick excepted,) consisting of four hundred and seventy-nine members, who worship in nine chapels scattered over the island. Deep was the interest and solemn was the hour.

It was the first time that they had ever received this sacrament, which they called *kai ma,* "eating of bread." When we asked Paul, the governor, what he thought of this matter, he said, "This is the first day ever known in Niua. Why did not the *kai ma* come before?" He is a fine man, and a local preacher. At three we had public preaching, and at five we catechised the children of the schools, and were not a little delighted to see how much they knew both of Scripture and of the catechism. It was now dark, and with this, the sixth, service our day of real and devout worship was concluded. Such a day I had not seen before, and upon it I shall meditate with gratitude and delight as long as my memory shall last.

On Monday morning we were to cross again, and join the brig, which, without anchoring, was lying off and on, under the lee of the island. Before we started, however, the multitude came together with the *mea ofa*, tokens of love,—nuts, oil, clubs, spears, mats, combs, baskets, wooden pillows, shells, and many other things, of which they begged our acceptance. I was really glad of these *mea ofa*, as they will form part of a bazaar to assist the funds for our new chapel at Auckland. Having judged all their critical cases, and set all things in order, leaving our good friend, Jehoshaphat, as head teacher, we moved off towards the sea, the far greater part accompanying us, and bearing on their shoulders the *mea ofa*. Their petitions were very earnest for a missionary; and certainly a lovely field is ready for his cultivation. This people might be moulded to anything at present; but if a Romish priest should land there, what will become of our fair blossoms?

Thursday, August 26*th*. Having returned from Niua Foou to Tonga, I proceeded to Hihifo, accompanied by Mr. Miller. The passage lay over a sheet of water of about fifteen miles' extent, and very wide inside the reefs, but seldom more than three feet deep; to the eye, however, it appears an open sea. This visit was very cheering in all respects. The place is dignified and grand, being rich in soil, abounding in fruits, and ornamented with immense trees, which seem to have undergone no alteration since I saw them twenty-five years ago. The mission-premises are neat, and have an air of comfort about them far superior to those occupied by Mr. Thomas. The people are intelligent, obliging, and united. The work of God is flourishing, and the members seem quite alive and in earnest. The children in the schools present a scene of cheering encouragement, having advanced in their knowledge of the Scriptures, and, in point of order and diligence, being fully equal to those in the best schools in these parts.

Mr. and Mrs. Wilson have a fine family of well-conducted children, for whom they begin to show great anxiety relative to their education. A good school at Auckland for the children of missionaries is the thing now most urgently pressing itself upon our attention. Surely, if the parents give their lives to the missions, they have a right to ask a good education for their children in some locality as convenient to them as possible.

27th. I went to Homa, a distance of nine miles, to see the old chief Via, whom I had known rather intimately aforetime. He is still a heathen, and is somewhat under the influence of a Popish priest. Messrs. Wilson and Miller went with me, and fifty local preachers, who offered to carry me thither and back; but I preferred walking the greater part of the way. Via was sick, but glad to see us. He expressed great kindness towards me. I delivered to him and to his people a faithful epitome of the "way to the kingdom," to which they listened with great solemnity. I found we had some members in this heathen *colo*, (fortress.) The appearance of this place, in its grim and gloomy hue, contrasted strongly with the clear and cheerful air of the neat *colo* we visited at Faahefa, where we opened their first chapel, and where they were all heathens only two years ago.

FAAHEFA is a beautiful place. The trees exceed in majesty those of most places that I have seen either in England or in Ireland; and the people are simple, loving disciples of Christ. After the chapel-opening service at noon-day, I found that many heathens were present, who had also assisted in building the chapel. We may hope that heathenism in these parts is rapidly declining. Popery waits to take its place; but we trust that "disappointment will laugh at hope's career." After the service, in which we all took part, and in which I preached, there was no collection; for they who were to use the chapel had built it at their own cost. A lovely edifice it really is, large, strong, and elegant. But by far the most singular thing, to us who form our tastes in England, was, that the friends who attended from other places were not only not asked for a collection, but were regaled by a feast, which consisted of thirteen fat hogs, and about twenty baskets of fowls, turkeys, yams, and cocoa-nuts. Such a chapel-opening may be very useful, and I believe this was; and it did not need a Dr. Newton to make it popular. To this occasion the Rev. Matthew Wilson has reference in the following extract:—

"When I returned this morning from the place where I saw you in the boat, I met several local preachers who were wishful to have seen you again, but were deprived of that pleasure by your starting so early. Among them was Apollos, the local preacher from Haafeva, where the chapel was opened yesterday. He communicated to me the following information:— After you left us yesterday, we spent much time in conversing with our heathen relatives who had come to the opening of the chapel. One heathen chief said, 'There was only one thing that was bad to me in Mr. Lawry's sermon, and that was, it was *too short.* We wanted to hear him.' Another heathen chief went to Apollos and Bunou, in the middle of the night, and said, 'I am come to *lotu;* let us kneel down and worship God; for the first words which Mr. Lawry spoke to-day darted light and conviction through my mind, and I believe that there is a God.' Perhaps, sir, you will remember that the sentence to which he refers is this, being the first which you spoke: 'One only is great, and he fills the universe. This is our God who is here to-day; and if you saw Jesus Christ walking on this side, and on that side, through the congregation, he would not be more certainly present, reading our thoughts, and watching all the desires of our minds, than he is now, though we see him not. Lo! God is here!' Apollos believes that the man's wife, children, and relations, will all soon follow in his steps and embrace the truth. Notwithstanding the toil and danger which must have attended your return this morning, I trust that you have sustained no injury."

On our return to Hihifo the schools, composed of *the entire population*, came to us in a procession, and made me a very handsome *mea ofa* for the New-Zealand Bazaar, consisting of shells, tortoise-shells, pearls, combs, native axes, native fish-hooks, clubs, spears, and wooden pillows. Their dresses were very fine; and as one party returned through the lawn, from the summer-house where we were sitting, and another entered singing a hymn, the effect was all but enchanting.

28*th*. We paddled fifteen miles, against a strong wind, to Nukualofa. On this day, as on the former, we started by the light of Jupiter, Saturn, and Mars, and were many miles on our way before the sun had risen. I record, with great satisfaction, my full approbation of what I saw at Hihifo, under the control of Mr. Wilson, both in his domestic circle and in the Church of God.

Sunday, August 29th. NUKUALOFA.—A large congregation attended the morning prayer-meeting at day-break, in the large chapel at Nukualofa. I preached at nine o'clock; the chapel was crowded, and many remained outside. At eleven o'clock we had English preaching, at which twenty-seven persons were present. At three o'clock we had native preaching again, which was well attended. At five, P. M., we had another English service, and many prayer-meetings were held. The people all go one way here. The Sabbath is fully observed, and God's house is thronged. At this place we have a population of about two thousand, of whom five hundred and forty are members of our society. The two missionaries visit twenty-eight places, of which Eooa is one, distant in the open sea some fifteen miles. They have no boat fit for such a voyage, and their lives are often in peril in the frail native canoes. A boat must be provided at Auckland for this station; and if the same were done for Hapai and Vavau, it would be a great security against the risk to which our brethren are now exposed in their frequent voyages from island to island in the open sea.

Tuesday, August 31st. MUA.—I went again to the Mua, and fully delivered my soul in the midst of this people. This was the place where I opened my commission a quarter of a century ago. It has always been the stronghold of pagan superstition in the Friendly Islands. We have now again entered this *colo;* and Mr. Miller's residence is on the very beautiful spot which I formerly occupied. The chief with whom I lived as my protector, died calling upon the Saviour, and professing to trust only in him. His wife lived and died a steady believer in Christ.* The present chief, Tungi, is their son, and has had powerful convictions and loud calls; but though he is friendly towards us, he has not yet yielded himself to the Lord. One higher in rank than he, is Eliza Ann, the eldest daughter of the late chief. She tells me in one of her letters that the good seed sowed in her mind, when I was there at first, has sprung up. She is now one of our steady leaders, and a powerful chief as to rank, character, and influence. I delivered a discourse to a full house: most that were present were our people; but many heathens also were there. The power of the gospel, which was "present to heal," will yet overcome all opposition at poor superstitious Mua. I trust the labors of Mr. Miller will be greatly owned of God in this place. His prospects are fair; and, being a medical man, he will be able to win some who would otherwise stand aloof. A Popish priest has settled here, by consent of the *Tui Tonga*, for the pur-

* The narrative of Mr. Lawry's residence in Tonga, in 1822 and 1823, will be found in the "Missionary Notices" of 1823 and 1824. He thus describes the scene on his departure:—"*October 3d*, 1823. We have this day embarked for New South Wales; and the scene of our departure was truly moving. PALOO was scarcely able to open his mouth for weeping; vast crowds collected round our house, and carried almost all our luggage in their canoes to the ship, a distance of seven or eight miles. Just as we were stepping into our boat, the natives formed themselves into a regular *cava*-ring, and desired me to stand in the middle of it, while one of the chief speakers addressed me to the following purpose:—'We thank you for coming among us. Before you came it was dark night on Tonga; now it begins to be light. Your friends in the foreign lands have sent for you: well, go; and tell them that Tonga is a foolish land, and let them send us many teachers. Our hearts are sore, because you are going from us.' Here they burst into tears, and I could bear the scene no longer."—EDIT.

pose, he says, of dispensing medicine: we shall see. At the Bea, a chief, named Lavaka, has, I am told, embraced Popery: but he retains his wives as before. Is not this a great *privilege?* Who beside antichrist can reconcile sin with safety?

While passing up between the islands and reefs on the way to the Mua, and while there, what a succession of recollections and emotions passed through my mind! Many a time have I sat and heard the chiefs discuss the question, whether we should be killed and our boxes taken, or whether it might not be better to await the coming of our vessel, by which means they would have greater gain. Almost every new spot recalled some instance of injustice, insult, or menace, practiced upon us in those times of their ignorance. But, enough! Tonga has heard the gospel, and that has leavened all Vavau, all Hapai, and by far the greater part of Tonga; and still the leaven works, until the whole lump shall be leavened! Was it to be expected that such a triumph could be won without a struggle?

It was not a little gratifying to see the young people, whose dwelling was under my roof at the Mua in days gone by, coming with their *mea ofa*, (offerings of love.) Among them was Malungahu, now called Malachi, who accompanied me to Sydney, but is now a leader and local preacher. There was Watson Now, who went to London with me; he is also a local preacher. And Eliza Ann was there, a dignified female chief, and a Christian class-leader.

Since this visit one man from among the heathen has bowed the knee to Jesus.

September 1*st.* I examined our school-operations

here, as I have done those in every other place. The children were few in comparison with every other that I have witnessed, and the system adopted did not seem to interest the people generally. Mrs. Thomas has exerted herself to the utmost; but from various circumstances, our school-operations languish at Nukualofa, while they prosper in other places. The arrival of Mr. Amos at this time may be considered as most providential; and hopes are entertained that in due time his efforts will be crowned with success, and that a better state of things will be seen among the youth of Tonga. At Hihifo the schools are already yielding a rich harvest; and why should we despair of any other part of the island? I think the Glasgow system will go far to meet the taste of this romantic and showy people. They must and will have varied evolutions and processions, displays and changes, which, as they are capable of being kept within the bounds of innocence, may very well subserve the ends of the schoolmaster, and prove the handmaids of instruction. No one can deny that where these have been admitted, and properly regulated, the schools have succeeded; and where they have not been adopted, but the old sombre plan of village schools in England adhered to, the trial has proved a complete failure. Our difficulty is to get the natives to put up suitable erections and fences, for the purpose of our training-school here. They are unwilling to labor, and extravagant in their demands for payment. They have before their eyes the ruins of the old school, but say they should like to see what Mr. Amos will do, before they expend their time and labor on large and troublesome buildings. They do not seem well to comprehend our meaning when we urge that he must have a suitable building before he can bring his system to bear upon them. This doctrine is not easily grasped by a people who can perform all their deeds on the sand of the sea-shore, or under the ample shade of their forest trees.

2d. The king has just now announced his intention to quit Tonga, and live at Hapai; but he intends first to visit Samoa, and to carry the teachers thither.[*] This has operated all at once as a thunderbolt. On the part of the congregated chiefs there is consternation. Yesterday I delivered a lecture to them and the king on various public matters, connected with education, laws, government, and public morals; all of which ought to be in accordance with Christianity. About five hundred persons listened with marked attention for an hour and a half. The matters then discussed have since been fully canvassed, and pronounced to be "the truth, and just what they required." Some chiefs have just called upon Mr. Thomas, to say, that if I will step in at this critical juncture, and say, "King George, you should not leave Tonga at this time, but stay where you are for the good of your people," he will hearken to my voice, and do as I say. In this opinion Mr. Thomas concurs: both he and I feel extremely anxious, and are looking up to God for his aid and direction in this important and delicate matter.

The king has not been treated, by his people while at Tonga, as he has been accustomed to be treated while at Vavau and Hapai; and he very naturally

[*] This Christian sovereign is the ruling chief of the Hapai and Vavau groups of islands, as well as of Tongatabu.—EDIT.

feels it. At the same time he is most needed here. The prospects of Tonga brighten daily under his Christian reign; heathenism everywhere nods to its fall, and Popery, its first cousin, is anything but prosperous. As the king will dine with us to-day, I shall reason the matter over with him, and pray that right words and right views may be given me. Every eye is now turned this way, and the issue is waited for with sleepless anxiety.

3*d.* I have learned from the king that he only intends to turn his back on this offending *colo* for a season, till they become penitent and sue for his return. There are also reasons which may not be named, but which weigh upon his mind, and I cannot say another word to him about staying.

Mr. Thomas has this morning signified to me his wish to return with Mrs. Thomas to England, and I have consented to his doing so the next time the brig shall visit the islands.

4*th.* The king of Niua came to pray for a missionary, and promised how many things they would do for his support. I urged him to come away with all his people to Vavau, where there was land enough, and where they could have all that they desired respecting the holy ordinances of religion; for there we had sent a good supply of missionaries. He replied that "such a thing might be very good, only it could never be done. Was it ever heard that a people had abandoned their country, where they and their fathers had lived happily *ever since the land was drawn up out of the sea?*"

I wish we could spare a missionary for this people. We have there one of the most pure and prosperous churches I have seen in any land, at home or abroad. In it the gospel leaven has done more than in any place I have yet seen, towards leavening the whole mass of the population. A missionary might guide them into all truth, no man gainsaying. These people, without a pastor, will find weeds and tares growing up among them: and upon us lies the solemn responsibility of caring for this little flock surrounded by the ocean.

King George has committed to me a letter to his Excellency Governor Grey, of New-Zealand, desiring to be under the shadow of British power, and asking the governor to inquire respecting a letter which had been sent by a former king of Tonga to the queen, but to which no answer had been received. The king renews the proposal therein made, that he and his people become not merely the *allies*, but the *subjects*, of the British crown. This is done because they fear the French, whose base conduct towards the people of Tahiti is fully known here. I am glad the king has taken this step; inasmuch as I am satisfied Governor Grey is just the kind-hearted and far-seeing man that will befriend a fine people who seek to be kept from the spoiler.

A man called on Mr. Thomas to mend a pair of spectacles, supplied from the mission-store some time ago, but which, he said, did not answer very well, though he had taken the greatest care of them, *covering them all over with cocoa-nut oil.* Another had come for some medicine, which was carefully wrapped up in a pretty substantial piece of brown paper, and accompanied with this verbal direction, "*Take this* when you get home." The man accordingly did so; but complained to one of his neighbors, that the medicine (a small portion of calomel) was very difficult to take. The other said, that, as to the difficulty, he, for his part, had taken the same kind of medicine, and found no difficulty whatever. To which the first replied, that he should not have minded the mere medicine, but he found it very hard *to swallow such a lump of brown paper.* This poor Tongan seems to have reasoned very much like those who are able to swallow the dogma of transubstantiation.

Respecting the cannibalism of these people, I have long had abundant evidence; but the testimony of one of our most holy and useful chiefs, called David, who was one of the *Tui-vakano* family, and in his early days a mighty man in battle, may be worth recording. David died in the Lord, after many years of deep piety and eminent usefulness. Before his health declined, he often related the following incident in his early career:—He was engaged in a sanguinary war at Faahefa, where he was hotly pursued into the wood by several strong warriors, fell under their powerful clubs, and was left for dead. After a while, however, he found himself able to crawl away upon his hands and knees into a small native hut, where he arrived in the dark night, with all his swollen wounds and bruises thick upon him. In this state he was unknown to the family whose dwelling he had reached. He was permitted to remain for some days in quiet, and partook with them of a little food. But one night he observed them preparing an *umu,* (to cook food,) which is not a usual thing under such circumstances. His apprehensions being awakened, he listened, and overheard them making arrangement to cook him in the heated oven, and then to eat him. The case was so clear, that mistake was out of the question. But David was a man of great resources in himself; and while they were outside preparing the oven, supposing their victim quite safe, he crept away, under cover of the night, and ultimately made his escape to his friends, by whom he was received as one alive from the dead. To them he related the affair of his escape from the cannibal jaws of the native family, who were sent for immediately. They there and then confessed the truth of David's report, but excused themselves on the ground of their not knowing that he was the person they now found him to be; for it was not then their custom for poor people to eat a chief. On this ground their punishment was mitigated; but the mere cannibal part of the business was no matter of surprise to any party.

We are busy to-day embarking the families for Feejee,—with Messrs. Ford and Malvern,—to proceed to their field of labor. They are thoroughly tired of their Tonga sojourn of three months, and sigh to reach their destination. One full year will have passed away from the time they left home to the period of their settlement in their stations at Feejee. Having now completed my work in the Friendly Isles, we are getting all ready to sail with the first fair wind for Ono, Lakemba, and Vewa. The native fleet of six canoes, with about six hundred men on board, will sail for Hapai about the same time, with King George and King Melchisedec Takapontolo: the latter is king of Niua Foou.

The wind being from the north, the heat and musquitoes have been tormenting. The children are blistered by the sun; the prickly-heat has broken out upon them; and now the sting of the never-tiring musquitoes leaves scarcely a sound place in their skin, where it is at all exposed. This is rather a severe seasoning; but I hear no murmur: all hands are assured that the worst is yet to come in torrid Feejee.

5th. The Lord's day. Our large chapel here was filled from end to end at the early-dawn prayer-meeting. At nine I preached, Mr. Thomas interpreting. The chapel was not merely filled, but, outside, the green grass was the seat of a multitude. These could both see and hear; for our chapels here are not encumbered with walls, seats, doors, and windows. There is a beautiful roof above, and the earth is covered with clean mats below. There are no pews, nor any seats but the mats, which are all they desire. They all seemed to hear with solemn attention, and deep interest; and the power of the Lord was evidently there. At eleven o'clock, the English service was conducted by Mr. Amos: about thirty persons were present, and felt that it was good to be there. Several of these were converted seamen from the brig, and others are *runaways*, who have become religious while living among the natives. At three o'clock our native love-feast began: it continued till sundown. The chapel was thinly sprinkled over with from five hundred to six hundred members, among whom there was great order and solemnity. The speaking was without any long intervals, and no one seemed devoid of interest during the time occupied by those who bore their testimony that Christ had saved them, and that they loved him in return. Mr. Thomas took down the following:—

1. Louisa Majiva, the class-leader from Holouga, said:—"I rise to make known the state of my soul. I have been looking forward with pleasure to this love-feast, and expecting much from it. Now I rise up, not, however, in pride, but with feelings of joy. I rise to speak before his ministers, and the friends of the Lord now assembled together, of what he has done for me. My soul is now happy, and I love the Lord Jesus. It is he, and only he, that I set my mind upon. There is by no means any one thing in this world that I trust in, or expect anything from, but him only. I wish to do so always; and am looking forward and trusting in him, that I shall be in that great love-feast which is held in heaven above."

2. Solomon Naa, of Nukualofa, an old chief, spoke as follows:—"I stand up before you. I am very happy. I thank the Lord Jesus. I praise him much. I do this; yet I am not wise, but a very ignorant, uninstructed man. My mind is yet dark and foolish, and I am nearly blind: I cannot read the sacred Scriptures; this I regret. I am a poor, weak, ignorant creature; yet I love the Lord Jesus. I love his ministers and his people, and am very happy and comfortable. It is true that there is evil at Nukualofa; but it does not spring from the religion. There are many disorders here; but I love the Lord, and look to him."

3. Mary Taukeiako, a class-leader of this place, rose, and, with a strong, clear voice, said:—"I rejoice this day in the Lord. I am very happy to be at this love-feast this day. Praise the Lord! My Christian

friends, I am very happy this day. This day is a day which causes joy, not vain and worldly, but joy in the Lord, in his love. Here are his ministers likewise, whom he has sent to us. I praise the Lord, and give him thanks. I know he has saved my soul. My soul is very happy, and I have got up to speak before you all of what the Lord has done, and is still doing. It is not on account of anything else, but on account of the death of Christ, that my soul is saved. The death of Jesus is the cause of my soul's life from the dead. This is the cause of my joy. And is it unbecoming in me to be joyful? Do angels rejoice in heaven when a sinner is converted to God, and shall not I rejoice when God saves me? I, who am a sinner, a condemned slave, once in danger of everlasting death, shall not I rejoice? I will rejoice,—I do rejoice in the Lord, who came that I might be saved."

4. Philip Jiji, the head teacher, from Niua Foou, said:—"I rise up to speak of the state of my mind. I know that God has saved my soul: my sins are forgiven, and I am happy. It is not for any works of righteousness which I have done; for I have been a great sinner; but he has had mercy on me, and saved me from my sins, and I still know his love. I still retain this sense of the love of God to me. In reference to my situation as a teacher, I find nothing difficult to me, either to remain at my post of duty, or to leave it for another to take. I have seen what the Lord has done at Niua Foou, and my heart has rejoiced. I set off, because I was directed, for Vavau, where I saw the work of the Lord, and rejoiced. I then came to Hapai, where also I saw the work of the Lord Jesus amongst his people, and was glad. And

now, having reached Tonga with the *Tui Niua* and his people, even here I see the work of God and his ministers, and am happy. My soul is happy in the Lord. I make known this work of the Lord in my heart. I know the forgiving love of the Lord Jesus. He does now save me, and I do trust in him that he will save me to the end."

5. Benjamin Luani, a chief of this place, said:—"I stand up before you to make known my feelings on this occasion: not, however, in pride or show, but simply to declare the work of the Lord in my soul. When I heard of this religion, I thought it was a good thing, and began to attend, so as to find out. I soon found out many things which I did not like, and which were hard to be endured. I then said, 'Religion is an evil thing:' but I was not happy; I was very foolish. I sought again to try to find out. Then I found that religion was true. The Lord pitied me, and has saved me; and I am now happy, yet very weak and ignorant: but I wish to be separated from the world, and to live for the Lord only. I wish to do that which is right before the Lord, to fear God, and to act as becometh his holy word at all times."

6. Joel Mafileo, or Tui Hapai, rose and spoke as follows:—"I had lived in all kinds of sin; but when the true religion began to be known at Tonga, and the true God spoken about, I was afraid, and began to seek God. Still I lived in sin and wickedness, and found it hard to practice that which I knew to be good; but I sought again and again, and the Lord made himself known unto me, pardoned my sins, and made me happy. Then it was I learned how easy it is to practice that which is right and good. As I

love God, and delight myself in him, the Lord is carrying on his work in my soul. I am happy, and find it good to be here. I find it good to draw nigh to him in secret: the Lord is there; he is in my soul. In voyaging from Hapai hither, I found him with me. My spirit rejoiced in him. He is near me. I am happy. The morning sermon was very good to my soul. I love the family which was then spoken of. I am one of that family! Praise the Lord! I do not wish to do my own mind or will, or to walk in my own way. I wish to endure all things for the Lord's sake, and endure unto the end. This is a joyous day. I am glad to see the ministers of the Lord and his people this day. Praise the Lord!"

7. Rhoda Ungounga, a leader and chief, from Vavau, said:—"I was ill yesterday, and feared I should not be able to attend this love-feast, and I prayed to the Lord about it; for I much wished to be present, lest I should suffer loss by it. And now I praise the Lord, who has heard me, and brought me here. This is a great day, and a good day to my soul. I am happy now. I was blessed at Hapai, on my way hither, and have found the word very good here; my soul has been made very happy. I do not fear to die. I love the Lord, and he loves me. He is with me. I thank him that I have come to Tonga at this time. I am nearly blind; but I bless the Lord I am happy in him. I believe I shall praise him forever."

8. Jone Faubula, of Vavau, the Feejee chief, said:—"Friends, I rise to thank the Lord, and to speak of his work in my soul. I love the Lord, and praise the Lord, and will continue to praise him. I belong to Christ. I give up myself to him, and to his work.

'I live, yet not I, but Christ liveth in me.' I am his; let him do with me as he pleases."

In the evening I preached in English, expecting to depart on the morrow. This parting of the mission families, who had been so long together, was not without *feeling;* which could not be wondered at, considering the trials of the way, and the untried scenes upon which they were about to enter. But they trust in the living God, and follow the Master who never deserts, nor fails to succor, his servants.

A copy of those parts of the Scriptures which are already in print in the Tonga language, was placed in my hands by the chairman of the district, with the following inscription:—

"To the Rev. Walter Lawry, General Superintendent of the New-Zealand Missions, &c., and the first Wesleyan Missionary in the Friendly Islands: presented to him on the first official visit to his old station, after twenty-four years' absence, by his unworthy brother and fellow-laborer, John Thomas."

On leaving the Friendly Islands,—where my life was held in jeopardy, when, in the prime of my days, I came to ascertain whether a door was open among them to receive the message of mercy at the hands of missionaries, or whether they were disposed to murder them now, as they had formerly murdered those of the London Society, sent out in the "Duff," —I may set down a few of the impressions which this visit has made on my mind, while I have been observing everything in connection with the natives and the mission with the attention of deep interest and earnest solicitude.

In point of civilization, their advance, at first,

appears but small. The natives of Tonga are an idle people; and, as such, they must of necessity be, less or more, a degraded people. But at the same time their love of ease, rather than of toil, arises from the wasting heat of their climate, which unfits them for labor, as labor is performed among us. They are not so strong as they are well-grown and beautifully formed; and having such abundance of fruit on their luxuriant trees, their bays also and shores teeming with various fish, they have all that they need, and almost all that they desire; therefore they cannot, in their present state, have any adequate motive to endure wasting labor. Their soil is rich, and sends forth food with little culture.

What they need to make them industrious, is education, and instruction in the useful arts, which will lead to new wants; then they will not only desire books, but commerce also. They will begin to imitate those who are above them. This, indeed, they have begun to do: the chief men and teachers wear an upper linen garment, in addition to their usual dress; the females often do the same. This will spread, and require them to get cocoa-nut oil, and the like; as they have already begun to do. Many tuns per year are being shipped off, for which they get calico and cutlery. Here is incipient commerce. They are certainly not merely keen, but greedy, traders. This arises partly from a desire to have our wares, partly from their ignorance of the relative value of their articles and ours, and partly from the foolish, and worse than foolish, things which they have picked up from foreign traffickers. They have been often duped, and not unfrequently misled. In these matters they are spoiled children, which is a cause of grief and trouble to their pastors. Their country has resources of wealth to a great extent: beef, pork, and poultry might be raised in abundance; cotton and sugar-cane thrive well here; to the cocoa-nut there is hardly any end; cordage and shells are plentiful. Perhaps Divine Providence will favor New-Zealand and the Australian colonies with these islands as *their* West Indies.

The comparison which I have been able to make between the heathen fortresses and the Christian villages, is greatly in favor of the latter. These have comforts about them, and an air of superiority which leaves the Pagan far behind.

They are now in a transition-state: their old habits are broken up, and their new state of things is only formed in embryo. Formerly they were ruled by terror: the chief dealt death to whom he would with the end of his club; a man who was found refractory was quickly dispatched. But, now that they are freed from the reign of terror, it would be too much to expect that such an emancipation would not be abused. It is abused by certain young chiefs, who are merely nominal Christians; and it is also abused by a few disorderly persons here and there: but order is rising out of disorder. A code of laws is under consideration; and I am to seek assistance from one of our judges, on my return to New-Zealand. Governors are appointed at Vavau and Hapai, and courts of justice are set up. All this needs much to make it complete: but the matter is advancing as fast as such matters usually do, and the movement is in the right direction.

As to EDUCATION, I have no fear whatever. There are and will be some obstacles in the way; but the mass of Tonga children and adults are not merely willing to be at school, but they delight in learning. They have both leisure and capacity, and, being densely crowded in their *colo,* we need little more than a good system and a proper teacher, and all will go on cheerfully. These we now possess; and the fields are white unto the harvest.

As to the success of our MISSION in the Friendly Islands, I am far from thinking that it is as great as it might have been, because I am familiar with some hinderances, which could not fail to check the great work of the Holy Spirit among this people; while, on the other hand, I am bound to record my testimony, that a great work of God is manifest on every side, and that there is much more to cheer than to discourage those who labor among the Tongans. The spirit of the people is generally open and benevolent, cheerful and happy. In their devotional exercises they are solemn and earnest, like men who think as well as feel. Their attendance is generally very good, fully equal to anything I have ever seen in the best days of Cornwall, when the Spirit was specially poured from on high. The morals of these islanders are greatly improved, not to say revolutionized. They were much given to lying and theft, to treachery and uncleanness. But now they are for the most part truthful and straightforward in what they say. I am not aware that they are a whit behind the New-Zealanders in their high sense of justice and integrity: a double-dealing man is pointed at by public consent, and impurity hides itself. I speak of the *general* state of public morals, when I say that I have never seen the wheat so free from chaff in any part of the world, as I have seen it in these islands. Of course, there are some scapegraces here as everywhere; but the Sabbath is observed as a holy day, consecrated to the Lord, and there is a conformity of heart and life to the Christianity of the New Testament, surpassing all that I have elsewhere seen, and such as it is truly gratifying to witness. In passing up and down among them, I often ask myself, "What but the gospel of the Lord Jesus Christ could have produced such a change in this once deeply-polluted people?" Surely acts of Parliament could not; counting beads and making crosses could not; baptismal regeneration and priestly assumption could not; the teaching of a Christless morality could not. No: the Author of this work is God; and the work is worthy of him; and those whom he has honored as his agents in this mighty moral change of an entire people can change places with but few on earth, without being losers by the change. "They that be wise shall shine as the brightness of the firmament; and they that turn many to righteousness as the stars forever and ever."

CHAPTER II.

VISIT TO THE FEEJEE ISLANDS.

Wednesday, September 8th, 1847.* I left the Friendly Islands, and proceeded with Messrs. Ford and Malvern, and their families, to Feejee, their ultimate destination. All the party was sick, as usual; for the wind was high, and the sea boisterous.

10*th*. We made Ono, and received a note from Mr. Watsford, but could not anchor the vessel, as the small opening in the reef only admits a boat at certain times of tide, and through this opening there is generally such a rush of the waves from without, meeting the mighty flood from within, that the passage is not merely dangerous, but awfully terrific. The same precisely is the case at Lakemba, where we had to "shoot the gulf" in our whale-boat, with four oars, and Captain Buck at the steer-oar, all of which were

* "The details here given of the cannibalism of these islands, we are aware, will be almost too horrible for many readers; but we feel, notwithstanding, that the facts of the case *ought to be made known*, in order to show to Christians what pure heathenism really is, and thus to make them more fully recognise the solemn duty of sending the gospel of Christ to the pre-eminently wretched and perishing inhabitants of those many 'dark places of the earth, which are the habitations of cruelty.' The perilous circumstances by which our missionary brethren are daily encompassed, their manifold privations, their self-denying labors, and their Christian heroism and patience, so touchingly described in this journal, call for the deep sympathy and earnest prayers of our friends at home, and will furnish ample topics of powerful appeal, and *texts* for practical addresses, in missionary meetings."—*Wesleyan Missionary Notices, November*, 1848.

knocked about as a leaf is tossed by the mountain torrent. In vain was the cry of "Larboard oars," and then "Starboard oars:" for, when all was done that skill and strength could do, the war of the elements set us at naught. Then Providence sent aid to maritime skill, without which we could not have re-entered the open ocean on our way to the brig. Our work is rendered very trying by these reefs, where no harbor exists for the vessel, and only such rapid gulfs for our boats.

But Ono is a little gem in the Christian's eye: for nearly all the adult population are consistent members of the Christian Church, and all the children are under instruction. The total number of souls is four hundred and seventy-four, and of Church members three hundred and ten.

There is one thing not a little singular in the early history of Christianity here.

About six years ago, the few who believed the word of God at Ono were violently persecuted by the heathen; but in the midst of the storm, their numbers kept increasing, until they concluded that they would take up arms against their enemies. They did so; and the heathens fled before them to their strong fortress on the mountain. The Christians followed, and took the town. Scarcely any one fell on either side; and, instead of killing the vanquished, the Christians ran to the others, fell on their necks, and wept over them. These, in turn, were so affected by this new and extraordinary treatment, that they fell on their knees and *lotued* at once. Aforetime, they would have been eaten. Now, they are not merely preserved alive, but also wept over by their conquerors.

The fear of them fell upon the Pagan warriors, Christian love bowed their hearts as the heart of one man; and Christ was glorified both in the conquerors and in the conquered. How wonderful will be the history of his conquests in that day, when he shall appear in the clouds of heaven, and every eye shall see him, and every knee shall bow before him!

The Rev. John Watsford, with his wife and two children, came on board, on their way to the district meeting, and to their new station. These very excellent persons are the fruit of our mission in New South Wales, whence they were taken out four years ago. A more efficient missionary than Mr. Watsford will not often stand forth, as, at once, a fruit of our missions, and an ambassador sent to the heathen.

Sunday, September 12th. We made Lakemba, and I preached in the chapel in the afternoon, Mr. Calvert interpreting to a most attentive congregation. At Ono the natives partake much of the Tonga character, dress, and color; but here we were met by the dark skin, almost entirely without covering, of the unmixed Feejeean race. They appear less lovely in their features, and far less symmetrical in their form, than the Tongans; but they are more willing to lend a hand, and upon an intimate acquaintance show a keener intellect, than the Friendly Islanders. The Feejeeans are comparatively an industrious people, and they are polite and obliging in their manners, far beyond all that I have seen in these seas; but their nude appearance, and their strong ill odor, make them thoroughly disgusting to persons newly arrived.

13th. Lakemba from the sea commands unqualified admiration. Its wood, and hill, and dale, and sunny

WESLEYAN MISSION-HOUSE, AND OTHER BUILDINGS, AT LAKEMBA, FEEJEE ISLANDS.

shore, cannot fail to strike the eye of him who has a taste for the beauties of landscape. Yet this fine and picturesque island has many a barren hill; most of its flats are bogs, teeming with swarms of mosquitoes and stinging flies; and, worse than these, the miasma, arising out of the swamps, cannot fail to be more or less injurious to those who breathe its atmosphere.

The island is high, and measures about thirty-five miles in circumference, with a population of about fifteen hundred, of whom two hundred and fifty are Christians, whose children are trained with care, and in the fear of the Lord.

Mr. and Mrs. Calvert gave us a very kind welcome, and showed us a mission-house and premises, which sufficiently established their reputation for good taste, sound judgment, and untiring industry. Their children also were such as the children of a Christian minister should be, "in all subjection, with all gravity."

Accompanied by Mr. Calvert, I visited the king, another Eglon, rolling in fat, and surrounded by many wives. He lives in a very large house, in which a fire warmed the family, while I could with difficulty bear the temperature without any fire: my friend Calvert, however, enjoyed it: such is the force of habit. I saw nothing but sombre wretchedness at this palace of a pagan. Through Mr. Calvert I lectured to him on the truths of Christ, faith, and eternity; to all which he, and those who were with him, listened as though they tolerated, rather than enjoyed, what was said.

This chief city of Lakemba is another Venice, intersected with water in all directions, which cannot be healthy under a vertical sun. I was sorry I had not brought my powerful microscope, that I might inspect the abounding animalculæ, which inhabit these stagnant waters. Several of the king's household attend the services, and some are members of our society; but this mighty cava-drinker sits still, and treats Mr. Calvert pretty well.

From the top of a hill we could see several of the islands comprehended in the Lakemba circuit, where we have many members. Many more lie so distant as to be far beyond the horizon of view, and all have to be visited in the feeble native canoes. The number now visited is considerable, and on each of them we have native teachers and Christian churches.

I consider that the mission at Lakemba has been conducted with sound judgment and considerable success. A colony of godless Tonga natives is a drag upon our wheels at this place; and a Romish priest will not afford us much help, unless it please Divine Providence to make the wrath of man to praise Him, and the rest of wrath to be restrained.

We left Mr. and Mrs. Malvern here, at least for a season, that they may have the valuable aid of Mr. and Mrs. Calvert, and with them take part in the work of this very extensive circuit, as soon as they shall have sufficiently studied the native language to be able to communicate with the natives.

15*th.* I sailed for Vewa with the missionaries, to attend the district meeting. This island is a mere insignificant speck in the Feejeean group; but is very near the large island that measures three hundred miles round, and is the key to a very dense population. Besides which, it is within sight of Bau, the imperial heathen city, with which a daily intercourse is maintained. It seems that the great chiefs of Feejee prefer living on small islands, near the large land.

We landed at nightfall, and were received by the families of this interesting mission with a most cordial welcome. Messrs. Hunt and Lyth came on board, while Mr. Jaggar prepared for us on shore. We were now surrounded by man-eating, dark-colored, and almost nude men and women, whose appearance made nothing in their favor, and whose history scandalizes human nature. In addition to what they were born in, they possess a fine set of white teeth, and a large bushy head of hair, which some of them take great pains to set off to advantage. One has his natural hair set up and powdered gray, like a judge; another spreads it out like a forest oak in full foliage; while a third has the front white, and the back part jet black. Surely the *beau idéal* of hair-dressing must reside in Feejee. They have an apology for a belt round the middle, and the rest of their covering fits exactly as tight as the skin.

The country presents a fine appearance, from its richly wooded and uneven surface; but, like New-Zealand, its hills and gullies are too rapid and precipitous to be easily traveled over, and will, in this respect, bid defiance to the plough and to the wheel vehicles of old England. The productions, however, of its rich soil are procured by the natives to an extent which fully satisfies them; and a population estimated at three hundred thousand might be multiplied ten-fold without exhausting the resources of these islands. But should emigration ever flow to Feejee, even after the Christian missions, now being planted with so much hopefulness, shall have changed the character of this people, it is more than probable that the first generation of bold adventurers would fall a prey to the many devouring jaws of destruction, which could not but await them in such a country and in such an enterprise. The Christian missionary lives wherever God sends him. From the beginning the natives say, "This *lotu* is a great thing!" and the Lord puts the fear of it upon the public mind. These self-denying men never interfere with the secular affairs of the natives, and are men of strict integrity and benevolence of character, devoted to the good of the people. This they plainly see and readily acknowledge. These servants of the Lord go forth in the name of their Master, and he is with them as a wall of fire round about, and concerning them he says:—"Touch not mine anointed, and do my prophets no harm." These are their circumstances, and sufficiently explain the secret of their safety: but are these the circumstances of those who emigrate to foreign lands for purposes of civilization? Most certainly not. They may be, and often are, very respectable persons; but they are mixed, and their objects will, sooner or later, clash with the wishes of the natives; and other causes, arising from intemperance, want of caution, ignorance of the language, inordinate love of gain, and heedless breach of native law and usage, will cause their defense to depart from them:—then it is too late to repine that they had begun in ignorance a career that must end in a beacon to warn those who succeed them. Who can number the white men slain in Feejee? Nor has this

WESLEYAN CHAPEL, MISSION-HOUSE, AND HEATHEN TEMPLE, AT VEWA, FEEJEE.

ceased; it still goes on: the intervals are brief between these cases of violence and destruction. How grateful should we be for the preservation of so many mission families during a period of nine years! Not one of them has been injured, though they have stood in the front of danger, and in the midst of devouring cannibalism, all these years! At the same time they continue in jeopardy every hour. While I am writing these lines, there are canoes in sight, proceeding to murder certain persons of this place; and any boat's crew of white men landing at the opposite island, about seven miles away, would be immediately cut off. This they meditate in consequence of five men of their number having been shot by the natives, two days ago, at the instigation of a white man resident at Vewa: so the natives assert. Such to this hour is the insecurity of human life at Feejee!

Vewa, Sunday, Sept. 19th. Mr. Calvert preached at eight o'clock to a very well-behaved native congregation, who evidently entered into the spirit of religious worship. The well-built native chapel was quite full. The Feejeeans observe better order and more solemnity than most congregations that I have seen. At eleven o'clock I preached in the same chapel to the mission families, and the crew of the brig. We were all professing Christians, and, being met under rather peculiar circumstances, the interest of the occasion was somewhat strong and lively. Our friends were glad to see us among them, and shame upon us if we did not cherish a deep interest in these heroic servants of the Lord! While those fine spirits, Messrs. Hunt, Lyth, Calvert, and Jaggar, with their wives, stood before me, with the junior members of the mission, I could not but reverence and honor the men whom God had so greatly distinguished in this scene of activity, danger, and usefulness. In the afternoon, Mr. Watsford preached to the natives with a fluency and effect that astonished me. His swarthy audience was not merely impressed, but riveted to the subject, so well handled by their preacher.

Elijah Varani, the second chief of this place, and a thoroughly Christian man,* has just told me that he has been negotiating, with the few heathens left in Vewa, for the *'Mburi*, or god-house, of this town. Most of the people are become Christians, and, among them, all the priests, save one, and he has run away. Varani remarked to the heathen, that they could now have no service in the temple, and that he and his Christian friends would like the use of it for the purpose of reading the Scriptures and repeating the catechisms. "The appropriation of it in this way," Varani said, "will give your gods an opportunity of being avenged on us, if they are able, for driving them out, and bringing in another worship. Let them try what they can do," said he; "and be assured we are not afraid of them." So the matter is settled; the temple is now for the use of the Christians. I went to see it, but found little to interest, and nothing to admire. Its situation is good, and great pains have been taken to make it showy; but still it bears all the dingy gloom of heathenism through every part of the interior. Thank God, this scene of devilish imposture will now be lighted up by the oracles of divine truth and mercy.

* For an account of the character and conversion of Varani, see note A, at the end of the volume.—EDIT.

20th. From Varani I learned the true state of the case in reference to five murders, which have just now taken place. The report is, that a Manilla man, living here, had a wish to obtain a barrel of oil which the natives of the coast, seven miles hence, had found drifting toward their shore. He went and made an offer for the oil, but was refused. He then went to Navingi, a Bau chief, and, presenting him with a musket, requested that the people having the oil might be compelled to give it up to him. The chief sent to them to do so; but they refused. Another party was sent to demand the oil, and, if it should be refused, to kill the people. They did refuse, and five unoffending people were at once murdered. The white man, as the natives call him, was the cause of this outrage, as the natives assert; and the friends of the deceased who survive say they will be avenged on white men, the first that they can lay hold of. The Manilla man has given out that Varani told him to do as he has done. The falsehood, however, cannot stand before the well-established character of Varani. But should a crew from the "John Wesley" be found on their coast, no doubt every one of them would be put to death: and this is by no means impossible, as the vessel has gone to Uvalau for the purpose of taking in ballast, and can know nothing of this awful state of things. Such is life in Feejee!

21st. I learned from my friend, the Rev. John Hunt, several facts illustrative of the Feejeean character, but they cannot be recorded: "for it is a shame even to speak of those things which are done of them in secret." There are, however, some others which I will venture to put on paper under the head of

HORRIBLE CANNIBALISM IN FEEJEE.

It is by no means a rare occurrence for a number of natives to fall upon a fishing party, and kill as many of them as cannot escape. The following case occurred not long ago: seven persons were clubbed in a most brutal manner, near the spot where I write. Their heads were crushed by heavy blows, and their bodies mangled with axes. When the men had done, the boys began, and did as they had seen the others do in the work of mangling the bodies. In this state they lay for three days, broiling under a tropical sun, until all who desired had gazed upon them, and their smell had became all but intolerable; then the cooking and eating proceeded, until the whole was devoured. It is proper to remark, that these very people turn away in disgust from a piece of pork which may happen to be only slightly tainted!

It is not at all unusual for the Feejeeans to inter a human body, or a part thereof, and especially the heart and liver, under the earth, in the place where they keep their bread, during any period they please; and when they have an occasion for preserved flesh, it is exhumed, cooked, and eaten! Nothing is done, but to put it under the earth, and then to take it up again as a dainty dish!

These are the days of education, and in their way the Feejeeans are on the alert: they rub human flesh over the lips of their little children, and put a portion into the infant's mouth, that it may be nourished by its juice and trained in the practice of cannibalism!

A mighty chief, now in power, eats human flesh, cut off limb by limb from the man whom he has selected, and that while he is yet alive; and he compels the remaining part of the mutilated man to look at the process of his own limbs being cooked and eaten by his own chief! But these cases are rare.

There are parts of Feejee where they not merely kill and eat their enemies, but where the chief lives upon his friends; and these are frequently eaten raw! This cannibal of Ragi-Ragi has been known to have a good supply of human flesh in his box salted down, and has lived upon it as his daily food, seldom eating any other kind of flesh.

In some few cases they bake their enemies *alive*, and many of them together. But it is more common to take them to the capital, there by torture make sport for the public, and then kill and eat the captives.

One way of obtaining food is to lie in ambush, and seize upon females, as they return with water, or from bathing. These are killed and taken away; and there is a rule among them to this effect,—that, in case a man can succeed in pouncing upon a female from the place of his concealment, and strike the death-blow so suddenly that no one, friend or foe, shall hear or know anything of the matter, and then open the body and cover himself with the contents, that covering shields him from the claim of any one to have a share: he eats as much as he can, and buries the remainder, to be exhumed for his own future use. While Mr. Jaggar was living at Rewa, the following event took place there, and was well known to all:—The king of Rewa became angry with one of his young female servants, and commanded that one of her arms should be cut off. This was done accordingly. He directed that the girl should be compelled to eat her own flesh, or die. She did eat part of her own arm, after it had been cooked, and proceeded till she became very sick. She was then permitted to live.

There are some circumstances in connection with these facts, which I am not able to set down: they are before me; but a veil must cover them! The whole of these things, and many more, are related to me by many witnesses, persons who cannot be deceived, and who would not deceive. I set them down on the spot, where no one doubts, or attempts for a moment to deny, their truth. They are far enough from being an inventory, but are merely given as specimens.

There is one thing remarkable in the revolting accounts which this people give of their man-eating career; that is, that the flesh of human beings is really very good, and they like it. The flesh of women is rather better than the flesh of men; and when the chief wants something very delicate, or in case many bodies are before him, a child is roasted for his repast.

A Rewa canoe was wrecked near Natawa, and many of the crew swam to the shore. The Natawa people found them, took them into the town, and at once began to make preparations for cooking them. They did not club them, lest a little blood should be lost; but they bound them until the ovens were heated. Some of the cannibals could not wait, but plucked off pieces, such as ears and noses, from the bodies of their victims, and ate them raw. When the ovens were ready, they began to cut up the poor wretches, who were crying to their murderers for mercy. They first cut off their legs as far as the knees, afterwards the arms, and then the trunks. While they were thus engaged, they had dishes placed under the different parts to catch the blood; and if a drop happened to fall on the ground, they licked it up. The different parts were then cooked and eaten. The whole of this was seen by an intelligent Christian native, named Micah, or, in Feejee, Maicha, who is on the spot where I am now writing.

The Socinian says, that human nature is very good; and the Feejeean says, that human flesh is good, for he has eaten it, and likes it. But perhaps the Socinian will not receive this testimony: whether he receive it or not, one fact is clear, that these people are in a state of nature, and are quite free from education and religion. The apostle, writing to the Romans, describes human nature just as I see it in Feejee. "When they knew God, they glorified him not as God, neither were thankful; but became vain in their imaginations, and their foolish heart was darkened. Professing themselves to be wise, they became fools, and changed the glory of the incorruptible God into an image made like to corruptible man, and to birds, and four-footed beasts, and creeping things. Wherefore God also gave them up to uncleanness, through the lusts of their own hearts, to dishonor their own bodies between themselves: who changed the truth of God into a lie, and worshiped and served the creature more than the Creator, who is blessed forever. Amen. For this cause God gave them up unto vile affections;" (and are not the facts above narrated a clear comment on what is meant by "vile affections?") and because of these things, "God gave them over to a reprobate mind, to do those things which are not convenient; being filled with all unrighteousness, fornication, wickedness," (far too gross and revolting to be placed on paper,) "covetousness, maliciousness; full of envy, murder, debate, deceit, malignity; whisperers, backbiters, haters of God, despiteful, proud, boasters, inventors of evil things, disobedient to parents, without understanding, covenant-breakers, without natural affection, implacable, unmerciful." Rom. i, 21–31. Here we have a perfectly accurate portrait of human nature as it was in Egypt and Moab, in Greece and Rome, and exactly as it is at this hour in the heathen parts of Feejee. But he must be a man of strong prejudice, who is able to believe that this human nature is very good. On such a mind the evidence of facts must weigh just as little as the testimony of Scripture. And when the goodness of human nature is preached up, the understandings of those who hear must be trampled under foot.

Mr. Hunt asserts, and the other missionaries confirm it, that the Feejeean language contains no word for a corpse; but the word they use, *bakola*, conveys the idea of eating the dead. This is their war-cry, when one of the enemy is slain, and his body found: "Here is a dead body to be eaten:" the word they use is *bakola*.

They also affirm, that within the last four years, fully one thousand people have been killed within twenty miles of Vewa; and that they keep far within compass when they say, that, of these slain, five hundred have been eaten. As to the total number eaten in that period in all Feejee, it would not be easy to form a conjecture, inasmuch as many devastatory wars have been going on beyond the limits of twenty miles.

It seems that at Ngau, an island within sight of the place where I am writing, they prepare the human body, about to be cooked, in any form they may desire. The limbs are tied, say in a sitting form, and there they remain; the body is roasted, hot stones being placed within, as in the case of other animals; when dressed, they take the body up, paint the face red, place a wig upon the head, put a club or fan in the hands, as they may happen to fancy, and then carry the whole as a present to be eaten by their friends. They sometimes travel far with this spectacle, which, when met in the path, may easily be mistaken for a living man in full dress. When the carver commences his work, he observes the same rule as in dividing other food, only the *cutis*, or outer skin, is first removed, leaving what remains white. A man here, not long since, killed and roasted one of his wives, who had offended him in the preparation of some food: he ate a part, and hung up the rest in a tree in front of his house, for the other wives to see; and there it remained. He did not say, like Abraham, "Bury my dead out of my sight."

How correctly does the inspired book portray this degraded people! "They are all gone out of the way, they are together become unprofitable; there is none that doeth good, no, not one. Their throat is an open sepulchre: with their tongues they have used deceit: the poison of asps is under their lips: whose mouth is full of cursing and bitterness: their feet are swift to shed blood: destruction and misery are in their ways: and the way of peace have they not known: there is no fear of God before their eyes." Romans iii, 12–18. There are, however, a few in Feejee, who have now the fear of God; and they, to a man, abhor their former practices, and insist upon it, that though cannibalism is a very ancient custom among them, yet that it did not formerly obtain to the same extent that it has done latterly; that the present overflowing of this tide of blood, this abounding of iniquity, is of recent growth. Varani fully believes, and confidently asserts, this *revival* and extension of the works of darkness, these frightful and startling deeds of blood. He says, all the old people, and especially his own father, used to tell him, that these bloody wars and this eating of one another, upon the present enlarged scale, sprang up in their days, and did not obtain to such an extent in the generation before them. All testimony speaks to this effect throughout Feejee; so says Varani. His friends support him in this view; and it is difficult to imagine how the human race could long exist, where violence had become so rife, and death ruled as the king of terrors over the children of pride, whom he permitted not to live out half their days. The history of infanticide here is too revolting to be written: it may be enough to say, that it is very general, and has not merely become an abominable custom, but is reduced to a system. The chief women recommend the practice to the common people; and there are persons whose profession it is to aid and abet them therein.

In the days of our Saviour, "the unclean spirit entered into many," and cases of possession became so alarming, as to clear whole neighborhoods; "for no man might pass by that way." But here the reader of Holy Scripture is presently cheered by the appointment of chosen men to preach the gospel. "Go your ways," said the Lord Jesus; "behold, I send you forth as lambs among wolves!" The effect of their preaching among these "wolves" is recorded immediately after that appointment: "And the seventy returned again with joy, saying, Lord, even the devils are subject unto us through thy name! And he said unto them, I beheld Satan as lightning fall from heaven." He was permitted to demonstrate his power and tyranny among men, and then he fell before "the sword of the Spirit, which is the word of God." Satan perhaps might see the agency of his overthrow at hand, and he came down in great wrath because he had but a short time. Wherever Christ's gospel is preached with purity and power, there Satan falls, whether it be in India or in Feejee. The divine permission for him to rally all his force, and put forth all his energy, as the old murderer, serpent, and destroyer, is clearly enough set forth in Scripture. His availing himself thereof, and doing his worst, "in great wrath," and "as a roaring lion," are also explicitly revealed; and all this rage is increased and poured forth, because he is doomed to fall before the word of God. He knows this full well, and never loses the least opportunity allowed to him to assert his evil reign, and support his infernal kingdom. From the moment when the eye of Christendom first beheld the nude savage of the south, Satan saw his kingdom fall, because he knew that that eye would pity such wretchedness as would show itself where Satan had his seat; that the Christian sympathy thus awakened would send that mighty remedy for man's misery, the gospel of the blessed God; and that this gospel, which is never faithfully preached without avail, would most certainly overthrow and banish the kingdom of darkness, and rescue the slave of sin and Satan,—as it is written in St. Paul's commission, and in every Christian minister's commission, "I send thee to open their eyes, and to turn them from darkness to light, and from the power of Satan to God; that they may receive the forgiveness of sins, and an inheritance among them which are sanctified by faith that is in me." Acts xxvi, 17, 18. Satan is enraged at this loss of his dominion; he hates the doctrine of the cross. What our Christian natives say of the time when their wars and cannibalism received a new impulse, and raged with new vigor, a vigor unknown to the former generations, and startling even to themselves, exactly corresponds to the period of their becoming known in Christendom; and the hopeful conclusion to which I am conducted is, that Satan, who held his goods in peace aforetime, now that he witnesses their discovery, and knows that a stronger than he will soon claim his goods, resolves upon a last struggle and mighty effort; and surely what is now in progress throughout these islands supplies a sufficient illustration of the energy that now worketh in the children of disobedience. Of this our own brethren here are fully sensible; and to them is the word of Scripture applicable, which saith, "Finally, my brethren, be strong in the Lord, and in the power of his might. Put on the whole armour of God, that ye may be able to stand against the wiles of the devil. For we wrestle not against flesh and blood, but against principalities, against powers, against the rulers of the darkness of this world, against spiritual wickedness in high places." Eph. vi, 10–12.

How awfully grand must these transactions appear to the ministering angels, who take such deep interest in men redeemed by the blood of the cross! And what a mystery is it, that, in neighboring islands, the prey should have been taken from the jaws of the mighty; and that, after they had clean escaped out of the snare of the devil, they should again be brought into bondage, by the importation of an old form of heathen idolatry, under the Christian name; and that customs and forms of sin, long abandoned, should now again be revived, perhaps in forms somewhat less revolting, but not in the least more pure; and that a life of sin should be pronounced reconcilable with an end of safety! Surely he who hath done this must be the "Man of sin!"

VEWA, *Sept. 22d.* We are now fully engaged with the business of the district meeting. All the characters of our brethren stand fair in every place: and, except at poor Somosomo, the great work prospers. The language has been mastered by most of them, and they speak it with surprising fluency. The New Testament is translated and printed in the Feejeean language. Measures are taken for the translation and printing of the Old Testament forthwith, and for a more extended system of education. Considering the heat of the climate, I am thankful to find the mission families in such health as they are. When I look at the very great and formidable difficulties with which they have had to grapple, in their perils by sea, perils among false white men, and perils among the heathen, this little band of Christian missionaries exhibits to me many signal proofs of the special providence of God over these precious sons of Zion, comparable to fine gold, though esteemed as earthen pitchers, the work of the potter's hands. Great, indeed, is the honor which the Master has put upon these his servants; great is the work already accomplished; and great is the labor which they have resolved to bestow upon this long debased and bloody people.

In the next world, a faithful missionary from Feejee, with his quenched brands of saved sinners attending, who shall be his crown of rejoicing in the day of the Lord Jesus, will stand so near the apostles, and prophets, and martyrs of the Lamb, that ordinary Christians can hardly hope to rank with them, so near the throne of the world's Redeemer.

Among other entries in the minutes are the following: "Are the regular contributions made in the classes, and at the renewal of the tickets, for the support of the work as far as possible? Yes; contributions have been made in the Vewa Circuit, consisting of mats, native cloth, pigs, yams, &c., amounting in value here to £16 2*s.* 10*d.*"

The following is an extract from the minutes of the district meeting now holding, on a very important subject:—

MISSIONARIES' CHILDREN.

"What can be done for the education of the children of the missionaries in this district? Answer: Feeling as we do the extreme difficulty of educating our children in Feejee, we most gladly enter into an arrangement respecting a school establishment for missionaries' children, made by the brethren of the New-Zealand District in connection with our excellent general superintendent, the Rev. Walter Lawry, for the following reasons:—

"1. Our children will be under the immediate care of Mr. Lawry,—a point in our estimation of the utmost importance.

"2. They can be conveyed to New-Zealand without expense to the committee.

"3. They will, we are persuaded, receive a suitable and sufficient education, and, which is equally important, they will have good society,—a thing which they cannot have in Feejee, except in their own families. We find that our utmost efforts to prevent them from being injured by the example and spirit of the natives are unavailing.

"4. The brethren will be comfortable in their work, until age, or sickness, or some such cause, may point out their providential path to leave the islands. The brethren have been particularly concerned respecting this point. It seemed necessary that, without such a provision, they should return home much earlier than they otherwise desired, on account of the education of their children. The plan of educating them in New-Zealand fully meets the case.

"5. After residing in a torrid climate, it is desirable that the children be removed to such a place as New-Zealand, where the air is peculiarly healthy and salubrious.

"6. We are aware of the difficulties connected with this plan,—suitable buildings must be erected, and everything requisite for such an institution provided, which will involve considerable expense: but we are willing to bear our part of the burden, so far as pecuniary means are concerned; and Mr. Lawry has nobly engaged to be at the trouble of superintending the whole undertaking.

"7. We sincerely hope, that the committee will encourage this plan, as it will, we are persuaded, be advantageous in a high degree to the good cause in which we are engaged: our children will be educated, the mission funds in the end materially saved, and we shall pursue our public duties with the satisfaction that we have not to neglect our families in order to attend to the interests of others.

"8. In addition to sending out two suitable persons to be at the head of the establishment, and furnishing the necessary school apparatus, and also allowing the Rev. Walter Lawry to draw one hundred pounds for the first two years, if required, we beg to suggest that it would be very acceptable to us if the committee would send out such linen and woolen articles as may be necessary for such an establishment, for bedding, &c., which we will most cheerfully pay for, if we have funds, but, if not, we hope our committee will provide us with them.

"9. Mr. Lawry will make you fully acquainted with all particulars respecting the plan."*

* It will be satisfactory to the reader to know, that the plan thus recommended was adopted by the Missionary Committee. The Rev. Joseph H. Fletcher and Mrs. Fletcher, both highly qualified for the important duties of an educational establishment for missionaries' sons and daughters, sailed for Auckland, Dec. 22d, 1848, with an ample supply of school furniture and materials. They were accompanied by Mr. and Mrs. Reid, the principals of a native training institution for the New-Zealanders.—Edit.

September 23d. This is our vernal equinox; the trade winds blow strong, fully a nine-knot breeze; the season is considered rather cool, but the thermometer is 82° in the shade. The new comers are all melting with the heat; but the natives have a good fire in every house, and the old missionaries button up their warm clothing, and say to us, "Wait till December and January." The process of acclimatizing is fearfully distressing, but afterwards all is easy and natural: not that this torrid heat does not produce a wasting prostration of strength and health, which now and then require a removal, in order to recruit again; but the feelings seem to be in some sense destroyed, and, though death worketh, and the patient sinks, all around him seem more sensible of what is progressing than the man himself.

An occasional trip to New-Zealand will be necessary for these Christian heroes; and such a trip in our own vessel will be inexpensive, and, by God's blessing, will fully meet the case.

24th. I received a visit from Thakombau, *Tui Fiti*, or king of Feejee, who is about thirty-five years old, above the middle size, of a very dark complexion, but rather comely. He has many wives, and knows no restraint: two were killed in his house lately, because a house of his had been burnt, and they *might* have done it! He is an absolute ruler: whom he will he kills, and whom he will he keeps alive. Upon the whole, he is rather favorable to our mission here, but does not *lotu*. He professes great dislike to the introduction of Popery. War is his delight, and feasting on the bodies of the slain. He is sitting by my side while I write, and is urging me to persuade Governor

Grey to visit him in a war-steamer, in order that they may be allied friends. He reposes confidence in England, but not in France; for the barefaced outrage of *protecting* Tahiti is known to him, and heartily denounced. He and his chiefs say that they shall one day *lotu*, and that the gospel will triumph in *Fiti*, (so they pronounce the word Feejee.) They seem to think that they shall be overcome and submit to it, rather than seek unto the Lord that they may be saved. Their two great obstacles are,—casting off their many wives, and wearing decent clothes to hide their shame. But for these formidable difficulties, many of them would openly avow what they now secretly whisper,—their belief in Christianity.

This pagan king has very little majesty, having little cultivation; but he has a feeling of pride or consciousness of power, which oozes out at all points. He has ceased to blaspheme our holy faith, as was his custom formerly. His hair is neatly dressed, and he has a small bandage round his loins, with a string of blue beads round each arm and round his neck, to which is suspended a circular boar's tooth. These are all his clothes and ornaments, except a strong black beard projecting about eight inches from his chin, and an abundance of oil besmearing his sable skin. His attendants, smoking about the mission-house, are few, and not over-dignified; but the court ladies are still more offensive than the men.

It is, however, due to this people to say, that first impressions concerning them are generally the worst; for, while their character and customs are full of contradictions, they unquestionably possess many fine qualities.

Sunday, Sept. 26th. In the native prayer-meeting at sun-rise this morning, one said in his prayer, "Lord, help us to bear our cross; and, if it be heavy, help us to move on still, bending slowly. Untie the load of our sins. If this load were tied round our loins, we could untie it ourselves; but as it is tied round our hearts, we cannot untie it, but thou canst. Lord, untie the burden now!"

At nine I preached to this sable congregation, Mr. Hunt interpreting: both he and Mr. Calvert interpret with amazing ease and fluency. I was surprised to see this clumsy way of preaching produce such effects. All were listening with fixed and solemn attention; and many, very many, were suffused in tears: among these I noticed the Queen of Vewa, and Varani. In this respect, as in many others, the Feejeeans and New-Zealanders very much resemble each other, and come much nearer than they do to the Friendly Islanders. These go in multitudes to the public worship; but they are less orderly, and are neither so much impressed, nor melted down into subdued weeping, as I have seen both in New-Zealand and in Feejee. It must not, however, be supposed that in the Friendly Isles they have not order and feeling in their public worship: they have both; and there are times when they send forth a strong and bitter cry. I have seen a congregation of worshippers so excited, that their cry might be heard as far as the full voice of a multitude could reach the ear.

In the afternoon Mr. Jaggar preached in the chapel, with ease, energy, and full compass of voice.

27th. I am surprised at the difference between the native servants in the Friendly Islands, and those of

Feejee. In the former, they can only be obtained in rare cases, and for a short time; and then they do little, and expect much: moreover, they are so trying in Tonga, that Mrs. Thomas can just as easily do her own work, as suffer the plague which they give her. At Feejee the mission families are well supplied with both male and female servants, who are respectful and kind, every way answering the end for which they enter the premises. The truth is, the Feejeeans are far more industrious than the Tongans, who, though they are more comely in our eyes, are not so sharp, nor so well disciplined, as the Feejeeans. Here they have no difficulty in landing goods from the vessel, and getting them conveyed to the mission-stores, almost for nothing; but in the Friendly Islands such matters sadly plague the poor missionaries, who have to pay most exorbitantly for all they get done by the natives.

The severe system of subjection to the arbitrary club-law of the Feejeean chiefs, who strike every one dead who offends or disobliges them, may in part account for this difference. No eastern tyrants can rule with more absolute terror than the chiefs do here; and few people are more thoroughly enslaved and trampled upon than are these islanders. They are the subjects of a grinding system of oppression, hard labor, demon-worship, and most debasing superstition. But the Christian natives are free from this thraldom, and they prize their liberty, and love those whom they know to be their liberators and their true friends. The present aspect of Christianity in Feejee is in no respect discouraging, and in some places it is exceedingly cheering.

28th. This morning early I walked over the little island of Vewa, containing probably about four hundred acres. It is removed from the large land by only a narrow sheet of salt water. If we are to judge of the soil by its productions, this land must be among the richest I have ever seen. The bread-fruit abounds. The banana also is everywhere seen in great perfection. The pine-apple and sugar-cane luxuriate here. The land is almost covered with trees, fine and stately; but not mere forest-trees; for most of them bear fruit, and the fruit is the food of man.

The shores teem with excellent fish; and the women are the chief fishers, when the net only is used: the men fish with baskets, spears, and hooks. One would think that everybody here would have enough and to spare; but such is not the case. The chiefs demand more than they need, the people are improvident, and war is not merely a destroyer of life, but also of the bounties of nature, bestowed by the Lord of all the earth.

29th. A singularly clear case, illustrating the indirect influence of the gospel, is stated by Mr. Calvert. One of the native teachers, sent by him to a heathen part of the island, tried to prevent the people from going to war; but they would not hearken to him. All things being ready, they were starting for the battle-field upon the Sabbath day, when the teacher warned them of the sin they would commit, and of their exposure to danger, closing his address by saying, "If you *will* go on the Lord's day, should any of your opponents fall into your hands, the least you can do is to keep them alive and bring them here." Two of their enemies did fall into their hands: they brought them home alive and well, and exhibited them to the teacher, who said to them: "You did well not to kill these men: my advice to you now is, to let them go home to their friends, that they may tell them what a fine religion this is, that teaches us to love our enemies." They were accordingly liberated, instead of being cooked, and are gone home to report what has not often been so reported in Feejee. The parties have not since been heard of; but no act of parliament could have produced such a result, as this silent teaching by facts, clothed with benevolence and light. The moral hereby conveyed to this gross people will be much the same as that which our Saviour taught to the gross Gadarenes, when he said to the man who had been possessed with devils, "Go home and show what great things the Lord hath done for thee."

NATIVE TEACHERS.

Thursday, September 30th.—I am preparing to send forth some native teachers. This is a very important part of our work in these islands: the selection requires great care, and a sound judgment. Nor is this all; for two extremes should be avoided,—that of making no use of native teachers in any department of the great work now in progress, and the opposite one of intrusting too much power and authority to men not sufficiently informed to bear it. They are hereby injured themselves, and the flock intrusted to them is mangled, and not fed. A native agency should be *trained:* without this it will never come into full efficiency. They should first be taught, who would teach the things of the kingdom of God.

The *lotu* is an entire disruption of the whole order of things: wives must be put away, in all cases of plurality; the reign of terror ends, and the rule of love comes in its place. In this moral and social revolution, some strange things occur, such as are far too difficult for the decision of a poor native, who, though he has "passed from death unto life," has had no experience, and will form very crude notions of this order of things. I could set down twenty cases illustrative of this matter; but to conceal is better than to uncover the frailties and errors of those who mean well. There are three ways in which the agency of pious natives may now be employed with advantage:—

1. To conduct schools, when they themselves have been instructed and trained sufficiently; and it is all the better, if they are under the superintendence of a missionary.

2. They are useful in opening new places where the heathen desire to be instructed, but are still ignorant of the *lotu*. In this case a pious native teacher will be of great use, and will prepare the way of the Lord. The occasional visit of a missionary will be required even here, and that at an early period of the new station, or else blunders will be made, and the work will be marred. But under the occasional inspection of a missionary, the work may go on well for some years, as in the cases of Mua and Ono.

3. A native agency works admirably under the eye of a missionary. Here is its great field of usefulness. Our local-preacher system comes in at this point with great efficiency. A superior native, having the charge of an island, or a town, conversing once a

fortnight with his pastor, and having frequent visits from him, will never fail to be more or less efficient. The native teachers are seldom any trouble when they have access to the missionary; for they submit every case to him, and are entirely under the control of their pastors.

The Friendly Islands have produced one assistant missionary in the case of Benjamin Latuselu; and the Feejees also will, I am fully persuaded, supply their preachers of the gospel in due time, who will be duly qualified, and regularly sent forth as the messengers of the churches, and the glory of Christ.

I cannot but admire the order of God in these islands; where he opens to us doors of usefulness just as he gives us agents to enter into them, and the native teachers are multiplied just as they can be of use, by having due supervision from the missionaries. The openings generally increase rather faster than they can be occupied. All the laborers are on full stretch, and open new ground so fast as to be in danger of leaving such lovely flocks as that at Ono to be scattered in the evil day, when the wolf shall find them shepherdless.

FEEJEEAN PROPHETS AND PROPHECIES.

Among many other things, which suggest to me the notion that the Feejeans have derived some of their religious ideas from the same source as the Jews, one is remarkable; namely, the existence of prophets, as well as of priests. The priests are generally prophets, one part of their work being to predict the success that will attend warlike expeditions, &c. But there are others who are more particularly prophets, who profess to foretell distinctly events which appear very improbable to any one but themselves, but which seem to come to pass in a very remarkable manner. The name of this class of persons is *Rairai*, ("seer,") from *rai*, "to see." This word has a very similar sound to the ancient name of the prophets, who, we are told, were called seers at the first: (1 Sam. ix, 9:) the resemblance is to be found in the sense as well as in the sound, and is certainly remarkable. The Hebrew word for seer is *roeh*, which is the participle of *raah;* and this is certainly much like *rai*, and means precisely the same. *Rairai* is the same word reduplicated, and means precisely the same as *roeh:* both designate a person who sees preternatural things, yet not always by the bodily sense, but in a preternatural way; that is, by means of alleged inspiration. Sometimes the Feejeean seers describe what they predict in a way exactly similar to the ancient heathen sibyl, expressed in the following lines:—

Bella, horrida bella,
Et Tybrim multo spumantem sanguine cerno.

"I foresee wars, horrid wars, and Tyber foaming with much blood."

The Feejeean seers profess to see a town in flames, when foretelling its destruction, and sometimes declare that they feel the clubs of the successful warriors do the work of destruction on their own heads.

FEEJEEANS IN SICKNESS, AND ABOUT TO DIE.

The Feejeeans have a custom which resembles, in some respects, that of the ancient patriarchs, who blessed their children on their death-beds, and foretold their future destiny. When a Feejeean is about to die, he calls his children around him, and takes leave of them in some such manner as the following: "I am going to die, you will remain behind: you will look well to our affairs, and you will continue to prosper," &c. "But such an one will die," (referring to some one he dislikes,)—"some disease will overtake him, or some calamity will befall him, and he will be destroyed." The dying person mentions the name of the party, and produces considerable concern in his mind by these predictions of evil; as it is understood that when the spirit of the dying man arrives at the other world, he will have both liberty and power to return and bring to pass what has been predicted. Sick people are feared on this account, and are often strangled, that these malevolent prognostications may not be uttered by them.

When a Christian approaches the other world, his spirit becomes more and more subdued and elevated, and his hope of future bliss brings a large portion of heavenly purity and love into his spirit: and it would appear that, as a heathen approaches his end, the malignant cruel spirit impresses more fully his image on his soul; his friends become afraid of him; and this is one reason why they strangle the sick, according to their own account of the matter.

I have mentioned one way in which the sick show their malignity by devoting to destruction those whom they dislike. Another thing, which is quite in point, is their custom of getting up in the night, when all the members of the family are asleep, in order to pollute the drinking-vessels with their saliva, that they may thereby communicate their diseases to the other members of the family. When they are left to themselves, as they frequently are in the day-time, the people of the house being employed in their gardens, they will go and lie down on the mats of those whom they wish to injure, thinking that by this means they can communicate their own disease to them. In some instances they get so out of temper with all about them, that they will use means to destroy themselves, if they cannot persuade their friends to strangle them. A case of this kind occurred a short time since. An old woman, who had been ill some time, persuaded herself that the members of the family were always speaking against her, and, being deaf, she could not believe that they ever conversed on any other subject, not being able to hear what they said. She made herself so miserable, that existence became intolerable. She then took a stone, and almost succeeded in beating herself to death; but her friends prevented her from accomplishing her design.

I do not think that these are the only reasons why Feejeeans strangle the sick; but it is one view of the question. It is generally supposed that the only cause of this horrid practice is the cruelty of their friends: the preceding details will show that the malignant spirit of the sick has something to do with it. The vile practice of the sick lying in the beds of others will account for the general custom of putting the sick into a house by themselves. How true is the saying, "Hateful and hating one another!"

FEEJEEAN AVERSION TO CHANGE.

I contrast the civilization of the Friendly Islands now, with the state of things which I observed a quarter of a century ago; and certainly the Christian *kolo*, or village, is far advanced above its former heathen state. But the difference is far more mental than physical; the mind is changed, while the outward circumstances are only slightly improved. The same is the case in Feejee, after a ten years' residence of the missionaries. In both cases the natives' houses remain just as they were, notwithstanding the erection of a mission-house with stone walls, and an upper story; and another of wood, with a large verandah. These, the natives say, are very excellent houses; but "why cannot they live in houses such as their fathers lived in?" Their canoes are the same: our vessels and boats are here, and are better than their own; but still they will be contented with what they have. Their mode of dress, or shameless undress, will also do for them; "they are as the former generation was, and why should they depart from the custom of their fathers?" They taste a piece of beef, and say, "It is very good." "Then why not keep some cows?" the missionary asks; and they reply, "Because we can do with what we have; and the cows would eat of our vines, and of our sugar-canes, and we are not fond of fencing in our cultivations. We prefer to lie down and talk, or sleep, or smoke." It is in vain that you urge upon them the very great advantages of our calico over their mere paper-garments: they say at once, "We will have your calico if you will give it; but otherwise we will do as we have ever done." If you say to them, "Your land is rich—you can cultivate arrow-root, coffee, tobacco, cotton, and indigo, which grow here; and you can make cocoa-nut oil, and preserve fruits almost without end; your cordage, tortoise-shell, and sandal-wood, would sell in the colonies at a good price; your *bêche de mer*, and other fisheries, might be very productive to you, and you might have ships of your own, and dwell in houses, and wear clothes, as white men do, and live on better food and more peacefully than you have ever done aforetime:"—to all this they will generally yield their assent, but make no effort to improve. They praise our superior habits, but continue to practice their own.

THE "JOHN WESLEY" IN DANGER.

Oct. 1*st.* Yesterday was an awful day of weather; and last night it blew such a storm, that I got up to watch its progress, and to pray that protection might be afforded to the brig, on her voyage from Somosomo, with the mission-families on board, now withdrawn, at least for a season, because the king will not permit any of his people to *lotu,* while many are calling out for gospel light in other parts of Feejee.

Early in the morning, I saw the "John Wesley" threading her way in between the reefs, under reefed topsails, having been out in all the fury of the storm. Captain Wallis, of the American bark "Zotoff," was standing with me watching the movements of the brig, when he observed, "I should not be at all surprised, if she gets upon some of those reefs. The water is foul from the late rains, the clouds hang heavy overhead, and the air is in that state that makes objects look large, and Captain Buck thinks he is nearer shore than he really is. I see him at the mast-head; but he cannot see the reefs to-day." The next minute he cried out, "The brig is ashore on the reef!" We lost no time in getting off, with all our native teachers, and others, that could be mustered quickly. Captain Wallis, with a boat's crew, afforded most seasonable and valuable help. The vessel lay full two miles from Vewa; but we were soon on board, and found the furniture of the two mission families, and part of their houses, covering the decks. The vessel was bumping, and the stony bottom visible. She struck at high tide, and the tides were "taking off." The wind blew very strong, and it was right aft, with much sea on. Captain Buck had just before taken in his full quantity of ballast; and the long boat was crowded with all sorts of things from Somosomo. There was great difficulty in getting the main hatchway clear, in order to throw the ballast overboard; yet an effort was made as quickly as possible, and her anchor carried out astern; but it was of no use, the tide having begun to ebb. There we were, hard and fast. One said, "She must be shored up, to keep her from tilting over as the tide ebbs out: it falls six feet here." Another said, "She is hung in the middle, and will probably break her back." A third could "see coral rocks, that in all probability would find their way through, and the vessel would thus become a wreck." A fourth could "see the brewing storm, that rendered our case additionally perilous." One came up to me, and said, "There are large war-canoes coming off, and the natives have painted their faces red: with them it is law to seize every vessel wrecked on their shores."

These were our circumstances! That was an hour of trial! We knew that prayer to God, and united effort, would be our course; and many a brief but hearty prayer of, "Lord, help us!" went up to the Advocate above. The decks were crowded, and must be cleared as soon as possible. The wives and children were sent ashore. Every canoe that came alongside was employed to convey ashore the articles which crowded the decks. The chiefs remained aboard, and were set to work, throwing ballast overboard. This kept all parties out of mischief. The yards were sent down, and a large anchor carried out astern, to heave upon when the next tide should serve, which would be at midnight. All•hands worked well, and every step was taken to lighten the vessel. At eight o'clock all the missionaries, and as many as could be spared from their respective stations, were at prayer in the cabin, which resounded with deep-toned and solemn Amens. At half-past nine, we began to heave upon the anchors astern; the wind lulled, and the lightning played at all points of the heavens. At last, when the tension of the hawsers had been brought to a high pitch, and the tide was within an hour of high water, the "John Wesley" sprung astern, and floated off in fine style: then went forth the cry, "The vessel is off!" "The ship is afloat again!" We have not ascertained that any material injury was done. At midnight the missionaries all came ashore in a native canoe, and left the crew to secure the brig. They did well, and are exhausted enough. Captain Wallis was of great service; and the white men in Vewa lent a hand. We left Captain Buck happy once more; but he said he should have to be at work nearly all night.

Time was, when not one man on board that vessel would have escaped the oven, and the open-throated sepulchres of these barbarous people; but now they came and rendered us the most efficient help, and not one thing was said or done by any of them to give us pain. This effect would not have been produced, we think, by legislation, at home or abroad, nor by any bulls from Rome, nor by all the dancing-masters of France, nor by counting of beads, and mounting of crucifixes; no, nor even by preaching the necessary efficacy of the sacraments, and the sacredness of those who are said to be successors of the apostles. But the word of God, the simple preaching of Christ, has accomplished this moral miracle, this mighty revolution in Feejeean manners.

On our return to Vewa, a little after midnight, in a double canoe under the command of Varani, we were lighted over the waves by the old and modern friends, Orion and Pleiades, who were going down in the west; and Venus, the evening star, was following them toward the horizon; while the Southern Cross and the clouds of Magellan were looking down from their lofty position in the south, and, with the hosts around them, lending us their aid to bear the cheering news to the wakeful natives who stood on the shore, and to the anxious mission families. We retired, thankful to the Lord, who had delivered us out of great trouble, because "his mercy endureth forever."

October 2d. I went over to the imperial city of Bau, with Mr. Hunt and several missionaries. Here we saw the *élite* of Feejee. The king says, that the *lotu* is near, but that he has a few more towns to burn, before he and his warriors *lotu.* Bau is a small island, not containing more than two hundred acres; but the town contains nearly one thousand souls, most

MBAU, OR BAU, THE CAPITAL OF FEEJEE.

of whom are chiefs, and the houses are far superior to anything else I have seen in the South-Sea Islands. The large double canoe of the king will carry from two to three hundred men; and they are just now preparing to start on some warlike expedition. Their spirit-houses are finely ornamented; but when I told one of the priests that unless Jehovah saved him from the burning fire, no other god was able to do so, he fell into a passion, and we left him. The men paint themselves, and both they and their many wives go nearly naked. We have preaching at Bau, and shall, by God's blessing, soon have a missionary there. Bau is the lion of Feejee; and dark are the deeds of which it is guilty. It sends out its little war-parties, who fall upon men, women, and children, as the case may be, and the carnage is all their own. I do not find that Feejeeans are at all celebrated for courage; but quite the contrary: their way is to fall upon the defenseless, and to overcome by numbers, rather than by personal bravery. It is, however, very encouraging to observe a gradual melting down of this icy mountain, and a breaking-up of their iron system of cruel tyranny. The light is breaking in upon them, and the power of the truth is felt by many.

REMOVAL OF THE MISSIONARIES FROM SOMOSOMO.

We have withdrawn the missionaries from Somosomo, by the united voice of the whole body of Feejeean missionaries. The old king behaved very well, and opposed no difficulty in the way of their removal, as some of us had apprehended. He said, "The wars are not yet ended, and there is no use in your staying here. I shall be glad for you to come again, and we will all *lotu* then." Messrs. Lyth and Calvert, who went over to assist in the removal of our brethren, could see a marked improvement in this people; and are fully persuaded that our labors there have not been in vain, although the influence has only been partial and indirect. Messrs. Williams and Hazlewood felt much at leaving this place and people, and would not have done so but for the authority of the district meeting. We have none of us any doubt of the whole matter being right in the sight of the Lord, as far as we are concerned, in reference to the removal of these suffering servants of Christ. What the result will be to Somosomo, time will show: but the natives say that the people will now be cut off, because their protection is removed from them. Both Christians and heathens say that this is a thing not to be called in question. Messrs. Williams and Hazlewood say:—

"In the month of January we were permitted to witness a remarkable movement in favor of Christianity. There was a shaking among the dry bones. We thought breath was entering into them, and that they would live. The emotion was not a thing of a day; it continued some time, and in a greater or less degree, pervaded all classes. Since the occupancy of this station, the Somosomo people have more than once said, that the time of their becoming Christians was near: not that they desired it, but because they thought circumstances would induce their chief to become a Christian; and then they, as a matter of course, would become Christians too. But the present movement was of a different kind. It had more of principle in it. Some of the people desired liberty of conscience, and an effort was made to obtain it.

"Tuiilaila was informed by persons composing part of his council, that several of his subjects wished to abandon heathenism, and requested his undisguised permission to do so. He was also asked to allow all who chose to become Christians. On hearing this, we were greatly revived. We thought the many prayers offered for the prosperity of the work here, were now to be answered, and we said, 'Better days and brighter prospects break upon us.'

"It was an easy thing for Tuiilaila to deny his being an obstacle to his people becoming Christians; and he did so; and, to support his assertion, ordered his favorite wife and some others to *lotu*. This, however, was only a feint, designed to quiet the unwelcome visitors; and this cheering glimpse of a better state of affairs ended in a stronger confirmation, that Tuiilaila maintains a determined opposition to the cause of Christ, not the less effectual for being partially covert.

"Several islands and districts have been visited, and generally our message has been well received. We are disposed to the opinion, that if Tuiilaila would withdraw his opposition, we should quickly have a call for teachers from six different places in this circuit.

"War continues to occupy a large share of the people's time and attention. But the language of Isaiah is applicable to them, 'For the leaders of this people cause them to err.'

"The Lord has been very mindful of his servants, and of their families; and whilst endeavoring to serve him, he has blessed us with bread and water, and defended us in the hour of danger. Though painfully conscious of the absence of that success which we earnestly desire, and which we feel warranted to expect, we have proceeded with our labors, remembering the injunction, 'In the morning sow thy seed, and in the evening withhold not thine hand: for thou knowest not whether shall prosper, either this or that, or whether they both shall be alike good.'"

I received the following letter in the Tonga language from our excellent teacher at Nakorotumba. He came from Tonga a long time since, and is useful in Feejee:—" Mr. Lawry, I, Paul Vea, I like to make known that I very much like your face. I rejoice exceedingly to hear that you have come to this land, and I desire to come and see you; but I am very much engaged in the work. Love to you from my heart and mouth. The love of truth to thee, Mr. Lawry, my father in the gospel. Come thou, that I may look upon thee, and also the *lotu* people here. This is the end.—*October* 1*st*, 1847."

Sunday, 3*d*. I held the usual worship at sunrise; took breakfast a little before seven; and attended the public preaching at half-past eight, which was followed by a love-feast. The natives spoke freely, though not in so lively a way as they sometimes do. Mr. Hunt, at my request, set down the following

LOVE-FEAST TESTIMONIES.

He remarks: "The speeches at the love-feast were not characterized by much that is unusual. The principal thing that struck me was the entire absence of all boasting and self-confidence; a simple dependence on the Saviour, and love to him, his servants, and his cause; with a desire, sometimes feelingly expressed, that their friends might all enjoy the blessing of salvation."

1. The first speaker was an aged man, named Paul, a man of much simplicity of character, and one of the first who embraced Christianity: what he said was to this effect:—"I shall speak my mind about Jesus. When Wesley and Mr. Cross came, we embraced Christianity. The *lotu* in my mind has been something like a tree, that grows up by degrees, and grows quite straight: it is not turned aside by any thing. Such is my mind—nothing turns it out of the way. I am happy in the *lotu.* I think much of my friends who do not *lotu.* On their account I am pained; but in the *lotu* I rejoice. I rejoice in mind and heart, because the missionaries have come to our land. I have found the benefit of being a Christian. I know the love of God in Christ. I was a bad man; but God loved me. The wind blows on me, that is, the evil words of men; but I am like the tree that moves not. I praise God only. I wish to get to heaven. I am afraid of hell. I only wish to live that I may hear the word of God, that by it I may be convinced of all that is evil, and put it away. I rejoice that missionaries are here, that I may hear the preached word. I cannot read; but the word I hear from the missionaries is the food of my soul. Such is my mind."

2. The next in order who spoke was Lydia, the wife of the chief of Vewa. She is a woman of high rank, being nearly related to the King of Bau, and was for

a length of time, after she became a professing Christian, a very troublesome woman. She was, however, truly converted on Whit-Sunday, 1844, and since that time has been " walking in the fear of the Lord, and the comfort of the Holy Ghost." What she said was to the following effect:—" I wish to speak my mind, and I wish to say that I know God is true. If he had deceived me, I would say so; but he has not; I have proved his faithfulness. I desire Jesus. God is near me every day. I do not wish to have the praise of men. I wish to put away sin, because it is offensive to God. I wish to trust in Jesus, and to love him. I rejoice in being where the missionaries reside. It is the custom of our chiefs to send their daughters to different lands. I rejoice that I was sent to Vewa, that I might find religion. I desire to be in earnest, because of what Jesus has done for me. Such is my mind."

3. The next who spoke was a person who has been with Mr. Williams at Somosomo in the capacity of a servant: his name is Bartimius. He said:—" I have peace with God. I rejoice in going to Somosomo. We have been long like slaves and prisoners at Somosomo. I am now very happy. The land where Mr. Williams lives is where I wish to live. I do not wish to leave him. Such is my mind."

4. Luisa, a woman from Somosomo, spoke next; but as she spoke in the Tonga language, I did not understand all she said. The purport of her speech was to congratulate the Vewa people on their privileges in being allowed to worship God in peace, and to express her own joy in seeing so much of religion. She is a Uean.

5. The next was Jacob, who, from a fierce warrior and cannibal, has become a consistent Christian. He was induced to embrace Christianity from some remarks made by the missionaries when burying one of his children, who had been induced to *lotu* by some Christian relatives, and afterwards died. He found the peace of God in the most extraordinary manner, during the religious revival of 1845, and is now a steady member of the Church. He said :—" I greatly dishonored God formerly. If he had despised me as I despised him, I should have been ruined. I am now humbled on account of his love to me. He has not done to me as I have done to him. I have despised him; he has not despised me. Such is my mind."

6. Joshua, a Matuku man, who has been residing with Mr. Hazlewood, said :—" I formerly followed a way that was not good. I used to spin nuts to know whether Jehovah was the true God or not. I have now abandoned all these things. I know that God is with me. He was with me in my own land. He was with me in Lakemba. I know that nothing else is of any use whatever."

7. Koroitukana, a Bau chief, spoke next. He is of considerable rank, and had a favorable opinion of Christianity long before he embraced it. His good feeling exposed him to the wrath of the other Bau chiefs, during the persecution of 1845, and he was ordered to take up his residence in Vewa. After he had resided in Vewa some time, he renounced heathenism, and has since been consistent as a professor of religion, and, I trust, is sincerely seeking the Lord. He said :—" I did not first begin to think of Christian-

ity in Vewa. I began at Bau. I was in Vewa some time before I renounced heathenism. At length Lydia persuaded me to be a Christian. I wish to follow Jesus on earth, and then to see him above. I desire that my friends may *lotu.* I have now no God but one. We formerly thought sin right; but we have learnt to think differently. We now see sin in the light of the Lord, and we desire to follow his steps. We are now concerned about our friends, who are eating one another. This is my mind."

8. Daniel, a Vewa man, was next. He said:—"I am very happy, because this is a spiritual assembly. We used to rejoice in our worldly assemblies; but we now meet to speak of Jesus. I am now happy on account of Jesus. I know we did not sail to another land in search of missionaries; you came to us of your own accord. We are but a small people; but we know in an acceptable time the true religion. I wish to die in this age, a good age for us; others are living under a different age. Such is my mind."

9. Elijah, the Vewa chief, was next in order. He said:—"I wish to speak my mind, which is to follow God, and to trust in him. Let me speak of the love of God to me. I have nothing else to speak of but the love of God. I professed religion sometime before I knew his love: but now I know it. Now I wish to do what he approves, and to hate what he disapproves. I desire to do something for him, and am much pained because I do so little. I rejoice, because of his love to me, and to our land. I wish to spend my whole life in doing something for Jesus. I do not wish to remain in my own land. I wish to do something for Jesus. I do not wish to die be-

fore I have done something for him. Such is my mind."

10. Luke, a Bau chief of high rank, who was formerly a great persecutor, said:—"Formerly I resided at Bau. I knew then that Christianity was good. What I desire to say in the presence of you, servants of God, is, that my desire is to follow Jesus; to do that which is just and right; and that I pity those who are in darkness. Such is my mind."

11. Susanna, a woman of sincere piety, and much respected by us for her kindness to Mr. and Mrs. Cross, came next. She said:—"What I wish to say is, that I am a great sinner. I am not conscious now of living in sin. I know I have repented of my sins. I wish to trust in Jesus. I desire to give him my heart, that I may not be separated from him."

12. Joshua, an old native teacher of excellent character, came next, and said:—"I wish to show my love to Jesus. I know of no other Saviour. I went to Tonga formerly; but I did not find the Saviour. I have now found him; not for my own sake, but through his love alone. I was a long time before I began to meet in class. I thought that this is the reason why I do not find Jesus. I went to class, and found what I sought. I now desire to tell others of his love. I pity my friends who do not *lotu*. I have great love to the missionaries. Such is my mind."

13. Satareki, (Shadrach,) a good servant of mine, was next. He said:—"I was very near death, and I then thought, 'Shall I go to heaven or hell?' I prayed to God: he heard me, and I lived. I desire now

to live and serve him. I know religion is useful to me. I see religion in others, and rejoice. I wish to live in the land where the *lotu* grows."

At eleven o'clock, we had English preaching, when Mr. Hunt delivered an excellent sermon, on the parable of the sower. In the afternoon we held an ordination service. Both natives and English attended; and the season was one of deep interest and solemnity. There were twenty-five English children present on this occasion: no wonder that great zeal is shown by their parents for their future education; for "a troop cometh."

A case occurred in these prolific regions of a mother naming her child *Acts*, having already had Matthew, Mark, Luke, and John. *Revelation* may be reached.

INFANTICIDE AND POLYGAMY,—THEIR DESOLATING EFFECTS.

All the missionaries say that infanticide is very prevalent here, and that the children are mostly destroyed before they are born by means the most startling and revolting, but that many others are murdered after birth. This practice is under the sanction of the authorities, and is particularly acceptable to the head-wives, that the lower order of women kept by the chiefs may not have the care of children, and may not have any afterwards, but be at leisure to wait upon their superiors. They do not attempt to stay the general polygamy and licentiousness; but they cut off the children with an unsparing hand. So manifest it is that polygamy will not be followed by increased population; but, on the contrary, the more the wives are multiplied, the more the children are murdered. In order to "replenish the earth," the law of nature and the written law of God must be obeyed, "Let every man have his own wife." It is clear to me that heathenism could never people the world. Life is not sufficiently sacred in its eyes; it is Christianity that gives sacredness to human life, and creates principles, motives, and energies, that will tend to the preservation of the race. This is what God is now doing in these seas. The heathens will melt away, some by conversion, others by sin; but their days are numbered as a pagan race. The benevolent religion of Christ will *tame* them, and it will be easy for white men to live in their land. Colonization in one form or other will certainly follow in the train of Christianity. The people will mix with each other, and the original race will cease to be a distinct people. The new character they will take must depend upon that of their colonial neighbors, whether true Christians, nominal Protestants, or ignorant Papists.

The preservation of any one of the families of the extensive Polynesian nation in their distinct and present form, seems to me unlikely. Others have melted away; and what is there to prevent these from sharing the same end? If they remain heathen, they will fight and destroy one another, until their land shall tempt some powerful adventurers, without any concern but that of gain, to enter their country; and the collision that will follow must end where such collisions always end:—ferocity falls before skill. But if they receive the gospel, as they are almost sure to do where

6*

it is clearly and faithfully preached to them, they will become new creatures, and will no longer engage in devastating wars, but will sit down peacefully, enjoying their new and improved condition. They do not all at once become industrious, for they have no motive to engage in wasting labor under a vertical sun: they already have all they need; and the habits, usages, and practice of their nation are adhered to. Civilization is a thing of slow growth, and requires several generations before it will be worthy of the name. Nations do not readily change their ways, and especially tropical nations, where industry is rendered fatiguing by the heat, and is the less needed on account of the fertility of the soil, and the abundance of fruit-trees. Very little progress has hitherto been made in the civilization of the South-Sea tribes in the Friendly Isles and Feejee; nor are the signs at all encouraging in this matter.

The expectations entertained in England are by no means realized on the spot,—at least not with the rapidity which hope had painted, but left experience to correct. I am of opinion that the probable working out of the problem will be this: That the gospel preached by our devoted countrymen will save the souls of multitudes in these isles; that this grace will soften their hearts and change their national character from warriors to men of love and peace; that the tide of emigration will sooner or later flow to their shores, and that a fine new race of civilized, mixed people will cover this part of the earth. Thus, while a remnant of them shall be saved, God will show mercy to all who will accept it; and his retributive providence will be seen in the extinction of a nation (as such) that has been so deeply stained with the orgies of idolatry and with blood.

The Bishop of New-Zealand informed me that he took the census of the population of Waimate before the war, and while his establishment was there, and order and regularity reigned: the result was a decrease of five per cent. In many parts of New-Zealand, the natives are melting away; but they are not lost—they are merging into another and a better class. In this process there lacketh not sin; but Providence will overrule even this, and bring about an order of things which shall be better for the world, better for the Church, and better for the new race destined to people parts of New-Zealand.

In the Sandwich Isles the American missionaries are said to have been very happy in their work, and in the fruit of their labors. They have preached the gospel efficiently, educated the people with diligence and general success, and they have been visited by a small colony of respectable people, English and Americans, well instructed themselves, and having the fear of God before their eyes. The effect of these three causes (namely, the gospel, education, and colonization) is just what might have been expected. The natives are beginning to show a taste and a liking for the manners and customs of civilized men. With these they will become mixed, and by the mixture they will be preserved and civilly improved. Their moral improvement will depend very much on the character of those with whom they mix.

Oct. 4th. The heat is now 82° in the shade, at seven o'clock in the morning: at noon it is higher:

but no inconvenience is complained of by the mission-families. When I speak of being distressed, melted, and prostrated, they simply observe that they have a few hot days in the summer months, but that the present temperature is quite agreeable to them. Acclimation is the painful process by which these families have attained to this state of ease and accommodation to their circumstances. A stranger is constantly annoyed by gnats and musquitoes, whose stings convey great misery; but the old residents scarcely notice them at all.

5th. The school-examination took place at Vewa. The procession was composed of almost the entire population. The chief, with a gray beard, walked before; each person, whether old or young, bore a thank-offering,—a mat, a club, or an earthenware vessel of native manufacture, &c. These, by the kindness of the missionaries here, as everywhere, were handed over to me for the Auckland Chapel Bazaar. This part of the business done, the whole body moved onward towards the chapel, which stands on a high mound, in the midst of lofty evergreen trees. In the hands of many were carried branches of trees, and they sang sweetly as they moved slowly along. In the chapel they chanted the rules of the society and the catechism, one part taking the questions, another the answers. They then stood up, one by one, and rehearsed chapters of the New Testament with great propriety and accuracy. The queen did her part, the missionaries said, better than any one beside. These are the early days of purity and simplicity here. One thing strikes a stranger on entering Feejee, which is, that all the Christians appear at heir worship in full dress, their sable bodies being decently covered, which thing their heathen neighbors utterly detest.

It was pleasing to see a good sprinkling of the heathen looking at this spectacle with intense interest; and, at the conclusion, I addressed both parties on such points as I deemed appropriate to them and to the occasion. These islanders require indulgence in this way: they love exhibition and display, and act most efficiently when they act in concert. I observe that in those places where the taste and good sense of the missionary permit them to enjoy this innocent preference, there everything flourishes, and success attends the mission; and that the contrary is equally true where a cold and merely northern taste prevails. Our excellent and promising chief, Elijah Varani, was very conspicuous and happy in the proceedings of this delightful day.

7th. Captain Buck attempted to get water at a heathen place, where there is a fine water-fall; but the miserable natives demanded such large payment for the water, that he was obliged to come away without it. This, considering the very great difficulty of obtaining any water at the places we visit, is a heavy disappointment. Feejee is generally high land; but the shores are surrounded by reefs and mud flats, so that few places are accessible to boats. In the low and flat islands the difficulties are still greater. Water is very precious here.

8th. There are now six-and-thirty persons at Vewa, belonging to the mission-families of Feejee, met at the district-meeting; and for these there are three small houses, just sufficient for a small family in each. How the ladies contrive their part of the business, I am at a loss to know; but the families have been long since they saw one another, especially Messrs. Williams and Hazlewood, from Somosomo, and they seem never to know anything about inconvenience or trouble. They are met together with Christian views and feelings, delighted once more to see each other, and to indulge the social principle so long shut up in solitude, to talk over past events, escapes, and mercies, to project new plans of useful enterprise, and to "edify one another, as also they do."

I observe that each wife has her hands full from morning till night, attending to the children, superintending the native nurses, the native cooks, the native washerwomen, and many things beside, among which is the doling out medicine to the sick, and carrying on the marketing with the natives who come to sell yams, fowls, and other food needed for the house. I would, therefore, earnestly advise all the young females, who may hereafter enter upon the mission work, to give up at once all thought of a piano, or other heavy instrument intended for amusement. Forsake all such things, which will be worse than useless in such stations as Tonga or Feejee; forsake them utterly, as those now here have done, and seek all your pleasure in your duties, in serving God and his servants, and great will be your reward in heaven.

I may also say a word to my junior brethren who may have thoughts of entering upon the mission work. There are two classes of men who should never dream of entering upon the South-Sea mission work. The first is, those who feel a thirst for popularity, and who would like to shine before the people. Be it known to all such persons that they will never get one particle of applause from any one in these seas; and that the whole cargo of such desires must be thrown overboard at the very entrance, or disappointment will attend on this popularity-man to the end of his days. A second class of persons who should never come to these stations are those who have been bred and cooped up all their days in artificial society, who have everything to learn concerning the common affairs of life; they are strangers to traveling by sea or land, they cannot build the house, or contrive its simple furniture; whereas many of our best missionaries can do these things with ease and expedition, and many such like things they actually do: the consequence is, that they are happy at home, and they are at home anywhere, where duty calls them. They are willing to live any how and die anywhere. Their conduct has the best effect on the natives, who are keen observers of external matters. They go in and out before their people. They have time to learn the language, and to teach religion, and are happy and useful in their labors: while the mere artificially-trained man is always busy in preparing to learn the alphabet of common life; he is ever learning, and never able to come to an adequate degree of practical knowledge; he soon becomes miserable and discouraged. His home is in confusion, and he spends his strength for naught, and in vain. The poor man has no resources in himself; for he does not understand how to begin to work with the mere raw material, and there is none to prepare it to his hand. Such a man is not qualified to be an apostle to the Gentiles of the Southern isles.

I have cases and facts before me at this moment, which, were it proper to record them, would illustrate and establish these views, beyond all doubt; but I prefer to conceal the particulars, lest I might wound the Church of Christ, and give pain to living men. Be assured, it requires rare qualities to be a happy and efficient missionary in these islands. A man and his wife set down in a wood on the island, having none to communicate with, but the staring, pilfering, idle, nude, and deceitful barbarians, must have patience, courage, wisdom, and resources within them, of no ordinary kind and degree. "And who is sufficient for these things?" The answer is, All those whom the Master calls to this great work; and by his mercy and gracious providence we have many such in the work, and other angels are no doubt preparing to sound their trumpets in every part of the earth. Let us more and more pray the Lord of the harvest that he will send forth laborers into his vineyard; for the harvest truly is great, and the laborers few.

9th. I was surprised this morning to learn from Mr. Williams, that he knew one *white* man at Somosomo, usually known by the name of Tom, who went about with nothing to cover him, save the small strip of native massi which the Feejeeans wear, and he ate human flesh as eagerly as any Feejeean cannibal would do.

It seems that our brethren have had several narrow escapes with their lives at Somosomo. Mr. Lyth, when sent for by the late Tuithekau, talked to him so closely about the interests of his soul and eternity, that the savage became enraged, and laid hold of Mr.

Lyth's garment, calling out for a club that he might kill him. Mr. Lyth left the skirt of his calico coat in his hand, and escaped away to his own house. The sick man relented, and sent to beg pardon, before he died. Mr. Lyth had been sent for by this chief in the character of a medical man; but even this did not screen him. Another case occurred the other day, when Mr. Williams was getting his baggage on board the "John Wesley." A chief who had been attempting to steal, and was prevented, ran up to Mr. Williams, shaking his club over him, and shouting that there and then he would settle him. Mr. Calvert stepped up to the succor of our brother, and prevented the fall of the club; but so frightful was the sight, that the ship's crew cleared off to the brig with all convenient speed. Mr. Williams says he never felt any fear. The same chief, on a former occasion, wanted to get into Mr. Williams's house at the time of taking dinner, that he might assist them in eating the food; but a large dog was chained in the passage to secure the family from intrusion, at which the savage became so enraged that he took up one of Mrs. Williams's little boys, about two years old, and threw him with great violence at the dog. The mother saw it with the feelings of a mother! The child was injured, but not seriously. Good nerves, and full confidence in Divine Providence, are necessary here. God has hitherto kept his servants, and all belonging to them, in Feejee; so that they have not yet received any fatal injury from the warlike eaters of one another.

Sunday, October 10th. The Sabbath day. The fleet of Thakombau sailed out this morning, with not less than two hundred warriors on board each canoe. They are bound for Natewa, a part of Somosomo: their object is not clearly known.

Our services closed with the Lord's supper; and it was good for the sailors and mission-families to be there.

11*th*. It seems necessary that extensive and Scriptural revivals of primitive Christianity should be looked for and promoted among this people. They cannot be made practically Christians without sound New-Testament principles; but in order to this they require an impulse, which must rise in power and energy sufficient to bear on high these sunken, heavy "vessels of wrath fitted for destruction," but now taken up from their low estate, because "His mercy endureth forever." In the last religious revival at Vewa, the anguish of many was awfully severe, and showed the work of the Holy Spirit to be very deep and powerful, producing such pungent sorrow for sin as to startle even the men of God who witnessed what was passing. Their cries and agony admitted of no control, and seemed incapable of restraint. They said a fire was consuming their vitals, and their souls were filled with horror at the sight of their sins. Mr. Hunt pointed out one man to me whose sister had buried her husband, and strangling was to be her lot; and this was to be executed by the hand of this brother. Two missionaries did their best to prevent this atrocity, in which they only succeeded while they remained present with the savage; but no sooner were they gone, than he twisted a piece of native cloth, and, placing it around his sister's neck, she was strangled instantly. This man was convinced of sin in the time of the general religious awakening here; and who can wonder if "the pains of hell gat hold upon him?" His bitter howlings could not be described, and none could pacify him but the Lord Jesus, against whom he had so long rebelled. When he did find peace through believing, his ecstasy was equal to his former anguish, and he did not cease for a long time together to shout with heartfelt joy. About seventy such cases in one small town would create no small stir about "this way;" and many heathens came to see what was going on, several of whom seemed to be solemnly impressed. In Tonga they were slightly persecuted under similar circumstances, and several wild young men came to the chapel with the intention to interrupt the praying people; one of whom, being exceedingly filled with the power of truth and love, went boldly up to this band of scoffers, and commanded them with a loud voice to *boono*, that is, to kneel and pray; and such was the spiritual influence with which he spoke, that they all fell down on their knees at once. I do not know that they became pious, but they went away and reported that God was in the *lotu* people.

This people will require rousing from their deep slumber: like Noah, they must be "moved with fear." They are so firmly attached to their old customs, and so generally careless and thoughtless, that ordinary means will not be sufficient to gain their attention, and keep hold of their hearts, that they may be converted. Our missionaries seem fully aware of this, and therefore look for the promise of the Spirit, and teach their people to expect and pray that the Spirit may be poured out from on high;

that the valley of dry bones may have a shaking among them, and that breath may come into them.

12*th.* In passing through a native village to-day, I witnessed the opening of two caves, or deep holes, containing bananas and bread-fruit in a state of fermentation, and, as must be the case with large masses of decayed vegetable matter, sending forth a very offensive odor. My surprise was great to find that this store belonged to white men, who lived near the spot: but the life of the white men in Feejee, unconnected with our mission, is not only very precarious, as they are frequently cut off, but is wretched beyond all that I have seen among the islands. Wicked men from civilized lands have done great mischief to the barbarians, and the barbarians, in turn, have done much damage to them; by far the greater part have fallen victims to the club, and most of these in consequence of their own demoralizing conduct.

Cutaneous complaints, and wide-spread sores, are very common among this people; and the general opinion seems to be that such eruptions proceed from eating the vile fermented vegetables, and the flesh of man. They sometimes keep their fermenting bread-fruit and bananas under ground for many years together. Both leprosy and elephantiasis, or swollen legs, are among their dire diseases.

13*th.* I observed to-day a party of heathen natives engaged in building a new printing-office for the mission here. As they seemed more diligent, cheerful, and contented in their labor, than is usual in the Friendly Isles, I inquired of Mr. Hunt, what he had agreed to pay for the work: he said nothing was agreed upon; but when the work was done, he should hand over to his chief, Varani, what he deemed sufficient, and Varani would pass the same over to their chief, and all would clap their hands and walk away, quite pleased and fully satisfied. How different is this from the state of things in Tonga! There they will do nothing for the missionaries without murmuring and exorbitant payment. It is very difficult to get those idle natives to work at all; and, when they do perform a small amount of labor, they can hardly be satisfied, however much you may pay them. There are some honorable exceptions in the Friendly Isles, but they are very few; as I had full opportunity of witnessing as I passed from island to island, landing the stores, and sometimes changing the missionaries, who deeply feel this sad state of the native mind, and do their best to correct it; but up to this period they have not succeeded.

As in Feejee the people work, and in the Friendly Islands they are idle, so in New-Zealand the active and energetic character of the natives is about to produce a transition in their social condition, from extreme barbarism to initial civilization. Just as I was leaving Auckland, I passed a multitude of our own natives working on the high road, and another party was building a stone wall for the military barracks. I asked one of the young men what his object was in hiring himself at one-and-sixpence per day: he answered, "I have set my mind upon having a horse, and shall work till I can buy one." I went farther, and proposed the same question to another young chief: and the reply was, "I am working to get money to buy a cow." This employment and money given to the natives bring crowds of them to Auckland, and some moral evil will incidentally spring out of it; but his Excellency, the Governor-in-Chief, is bringing a bill before the Legislative Council, to prevent persons from either selling or giving anything intoxicating to any one of the native race. Under so wise a rule as that of Governor Grey, the interests of the natives will not be neglected, nor the efforts of the devoted missionary trifled with and frustrated, except in cases to which the eye of government does not extend, and then never without regret.

Now, in the scale of elevated men, the case will probably be seen at a future day in the following order; namely,—

First. The New-Zealander, whose improved moral condition is founded in Christianity as brought to him by the missionaries, and whose social state will have been further improved by a paternal government, and by his association with civilized men.

Secondly. The Feejeean, whose moral necessities will be met by our Christian mission to his country, and whose social improvement will have grown out of his moral renovation and industrious habits.

Thirdly. The Friendly Islander, whose idleness placed him far in the rear of New-Zealanders and Feejeeans, when in many respects he stood before them both; but without labor there is no profit under the sun. I shall not despair, however, of that fine, elegant people, although at present they seem almost ruined for want of industry. The gospel has done much for them: education will now become the handmaid of religion; and wise laws will soon be introduced, which will act powerfully on the whole nation.

They now cease to be subject to club-law; and it is not to be wondered at, if a considerable amount of something bordering on licentiousness should here and there show itself. These interesting people are in a transition state, and will soon take a new cast and mould, to abide during all the future days of their existence.

14th. I observed some of the natives trying to dress after the English fashion; but the failure was complete, and the effect all but ridiculous. An English bonnet, instead of the beautiful way in which the natives dress their hair, causes a sad falling off in their dark faces. A white shirt, and a sable skin above and below, contrast rather unfavorably. But in Feejee, where the native fashion is to go very nearly without clothing, and where the sons and daughters of chiefs are not allowed to have anything to cover them until they are grown up, Christianity has done its proper work; and where there are Christians, the naked are clothed: with these the native cloth serves; but they highly value our cotton and calico to wrap themselves round with,—it looks better, and wears longer, than their own poor fabric made from the bark of a tree.

I have seen their earthenware, in the manufacture of which they have made considerable advancement. They confine themselves to coarse brown ware, some of which they make for culinary uses, and others are fancy articles. Double canoes and drinking vessels are made in small models. Some of their large cooking vessels will hold a hogshead; others restrict their capacity to a couple of quarts. The clay seems good; but, as there are no ovens or kilns here, and they are only burnt by loose fagots of wood thrown round them, they are necessarily deficient in strength. Still, with care they last a long time, and are a great addition to the usual artificial comforts in the islands of Tonga, and of some other groups. I have procured some specimens, which shall be forwarded to Messrs. Venables and Co., and Barker and Till, of Burslem, who, I am sure, will readily send me out such suggestions as may be useful for the improvement of this art as now practiced in Feejee.

15*th.* I have procured three Feejeean wigs of different sizes, and colored variously. They are certainly an exact imitation of the several ways in which the chiefs dress their natural hair, or rather get it dressed; for many hours are spent over this work, and there are professed hair-dressers among them. In general the natives of all these islands dress and wear their hair very beautifully; and when they try to imitate us by wearing hats or bonnets, they appear quite degraded, and sometimes ridiculous. The wigs which I have procured would add dignity to almost any wearer, and are done up as tastefully and elegantly, as if they were designed for English bishops, counselors, or judges. When these people embrace Christianity, they cease to disfigure themselves, by burning their skin, and cutting off their hair: they also cast aside such pompous trifles as fine wigs, and showy ornaments worn on their legs and toes.

16*th.* Mr. Jaggar presented me with some native-made salt, weighing about eight pounds. They make this from salt water: by the application of heat, they evaporate the water, and retain the salt in their earthenware ovens, or cooking-pots. The dampness of this climate is such, that the salt, as well as sugar, very quickly becomes moist; but they guard against this by hanging their salt, very much in the form of loaf-sugar, over their fire-places: this prevents it from melting, but turns it black outside.

As the sugar-cane thrives well here, the time will, no doubt, come, when these people will be taught to turn this article to good account; as also many others, which their fine, well-watered country produces without the aid of the cultivator's hand,—such as the tea-plant of China, carraway-seed, the lofty nutmeg-tree, turmeric, arrow-root, capsicum, and the sarsaparilla shrub. All these, and some others, I have seen and handled. The large and beautiful bread-fruit tree abounds here, with very many other native fruit-trees, most abundant in excellent fruit for the use of man: yet *this* is the land where sin has triumphed over the fallen race to such an extent, that the "vile affections" are not satisfied until the reeking murderer has eaten the man who was his neighbor, brought up with him. But the Liberator is come, the Redeemer is proclaimed in Feejee, and the ransomed of the Lord are beginning to appear, "clothed at the feet of Jesus, and in their right mind."

Sunday, October 17th. The early prayer-meeting was well attended, notwithstanding the heavy rain. At half-past nine I preached to a very interesting congregation. Mr. Hunt interpreted with great facility and energy. Twelve adults and three children were publicly baptized, and great was the emotion manifested throughout the congregation. Surely "the power of God was present to heal." The private houses were generally vocal with songs of praise; and the voice of prayer, "with strong crying and tears," prevailed throughout the holy day.

18*th*. An elderly woman has just called here to exchange her native dress, about eight inches wide, made to wrap round the middle. For this she wished to obtain some calico to cover her person; as she began to *lotu* yesterday in the metropolis, next door to the king. Mr. Lyth was preaching there. The *lotu* people are increasing, and "of chief women not a few." Of course, we gave her the calico; and I shall take her *lego*, or garment, to the bazaar at Auckland, to assist us, by its sale, in building the house of the Lord. It is cheering to witness in all persons who *lotu* here, that two things are desired by them; namely, a garment to appear decent in, when they assemble with the worshipers of God, and a book from which they may gather further instructions. Thus the body and the mind are cared for at the same time, and the principles of initial civilization and social comfort are fostered by Christianity.

When the melting heat will permit me, I ramble among the luxuriant woods and hills of this very picturesque country, more like New-Zealand than any other land that I have visited, in its uneven surface, and rich clay subsoil. Next to the mighty moral enterprise now in progress in the hands of my devoted brethren, by which a nation shall be induced to change its false gods for vital and pure religion, are the developed works of God in the kingdom of nature. In these I find a zest of delight only to be enjoyed in circumstances like mine, and by a person such as the Psalmist describes: "The works of God are great, sought out of them who have pleasure therein." Here everything is luxuriant and grand: the tree, the shrub, the flower, the leaf, are all fresh, strong, and brought to perfection. New and beautiful varieties meet the eye at every turn. Fruits and flowers teem by the wayside: the fruit is good for food, and the odors of the flowers defy description. Birds are few, and their song not very attractive; but, in general, their plumage is rich and gay. The insect tribes are seen here to great advantage, especially the *coleoptera.* Many large and lazy butterflies present the eye with gorgeous hues. The *libellula* of this land are of a ruby color; and I have seen here a beetle, the *staphylinus,* flying with eyes as bright as the Chinese firefly, emitting a clear light for a considerable distance. But if the botany and entomology of the tropical isles present us with extraordinary specimens of natural history, what can be said of the Feejeean conchology? It is here that we enter on a world of wonders, the more valuable because they can be secured and preserved: whereas, the heat and living insects render it very difficult to preserve specimens of botany, and still more so of entomology; but the shells, though rare, beautiful, and valuable, are easily preserved. Of these I shall take such as may be available for the chapel-bazaar; and a few, perhaps, of the most beautiful and valuable, for other purposes. The harp-shell is found in great perfection among the islands: the nautilus, and a few of the orange cowrie, with many other valuable shells, are found by the natives on the reefs; *we* cannot find them, but must depend on those who have had time and opportunity for such tedious pursuits; and they sell them at a price by no means trifling. Ships-of-war from America and

France often call here, and buy such things at a random price, and to the astonishment of the natives themselves. Our ships-of-war very rarely call, though by doing so they might accomplish much good, and make a proper impression on the native mind. But, while science brings the American ships-of-war, and a zeal for planting Popery, where we have prepared the way, brings the navy of France into these seas, there has yet been no inducement strong enough to bring British men-of-war into this group, or, if they have come, the natives did not know them. One would think that the murder of so many white men, and the horrid cannibalism of Feejee, where so many mission-families reside, might be sufficient to induce a call from ships-of-war now stationed in the vicinage of these islands: but what are these considerations to officers who love their anchorage and the port? Beside, who and what are these mission-families? Mere sectaries! Who ever dreamed that they were subjects of Great Britain? We know that the gospel needs not the aid of great guns: but there are times when refractory white men may be restrained by the presence of authority; and even the natives themselves may receive a wrong impression when other navies give countenance to those who are of their nation, while the English Protestant missionary, living where war and cannibalism are the common practice of the people, is not favored with the countenance of any part of the navy of his country. The Popish priests know well how to avail themselves of such an argument, for the purpose of lowering our missionaries in the eyes of these warlike barbarians.*

* The visits which British men-of-war have paid to the Feejee

19th. The wind is from the north, and the heat is, therefore, intense. Multitudes of the native women and young people are on the reefs and in the sea, gathering sponge, and bringing it to me,—about twenty large pieces for an empty quart bottle. A good boiling is required to extract the particles of salt from the sponge. The day may come, perhaps, when this, with many other articles, will lay the

Islands, are remembered with gratitude. December 1st, 1836, Mr. Cross writes:—"His Britannic Majesty's brig, 'Victor,' Captain Crozier, arrived at Lakemba. The principal object of this visit is to inquire into the murder of a boat's crew belonging to the 'Active,' lately anchored in this group. Captain Crozier, having called at Vavau, kindly brought us letters, and a providential supply of various articles of which we stood in need."

"The officers of men-of-war who have visited these islands, have generally been so kind, as to prove to the natives that they are the friends of the missionaries, and well-wishers to the cause which they are sent to promote. It is at all times a cause of joy to us when we are favored with their company; and a more frequent repetition of such visits would greatly tend to promote the interest of the natives, as well as completely keep them in fear of doing mischief. The boldest of them tremble at the sight of a queen's ship, especially when conscience accuses them of having merited punishment. The opinion of Mr. Cross, that no one who heard the report of the 'Victor's' visit would be guilty of murdering Europeans, might be a true one; but very few would hear of it.

"In 1840, two officers belonging to the United States' squadron, then surveying these islands, were most barbarously murdered at Malolo, a small island to the leeward. They had gone ashore in a boat to purchase fruit, &c., when the natives attacked and destroyed them without any provocation whatever having been offered. They did not escape punishment. Refusing to give up the culprits, the town was destroyed; many of the inhabitants perished in the contest; and the rest, having humbled themselves, were spared. The conduct of the American officers in Feejee was praiseworthy. They manifested great kindness to the missionaries, and an intense desire to promote the interests of the natives." (*Memoirs of the Rev. Wm. Cross*, pp. 81–87.)—Edit.

foundation of a brisk Feejeean trade, to be carried on with civilized countries. The wicker-work baskets of Feejee are strong, handsome, and useful, beyond any that I have seen at home or abroad. They sell a good one for two yards of calico; a mat of good firm texture, and about eight feet square, will cost the same. In such articles of manufacture these people excel. The clubs and spears of Feejee are very neatly formed, and awfully ponderous. Their bows and arrows also are excellent; but they know how to put a good price upon them. I have not purchased many, as they give the best they have to those they love; and who are so likely to stand high in their esteem as their benefactors?

20th. We have been fully engaged to-day in sketching our plans for the Auckland school, to receive the children of missionaries in these seas; and also in laying down an educational scheme for Feejee; and the rules for civil government, which shall be recommended to the consideration of the Christian chiefs, at a period as early as may be necessary.

21st. How the missionaries can study, or exercise themselves, in this oppressive climate, is scarcely conceivable; yet they do both, and complain not: but those who are newly arrived feel greatly distressed, until they become seasoned against the heat and the musquitoes. I not only feel very much inconvenience from the heat, but the perspiration flows down over my bald head, and the evaporation from the rolling stream, as it passes down over my face while writing, spreads a dense mist over the spectacle glasses, so that I am unable to proceed, until I have cooled myself by a plunge into the water.

The old store at Vewa having been joined to the printing-office, and both having fallen into decay, a new printing-office is now being erected under the eye of the missionaries. A tribe of natives from the neighboring large island is engaged for this purpose: they are to find the material, and build the house, trusting to their employers for a righteous compensation when the work is all completed. This, I am happy to say, they readily and uniformly do in Feejee, where our credit stands sufficiently high to secure their full confidence.

This house is erected of strong timber, for the frame-work, and of the large and long bamboo which abounds here, for the side-walls and roof: the lower part is thatched with the leaves of a tree, and the upper with the sugar-cane leaf, fastened to small straight canes. The whole looks very well, both within and without, and will stand firmly for six or seven years. The size of this office is twenty-one feet by twenty-two, and the entire cost, except the windows and door, is £2 10s., in mission property. The number of men at work is sixty, and the time they take is three days.

We have a stone-built house, and one of timber, in Vewa, erected, of course, by white men. We shall forthwith get title-deeds from the king, or chiefs, as the best thing that can be done under the club-law system: but in case of a war, deeds, lease, and all may be destroyed.

We shall, however, feel it a duty in every place to set apart a piece of land for mission purposes, and pay for the fee-simple thereof, to the amount of from three to ten acres, at a price averaging a pound an acre. This may now be done in Feejee without any difficulty; but who can say what may be hereafter?

22d. Our missionaries here are hard-working men, and men of all work. They rise early and translate the Scriptures, or prepare other good books: they teach the natives useful arts, and guide them in all they do: one part of the day is devoted to native schools, and another to the schooling of their own children. They preach the gospel to all who will hear it, morning, noon, and night. They administer medicine to the sick, and settle disputes for all parties. They are consulted about every important enterprise, and have their hand in everything that is going-on. They are lawyers, physicians, privy-counselors, builders, agriculturists, and frequent travelers on the high-seas in the frail native canoes. They are men

> "Whose path is on the mountain wave,
> Whose home is on the deep!"

They study hard, that they may give a faithful translation of the word of God; several of them daily read Hebrew, Greek, and Latin, for this end; beside their constant application to the perfecting of their knowledge of the native language, in which they preach and converse daily with ease and fluency. These things they do in the ordinary course of their regular labor as pastors of the flock of Christ; beside the oversight they are obliged to take of their own domestic affairs, where the busy housewife plies her care, and where the tedious natives crowd around.

Such is a very faint picture of the devoted men employed in these missions, of whom it would be wise to say, what we often hear said in a very different sense, "They may do to go abroad, they may be fit for the mission-work." Whoever has been tempted to think that inferior men are good enough to send out as missionaries, cannot have estimated the cost of sending them, the mighty obstacles they have to overcome, the versatility of gifts and graces they need, and the untold evils which must result from an unqualified standard-bearer. Let no young superintendent propose, nor any quarterly meeting pass, a candidate for the Christian ministry of slender abilities, and questionable qualifications, under the absurd and inexcusable impression that such a man, though not fit for the home work, "may do to go abroad." Our work abroad requires men of all the wisdom, courage, and piety that can be obtained. *No man is too good for the mission work.* This field will give full scope to all his energies and powers, no matter how much they may have been cultivated, improved, and refined. If possible, the man who is to spend his life in learning a strange language, and in raising and ruling new churches, far away from the wise counsel of his fathers, should have his full time in one of our admirable institutions, and there be instructed in those things which may prepare him rightly to discharge the duties of the pastoral office. These are not mere probabilities: I write the observations which are pressed upon me in my every-day movements, in the discharge of my duties, among the South-Sea mission stations.

To show how thoroughly an Englishman may become inured to the heat of the tropics, I set down the casual remark of Mr. Hunt, made to me last evening, when the perspiration was oozing from every pore, as we stood under the vertical sun. "The house," said he, "which the natives have constructed," will not admit any air, and will be very warm and comfortable."

23d. We have just learned that a whole town has embraced Christianity, near Bua, the new station for which we are to sail next week. It seems that this people have heard one of our simple native teachers propound the gospel to them, and they have in a body thrown away their heathen gods, just at the moment when we are preparing to take Mr. and Mrs. Williams there, more fully to explain to them the way of salvation. Who can deny that the finger of God was here? Here are a people prepared of the Lord, and here is a missionary prepared for this people. Neither party knew what the other was doing; but the Lord was present with both, giving seed to the sower, and bread to the eater. "Go, preach the gospel to every creature: and, lo, I am with you alway, to the end of the world." It is in this way that his work *appears* unto his servants.

Bau will surely *lotu* before long; and then, Mr. Hunt says, full one hundred thousand souls will be waiting for the word of life at our hands. It is estimated that in Feejee there are three hundred thousand souls, who at present bid fair to be cast upon us for religious instruction. I have sometimes heard comparisons instituted between our different mission-stations, and the palm given to those where the multitude was greatest. True it is that all souls are the Lord's; but we do not see him always saving men in the greatest numbers, where they are the most densely crowded. There are some places where the people receive the word of God with all readiness of mind, and multitudes there are added to the Lord. Where he works, the mission prospers; and the prosperous missions ought not to be lightly esteemed, seeing that the Lord hath delighted to honor them. The Friendly Isles and Feejee are of this happy number. The triumphs won here are truly illustrious. Such cannibals and bloody men are seen fully saved!—yea, suffering the loss of all things for Christ's sake! They flee to Vewa that they may enjoy quiet from without, and read the New Testament, which is now complete in the Feejeean language. Several of these men are chiefs of high rank among their countrymen, whom they long to instruct in the things concerning the kingdom of God. To train them for this purpose, a native institution is in operation here, and the angels with their trumpets are preparing to sound. These are the things which Christ, by the power of his gospel, is doing in poor heathen Feejee. And who hath despised the day of small things?

In one of the distant towns, where we have two hundred members, it happened that the chief of the place was also the priest. He was taken ill, and did all in his power by enchantment and by Feejee medicine; but, when all had failed, he sent for some medicine from the missionaries, which issued in his recovery. He then said:—"I tried my god, and he could not help me; but your God has cured me. I shall therefore *lotu* at once." He did so; and many of his people are being instructed, in order that they may be saved. Mr. Hunt related to me a second case, very similar to the foregoing, where the priest was brought to receive Christianity by reason of a cure which had resulted from his taking medicine prescribed by the missionaries. And even imperial Bau has changed its haughty tone towards us, since some of their children, and others, have been cured of sore diseases in this way. This is just what one might expect from such people, influenced by the kindness and benefits received at the hands of Christ's messengers; and it shows that medicine for the body should be liberally supplied to mere heathen stations, and that, in the hands of careful and duly-qualified men, such medicine may prepare the people to hear of the spiritual remedy that saves the soul.

24th. The Lord's day. I preached to a full and well-behaved congregation of Feejeeans; and the word was devoured by them. They seemed to bow before the Lord, and fully to enter into the spirit of Christian worship. There is evidently a great work now in progress here, and I expect soon to "see greater things than these." The brethren are repairing to their respective stations as fast as the vessel can take them, and are encouraged to expect that happy effects will crown the labors of this year. They are full of zeal and hope themselves, and are, I believe, likely to be extensively useful in their respective islands and circuits.

Mr. Hunt is appointed to translate the Old Testament into Feejeean; and Mr. Lyth to read and revise the manuscript: it will then be seen by as many other brethren as can conveniently inspect it, and immediately pass through the press, so as in three or four years to be completed. This is a great work, and God has provided for it, by giving us instruments, who seem every way qualified for its performance in a manner the most creditable to themselves, and satisfactory to all concerned. The New Testament now in print gives very general satisfaction.

The stations of the missionaries in Feejee are already so extended, that, to visit them all, I have to perform a voyage of about seven hundred miles. In a year or two more we shall, by God's blessing, have taken possession of both the centre and the circumference of the entire group. In all parts the seed is beginning to grow, poor Somosomo excepted; and even there we are by no means without hope that what has been cast into the ground, and buried there, may one day spring up, and ripen to the gospel harvest.

25th. A female came this evening, with several other sick persons, in the usual way, to be cured of her disease. It appeared that her arm was disabled, and rather painful, from the extraordinary course which this poor silly heathen had adopted. The case was this:—One of her fingers had become painful, and she had proceeded in the most deliberate manner to cut off the finger next to it; but, as the pain in the diseased finger did not abate, she cut off another finger; having now only two left, and one of them diseased. The pain, however, had left the finger, and settled in the arm, when she came to Mr. Hunt to be cured. Such a thing, I am informed, is by no means unusual among the Feejeeans. They use the knife very freely upon themselves when affliction overtakes them. Medical knowledge has done much to prepare the way for the truth in these islands; and, as Mr. Lyth is a surgeon, most of the brethren have taken a leaf out of his book.

One of the most painful and barbarous facts connected with any mission family in these seas, has just now come to light. Our excellent young friends, Mr. and Mrs. Watsford, who have been at Ono, one of the out-islets, during the year, have come in for their full share of domestic trial, arising from the want of servants. The natives there have no idea of serving in a family, where all their time would be occupied, and where everything would appear new and strange. The King of Ono, however, sent one of his young daughters as a child's maid; and this girl has showed herself a thorough Feejeean for cunning and cruelty, in which these people surpass all others that I am acquainted with. Her cunning led her to invent such strings of lies as really surprise one; and all of them tended to ruin the character of Mr. and Mrs. Watsford. To this vile practice she added the most shocking cruelty, about which there can be no mistake; for the whole affair has been openly confessed, and too clearly demonstrated to admit of any question. It appears that she intended to murder the babe of Mrs. Watsford, and to conceal the fact. Her plan was to avail herself of those times when the child was cross, to hug it in her arms so strongly as to crush its frame together! She proceeded in this work to a sad extent, and was then discovered, and made full confession. The babe is not dead, but seems to pine away, and shows great difficulty of breathing. No doubt the injury is considerable; but whether, under the judicious treatment of Mr. Lyth, its life can be preserved, time will show. I fear the effects will remain co-eval with life.

It is a fixed opinion in the minds of our missionaries,

that men in their wild, heathen state, are generated with a more depraved and vicious nature, than is the case in Christian and civilized countries. I am not aware of any reason why this may not be the case. Human nature is fallen and corrupt all the world over, and there is none that doeth good, no, not one; but does it therefore follow that there are no degrees of wicked men, and of vicious natures? Mr. Fletcher observes, that oak-trees are oak-trees all the world over, but some grow more crooked than others. The oracle says, that "the wicked shall wax worse and worse." And analogy says the same: take the wild fig, and compare it with the same shrub and plant in your garden. Do the same with the crab-tree and the apple; or compare any wild shrub, flower, or tree with those that are cultivated and trained. Go from the vegetable to the animal world, and compare your domestic poultry with wild fowl, wild rabbits with tame ones, wild cattle with tame ones, and so examine any other analogies: then say whether the wild ones do not come forth as the inferior and degraded offspring of the wild families, and whether they can be elevated to the higher condition of the family, until, like them, they have passed under cultivation. The state of the poor heathen is awfully degraded, and has strong claims upon Christian pity and benevolence; and those who devote their lives to the missionary work should have a place in the prayers and other kind offices of all churches and good men everywhere, and at all times.

The King of Vewa sent one of his men to-day, begging Mr. Hunt to give him a piece of pork for his dinner! Both the queen and himself are professed

Christians, and bear the fruits of faith and love; but they are not very wise in their economical affairs. Their command of Feejee riches is very great; but still they are often without a meal when they are hungry. The king's name is Melchisedec, and his history will vie with that of the most bloody of his race; but in the arts of cunning and deception he stands unrivaled in the annals of Feejee. The conversion of such a warrior might be expected to excite the wrath of his compeers; and it did so for a long time, during which the haughty chiefs of Bau meditated the destruction of Vewa; but, it seems, the mission establishment there was its wall of defense; and is it not true of all God's servants, that He is a wall of fire round about them? How else could our missionaries live in Feejee? It is the common remark of all the white men in Feejee, that they are only safe when they are under the wing of the missionaries. Some live, therefore, as near the mission premises as they can; and so gracious is the Lord, who hath redeemed all men, that a few of these runaway sailors come under the influence of divine grace and truth, both at Tonga and Feejee. I am glad to find that our brethren, for the most part, treat this class of persons with kindness, and afford them many helps, which they could not obtain elsewhere. By such means the Christian minister is most likely to win souls, and to exalt his Lord and Master.

26th. This morning, a case of printed calico, a private order of Mr. Williams's, which had been lying sometime in the store here, (because it was not safe to have many things at Somosomo, where he lived,) was found drenched with wet, in consequence of the bad roof of the common mission-store. Many of the articles are stained and spoiled. These things, being his barter, are of great consequence to him. Not long since, a case of axes was lost at Somosomo, when they were in the act of landing them. In this way our brethren have their patience exercised, by losing their supplies just when they are most needed. When the case was opened, Mr. and Mrs. Williams were both present, and preparing to move to their new station at Bau; but not one syllable of complaint or of murmuring escaped their lips: they meekly submitted to their loss as to one of the light things which they were accustomed to, in bearing the burden of the Lord in Feejee.

I have a full opportunity of observing how the mission-families live; being at their houses from month to month. Their table presents pork and yam, with water, (the best they can get, but often far from good,) and pork and yam again, with tea and sugar, as the main stand-by comfort of their frugal board. Poultry and fish are obtained, now and then, and bread-fruit when in season. A missionary's suit in general consists of a thin pair of cotton trousers, and a calico coat, (besides his usual linen,) and over all a wide-brim straw hat. They neither dress in costly array, nor fare sumptuously at any time; but, having food and raiment of the plainest kind, they are therewith content, and pursue their high and holy vocation, preaching the gospel, the whole and pure gospel, justification by faith, and entire sanctification or perfect love, holiness brought into the heart by the Holy Spirit, received by the earnest, praying penitent, through simple faith in Christ, exercised in full expectation of a present salvation. These things they teach and exhort with all long-suffering and doctrine; saying, "Save yourselves from this untoward generation." And the Lord works with them, and signs follow in them that believe.

28th. The heat is so great here to-day, that my going into a cold bath in the shade was quite agreeable at first; but, after a little, I felt a desire to be refreshed with a lower temperature; a thing that could not be, for I had got into the coldest element, in the coldest place to be found. The old hands say, "The weather is very hot now; but we can bear it very well, feeling little inconvenience, and suffering no injury." What a kind Father is "our Father!"

The brig returned from Lakemba and Ono, to which places she had conveyed Mr. Calvert and Mr. and Mrs. Hazlewood. On entering among these Vewa reefs, she struck the bottom, but did not stick fast. This navigation is really very difficult, and especially as the helps by good charts are few, and other marks of direction to the mariner, such as buoys, beacons, and lights, are not in existence.

From Ono the news is cheering; but owing to the rough sea, many things designed for Mr. Hazlewood could not be landed, and going without them for one year must be his hard lot. A change of clothes must be reckoned among the articles of which he is *minus.* Many of his things, such as furniture and supplies from New-Zealand, are broken and spoiled; partly, perhaps, through the frequent landing of them from place to place, and partly through the carelessness of the seamen who did the work.

The smashing of the poor missionaries' property is

really frightful, and must be reformed. The many voyages we have to make, the want of packing, in some cases, because the vessel cannot wait so long, and the habits of seamen, all contribute to make us suffer very heavy losses.

Frequent removals in the stations are not called for; and, as they involve both loss and expenditure, they should only take place in those cases where the prosperity of the work demands the sacrifice.

29th. The way in which God is pleased to work in Feejee would hardly be thought of by a person at a distance, however much he might be inclined to speculate. Medicine and children are our chief forerunners in this work. The gospel has been faithfully preached at Somosomo, year after year, without a single person believing a word of what was said: but the instruction of the children in our own schools succeeds in many instances in securing them; and when a cure is effected by the medicine of the missionary, a favorable impression is made respecting the God of this benefactor, as being superior to their own gods; and they therefore *lotu*, or come under instruction. When these are saved by the faith of the gospel, they go forth and preach, where no missionary would be heard, and their story is "salvation by the faith of Jesus, and peace and joy in the Holy Ghost." These heralds are now scattered abroad in Feejee, where many are opening their eyes to see the truth; and when they *lotu*, a missionary must go to them, either to reside, or as a visitor, whereby they become established in the faith, and excesses and errors are prevented.

CHAPTER III.

MISSIONARY CRUISE AMONG THE FEEJEE ISLANDS.*

Nov. 2d, 1847. We weighed anchor, and began a voyage truly apostolic in its character,—that of planting new churches in a distant part of Feejee. Our course lay among shoals and reefs, endless and without number; in consequence of which we took Elijah Varani as our native pilot, and a double canoe also accompanied us, under the command of the king of Vewa in person, whose native name is Namosemalua, and his name in baptism Melchisedec. These are two extraordinary persons, whose paths have been flowing with the blood of the slain for many years; but Christianity has fully subdued them, and in them there is a new creation. Having on board the families and furniture of Messrs. Williams, Watsford, and Ford, with goats, hogs, fowls, and a deck covered with

* The Journal now published relates to the perilous voyage from VEWA to several *new* stations in a populous district of Feejee, for which previous preparation had been made, chiefly by native teachers. It describes the landing of the missionary party in BUA BAY; the settlement there of Mr. and Mrs. Williams; and the landing of other brethren at NANDI. It also includes an account of KING NAMOSEMALUA, and of ELIJAH VARANI,—their former horrible cannibalism, and present character as Christian converts;—some topographical notices of *Vanua Levu,* or "Great Land" in Feejee;—a striking instance of the eager desire of the natives to possess and read the Holy Scriptures in their own tongue;—very interesting notices of the native schools at Bua and Nandi;—and other particulars. For these extraordinary missions, and for the invaluable laborers by whom they are conducted, let "prayer be made without ceasing of the Church unto God."

the wreck of [the mission property removed from] Somosomo, we steered away for Bua, the station of Mr. Williams. On our passage we ran close to the island of Ngainge, where the king above named was not long ago employed by the chiefs of Bau, to use his astonishing eloquence with this people, in order that the Bau warriors might gain the victory over them: a thing they had long tried to accomplish, but were not able. King Namosemalua went to them and gained a hearing. His speech was made in sight of the Bau fleet and army: but so persuasive was his address, that he induced the warriors of Ngainge to come out of their fortress unarmed. They were at once fallen upon by their enemies and nearly all cut off! According to the representation of the royal orator, these people were to have been taken to Ovalau, an island not far off; and, having remained there only a short time, were to return in peace to their own home; and, "See," said he, "here are the canoes all ready to convey you all to Ovalau." These canoes were the fleet of their destroyers!

A short time after we left Ngainge, we passed the island of Malagai, where the king of Vewa had met the inhabitants in pitched battle not long since. Terrible was the slaughter which he made among them, and the consequent eating of human bodies by Namosemalua and his renowned men of Vewa. Scenes like these are truly revolting: but grace has triumphed over this savage chief, and he now attends us in our work of evangelization from isle to isle.

Elijah Varani also is now a thoroughly devoted servant of Jesus Christ; but his former history is full of cruelty and carnage beyond that of the ordinarily vicious cannibals of Feejee. While I am writing this, he is standing on the foretop-gallant yard, looking out for the best passage between the reefs at the entrance of Bua, where we hope to be at anchor between the hours of eight and nine this morning, though at present we are at sea.

The spot over which we are now sailing is one which Varani will not soon forget. He was here, a short time since, in his terrible character of warrior and cannibal: and in one canoe he met and encountered a fleet of sixty canoes, one of which had a small cannon on board. The name of Varani struck terror into any ordinary force; but in this instance he was considered as being so completely over-matched, that his destruction was all but certain. He, however, thought not so; and making full sail towards the fleet, directed his men to fire into the canoe which had the great gun on board. He watched the man who had the fire-stick, and who was going to fire off this "gun to shoot the earth with," as they call it. Varani leveled at this man as his canoe was approaching. The fire-stick fell from his hand, and a general consternation seized the whole fleet, which fled precipitately, pursued and fired into by this terrible man. This was a gallant action in its way: but Varani was by no means satisfied, for by this time he had become hungry, and not a single man had fallen into his hands as a passing meal; so he took one man with him, and went ashore with his death-dealing club; but the sight of him cleared the coast, and not a man could he find, until at last two bold warriors came down upon them in great fury. This was very much to the taste of Varani, who said to his companion,

"You take the smaller man, and I shall see after the large one." They soon closed, and the little man was soon dead by a blow from the club. Varani, however, did not design to strike his antagonist, but was content with parrying his thrusts, until he saw the way clear to wrest the weapon out of the hand of his antagonist, and plunge it into his vitals. Both were presently in the oven, and served the craving appetites of Varani and his party. The next day Varani went ashore, and, entering the *mburi*, or god-house, where many were sleeping, he kicked them till they awoke, and then they were clubbed, not one escaping. Other houses were entered in search of human beings, who were destroyed like frogs, until they who slew them were weary of hewing down their victims. As soon as the presence of Varani was known in the town, there was no more spirit in the inhabitants thereof, who gave themselves up to destruction. Such was the man who is at this moment at the mast-head of the "John Wesley," conducting us to Bua, with one of our missionaries to begin a station there!

A circumstance of a rather curious kind may here be mentioned, as showing a different spirit from that above detailed. A small canoe, with a large *pulpit* on its deck, has come alongside of us, having many muskets stowed away therein. The case is this: Nala, the chief of Dama, having lately embraced Christianity, has had a native teacher called Ezekiel stationed with him. They have built a chapel after the native fashion, and have hired some white men residing at Solava to build them a pulpit, for which they have paid two hogs, and a bag of arrowroot: the whole being completed, they are taking home the pulpit, but do not perform even this voyage without arms. In *their* views the law and gospel may be very well associated; the preacher and the musket occupying by turns the same pulpit. Nala and Ezekiel having come on board, and cordially saluted us, we have again steered away for Dama, which will be one part of Mr. Williams's circuit.

3d. We came to anchor in Bua Bay, and proceeded forthwith to send goods, furniture, and goats ashore. As the reefs forbid our near approach to the new mission station, we shall have a long struggle to get everything on to the spot; for we can only land things when the tide serves. Varani has gone ashore in the first boat, in the service of a new Master, even the Captain of our salvation. No doubt the *lotu* people will rejoice to see the man who once destroyed them become a fellow-helper to the truth. I was questioning him about his conversion just now, when he remarked that Jesus Christ would not let him go. He kept hold of him, and shook him about so much, that he could not help yielding his heart to him. "God was my protector from all darts, when engaged in war," said he; "and after I had bowed my knees to Jesus, and was become a new man, the Bau chiefs were very angry, and resolved to destroy Vewa on account of the *lotu*, and especially on account of the king and myself, because we now refused to fight. Thakombau offered me very large gifts, if I would only go to war as before: but this was not now possible; I was the servant of the King of Peace; beside, I loved every one, and could not destroy any more lives. The king of Feejee then said he would kill me because of my *lotu*. I said, 'Very well; but you will soon *lotu* yourself, and then will the thought follow you, *I killed Varani because of his lotu.'* These great Bau chiefs tried in their anger to destroy Vewa, and came for that purpose. They arranged everything, and looked hard at the mission premises. We told them we should not resist them, but wait to see what would be the will of the Lord. I went to the king's house, that we might there die together; but the king of Bau went away without doing any injury; for the God of heaven, who protected me aforetime, was still a wall of defense round about the *lotu* people, and the mission families at Vewa. The heathen now say, that our God is certainly too strong for their gods, and that they too shall one day *lotu.*" (See note A, at the end of the volume.)

4th. BUA BAY.—All hands are busy landing the old parts of the houses and furniture brought away from Somosomo. Canoes and boats are all in requisition: stools with two legs; chairs without bottoms; tables with one corner broken off, and the smooth surface drawn by natives over rough stones; barrels with one end out; jars and bottles wrecked at all turns; boxes with the key lost and the hinges gone; iron pots used for drinking-vessels; and the tea-pot without lid or spout: but these are too good to be lost; and ashore they go, because there are no others to be had. This changing of stations is only to be tolerated here on the ground of being unavoidable.

The Feejee group consists of many islands; but there are two large ones, *Viti Levu,* (Great Feejee,) near to which are the small islands of Bau and Vewa; and *Vanua Levu,* (Great Land,) on which we are now planting three stations, having already several infant churches formed, and many native teachers employed. Each of these islands is larger than an ordinary English county, and is surrounded by very many smaller ones, generally well peopled, and exceedingly fertile. The peculiar characteristic of the Feejee Islands, is abrupt and lofty hills, interspersed with well-watered valleys and extensive swamps. In the low grounds the heat is intense, and the musquitoes numerous; here, too, are large trees and shrubs, and luxuriant vegetation. But on the hills, when very lofty, these are less abundant. That part of Vanua where we now are, is finely interspersed with plains and forests, hill and lowland. The fires by night, and the smoke by day, indicate a thick sprinkling of native villages: but the people seem of a low caste.

In the afternoon I went ashore with Mrs. Williams and her four children. Mr. Hunt and Mr. Williams were busy receiving the goods that were constantly coming ashore, and setting up doors, bedsteads, and other things required for immediate use. The natives were crowding round, most of them entirely naked, and the rest nearly so. If it were not for decency's sake, I am sure they are far more comfortable without clothes, in such a climate, and where they are so much of their time in the water; but in my eyes their appearance is very disgusting! Poor creatures, they peeped into everything, and seemed perfectly astonished, and somewhat pleased. They lent a hand much more cheerfully than did their more polished native brethren of Tonga. Some of them ventured off to the "John Wesley," and asked permission to go below that they might see the wood wherewith the temple of Solomon was built; meaning cedar, of course. These men stared at everything, letting fall the under jaw, and standing stock still in perfect amazement. When the others inquired what they had seen, their answer was, "It cannot be uttered; you must go and see for yourselves: when we have boarded other ships, why, there they were, a floating land; but here, there was a floating land, and so much beside, that we are afraid because we are struck speechless."

The station chosen for Mr. Williams in Bua bay is inland about a mile, on the side of a fine river, navigable to the door. The natives had built a mission-house sixty feet long, a chapel about the same size, and a good store. These three strong and commodious buildings cost next to nothing; for the naked native was willing to work that he might have a missionary. Native teachers have labored here for some time. The soil is very rich, but very little cultivated. The site does not please me at all; being only five feet above high-water mark, one is cut off from seeing anything that is more than a few yards from the house. To make it still more disagreeable, the trade wind cannot penetrate the dense mangrove forest between it and the sea, and the dwellers therein are consigned to the unmitigated heat of a vertical sun, and to the continual annoyance of swarms of flies and musquitoes. There is, however, no choice left to us: we must live where the people live, and among them who are willing to hear and receive the gospel when it is offered to them.

5th. Having finished landing the stores and furniture here, we proceeded to hold our school-examination. The school was composed of the entire population of the *lotu* village. Men of hoary heads were there, showing that they were beginning to try to learn. I was pleased with this meeting; for their order was as great as their solemnity, and all appeared well dressed for the first time since we arrived. Their knowledge of Scripture was by no means small; and one of them repeated one of Mr. Hunt's short printed sermons. They brought mats and oil as presents to Mr. Williams; and many fine pieces of sandal-wood were handed to me. These must go to the Auckland chapel bazaar.

The introduction of *lotu* at Bua bay was in this way:—The chief and two or three of his people went to Vewa, where they received religious truth, and soon became Christians. They came home, and were followed by a teacher, named Joshua, who had visited the Australian colonies with my excellent predecessor, the late Rev. John Waterhouse. Joshua was soon joined by a second teacher, whose name was Solomon. In those days a general war broke out over the whole island of Vanua Levu, and presently the storm gathered portentously over the *lotu* chief of Bua bay. An army of about eight hundred warriors moved towards this little defenseless village: but the inhabitants were not aware of their danger, or were not wise in their preparations. Solomon, however, the second teacher, had been a man of war from his youth, and no doubt he was the instrument of saving the village from utter destruction; for, while all the people were fast asleep, Solomon kept watch, and said nothing to any one. In the gray light of the morning he heard the approach of a multitude, and, concealing himself behind a tree, saw their advance, and, leveling his piece, brought down his man. The report of a gun, and the fall of a man, filled the invading army with consternation. They no doubt imagined a man with a gun behind every tree. They took to their heels in terror and confusion; some went one way, some another, but they looked not behind them, nor could they ever again congregate. From that day to this no enemy has had sufficient daring to come near Bua bay. Soon after the general peace thus strangely brought about, the whole place joined in the *lotu*, admiring the teachers who had cleaved to them in the time of their danger, and whose God was able to save them.

At the school-meeting, king Namosemalua delivered an address after I had done, in which he instructed this people how they ought to conduct themselves towards their missionary. Such matters would come well from him; and the people devoured the good advices which were given to them. On our departure down the river in a large canoe, many saluted us from the shore; a large group were singing a hymn; others followed us on the water. When we thought we had fairly got away, the crowd was seen again considerably in advance of us, having taken advantage of the bend in the river.

Here is a fair beginning for Mr. and Mrs. Williams, who have been severely tried by ploughing several years upon the rock of Somosomo. We have now good reason to hope that God has better things in store for them. They enter upon their work with cheerful earnestness. As I was leaving, Mr. Williams said, "I hope you will send me a boat, as good canoes are not to be had here, and my labors would be more efficient by this additional equipment; I can manage it, and the natives will soon learn to pull the oars."

As the "John Wesley" has been twice ashore, Captain Buck was anxious to know how the copper stood about the keel. Varani offered to go down and examine it. He and another dived down under the fore-part, and found a small patch gone. They came up, after a surprisingly long absence, and, having taken breath, plunged again below, and examined the after-part, which was not at all injured. They went under the keel, and passed from the middle to the stern, about fifty feet, and thirteen feet under water. I could swim well myself; but to live so long under water, and all the time to be making violent efforts to pass through the fluid, is more than I shall ever hope to perform. These people are behind us in many things; but among these must not be reckoned climbing, throwing, swimming, and diving. Varani said, "If a shark had come near me, I would have fought him on his own ground."

One of the natives on the Rewa river was attacked by a shark; and severe was the struggle between knowledge and strength. Sometimes the man would rise to get breath; but for the most part the antagonists were under water. The shark got hold of the man's arm, and frightful were the gashes made there; but the man got his other arm round the fish, and was steering him ashore. This was nearly accomplished, when the shark let go his hold on the man's arm, and giving a quick splash with his tail, disengaged himself from the man, and sheered off into deep water. The native's spirit was now up; and therefore, having taken breath, he pursued the shark, and in deep water they again engaged. The same tactics were pursued on both sides, only that the man clasped the shark farther back, and by this means kept his arm out of the mouth of his foe. In this position he had more power to steer; but being under water too long, he was obliged to let go, and rise to the surface for air. The shark did not pursue him, having, as the native believed, had enough of it. The man went to Mr. Jaggar to get his arm dressed, and seemed not much to care for his wounds; because he had established a clear claim to victory, inasmuch as the shark, by sheering off the second time, gave up the contest. But the poor fellow had paid dear for his triumph; for, by loss of breath, and loss of blood, he was within a hair's breadth of losing his life.

6th. We sailed from Bua this morning for Nandi, having to work our way directly against the trade wind, among innumerable reefs and sunken rocks. Surely there is no other part of the seas so broken and dangerous as this. I cease to wonder that such a fleet of vessels have been wrecked among these islands, sand-banks, and coral reefs. By God's merciful care, we have just come to anchor in twelve fathoms; but there is no shelter except from a distant reef. It is now Saturday night, and here we must remain toiling until Monday morning. Messrs. Hunt and Watsford are ashore at Dama, where the new pulpit which we saw at sea will be occupied by them to-day and to-morrow. Their families remain on board sea-sick. As we are on our Master's work, we shall look to him for safety, and for a blessing for all on board.

Sunday, 7th. We had family worship early this

morning upon deck, where we could breathe a little fresh air. At ten o'clock we began our public worship on the quarter-deck. All hands were mustered, both English and natives; I read the abridged liturgical service, and Mr. Ford preached a very excellent sermon on, "Simon, son of Jonas, lovest thou me more than these?" I know not when I have enjoyed an act of worship so much as this. The day was intensely hot; but we were in the open air, shaded by an awning, fanned by a strong breeze, and anchored about two miles off the shore. The hills and valleys, the plains and woods, the distant mountains, and the open ocean, lay before us: all was grand and lovely. On board all was stillness, order, and devotion. Our brethren were on shore, improving this fine opportunity among a people who were just in a transition state. Some *lotu,* others behold and inquire. On the morrow we hope to move off, and plant two missionaries on the coast. All these things fill my mind with gratitude, joy, and love. The Master is here, and shall be adored, reverenced, served, loved, and obeyed.

The heat is 92°, with thunder and rain in the afternoon.

In the evening I lectured on deck, upon the Paralytic healed. The power of God was present, and cheering our inmost souls.

8*th.* We passed up the coast from Bua to Nandi, directly against the trade winds, among reefs, seen and unseen. Twice we were within the ship's breadth of running upon sunken rocks, and in that case should certainly have been dashed to pieces; but thus far are we come by the help of the Lord.

On arriving at the mouth of Nandi bay, we anchored in fourteen fathoms, in the open sea, and on a lee shore; nothing else was open to us. The teacher, with some of the *lotu* people, soon boarded us. This man, whose name is Joel, is the very person whose encounter with the shark has just been narrated, of which the marks and seams appear deep on his arm. He is an excellent man, and has come here to teach the way to the kingdom of God. He is now more than a hundred miles from Rewa, the scene of his aquatic shark exploits. The main circumstances of the account he fully confirms, and adds the following:— The shark was from seven to eight feet long. He was bathing in the salt-water river when he saw the fish making towards him. It soon opened its wide mouth to seize him by the loins. Joel then said, "I am a dead man; but whither shall I go? Well, I am quite satisfied that Jesus Christ is my Saviour, and that I shall go to him; I have no fear of death. However, the shark is here, and I will fight him before I am devoured. Then," continued he, "I drove my arm down his throat, thinking to pluck out his heart. The biting was strong; but the shark lost his power, and let go his hold. He went away. I dived after him, caught hold of his tail, and steered him, intending thereby to steer him ashore; but he was aware of it, and rushed from my grasp." The man succeeded in lifting the shark out of the water, and was taking him ashore, the fish trying all the way to bite him. At last it slipped out of his arms. "The shark went away, and reported he had been well beaten," as the saying goes among the natives; "the result was, that a deputation was sent down the river to request the presence and aid of the old and chief sharks against their biped foes." Whether their belief therein be treated this way or that, it matters not; but shortly afterwards a native was bitten in two at the loins, and another had his thigh taken clean off by the sharks. Mr. Hunt, who, of course, smiles at their report, saw the man with the amputated thigh, which, he says, was taken round off, no doubt at a single bite. The man lived only a few days after he lost his thigh.

Mr. Hunt related to me the following anecdote:—A short time ago he took part of the New Testament, consisting of the Gospels and Acts, the remainder not being then ready, and proceeded to visit various places until he came next to Nandi, where he presented an axe, and stationed a native teacher, leaving only a small supply of books, that others might have the precious boon which he was bearing from place to place. At first, when they of Nandi found what was in the book, they would borrow a copy, and, uniting a few together, would retire into the bush, and read together for several days in private, until it was found that by this means they could not meet the calls for the book. They then agreed to divide it into three or four parts, each portion being in the possession of one party, who retired with his share thus obtained into some secret place, there to read alone its sacred contents; and they have so read it, that a great many have got the whole by heart. Most of the young men are of this number. They have since told my friend, that "though he had brought them an axe, and other rare articles, yet he had not brought them anything valuable except (or in comparison with) the book from the Lord!" In this dense population we have set down two missionaries, with a good supply of the entire New Testament.

9th. We have been landing goods to-day from six o'clock in the morning till eight in the evening. God's mercy has been our shield from evil, and the natives have done more in one day than so many Tongans would have done in three.

I write this at nine o'clock at night, with a simple covering of calico, and my bare feet on a cold sheet of lead; but, though my cabin windows and door are wide open, I am bathed in perspiration, and not a little prostrated with the intense heat.

10th. I got up at five o'clock, and went ashore to see the two mission-families settled there, and to meet the school, consisting of the entire population. They came in procession, as in every other instance, singing as they slowly approached, headed by their chiefs and teachers. Every one had his present in his hand; consisting of either a large mat, or a club, a spear, a shell, a *lego,* (female dress,) fowls, cocoa-nut oil, or some food ready dressed. They repeated the catechism, and some other pieces, very satisfactorily, and were all well dressed. I am told that thirty such families reside there; all these *lotu.* Mr. Hunt has so laid out his plans, as to have a mission-school at Solavo immediately. After I had said to the assembly what I had judged proper, the king of Vewa rose and said, "You will be wanting to see how these mission-families live, and will therefore be crowding into their houses: but you must not do so: and it is very bad to sit looking when they take their food: avoid this. When you catch fish, bring some to your pastors, and do not charge anything for them. Remember, also, that if you plant a yam, or a *taro*, and it die or be injured, then you can plant another; but if you lose a missionary, will another grow up in his place? Therefore treat them well, that they may live, and not go away, but stay here, till the *lotu* shall send its branches over all the lands. Many of the heathen are now like birds flying about, and have no place to alight upon; but soon they will hear of your happiness, and will come to find rest in the *lotu* tree."

At noon we weighed anchor, and passed down the coast to the westward, among the same reefs we had passed before. Shortly after we sailed, the rain came down in torrents, and the sea was perfectly calm. We knew of dangers everywhere, but could see nothing; and the ship was the sport of the currents. This day has been one of great anxiety; but at six o'clock the good providence of God brought us to a place where we could sound; and there, in ten fathoms, we anchored for the night, thankful for our preservation in the time of very great difficulty.

Within sight this morning, as I was going ashore, admiring the "morning spread upon the mountains," was the Bay of Waikama, or the boiling springs of this interesting island, very much resembling, I am told, those of Taupo, in New-Zealand.

11*th*. We are weather-bound between Nandi and Bua, upon a lee shore. The wet above, and the heat below, leave one to his choice, whether he will be wet with rain or with perspiration, besides being half smothered. But heat and wet constitute the peculiar fertility of this climate. The large flats between the mountains and the hills are composed of alluvial soil, perhaps twelve feet deep on the average; and, being level, the rain water, and the spring water also, are seen in pools in all the low places, with here and there a rill purling its way to the neighboring river. In these flats the natives grow their *taro*, about nine inches deep in clear water. Large trees grow everywhere, except where they are prevented; and the wild fig is seen here and there. Rice would grow well here. The broad fig shall come down from New-Zealand, with many fruits to beautify and benefit the mission-stations first, and then to cover the land. In coasting these islands, you scarcely ever see a house, or any indications, except smoke, that men dwell here. This, no doubt, is the result of their extended wars. The people live in the midst of the flats, which are approached, from the sea, by a creek running up through a dense bush of mangroves. Our new mission stations are by the side of these salt-water rivers, and are only just at high-water mark: having no elevation, and being close to the water, hemmed in by a dense grove, there is no view, and very little circulation of air; but heat there is to a very high degree, and swarms of flies and musquitoes torment the uninitiated. This state of things is very revolting to my mind, because it inflicts an amount of discomfort on the mission-families, which must be seen and felt to be at all understood. But at present we must suffer it; for the pastor must lodge with his flock, and these are the localities *they* [the natives] have chosen, and on which they have erected the mission-houses. When these are decayed, new ones may probably be erected on the rising ground by the sea-shore, where the breeze and the open view may be secured. The flocks will then follow their shepherds, especially as there will then be no fear of war, because the "son of peace" will be there. It is very remarkable that the health of our mission-families has been generally good, notwithstanding the local disadvantages under which they are placed. We are therefore warranted in concluding, that, upon the whole, the climate of these tropical isles is merely wasting, not deadly.

Poor Mr. Ford is suffering severely from headache. He and his family have been one year, save ten days, in passing from England to Nandi.*

We are now again at anchor in the fine bay of Bua, on our way from Nandi to Ba; for it is part of our tribulation to be obliged to come to anchor every night, or we should probably get on the reefs in the dark. The heat to-night is very oppressive; I am thoroughly overcome by it. Still all is well: my health is good, and my mind tranquil and joyful.

12*th*. We weighed anchor this morning, and started for Ba; but the wind met us, and we were compelled to give up the struggle among the reefs, and to return to Bua. The heat of the sun was melting; but upon the mountains the clouds hung heavily, and poured down torrents. There is one place on this large island where the natives say it rains nearly every day in the year; and at that place, Mr. Hunt tells me, is a very large river, called Wainanu, which takes its rise about the middle of the island, and runs into the sea both to windward and to leeward. The

* Mr. Ford's health has failed at this station, and he and his family have been obliged to remove elsewhere for their recovery. —EDIT.

native canoes pass through the island upon the bosom of this river; having to be lifted a little just in the middle. The Rewa river in Viti Levu is of the same kind; and the natives say that a large shaddock-tree in the centre of this river drops its fruit into the water, and some are carried into one sea, some into the other: for at that spot the ground is highest. New-Zealand is called a wet country; but I am well satisfied that more rain falls here than in New-Zealand, where, by the rain-gauge, it is clearly ascertained that the same quantity of rain falls as in England; namely, thirty-two inches annually.

STRANGE SUPERSTITIONS IN FEEJEE, — STORY OF RAVUYALO.

Among the many remarkable personages feared by the Feejeeans, because of their ability to do them harm, Ravuyalo holds a prominent place. Ravuyalo is his official name, and denotes his office; it implies the same as Abaddon, "the Destroyer;" only his name defines his work still more particularly, as it not only denotes that he is a destroyer, but a destroyer of souls. Ng-gilai is his proper name. It is not known whether he is the son of the arch-god Dengei, or not; but he is understood to have received his commission to destroy souls from him. He resides at a place called Nambanggatai, on the high-road to Bulu, or "the separate state." The town is inhabited by people of this world: and the town occupied by Ravuyalo and his sons, though in this vicinity, is nevertheless out of sight. The people of the natural town are nevertheless well acquainted with what is going on in the spiritual town, by means of a paroquet, which gives notice, whenever spirits are passing to another world. If only one is coming, he calls once; if two, twice; and so on according to the number. When a town has been destroyed, a great number are announced; and Ravuyalo and his family prepare for a smart contest. The Feejeeans, being aware of what they will have to meet with on their way to another world, make the necessary preparation just about the time of death. A person who is prepared to die, has a club in one hand, a whale's tooth in the other, or lying by his side: his face is painted, his body oiled, and his best dress is put on, &c.; just as if he was prepared for war. If he has been a great warrior, and has killed many, he has the honor of carrying the souls of all these, hanging at his spiritual club. Ravuyalo and party, on hearing the paroquet, prepare for action. Sometimes the contest is severe, and the natives declare that they can hear the sound of clubs in the encounter. This spiritual Robin Hood sometimes meets with his match, and is worsted. In this case the poor souls go on their way, and their opponent retires to his town. If, however, he is successful, he drags his ghostly victims to the oven, and feasts himself and family on his prey. It is confidently affirmed by the natives, that Ravuyalo is dead. He happened to meet with a misfortune sometime ago, which proved fatal. The paroquet had announced the approach of one or more spirits from this world, and Ravuyalo ran into the mangrove-bushes to await their appearance. He seated himself on the stump of some bushes, which had lately been cut down, and unfortunately one of the stumps ran up into his body, and nearly killed him on the spot. He was taken to the *Mburi;* where, after he had charged his sons to carry on the business after his death, this soul-destroyer expired. The news of this event is said to have been brought to this world by a man named Soli, who was lately translated to Bulu, or Hades, and has informed some of his friends of the event.

We shall now say a word about those who have the good fortune to escape the club of Ravuyalo. They proceed on their way to Bulu, till they come to the top of one of the highest peaks of the Kauvandra mountains. This mountain is called Naindelinde, and is so high that the ladies of the Kauvandra are said to stand on its summit to see the wars that are carried on in Feejee. On the edge of one of the precipices of this mountain two persons are seated, father and son, whose names I do not know. They hold a large steering oar in their hands, the broad end of which hangs over the precipice into the sea. When a spirit approaches them, they make inquiries to the following effect:—"Where have you come from?" Answer, "From the world." "What have you been doing there?" "O, fighting, feasting, and other things." The poor soul gives as good an account of himself as he can to this ghostly inquisitor, who invites him to take a seat on the flat end of the steering oar, that he may be refreshed a little with the cool air. The inquisitor, inquisitor-like, then suddenly tumbles him over the steep precipice into the sea, without giving him any reason for so doing; and the poor spirit makes the best of his way through the dark, deep waters into the other world. Some spirits are interrogated on their way to the precipice by those whom they meet, and, if they are found guilty of a

Feejeean sin, are punished accordingly. The punishment for not having killed an enemy in war, is, to beat a heap of human dung with a club; a thing as abominable to a native as eating human flesh is to us. Other punishments are awarded for other offences. In this manner the devil induces them to commit crimes of the worst kind, for fear of punishment if they do not.

Nov. 13*th.* At a quarter to six this morning, we got under weigh with a light land breeze, having to pass from one main-land to another, a distance of about fourscore miles; but there are many things to retard us,—not only shoals and reefs, but the wind is shuffling, being, no doubt, influenced by the high lands in different directions.

At three o'clock we came to anchor at the old spot, the wind having again become contrary. These disappointments are for the trial of our faith; and in a climate so thoroughly melting, no one can say, that to be kept here doing nothing, but suffering all over, is not a trial.

Sunday, 14*th.* In the morning I preached on, "If any man be in Christ, he is a new creature." During the reading of the Scriptures, and of the Litany, as well as through the entire service, a blessed unction rested upon us all. We had two native services; and in the evening Mr. Hunt preached a thoroughly Wesleyan sermon on, "Thou shalt love the Lord thy God with all thy heart," &c. He poured forth thought upon thought, so just, so weighty, so original, so luminous, that I sat upon the quarter-deck, looking at this wonderful man with amazement and admiration.

There was an energy and a simplicity about his appeals all but overwhelming. The scene was altogether lovely: the setting sun, the cloud-capped mountains, the placid ocean, the listening crew and native teachers, and the intelligent, zealous preacher, from whom were coming forth "rivers of living water," united in giving effect to the occasion, and made me willing to ride upon the mountain-wave, and feel at home upon the sea. This was none other than the house of God, this was the gate of heaven!

15th. To-day we came across from Vanua Levu to Viti Levu, through such a passage as I never sailed in before. Reefs, sunken rocks, and shoals encompassed us on every side. Screams were continually heard from the masthead, "Keep her away! Helm hard down! Steady! A rock right ahead! Rocks and shoals on both sides! Let go the halyards!" &c. Through all these, by a watchful Providence, we have been conducted in perfect safety; and now lie anchored off Ba. The day has been to me, and I believe to others also, a day of intense anxiety.

The brig did wonders; but eighty miles of such navigation, completed before three o'clock in the afternoon, requires better nerves than mine: I stood on the quarter-deck, with Mr. Hunt by my side, crying, "Master, help thy servants!" Elijah, the pilot, and the second mate, were at the masthead all the way.

Our exposures here, while taking the missionaries and the native teachers to their fields of labor, are such as still to call for the earnest prayers of our friends, both at home and abroad. Without special care by all on board, in addition to the special providence of God over us, we could not have calculated upon so many hair-breadth escapes as I have witnessed this day.

16*th*. We went in a boat from the ship to Ba, a distance of thirty miles there and back, leaving the sea, and entering a river almost as wide as the Thames. We passed one heathen town after another, until, about three miles from the mouth, we came to the town at which we had determined to leave a teacher and his family. Nearly fifty persons have embraced Christianity here, and we have blooming prospects among this dense population, having nothing but sin and the devil to oppose us,—no Popery, no Puseyism, no French skeptical vanity, no people spoiled by a bad religion. All here is fair sailing. The plain, powerful truths of the gospel, clearly laid before this people, lead them to repentance and to Jesus Christ.

This is by far the most beautiful part of Feejee that I have seen. A dozen British noblemen might find enough of everything dignified, rich, and lovely, for country-seats at Ba. The river is noble, the soil rich, the trees and plantations luxuriant, and a fine race of men are living here in great numbers. The prospect is most charming; the river, the groves, the distant and lofty mountains, with fruitful cultivations, and teeming fisheries, fill the mind with delight.

On our way to this place, Mr. Hunt told us of one of the Ba chiefs, who, having got on board an American vessel, was wantonly shot by the captain. The enraged natives say, that the first boat's crew they can fall in with, having a captain on board, shall pay for this outrage. He added, " Had I not been a missionary, no consideration should have induced me to venture ashore." No master of a vessel has, since that affair, come near them; and our position was not a very enviable one. However, we went into the mouth of the river, where many canoes were engaged in fishing. There were also many persons without canoes, wading to the middle in water, on the reefs, gathering shell-fish. They all were very noisy as we passed them. On the banks of the river, crowds were ranged to see this new sight,—a boat with four oars, and people with clothes on! Having reached the *lotu* town, Mr. Hunt preached under the shade of lofty trees. Many heathens looked on, sometimes talking and laughing; but, upon the whole, they behaved pretty well. Unhappily, the *lotu* chief was not at home, nor the teacher. When all our work was completed, and we were preparing to go, I observed that I was eyed with more keen glances than were quite agreeable to me, especially by a wicked-looking, angry cannibal, walking round me at a quick pace, carrying a musket in his hand. I afterwards learned that this man, and some others, mistook me for a captain, which fully explained their suspicious movements. The probability is, that Divine Providence put a restraint upon the heathens of Ba, and suffered us not to share the fate of men not employed by Him. But for this care of our God, how could we go on?

17*th.* We proceeded, against the trade-wind, to beat our way back from Ba to Ragi-ragi, and came to anchor in the evening under a small island, having worked our way up the coast about thirty miles. It is one of our peculiarities that we are obliged every night to come to anchor; otherwise we should not be safe among the reefs and rocks of Feejee. Such navigation is both tedious and fatiguing, to say nothing of its dangers. Every morning and night we call all hands to sing, read the Scriptures, and pray upon the quarter-deck, it being too hot to go below.

18*th*. We repeated to-day the efforts of yesterday, and, with the wind right ahead, worked our way directly up this coast of Ragi-ragi, among the reefs, and anchored in the bay of Nananu. Mr. Hunt took with him Varani, and went ashore to visit one of our stations under a native teacher. On landing, a stout cannibal attempted to ascertain whether Philip Johns, one of the seamen, was fit to eat, by laying hold of his leg and turning up some of his clothing, to see how the matter stood. Mr. Hunt called out to him, and the man stared angrily at him, while Johns got into the boat. The late chief used to salt men down, and live almost entirely upon human flesh, either fresh or salted. Through Mr. Hunt, I have procured the four-clawed wooden fork with which he used to feed himself. We have, however, a few sheep in this land of sin and cannibals.

Walking the deck this evening, I was charmed with the stillness of the scene: the men had retired, after a hard day's work, the trade-wind had lulled itself to sleep, and the heavenly bodies stood out in their full glory and magnificence. To these the language of the psalmist was so just and appropriate, as to recur to the memory with peculiar beauty and force:—"When I consider thy heavens, the work of thy fingers; the moon and the stars, which thou hast ordained; [Lord,] what is man, that thou art mindful of him? and the son of man, that thou visitest him?"

"Here," thought I, "am I, a mere leaf upon the rolling wave! But behold these brilliant constellations that dot the canopy on high!—the stars, so thickly distributed, that, as Herschel's telescope enabled him to ascertain, in a portion of the Milky Way, the moon would eclipse two thousand such stars at once! These all are suns, or how could I see their light, since it requires more than ten years to reach our world from the nearest star yet known? I am traveling about one hundred miles a day among these islands; the planet whirls me about sixty-five thousand miles an hour in her orbit, and another thousand round her axis! Look at these double stars, one red and another blue, revolving round each other, two suns in one system; and hosts beyond them, by heavenly machinery 'wheeling unshaken' in the nether skies! The centre worlds will surely have their planets; and will these be barren fields, or each a garden which the Lord hath blessed with intelligent inhabitants? Then come forth the nebular systems. These, I observe, stand thick among the constellations of the southern skies; and what are they, but congregations paying silent homage to their Maker, in company with countless others of the stellar world? These I see; but where is the outside of the universe, the boundary of the physical creation? Who has seen, in either hemisphere, worlds beyond which there are no other worlds? Improved glasses will give in their report; but high is the arch, and ample the sum of celestial worlds, the workmanship of our God! To be fully informed upon all these points, I must go on serving Christ their Maker. By his aid, I must go on spreading, as I best can, the savour of his grace among men, who are redeemed, though they know it not. For this reason we must go on in the work of instruction, that the Redeemer may be known, embraced, trusted, and adored.

> 'Let this my every hour employ,
> Till I my Master see!'

Surely, preaching the gospel is the best work a man can do, and saving souls the highest honor he can obtain! For 'he that winneth souls is wise;' and 'they that be wise shall shine as the brightness of the firmament; and they that turn many to righteousness as the stars forever and ever.'"

19*th.* The same work to-day as yesterday,—beating about among reefs. In the evening we came to anchor in Lomana bay. The natives here are at war; catching, clubbing, eating, as they go. The word "war" ill expresses their condition: they are at enmity, and carry on a system of kidnapping; but there are no field-days, no decisive battles fought among them. Perhaps one hundred warriors will be lying in wait for a man and his wife, going to their plantation. A rush is made upon them, and a shout of triumph raised, as they are shouldered off to the oven, where the whole affair will be discussed till the last morsel is eaten. They treat each other more like beasts than men, only they are more Satanic. Mr. Watsford told me a case, in which the same man took a pig on one shoulder, and a human body on the other, and bore them as a present to the chief, who told him to lay down the long animal; the short one he might take to the common people, as less delicate and less approved!

From our quarter-deck there is visible a large town, situate upon the very top of the highest sharp mountain in this Alpine part of Feejee. There, no doubt, they have built for the sake of greater security against their fellow-men. The difficulty and toil of ascending this lofty peak, at least three or four thousand feet high, must be a heavy tax upon them. But the gospel has reached their neighborhood; and soon "they shall not hurt nor destroy in all my holy mountain, saith the Lord."

Soon after we had anchored, many of these warriors appeared on the shore, distant about a mile, each man armed. Having come from their towns on the mountain peaks, they had no canoe; but this was no hinderance, for eight of them swam off to the ship with all ease: but as we were informed by Varani that they were all heathens, they were not allowed to come on board. They asked for powder, flints, and such things. Receiving none, they all swam off with cheerfulness, except one man, whose eyes glared as if he was disappointed of his prey. Their object may have been harmless; but the probability is, that, if they had been allowed to come on board, they would have watched their opportunity when we were off our guard; each one of them would have seized one of us, and thrown him into the sea, and the rest might easily have been disposed of.

Others came off upon rafts of bamboo, bringing bread-fruit, bananas, and sugar-cane, which we purchased of them for fish-hooks, beads, and empty bottles. They murder white men here with as little concern as they would destroy a dog; and such murders are every now and then taking place. The few that are now here have large families, that bind them to the soil; but hard is their lot, and bitter must be their regret that they ever saw Feejee.

20*th*. We passed along the coast to-day, and anchored at Nakorotumbu, where we have a teacher, and a goodly number of *lotu* natives. Here, therefore, we shall not need to watch with quite so much vigilant anxiety as we did last night, where danger was at our door, as the cannibals might think to board us under cover of the darkness; and several times in the night, I distinctly heard the beating of drums; but nothing was attempted, and we are away, safe and thankful.

As we were working up the coast to-day, we often approached within half a mile of the land, and could very distinctly hear the natives, who were fishing on the reefs below, shouting to each other; but we were amused by the extraordinary situations of their towns. The sloping high land hereabouts is very rocky, and, in some places, very abrupt. Such were the places selected to build upon: it matters not how high, or craggy, or precipitous it may be, there is their town on the crag of the rock. On the sharp top of the lofty mountain, you may literally see "a city set upon a hill, which cannot be hid;" and as we are bringing them the "glad tidings of great joy, which shall be to all people," we shall not be surprised at a future day to hear "the inhabitants of the rock sing!"

In the evening Mr. Hunt came off from the native settlement in a canoe loaded with teachers, chiefs, and *lotu* people. Their countenances were radiant with joy. "So many friends! come to see them in such a fine *vanka vanua* (ship)!" Having got up the side of the vessel, the first man that was introduced to me was Job, the next was Abraham, and the next Methuselah. These were all religious men, engaged in doing good, according to the light they enjoy. Paul and his wife Lydia also were present. These were Tongans, and knew me in bygone days.

It appears that a powerful chief has been here from Nandrona, which is on the opposite side of this large island; and his journey by water could not be less than two hundred miles. He wished to have a teacher to take back with him: but none could be found, save a boy, who was *lotu*, but he was a leper. "No matter," said the chief; "I must be instructed, and the boy shall go with me." This was done. The leper, however, sank under the journey, but the chief has embraced the gospel! The next time the vessel comes to the islands, a teacher must be taken to his district, and most likely a missionary will be placed at Ba. Thus the word of the Lord grows mightily and prevails. New fields open so fast, that we are in danger of rushing forward to occupy them, to the injury of those parts which we have begun to cultivate. Feejee must have more missionaries, or the loud and earnest cries for them by men who wish to cease from eating their fellow-men, and begin to seek salvation by faith in Christ, cannot be complied with,—at least, not by us; but the priests from Rome are waiting to step in.

Sunday, November 21st. I went, with Mr. Hunt, to the town of Nakorotumbu at nine o'clock, and preached to a fine congregation, of whom one hundred and twenty are professed Christians, the rest heathens; but even these listened with serious interest while I discoursed on "the dead, small and great, standing before God." Mr. Hunt interpreted with so much energy, that many wept aloud, and all were very attentive to hear.

At eleven o'clock we entered into the house of Paul, who was a boy when I was at Tonga, and is now here as one of our teachers. Paul married Lydia; and they are both serving Christ, and spreading his truth. At a short distance from his own dwelling, Paul had erected a small summer-house, of fine white cane and bamboo, covered with sugar-cane leaves, and floored with a mat, but open in the direction to receive the trade-wind. Its dimensions were about nine feet by seven. To this lovely little clean room, surrounded by evergreens and lofty trees, we retired between the services; for Mr. Hunt was soon to preach. In a few minutes after we had taken possession, one brought me a very antique and odd-looking elbow-chair, which had been made by Methuselah in his younger days. Then came a small table, covered with a nice white native cloth. A boiled fowl was set before us, with plates, and knives and forks. Yams, *taro*, and native salt completed the frugal, but wholesome, board. A vessel, with as pure a draught of water as it ever fell to my lot to drink, was brought to us from the purling brook close by. When we had finished our meal, a bowl of the same clear water was handed to us, that we might wash after dinner, *vakaviti*, or Feejee fashion.

Now, these two persons, who could place matters so tastefully before Englishmen, so clean, so well dressed, and exceedingly good, are the fruit of our missions, who, when I first visited them and their country, were grossly ignorant of all such things, and withal deeply depraved.

I take this to be a very hopeful earnest of good things to come, as the fruit of the gospel in these seas. May it please the Lord of the vineyard to preserve this field, now every way so promising, from the Roman "boar out of the wood," and from every evil worker, both foreign and domestic!

On Saturday, Mr. Hunt married one of the young *lotu* chiefs here, who, by being married, had one *wife* less than before. A circumstance of a rather curious character took place in this marriage affair. The young man had previously been living with two women, one of whom had several children, and the other had none. In balancing the point as to which of these he should keep, he concluded on marrying the one that had the children. This was made known to the parties; but no sooner did this lady learn her distinction and superiority, than she began to show airs, and make herself unusually disagreeable. The chief, seeing this, told her, quite calmly, that she had begun too soon,—he should now marry the other; and accordingly did so. It is probable that by this humiliating lesson she will learn in future to carry herself with greater moderation.

November 22*d*. We weighed anchor at sunrise, for the purpose of threading our way against the wind between the reefs on our way back to Vewa. Before the anchor was up, two canoes, filled with *lotu* natives, came off about three miles, and joined with us on the quarter-deck in our usual family devotion: after singing (and they greatly delight to hear our singing) and reading the Scriptures, I prayed in English, and Mr. Hunt in the native language. They then saluted us affectionately, and we parted.

After a dead beat of nine hours, we came to anchor in an open roadstead, called Mataikara, in seven fathoms' water. The day turned out wet, and the clouds hung heavy on the attracting mountains. The slopes of these looked green; and I should incline to the opinion that, for purposes of grazing, the land of Feejee, where there is so much wet and heat, must be admirably adapted; one acre here producing more grass and herbage than ten do in New South Wales. Fencing would not be at all difficult, as fine stone and timber everywhere abound, with excellent streams of water. The Friendly Isles are very rich in soil, and generally level; but they lack timber, stone, and water. They abound in trees; but still they are deficient in useful timber. It is rather singular, that neither in Tonga nor Feejee will the natives sell their land, although they cannot use one acre in twenty of what they have.

When the anchor was down this evening, I proposed to Varani that we should go ashore; but he said enough to satisfy Mr. Hunt that our flesh would be swallowed by the crowds as soon as convenient after we landed. We have a native teacher near them, and the kingdom of God is come nigh unto them. Their country would contain more than twenty times its present population: but they are still fighting among themselves, and eating one another. Yet for these the Saviour died, and his gospel grace is even now displayed among these savages. We have a Christian native called Benjamin from this very place, who will shortly come to his own people in the character of teacher, for which he has been receiving instruction and training at Vewa. The Lord has "his way" even in poor Feejee; and bright will be the splendor when his train shall fill the evangelical temple, now in course of building among these outcasts of men.

23d. We weighed anchor early this morning, and beat up to the roadstead under Moturiki, and the high island of Ovalau. At this latter place we have a small church of steady members, who, when they first embraced the gospel, were sent for by King Tanoa, to "come to Bau and be cooked." Their answer was, "We are here, and you can cook us if you please; but we shall not give up our religion to save our lives." The king spared them. Unhappily, a war is now troubling this fine island; and the high peaks of the cloud-capped mountains are the places where the people take refuge when their enemies are too strong for them. Cannibalism is still rife at Ovalau; but its days are numbered; for the gospel is preached unto them, and, therefore, a voice is heard saying, "Arise, shine; for thy light is come, and the glory of the Lord is risen upon thee."

25th. How truly perilous is the condition of such a voyage as ours in Feejee! Yesterday morning we began our work in the usual way, beating up to Vewa, which we fully expected to make early in the day. Varani and the second mate were on the fore-topsail yard, looking out for danger; and soon enough they found it. At ten o'clock in the forenoon a cry was heard from the tops, "Keep her away! A rock right ahead!" This was instantly attended to by Captain Buck, who had the helm; but it was too late. In an instant on we went, "bump, bump, bump," on a small coral rock, having deep water all around, and with an ebb tide. She hung by the middle, about one-third resting on the rock. The ballast was thrown overboard; but as the tide fell, the vessel heeled over, and her bilge struck hard at times upon the rock. We were all exceedingly terrified. There was, however, no help, but in putting our hands to the ballast, and praying to the Lord for assistance. As the people were in the hold, they could see the stones heaving, as though something were forcing its way up through. So much did they heave, that at times they were rattled one against another. This, of course, told a sad tale as to the contact between the side of the vessel and the rock. While things were in this posture, two canoes bore down upon us; the men being perfectly naked, and savage in their looks. They were ordered not to board us, as the vessel was at present *tambu*, (sacred:) they went off at first, but soon returned with an aspect of increased hostility. They were allowed to come very near; then our fire-arms were shown to them. At this exhibition, I shall never forget the glare of their eyes, as they made all haste to push off before the wind. They did not come near again. No doubt they intended our destruction; but God put the fear of our arms upon them. Meantime there we lay upon the point of a small sharp rock, so much heeled over as not to be able to stand on the deck without holding on. From ten in the morning till seven in the evening were very anxious hours with us, during which period many prayers were offered up; and I am well satisfied today that by the sadness of the countenance the heart is made better. As the ship had been considerably lightened during the day, the flowing tide, at seven in the evening, floated her off under sail, "bump, bump, bump," until we were in deep water. What damage may have been done, is yet unknown; but she makes no water. Never can I forget that moment, when from our deck the rock appeared astern of us. All hands and eyes were lifted up in amazement and thankfulness to God for such a deliverance. I felt power with God in prayer, and many a precious promise passed through my mind during the day. But that day was a day to feel one's own littleness, and to ascertain the small comparative value to be attached to property and to life itself. In one minute all was calm cheerfulness; in the next we were thunderstruck, and filled with dismay and horror.

In the early part of this day we made our way to Vewa, where we have to lay in wood and water, and to get the vessel ready for sea, on her homeward voyage; if it do not turn out that serious injury has been done to her while on the rock.

During this trip among the Feejee group, we have planted three new missions, and placed some native teachers in populous parts of the islands, where, though for the most part second to none in vice and ferocity, there are a few who are desirous of hearing about revealed religion, and some who have already bowed the knee to Jesus. Twenty-one times we have come to anchor; once we ran upon a rock, far from land; and it is impossible to say how many others we escaped by the skin of our teeth, as it were, while loud cries from the topmast, of, "Keep her away—we are almost on a rock!" caused every face upon deck to turn pale. Scenes like these shake my nerves; but at the same time they lead me to the Saviour, whose work I love, and by his grace shall pursue until he shall say, "It is enough: come up higher."

26th. Vewa is tranquil; but war is in the neighborhood, between Rewa and Bau. Two captives were killed and eaten within sight of our vessel, so late as yesterday; and two hundred others have been taken alive in the fall of a town called Notho. Many were slain and eaten; the town was burnt; and the captives await their fate.

A chief in another part of the island, not at war, said to one of his people, "Go, get me some bread-fruit, and cook it forthwith." The man went, and found none, which he reported on his return to the chief; who replied, "Very well, make haste and prepare the oven." The man did so accordingly, and, by order of the chief, was himself cooked therein at once, for no other cause than his not finding bread-fruit when his superior was hungry!

27th. Joshua, our native teacher, who had been sent over to Rotumah in an American vessel when I first arrived at Feejee, has returned, and reports that he found our teachers all well, and about eighty members in the society, anxiously looking out for a missionary. The population is estimated at about one thousand; and many of them would *lotu* if a missionary could reside amongst them. Some irregularities had crept in among the Tonga teachers, and also among the people, which were corrected by Joshua. He reports that two Popish priests have been landed there by a French ship-of-war, with this injunction, "Feed and treat these men well; because we shall call again, and, if there be any complaint, we shall punish you." But Joshua says the entire population strongly dislike Popery and the priests, and that not one person has joined himself to them. But to us they turn their speaking eyes in supplication for a missionary. I beg that one may be sent to poor Rotumah, if the state of your funds will permit you to incur the extra expense.

Both the master of the "Auckland" bark and Joshua state the following facts:—Two vessels from Sydney, of which the name of one was "Velocity," a schooner, had been engaged in obtaining men from islands hereabout at two pounds a-head by the year as wages; as they are designed to be shepherds and laborers in New South Wales. It is stated that forty of the natives, from an island called Uea, near New Caledonia, were on board when these vessels touched at Rotumah; where, not liking what they had met with on board, they all swam ashore. The chief was applied to, in vain, to give them up. He said he would not meddle with it; he did not bring them there, and should not interfere, one way or the other. The Europeans then resorted to harsh measures, with a view of compelling the chief to send back the escaped natives. A scuffle took place between the parties, and some were shot on both sides. The vessels hereupon sailed without the men, whom they had brought from their homes. I have no ground to doubt that these facts are substantially correct; but I hope that the government will not permit a system to grow up which is so deeply degrading to human nature, and so thoroughly anti-Christian and anti-British.

Vewa, Sunday, November 28th. The Lord is visiting his people in several places, and in separate islands. Showers of gracious influence are falling copiously on the older stations, as well as upon the infant churches. Conversions are by no means rare; and a general quickening is observable throughout the group. I have long since observed that a few clear and genuine conversions in any place will give an impulse to spiritual religion in that church. There is much unity of heart and purpose among the missionaries here; and their spirit is caught by the people.

29th. I left Auckland this day six months, and have been wandering about among the islands ever since. Though I have many mercies poured upon me from God, and favors from his Church, for which I trust I am thankful; yet so long an absence from home, combined with a sea-life, is by no means what I would choose. It is merely to be submitted to, for Christ's sake. Such a cause and such a Master will more than justify this little exposure of one's self, when the Lord hath need of it. This, after all, is not martyrdom!

A chief of Bau, within sight of Vewa, where I am writing, slew two women yesterday, merely for the pleasure of killing human beings. Notice may or may not be taken of these murders; but their blood crieth, and, "I will repay, saith the Lord."

CHAPTER IV.

REVIEW AND RETURN.

November 30*th*. Upon a review of our mission to Feejee, I am bound to say that its importance, in my estimation, increases with the increase of my knowledge of the people, the country, and the work now in progress here. There are two very large islands, with high mountains and fine rivers, each as large as Devonshire. Upon these the population may be reckoned at 150,000. Besides these, there are in the entire group about one hundred islands, with a population, Mr. Hunt thinks, of another 150,000, making a total of 300,000 souls in Feejee. I am well satisfied that twenty times the present number of people might easily find subsistence on these islands, and one hundred islets, not now inhabited. It is a remarkable provision of Divine Providence, that the two main articles of food in Feejee never fail together. If the season proves wet, the *taro* thrives well; and if it be dry, the yam abounds. When the gospel shall have caused their wars to cease, the industrious habits of the people cannot fail to secure abundance of excellent food, and, by consequence, a rapid increase of population. While this people have at present a rough exterior, and cannibal habits, they are possessed of activity, shrewdness, and the remains of civil distinctions, titles of honor, and courteous salutations of one another, which, in their fine and copious language, produce, the missionaries say, in a variety of ways, the most agreeable effect. The New Testament is now read by many, an edition having issued from the mission press in Feejee. The impression begins to be very general that Christianity is true, and that, of course, their system is false and destructive. Those who have embraced the gospel generally adorn it; and a goodly number of them go everywhere preaching the word. It is worthy of remark, that, notwithstanding the bloody and cruel ferocity of these pagan cannibals, no violence, even of the slightest kind, has been committed on the person of any of our missionaries. But the case has not been so with other white men dwelling among them, many of whom have been clubbed, maimed, and killed.

The character of our brethren for consistency and truthfulness, while living in Feejee, may now be considered as fully established. Whoever else is in jeopardy, the messenger of grace and peace is held sacred. The very devoted and spotless life of Varani, since he bowed the knee to Jesus, has done much to soften prejudice, and to cast a lustre on the Christian character. His friend and companion in arms, Thakombau, king of Feejee, was very bitter and earnest against the gospel, until he saw the true power of piety in this "living epistle." Since that time his tone has softened down, and his views have become corrected. He now says Christianity is true, and that he and his people shall soon embrace it; but there are some wars to be completed first! Both he and his people are well aware of the designs of the French priests, aided by the naval power of France; and deep is their dislike to both, but especially to Popery, the full display of which they behold in Tahiti.

The widely extended influence of the press; the diligent attention to the education of the people, and especially of the children, wherever we get a station; the increased instruction afforded to the most hopeful of the native converts; the multiplication of these in all directions, where the people are willing, and even anxious, to receive them as teachers; and, above all, under God, the successful preaching of the gospel, and the consequent outpouring of the Holy Spirit, now most earnestly prayed for by the excellent missionaries scattered among the islands—cannot fail to overcome the power of Satan, and to set up in Feejee the kingdom of our God and of his Christ.

At present it appears to me that our prospects are truly cheering, and that the day is not distant when this people shall be added to the triumphs of our blessed Saviour in the islands of the sea. Let us, therefore, go on, and, if possible, increase in prayer, in subscriptions, in collecting; and then we shall hope for one missionary for Ba, one for Nakorotumbu, and one for Rotumah. These doors are wide open, and the fields are white unto the harvest; and the harvest here also "is great, but the labourers are few."

There are two subjects which tend greatly, very greatly, to my comfort, as I pass from land to land, visiting the Churches, and planting new ones where the way of the Lord has been prepared. One is, that, with our connectional views of general redemption, I can confidently, and without any perplexity or secret misgiving, offer salvation, free, full, and present, to every man, and tribe, and people, with whom I come in contact, not doubting the power of the gospel to reach every case, and to become the power of God unto salvation to every one that believeth, whether Jew or Gentile, New-Zealander, Tongan, or Feejeean. Upon this point there is no misgiving, no mental reserve, no doubt. The commission runs, "Go ye into all the world, and preach the gospel to every creature." And to every creature of Adam's race, it *is* gospel, that is, "glad tidings of great joy to all people," when fully and faithfully proclaimed.

Another ground of consolation to me is, that prayer is made for us continually by the Churches of the Lord Jesus. We are here in the open ocean, without much intercourse with men; to the continuous solitude must be added dangers of various kinds; but the Master is here, saying, "I am with you." The prayers from the mission-house, from the missionary prayer-meetings, and from many a pulpit and family altar, enter into his ears; and he answers them by blessing us, and the springing field, as the case may need. It is in this way that we hold a spiritual correspondence, and are helpers of each other by prayer and by other modes of communication. From this reflection I derived no small amount of joy when our fine new vessel was bumping upon the rocks for nine successive hours. "The people of God," said I, "are praying for us, and our great High Priest ever liveth to make intercession for us." Such thoughts helped us, also, to pray, as they reminded us that we were not forgotten, even there, upon a solitary rock in the ocean.

December 2d. The murderer of the two Bau women fled to a town not far away; but the report had traveled faster than he did. The people of the place only knew him as a stranger; but they agreed to try their hand at a police stratagem, with a view of ascertaining from himself whether or not he was the murderer. They went to him, therefore, and said, "Have you been killing anybody belonging to Bau? because, if you have, we shall just throw up our fence round the town, and fight with those people. We have long wished to do this, but lacked a proper excuse. Now, if you have done this deed, you are the man for us,—we will have a turn with these Bau fellows." "O yes," said the man; "I killed two women yesterday, and shall now be content to abide with you." Instantly the people sent word to his pursuers, saying, "The murderer is here; come and bind him." This being done, the man was conveyed to Bau, where the women bit off his ears and nose. They did not try him, but prepared the oven, killed, cooked, and ate him this morning. The whole affair is just now concluded, within sight of the spot on which I write.

3d. Vewa was a "village in an uproar" this morning. One of the young men had offered some insult to a female, and the people collected to hear the case. It was fully made out; and there on the spot the offender was compelled to bow down at the feet of a strong man, who laid on him a certain number of stripes with a thick rope, all the people witnessing this degradation. This prompt investigation and punishment of crime is quite primitive, and, for aught I can see, not unbecoming even a Christian village in Feejee. It is rather remarkable that not one of the missionaries knew anything of the matter till all was over. I happened accidentally to pass by in the course of my morning walk.

4th. Mr. Lyth is just returned from Bau, where he has been preaching, and relates the following fact:

An apostate woman, living in the house of the king, offered in mockery to preach a sermon, and forthwith began; but the king, who was till lately very strongly opposed to Christianity, said to her, "You shall not ridicule the *lotu* here; religion is true, and a weighty matter, not to be trifled with." And he did not stop there, but proceeded to punish the scoffer in a way rather novel even in Feejee. There was a huge iron pot in the house, which he directed to be turned over upon the woman. She remained whelmed and coiled up under it all night. The iron pot, which had been taken out of a whaler wrecked here, would probably measure four feet in diameter. From under it she dared not stir till orders were given to that effect by the king.

Vewa, December 6th. We weighed anchor this morning for New-Zealand, after taking a most affectionate leave of the excellent mission-families at Vewa. They are accomplishing a noble work in Feejee, and a great door and effectual is open to them. Mr. Hunt is an extraordinary man, both in body and mind; and all his fine powers are devoted to Christ, and his Feejeean infant Churches, for the conversion of these energetic people. By his brethren he is very greatly beloved; and they in turn are much and deservedly beloved by their chairman.*

I have experienced nothing but the greatest personal respect and kindness from all the brethren, both here and in the Friendly Islands. I cannot re-

* The Society have now to deplore the loss of this able and admirable missionary: the obituary which appeared in the Minutes of the Wesleyan Conference for 1849, will be found at the end of the volume, Note B.—EDIT.

view my progress through these lovely groups, without ascribing praise to the Lord, for the work it has been my happiness to behold and to promote during my stay among them of between six and seven months, and for all the gracious interpositions of Providence in our favour until this day.

7th. Having anchored last night under Moturiki, not being able to clear the reefs yesterday, we are now opening the sea-gates, and passing out into deep water. During this voyage I have read :—

Barrett's Pastoral Addresses.—We need such essays; and they cannot be too pointed. These are times when plain dealing must be used, or Christ crucified will soon become a stumbling-block, and the gospel will be treated as "light food."

Dr. Fisk's Travels.—Interesting and instructive; but what a moral wreck is Europe! The author seems at home everywhere but in England, and there he is the American in the presence of his fathers!

Whewell on Astronomy and General Physics.—There is a fine compass of thought, and he settles the integrity of our system; but he sometimes attenuates to excess, and is always a mere philosopher.

Sir Charles Bell on the Hand.—Some just thoughts and original illustrations; but many passages are obscure, and the volume is a stream of text in a field of margin.

Dr. Dixon's Memoirs of Miller.—Food for the mind, and aid to devotion. I do not see the case of an aged minister becoming supernumerary in the gloom in which it is viewed by this excellent author. The position, in my view, is one of honor and ease; full of blooming hope and grateful recollections; far better than standing in the way of one who is strong to labor.

Horne's Memoir of his Wife.—An excellent woman, no doubt; but could so many domestic privations be necessary?—and surely they need not be published. The introductory remarks of the Rev. R. Young are excellent. We ought to see that the wife of a missionary be such as will serve the cause of Christ. More attention will have to be given to this matter, or evil will befall us.

D'Aubigné's Theological Lectures.—Generally good, but not equal to his "Reformation." He is sometimes mystical and obscure.

Treffry's Memoir of Benson.—Marrow and fatness.

Young's Lectures on Popery.—Admirable: the fair and honest argument sweeps along, leaving Popery no hiding-place.

Hoole's Personal Narrative.—This was looked over again, and found to be well worth the perusal. How much the natives on the coast of Coromandel resemble the Feejeeans! Their dress, attitudes, modes of doing homage, and bowing in prayer; their catamarans, and their general manners,—are the same; only the mind of the Hindoo is pre-occupied, but the Feejeean is open to receive the gospel.

These fine islands will, no doubt, one day be in the hands of civilized men, and almost all that the tropics can produce may be found and cultivated here; spice, tea, coffee, and almost everything that flourishes in the east may be produced in the south; and our Christian missions prepare the way of the Lord.

10*th.* We are at sea; but the wind is contrary, and I am ill: the numerous islets and shoals prevent our doing any good; and in the night our case is anything but desirable. In the evening, we put into the Rewa Bay, under Nugulau, till the wind shall favor us.

Within the last three years, not less than thirteen towns have been burnt at Rewa, and the people either driven to the opposite land, or eaten on the spot. One of these towns was a mile and a half long, and the rest were large, and full of people. The island of Rewa, now stretching out before me, is large, flat, rich, and fertile; but the people are cut off, and the conquerors do not occupy this very fine part of Feejee. The gospel was offered to them; but war broke out, and "death had swifter wings than love."

Just opposite our vessel is a small island, occupied by a few English and Americans, chiefly sailors, living with women, but not in marriage. These poor creatures must be very wretched; for, what have they to make them otherwise? A life of sin cannot be separate from misery.

11*th*. This morning the wind became more moderate and favorable, but only just sufficient to take us out between the rocks and foaming waves, in a passage so narrow, that we could not tack ship, whatever might come. Our good brig, however, went ahead, and was soon clear of rocks and reefs. On our going in through this narrow passage, the same kind Providence was over us; for in ten minutes after we had passed through the strait, the wind that had brought us in so propitiously, turned round; and, had we been then in the passage, nothing could have saved us from going ashore, amid rocks and surges, where the "John Wesley" would have been crushed like an egg-shell.

I feel very thankful to Almighty God that we are again in blue water, between Benga and Kandavu. Shortly we shall pass by the Pisgah of the last island we shall see, and all will be mountain-waves and open ocean. The many hair-breadth escapes which we have had during these very eventful voyages shake my nerves, but inspire gratitude and confidence in the Lord, who sent us forth, and has not left us to perish in the waters. Prayer and faith are of great value in such circumstances. Captain Buck thinks that a vertical sun is not favorable for seeing the sunken rocks and shoals: we shall, therefore, contrive to be here in future somewhat earlier in the season: about the time at which the "Triton" used to come is better; but the late arrival out from England of the "John Wesley" threw us back a little this year.

18*th.* We made the north cape of New-Zealand in seven days from Feejee, with an adverse wind all the way, and generally off our course. The American bark, "Auckland," is a fine, fast vessel; and it was thought a good run when she made Feejee from Auckland in seven days, with a strong fair wind all the way. The "John Wesley," however, has come up in a week, close hauled all the way, and without her proper amount of ballast. The "John Wesley" is a very fine vessel, easy, fast, and comfortable for passengers. The height of her 'tween-decks adds greatly to her otherwise excellent accommodations. She does great credit to all concerned in her building and outfit.

21*st.* We anchored at Auckland, after an absence of seven months, during which period we had made seven-and-forty voyages! Before the brig was at her station, we were boarded by my son and Mr. Buddle, with other friends, who in a few minutes opened up such a history of what had been passing in the world and in the church, as quite to bewilder my mind. It was the accumulation of seven months in one view! Here were ships-of-war, troops of soldiers, merchants' wares, crowds of natives, and all the usual scenes of an English sea-port in a distant colony. I was glad to get home; but at the same time almost sorry to be drawn out of the retirement and solitude of a sea-life, and to be plunged into an ocean of newspapers, letters, accounts, and matters of business, craving early attention.

Entering my cabin, I read from the Hymn-Book:—

"Thine arm has safely brought us
A way no more expected,
Than when thy sheep pass'd through the deep,
By crystal walls protected.
Thy glory was our rear-ward,
Thine hand our lives did cover;
And we, even we, have pass'd the sea,
And march'd triumphant over."

WALTER LAWRY.

AUCKLAND, NEW-ZEALAND,
December 21*st*, 1847.

NEW-ZEALAND CHILDREN.

TONGA AND FEEJEE.

SECOND MISSIONARY VISIT.

PREFACE.

THE narrative of the second voyage of Mr. Lawry exhibits the state of religion and civilization in the Friendly and Feejee Islands in 1850. The devout reader will observe with thankfulness and joy the marked progress which has been made, in both particulars, since Mr. Lawry's former visit in 1847. The work of God is deepened and established. The framework of society is improved and strengthened by the advance of education and the elevating principles of Christianity. The relative and social duties are understood and acknowledged. Just laws are enacted and administered. "Wisdom and knowledge are the stability of the times" of the Messiah, and are the foundation of the peace and comfort of these island communities. How vast the change which has been effected within thirty years! Great as have been the revolutions of Europe, and the advance of America within that period, in no part of the world has there been experienced so extraordinary a renovation as in the islands of the South Pacific. So greatly has God honored the prayers and labors of his faithful servants; and has borne testimony to his own truth, "The isles shall wait for his law;" and, "All the ends of the earth shall fear him."

One of the public prints, in giving some notice of the former Journal, suggests, that the valuable information it contains might have been given without being mixed up with quotations from Wesley's Hymns and the details of love-feasts. The writer should have known that it is the spirit breathed in the Scriptural hymns of the Rev. Charles

Wesley which has enkindled the missionary fire in the hearts of the Methodist societies; and that it is in those very details of love-feasts that we see exhibited the process by which the most barbarous and hateful of human beings have ceased to be savage and cannibal, and have been brought to their right mind, and are now sitting at the feet of Jesus. These islanders have not been first civilized, and then converted. They have been first converted; and their civilization is still in its infancy. The word of God has been preached to them, and they have felt its power. They have been convinced of their lost condition, and have sought and found mercy of God through Christ. Being new creatures in Christ Jesus, they are following after "whatsoever things are true, whatsoever things are honest, whatsoever things are just, whatsoever things are pure, whatsoever things are lovely, whatsoever things are of good report; if there be any virtue, and if there be any praise." The missionaries are aiding them in this pursuit; and it is hoped that the facts contained in the following pages will induce a continued and increased support to those funds by which the missionaries are enabled to follow up the work they have so happily commenced. If any independent confirmation of the statements contained in these volumes be considered desirable, the editor has great pleasure in referring to a beautiful volume recently published by a lady in America, relating her own observations and experience, and entitled, "Life in Feejee."

CONTENTS.

FRIENDLY ISLANDS.

CHAPTER I.

CHAPTER II.

CHAPTER III.

CHAPTER IV.

CHAPTER V.

FEEJEE ISLANDS.

CHAPTER VI.

CHAPTER VII.

CHAPTER VIII.

CHAPTER IX.

SECOND MISSIONARY VISIT.

FRIENDLY ISLANDS.

CHAPTER I.

APRIL 18*th*, 1850. We sailed from the waters of Auckland, and touched at the island of Kauau, thirty miles down the coast. Our little missionary meeting was attended chiefly by Cornish miners, who, in this distant land, not only dig copper from New-Zealand hills, but worship the God of their fathers, and, with enlarged means, contribute cheerfully towards the spread of the gospel. Their cordiality in this Christian work strongly reminded me of olden times in our fatherland.

20*th*. We sailed for the Bay of Islands, to obtain a suitable boat, and to land a member of Mr. Hobbs's family. In her former voyage the "John Wesley" had encountered an *afa*, or "hurricane," of the most fearful power and severity, during which she lost her jolly-boat from the quarter davits; and we called here, to replace it with a new one, which had been prepared to the order of Captain Buck.

The bay, when I visited it in 1822, was crowded with people. But, alas! what a change has come over this place! The Church mission was then strong at Paihia, at Rangihu, at Kirikiri, and several other places near at hand. But whalers touched at the bay; white men, escaping from a neighboring colony, came hither; settlers, who were in search of gain, left the sea, and located at the Bay of Islands. The natives, who, for the most part, had become only nominally Christian, learned the way of the foreigner. The instructions of the missionaries were enfeebled by a vitiating example from without. They found themselves *too soon* encircled by colonizing men, whose example caused a blight in the tender blade before it became mature. War followed in the rear, and both native and colonist were doomed to participate in its desolating effects. Out of four or five hundred white men, once resident here, not more than one hundred now remain, and these are in very humble circumstances; while the native population have almost disappeared, except Thomas Walker's people, a few of whom remain here, and occasionally a few others. The bulk of the white people have removed to the more suitable locality in and about the rising town of Auckland. It is much to be lamented that the excellent missionaries had not been left alone with the natives of New-Zealand other twenty years, when their Christian character would have been more established, and better fitted for the new order of things introduced by colonization.

22*d.* We launched forth upon the waves of the "great South Sea," and steered for the Friendly Islands. Mrs. Davis, who came up for the benefit of her health, and was much recovered, returned with us; and was the only person beside myself upon whom old fabled Neptune levied his heavy and long-continued exactions, while we did not dare to withhold our copious libations. These oft-repeated and comparatively little voyages make large demands upon me, especially when the wind and sea are rough and stormy. But as this sickness from the motion of the ship comes upon me in the way of duty, I may hope one day, if found faithful, to rest from this labor, and to receive my own reward, through the merit only of my great High-Priest:

> "No other right have I
> Than what the world may claim,"—

the right of access to the mercy-seat of Christ.

May 2d. We anchored at Tonga, after a run of ten days from New-Zealand, and were very affectionately received by the missionaries, Messrs. Webb and Amos, of Nukualofa, and by their intrepid wives. We were greatly delighted when we got ashore; not merely because we were, for the time, freed from the heavings of the ocean, but because of the manifest progress of the mission here, especially in its educational department. The mission houses and premises also looked so much altered and improved since I was last here, that the advance was marked and decidedly gratifying. At Mua the *lotu* has taken firm hold, while fair blossoms and much ripe fruit show themselves throughout the island of Tonga.

Education has received a most powerful impulse at the hands of Mr. Amos; and gracious dew descends upon the hills of our Zion, refreshing and cheering the minds of the ministers, and quickening the souls of thousands throughout this land. When King George heard at Haapai that Tungi and his people had embraced Christianity, he said, "This is the first canoe that has brought us any news of consequence for a long time: now the Lord makes Tonga live again."

The landing of stores used to be connected with great trouble and difficulty in these isles. The grief of the missionaries was great, and not without cause, aforetime. But now the scene is altered; the people are willing to work for the cause of Christ, and to assist their pastors. All is cheerfully and promptly done now, without fee or reward. Those heavy burdens are taken from the boat to the store by strong men, who bend under them, but do not complain. No doubt this change has proceeded from the Lord, and from the king. That which hindered formerly is removed out of the way. The change is truly wonderful, and shows the Christianity of the Friendly Islands to be that of the New Testament,—God's love producing ready and vigorous effort, and doing all without murmuring.

5th, Sunday. At day-break the prayer-meeting in the large chapel began. This fine temple has been erected since I was here last, the old one having been swept away by one of those devastating hurricanes, so frequent in the inter-tropical regions. At nine o'clock I preached to a crowded house on justification by faith, Mr. Webb interpreting. The serious devotional tone of this host of worshipers would bear a comparison with any congregation I ever saw in England; and their singing, though not quite equal perhaps to that at home, was greatly improved since I was here. The beautiful harmony with which they went through the responses in the morning service was very affecting, in tones like the sound of many waters! The females take their parts, and the males theirs, in this triumph of spiritual worship, where *deep feeling* is awed by *Christian principle.* Both the singing and praying were performed by the *entire congregation.* This, no doubt, is *pure Christianity;* and whensoever this cordial, loving unanimity shall be lost, then the glory is departed.

The Nukualofa chapel stands on a small mount, from which the eye takes in one of the most lovely views imaginable. The sea-shore is distant about two hundred yards; less than half a mile off the "John Wesley" rides at anchor in smooth water, within the reefs; the ocean is studded over with islands and islets of the most interesting appearance, covered with evergreen trees, some so distant that the tops only of the cocoa-nut trees rising above the horizon meet the eye; while the landing exhibits a forest of grandeur. To the trees which grow naturally here, such as the bread-fruit, cocoa-nut, banana, and twenty more, spreading out their luxuriant foliage, and laden with fruit, the missionaries have added the tamarind, orange, lime, and lemon trees. Coffee, cotton, and other shrubs, intermingled with thousands of pine-apples, adorn the enchanting scene which meets the beholder as he leaves the house of prayer.

The chapels are generally ornamented, and many of them very richly so, after the Tonga fashion; but there is not much progress made in the costume, or the dwelling-houses, since I first visited the Friendly Isles. The house of an ordinary person is a very poor affair, a mere roof standing on pillars in the midst of a grove; but many of the more advanced Christians have partitions in their houses, so that they can retire for secret prayer. Their clothes are the same as formerly—a piece of native cloth wrapped round their loins serves for all ordinary occasions; but our teachers wear shirts, and the females often have a calico dress from the neck to the waist; but, on high days, they ornament themselves in all the productions of their vine-groves, and that in a graceful manner. No doubt, they resemble the early inhabitants of our planet in this particular.

The great chiefs, many of whom are local preachers, appear in public with clean shirts on, which are carried under the arm during the long warm journey on a Sunday morning; and it has so happened that this appendage of the preacher has been omitted, through forgetfulness, to be put on before, and then it forms part of his first work after he has entered the pulpit, the whole congregation waiting! But such a thing would make little impression among these people, upon whom the extreme of civilization has not cast forth its magic shadows and sophistications; nor, on the other hand, has the refining and elevating power of the gospel yet had full effect upon these "little children," the lambs of Christ's flock.

6th. We attended the examination of Mr. Amos's Training School, which he conducted with skill and vigor, marching and counter-marching his pupils on the green, outside the school-room; and then taking them through the various branches which they have learned in the school.

The ground, about twenty acres, which has nearly sustained this institution during the past year, is laid out with good taste, and covered with yams and bananas; and the walks, which are at right angles, wide and clean, are adorned on each side with rows of delicious pine-apples. The ground is fenced, and the teachers' houses placed along in rows, straight, clean, and regular. The young men in the institution mostly live here: they are trumpeters preparing to sound,—twenty-six in number, with fourteen wives, and twenty children. In the school the number of persons under instruction is two hundred and ten; and the additional cost of all this to the mission fund, during the last year, has been under £30. But more will be required for the future, though nothing very serious.

These youths were examined in reading, writing, spelling, figures, and the catechism; in all which they quite astonished me. There is no lack of intellect, nor of application, in these persons, and their order would do credit to any school in any land; but when they repeated, by chanting, the multiplication-table and catechism, all at once, and keeping the most exact time, the same note was struck by two hundred tongues at the same instant, and the interest continued to rise, until the youths themselves became much excited; and, all present partaking of the enthusiasm, the interest flowed on till it reached its highest point, and swelled into a gust of rapture. The tears rolled freely down my face while I witnessed that most lovely scene, and I felt that such an exhibition would cast into the back-ground every lion in Europe.

Here is a fine garden for training our Tonga youth, and elevating them by education in secular, industrial, and religious knowledge. Most of the scholars are so poor that they attend school three days in a week, and the other three they work with vigor to procure food and clothing.

Those of them who possess a New Testament, show great satisfaction ; so much so, that when Jone Soaki, on Sunday last, was at public worship, and his house was burnt down in his absence, he came running to us, holding up his New Testament, and saying how thankful he was that the fire took place when the Book was out of the house. The house he could replace, he said, but not the Book. This was true enough; for, unto this day, a large portion of the population are without a copy of " the Book," arising partly from their want of education, and partly from the difficulty of getting books properly bound in the Friendly Isles. In future we shall meet this difficulty, by having them bound in New-Zealand.

I congratulate Mr. Amos on the state and prospects of the schools: and the co-operation of his brethren has greatly assisted him in this great work, so auspiciously begun.

The gospel has done its work in breaking down the pride of man, and leading him to the Saviour; and at this point the schools of instruction come in, and knowledge is made subservient to piety, and higher principles take hold of the youthful mind, aided by gospel truth, and growing up with the young people: a little leaven will leaven the whole lump.

Mr. Amos has succeeded beyond my expectations, and, by continuance in well-doing, will join with his brethren in giving Tonga a trained and greatly elevated population.

There are *infant* and *adult* schools in operation which I have not yet seen, but shall be sure to meet with in due time.

9th. Passing over from Nukualofa to Habai, we

anchored at Hafava, after a day of miserable sea-sickness and tossing. About two hundred praying people dwell on this small island, two of whom were married on board the "John Wesley" at dawn of day before we sailed.

10th. We passed over to Lifuka; but the wind was contrary, and "the sea wrought." The brethren going to the district-meeting were all sick. During the day we passed two small islands, which, at certain times, shake, tremble, and howl most awfully. They are within sight of Tufoa, the large volcanic island, and may have large caverns, which communicate with the sea; and the meeting of internal fire and external water may, perhaps, occasion the bellowing noise and tremulous motion, which frequently show the war of elements within. Both islands are of volcanic origin.

We came to Lifuka, and found the mission families well and glad to see us; Mrs. Miller was an exception, being ill of a fever. Poor Mr. Miller has had a year of affliction, both sickness and death having entered his family; but God has graciously sustained him. This day I called on King George and his queen, and I conveyed to him the message of Sir George Grey, the Governor-in-chief of New-Zealand, and viewed the new house which he has erected for his own use. The king then very modestly asked permission to go with us to Vavau in the "John Wesley," which, of course, was readily granted. He looks well, and is certainly doing a great work in these islands, acting like a Christian prince, and forwarding the great work of God now in progress through the length and breadth of the Friendly Islands. I was beyond measure surprised here at Habai, as well as at Tonga, to see the natives so readily taking the stores from the beach to the mission-premises, without being at all urged thereto by anyone. Aforetime they were sadly remiss in this matter, and most exorbitant in their demands for payment. All the information which I can obtain from the missionaries on this subject is, "We have treated them kindly, and showed them the reasonableness of doing what they are able to assist their teachers, who have brought them the word of life." The change is not only *marked*, but *delightful.*

This morning Buli·Uvea called upon me, and stated, that Booi and himself were the chiefs of Uvea; that his brother Booi had *lotued* with us, but he had received Popery; in which he had remained many days, until the falsehood and deception of the priests had opened his eyes, when he rejected them and their *lotu*, and fled to us; that multitudes of others were on the path which led to us in Uvea; that about fifteen hundred souls dwelt there, most of whom were ready to join our *lotu;* and he was come here to pray that a missionary might at once return with him, *that his land might be saved.* We tell him that it is very difficult for us to do as he wishes, now that Mr. Thomas and Mr. Rabone have gone, and left us feeble; but we will assist him, by sending with him a couple of native teachers, and, if they report favorably, it will be with our fathers at home to say whether a missionary can be sent to them when the "John Wesley" returns from her next voyage, which may possibly be to England. There is, I apprehend, no doubt whatever but the unequal conflict so long going on between the Popish and Protestant parties in Uvea is beginning very clearly to show that the Bible in the hands of our people there, who have as yet no pastor, is nearly a match for wily priestcraft. I pray that God may open our way, by an increase of funds, to send a missionary to Uvea, where they who worship with us have suffered so much, and so long continued firm. They are now about one hundred Church members, earnestly looking for a pastor. Uvea is known to navigators as Wallis Island.

Among the many novelties, which everywhere meet one in the new state of things in this semi-civilized society, one was told me to-day which may serve to illustrate manners here :—A shirt on the back of one of the local preachers being observed to be much shorter than usual, he was asked to account for this circumstance ; to which his reply was, " My wife, who is a leader, being destitute of a garment, I cut off the bottom of my shirt to make her a pinafore; hence you see my shirt is now rather short."

CHAPTER II.

MAY 11*th.* We sailed early to-day for Habai and Vavau, with the king on board, and many chiefs and teachers ; among whom was Joeli, who was one of my establishment at Tonga, eight-and-twenty years ago, and was then about eight years of age. He is now a local preacher, and governor of Habai ; a man of a fine spirit, and of an excellent character.

12*th,* the Sabbath. At Habai, at early dawn the

prayer-meeting began, and at nine o'clock the public service in our very large chapel there; the place was full from end to end, and their attention to Mr. Webb's sermon was admirable. I addressed them afterwards, and they heard most devoutly, and as men of thought and piety.

14*th.* We came to anchor at Vavau in thirty-five fathoms of water. This is too deep to be safe, beside the labor of getting up the anchor again.

15*th.* We landed early, and found all the families pretty well, except Mrs. Turner, who, I was happy to find, was not worse; at least she did not appear to be so.

Vavau looks very lovely after the late rains; and Messrs. Turner, Adams, and Davis gave us a most cordial welcome to the scene of their labors.

The luxuriant foliage and imposing landscapes of this group can hardly be surpassed outside of the Garden of Eden; but the heat is too great for me, and the musquitoes have no mercy on the newly-arrived.

I miss the schools which everywhere cheered one three years ago; their singing and rehearsals, which used to enliven every place, have been allowed to die away!

It is a great mistake into which those fall who, not being able to approve of everything which they see in the nurseries of education, are paralyzed in their efforts, and give up education altogether. These people have been preached to, and are craned up to the full extent of their present circumstances: the next thing is to enlarge their platform, by educating the rising generation, that wisdom and knowledge may be the stability of our times. The chairman of this district is much discouraged at what he finds here, as compared with what he left in Vavau three years ago. But while he cherishes his clear and proper views on educational operations, I shall hope well for Vavau under his pastoral supervision, and trust that, in future, no one will pull down what he builds up.

16*th*. We began our annual district-meeting at Vavau, with cheerfulness and solemnity. The state of the churches passed under review, as well as the state of the brethren.

21*st*. We completed our business, and have no opposing mind to contend with: all the affairs of the district, including those of translations and education, were harmoniously settled, and without any delay. Every missionary has his portion of the Old Testament for translation allotted to him; and the New Testament is to be revised and sent on to Feejee, that it may be in time to go home by the "John Wesley," with a view to an edition of twenty thousand copies being printed as early as possible by the British and Foreign Bible Society, provided that noble society concur in this measure. Mr. Kevern is requested to correct the press.

On the subject of education, there was but one opinion in the meeting,—that it had been too long neglected, and that now we must set about it with all our energy in every place.

The school at Tonga, under the direction of Mr. Amos, is doing so well, that we have presumed to request the committee to send out two additional trained masters, one for Habai and one for Vavau. May the state of the mission-fund be such as to allow of this very important addition to our laborers in this district! We must have schools in every place: we need one hundred trained native schoolmasters selected from among the local preachers, who should be at the head of our schools throughout this district, thus elevating the rising race, with the Bible in their hands, far above the darkness and baseness of heathenism, and the wicked intrigues of Popery. With a good supply of the Holy Scriptures, and the religious education of the youth of these islands, we have little to fear from the grand adversary of the truth, whether in the form of paganism direct, or of "the man of sin," with his lying wonders, under the Christian name, but with a mouth speaking blasphemies, and trying to reconcile sin with safety. Surely this great work, now in such hopeful progress in the Friendly Islands, where full *one-third* of the entire population are registered as members of our Church, and where all the rest who have *lotued* attend public worship and have family prayer, will fully justify the call of my excellent brethren for schoolmasters and Bibles! Nor will the societies to whom the call is made, fail to respond with promptitude, unless the springs of charity shall have been dried up in the Christian Church, by the clamorous voice of agitating men of malevolent spirits, who, having gone astray themselves, desire to lead others astray. How truly Satanic is this work of darkness! But it cannot stand! It must fall before the glowing love of Jesus Christ, who was lifted up, and will draw all men unto him.

I could not but notice the full tide of harmony which manifested itself in our district-meeting. There not only was no *distrust*, but there was a complete *confidence*, a brotherhood in the meeting, which, if I am not greatly mistaken, is full of hopeful promise as to future success. Thank God, our brethren are now eminently of one judgment and of one aim.

22*d*. I went to the top of Talau, from which nearly the whole group of Vavau was to be seen. The views were all exquisite in the extreme. The many islands, distant and near; the beautiful undulatory landscape on the island on which we stood; the hills intersected by bays and creeks, long and short; the rich and varied foliage in all directions; the distant ocean, with its rolling billows on the coral reefs; and the dotting villages, here and there throughout the land, with "the house of prayer," and the total population bending beneath the shade of Jehovah's protecting care:—these formed an accumulation of loveliness and grandeur, which I do not hope to see repeated until, by God's mercy, I enter into paradise.

23*d*. We put to sea with a head-wind for Habai, with the king on board, the teachers for the out-islands, the institution youths, and all the brethren from the meeting, where the king had met them, and fully conversed with us on the new laws which he intends to introduce into his dominions. They seemed to us well adapted to the circumstances of his people. As the day declined, the sea tossed about our gallant barque, and nearly all were sick.

The more I see of King George, the more I am convinced that his high reputation for wisdom, piety, and integrity has been well earned; and that, while he stands *first* in all these qualities, he is doing a great work in concert with the missionaries, in spreading the truth, and elevating the people under his dominion. He is a fine person, about six feet four inches high, and well-proportioned, with a fine glow of comeliness, intelligence, and Christian benevolence; he is of few words, and prompt in all his actions.

29*th*. We came to anchor in safety at Nukualofa, having had a rough and disagreeable voyage; every one of us was sea-sick. These *little* voyages, which occur so often among the islands, impose the heavy tax and sharp conflict of prostrated strength, agony of urging, and distressing head-ache. In my own case, the whirl and tossing motion of the vessel affects not only the stomach, but the brain. No wonder that few landsmen like repeated voyaging. To me it is a duty which I would gladly avoid, but cannot. The prospect of what is now before me, hangs upon my spirits like a night-mare. But, alas! what are *my little sufferings*, compared with those of the Redeemer, or with the glory which shall follow the good and faithful servant?

Many natives who sailed with us, and are never sick in their own canoes passing over the same ground, were prostrated on board the "John Wesley."

Our missionary meetings at Vavau and Habai were excellent; about ten persons addressing each meeting, the one half missionaries, and the other half natives. The king took the chair in each case, and the large chapels were crowded inside and out.

The following are extracts from the speeches of several of our native teachers at our missionary meetings held at Vavau, Haapai, and Tonga:—

JOELI MAFILEO spoke as follows:—"I am very, very

glad, my friends, to meet you in such an assembly as this. This is not a worldly or heathen assembly, such as we had in former times. We have met for God's work, and therefore my heart is dancing within me. My mind greatly rejoices in hearing of the good and great work which the churches in Britannia, and more especially our own, are carrying on throughout the world; and I hope, my friends, you are ready to help on the good cause this day to the utmost of your ability. I am very pained in my mind, at not knowing before I left Haapai that you were to have a missionary meeting here; because I cannot give a contribution, as I should have done had I known. I have not much wealth as to this world, but I am willing to give myself to God and to his Church. Here am I. I am willing to work for God's cause. I do not know why the missionaries hinder me. I am ready and willing to go anywhere to live and die in the work of God. And is it not right for us so to do? Let us love our missionaries, and do all we can to help and save our friends, who are still 'sitting in darkness and in the shadow of death.' Bring all the things you can as gifts to help the good work of missions. Do not keep the best things in your houses to sell some other day to a ship-of-war, but bring them here to-day. Bring them here,—your best mats and shells and dresses. Divide a portion of your worldly goods for the missions, and bring all with a willing mind. Think of the good you have received from the missionaries and from God's word, and think of your friends still in darkness and sin. *Oua naa tau kai vale be kai bo,* (a proverbial expression, meaning, 'Do not let us eat our good things foolishly or by stealth.')

Let us share our bounties with those who have them not, and God will bless and prosper us. And this is the end of my words to you this day."

JONE LATU, who is now recommended to be received as an assistant missionary, spoke as follows:—"My friends, it is very right for us to thank God for all the good we enjoy. We have heard, from the paper read by Mr. Turner, of the great mission-work going on in the different parts of the world. But whilst we are thankful for this, we ought also to remember that there are many heathens in our own land and in various parts of the world,—many, very many, who have never yet heard the sound of the gospel, nor seen its light. And why should we not love them? Is it not right? In former times we also were dark, like them. Great was the evil among us. Great was our ignorance and sin. But light has sprung up to us here in this land. God has sent us his missionaries and his word. But, O! how many souls are yet in the midnight of sin, and in the thickness of its darkness! And is it not right for us to try and help them out of the pit into which they have fallen, then lead them to Christ, and tell them the way to heaven? Have not the elders in England given of their money and their wealth, beside all their children, to bring us the gospel, and to carry it to the ends of the earth? and shall we sit still and do nothing? Let us this day do what we can. We are a poor people, but we can do a little. Let us not bring our offerings as a tax, or with a grudging mind; but willingly and freely, and then God will receive and bless them. Above all, we can pray. Never let us forget to remember the dark places of the earth when we pray to Jehovah;

and then he will bless us, and the year of jubilee will soon dawn upon the ends of the earth."

Each meeting was held from nine in the morning till mid-day, when all retired to refresh. At two the bell was rung for the *katuanga*, or "offering of love," to the society. One island sent forth its people in procession, all in full dress, singing a hymn, and bearing a gift: some a dollar, some a mat, or a few shells, clubs, spears, cocks and hens, yams, oil, wooden pillows, and native cloth. Of this kind of offering we packed up and sent on board the brig eleven packages from Vavau, and thirteen from Haapai; the chief part of which consisted of various shells, some large and handsome, others small and curious, but all less or more valuable.

The natives like this kind of thing, and no one is impoverished by what he gives. It comes easily and is given cheerfully. *All* give: no one is exempted, from the king to the poorest man, and from the oldest person to the youngest child who is able to walk. The pomp with which they advanced along the grassy lawn, surrounded by the beautiful evergreen tropical shrubs, and lofty wide-spreading trees, all adorned with new robes, and replete with cocoa-nut oil, headed by their chiefs, and accompanied by their native teachers with white shirts and a book exhibited, with the gift,—is one of those imposing sights which cannot be viewed without emotion, and no words are strong enough to paint the lovely scene.

The multitudes who have laid down their *mea ofa* (or "thank-offering") on the sward in front of the house of prayer, retire a little, and take their seats in the greatest order and silence; where they sit, beholding troop after troop advance, until all have come forth, and each individual, man, woman, and child, has deliberately and in public, under the full gaze of pastor and people, offered his gift. Nor is the eye of the Master closed to such a scene as this: for "he loveth the cheerful giver."

"They that dwell in the wilderness shall bow before Him; and his enemies shall lick the dust. The kings of Tarshish and of the isles shall bring presents: the kings of Sheba and Seba shall offer gifts. Yea, all kings shall fall down before him." "Blessed be the Lord God, the God of Israel, who only doeth wondrous things."

One small and dark spot in the distance had the effect of a shaded back-ground to this picture: three Englishmen, or Americans, stood outside,—men of the baser sort, who estimate the missionary as one who stands in their way. Men without character, living in society leavened with Christian morals, are happily doomed to be men without influence or consideration of any kind. But still their day is coming; and what will they say, when, side by side with these believing Gentiles, they shall stand before the judgment-seat of Christ and hear him say—"Behold, ye despisers, and wonder, and perish: for I work a work in your day, which ye shall in no wise believe, though a man declare it unto you?"

NUKUALOFA.—As Mr. Amos and I were walking by the sea-side early this morning, one of these men came up to us and desired to be married forthwith to a native woman, with whom, it appeared, he had been living for some years, and had several children. Upon inquiry, we found that he had been residing at the

Bea, a *colo* partly Popish and partly heathen,—if there be any difference between the two things. *There* men live as they list, and no one interferes: but now this man has come to Maofanga to live, which is a Christian *colo*, and not far from Nukualofa. One of the laws over all King George's sovereignty is, that persons are not allowed to live together in a state of adultery: hence this white heathen has complied with Christ's law, because the magistrates *require* him to do so. What reason can be given why every land claiming the name of *Christian* should not do the same?

I am urged to allow one or more of these islanders to proceed to England in our vessel; but I am afraid and ashamed to let them see the land dignified with the *Christian* name. We have a national Church, and churches many; but where are our national morals and piety? Alas! alas! Here we have a king who rules in love, and makes laws against overt sin; "in whose presence a vile person is contemned." What God has declared to be wrong, he causes to be refrained from, or punished when done; but *religion*, in all its operations, he leaves, where his God leaves it, between God and the conscience; but as the wicked shall do wickedly, so the magistrate is a terror to evil-doers. Is not any other establishment of religion both unnecessary and unscriptural? God has dominion over the conscience: the magistrate rules over men's conduct. For the sin of adultery God will judge the sinner hereafter, if he repent not; but, for the immoral example which adultery furnishes, the Christian magistrate will punish the adulterer in the present life, and thus drive evil away.

The French priests who are here have allowed the Tui Tonga all his wives, and other heathen practices; and yet have offered to baptize him and many others, and, by so doing, make them, as they say, real Christians, and not mere heretics, as our people are. When any contention takes place between the Papists and others, they threaten a French man-of-war, which shall compel submission to their will. This course has had its effect in some cases, but, generally, it tells against Popery; for the natives see clearly, that there is really no difference between such a religion and their old heathenism. As a system of fraud and falsehood, it gains a little at first; but when its real character is evolved, it shrinks back from the keen rebukes of a Bible-reading people. Popery in these islands has come too late: the *truth* was here before it; and now it merely exists, but does not thrive and grow. The missionaries at Tahiti say, that Popery there has its first convert yet to make from among the members of their churches. May we not gather strength from hence, and hope that the circulation of the sacred volume, now so earnestly in progress by means of the British and Foreign Bible Society, and other societies, will ultimately dry up the resources of the "man of sin," and be at the same time a wall of defense around the people of God?

These people say, almost with one voice, that our missionaries come with a Book in their hand, saying, "Here is our religion; all we believe and teach is here." "We read and see for ourselves, and know that this is true; but the pope's men come and dole out one thing now, and another then, and so they go on, telling us, all the time, 'This is *all*, we have nothing more to add;' and yet they add *confession*, and we know not what; it is lies, and we believe them not." When our missionaries come and go away, and another comes, it makes no difference; they all speak the same thing, the very same as the Book contains. How can the "cunningly devised fables," the mess of priestcraft, served up by the deluded and deluding emissaries of Rome, stand before the mighty force of facts like these, which every day, and everywhere, pass under the unsophisticated observation of the native mind?

30*th*. In conversation to-day with several persons, I was surprised to find how quickly they spring up and pass away. Several of those whom I knew by name twenty-eight years ago, when they were mere children, now rank among the *madua*, or "old people," yet cannot be more than thirty-seven or thirty-eight years old. We can clearly ascertain that the females are women at about thirteen, and grow old women before thirty. Their food is very simple, and mostly vegetable; but in size they far outstrip Europeans, so also, as they think, in personal attractions and beauty. But, alas! they quickly pass away and are gone. Diseases are very common among them, especially cutaneous complaints. War has ceased, for the present; but I do not learn that, so far, the population has much increased, although food for ten times their present number might easily be raised by a small amount of industry. The Tongans are, however, to some extent, an idle people; and how should it be otherwise? No man will labor hard, in a hot climate, without a motive. They get their few and simple wants supplied with little effort, and then lay themselves down on their mats. Two new wants are now creeping in among them, namely, books and clothes; to obtain these, they will have to put forth their energies and make cocoa-nut oil, which they can, if they please, produce to a very large amount. This they will do at no distant period; and then new wants will spring up, and with them new enterprise, until the idle, basking children of wild nature shall take their place beside the civilized nations of the earth. Their *morals* are already elevated by Christianity, and their habits and manners will as certainly rise; but these are of slow growth among an isolated people of barbarous origin.

June 1*st*, Saturday evening. We walked through this *colo*, but found very few persons, old or young. They had gone to their plantations for food, leaving only a few at home to sweep the premises. This is truly a preparation-day, and things show that the Sabbath is at hand. Everyone who is *lotu* seems to reverence the Lord's-day; and, less or more, the day is kept holy by the whole *lotu* people. Now, why should not this be the case in old England, by high and low, great and small, throughout the land? And so it will be, when the same gospel is as generally received there as here, and in the same spirit of love and obedience. While I am writing these lines I hear many families about me engaged in worship,—singing a hymn, reading, and prayer. There is not a family in this land, (save a very few Papists and heathens,) in which family prayer is not uniformly observed morning and evening, as it is now being performed in my hearing.

2*d*, the Sabbath. At day-break the bell rang, and,

family-worship having been concluded, the public prayer-meeting commenced. The hosts of the Lord were there, and not merely a *few* scattered over a large house, but the large chapel was nearly filled with worshipers, who evidently entered into the spirit of divine worship. Many prayed earnestly; and the singing was really good and devotional. At eight o'clock the Sunday school began in the large chapel; the attendance of teachers and young folks was pretty fair, but not up to my expectations. After a short hymn, the Lord's prayer was chanted, the teacher repeating sentence by sentence, and then the same was chanted by all present. This ended, the school was divided up into classes, without any noise or delay; the books were given out by the respective teachers, and all were fully engaged in their learning. When this was finished, the whole school was drawn up in order before the pulpit; and the head teacher, the son of a king, catechised the whole of those who were present, both teachers and children, out of the fourth section of the Second Catechism, they repeating the answers in a chant, with an accuracy and regularity which can never be surpassed.

At nine o'clock the chapel was full, and Mr. Amos preached, and then baptized five children. The whole of these services were conducted with order and regularity, and, I may add, with an intelligent piety which would delight our friends at home, and do no discredit to any Christian church in Great Britain.

In looking over the congregation this morning, I was pressed with the question which often occurs, namely, "Where did this people spring from?" The general expression of their countenance and their dress are Asiatic; so is their language, most unequivocally. Some of their customs seem to be Jewish, such as circumcision, the feast of first-fruits, and cities of refuge; which show, that, from whatever part of the eastern family they spring, Jewish rites are strongly impressed upon their national character. There are in some places curly-haired and Negro-featured natives in these seas; but they are not the most numerous race, though their number is by no means inconsiderable.

If one might indulge in conjecture, and add to the many which have been hazarded before, might it not be possible that the Ten Tribes, who broke off in the days of Rehoboam, and went towards the East, carrying with them some of their neighbors, the sons of Ham, from Africa, and proceeding *via* Hindostan, might reach the Malayan Sea, and thus people the Pacific Ocean? The Malay language and the language of these seas have a relation to each other, which this conjecture will perfectly reconcile, as it will also account for the Negro of these isles. These people are Oriental, as most men think, but they seem to have descended from different branches of Noah's family; and the difficulty of accounting for the Negro race mixed up with the Asiatic, and Jewish rites with pagan customs, has been the puzzle in this inquiry. All are here reconciled. Of course, the history of the islands and of their inhabitants is lost in a remote antiquity; but, so far as facts and circumstances throw their light upon this matter, it appears to me almost necessary to *suppose* something like the theory I have ventured to propound, in order to meet all the facts of the case, none of which shall be improbable, much less self-contradictory.

Here the people are, however; and here the devil reigned till the gospel came, and another kingdom was set up; and of this "kingdom there shall be no end; for He shall reign forever and ever."

CHAPTER III.

June 3d. I went up in a boat from Nukualofa to Mua, the place where I lived twenty-eight years ago, when we were acting as pioneers, and attempting to gain a footing among these warlike savages. Tungi, who was a child of about two years old at that time, is now the chief of this neighborhood, and has just yielded to the power of the gospel, after a life of more than ordinary sinfulness. With him God has been long-suffering indeed, and has visited him clearly, repeatedly, and powerfully, by dreams and by visions of the night, until at last he has cast away his sins and his idols together, (I bear his idols away with me to another land,) and now he is zealous for the Lord Jesus Christ. With him there have *lotued* about one hundred and sixty of his people; and others are daily coming from all parts of Ahagi. On the day of this *lotu* there was a solemn assembly of missionaries and praying people from all parts of Tonga; and public worship was held in the morning and other parts of the day. The place was crowded; and when Tungi entered the chapel, and fell on his knees with his people, the sobs and cries of the congregation were irrepressible. Some were called upon to pray; but no one could speak for some time, till the gust of overflowing feeling had subsided; and *then* they broke out as the sun when he ariseth. Papists and heathen were there; but they were overawed by the majesty of the Divine presence, and "compelled to acknowledge that God was in them of a truth."

4*th.* We spent six hours to-day in hearing the rehearsal of fourteen schools, already acquainted with portions of Scripture and our catechism, which they repeated with surprising accuracy and at great length. They advanced towards the chapel, (which stands on the very site where I lived at first,) and retired from it, in procession, singing a hymn, all in full dress, and well oiled. The surrounding foliage, and the smell of their flowers with which they were ornamented, added grandeur and fragrance to the deeply interesting scene. Messrs. West and Amos had come with me; and greatly were our spirits refreshed to witness the progress of the gospel at Mua, under the vigilant pastoral care of Mr. Daniel, whose wife is as fully employed in carrying on the work as himself. The day closed with devotional exercises, in which we all took part; a *mea ofa* (or "thank-offering") of shells, clubs, gods, &c., was laid at our feet by both old and young. In looking over the assembled multitude, it was affecting to observe the scars in their flesh with burnings, and many a stump instead of a finger, which had been cut off and offered to Satan in the days of his dominion over them. The night was spent in singing joyfully by these new converts, with the sound of the *lali*, or native "drum." Mua is now chiefly *lotu;* and all Ahagi is on the move towards the light of the glorious gospel, and the worship of the Lamb of God, the Redeemer of the world. "Behold, the former things are come to pass, and new things do I declare: before they spring forth I tell you of them. Sing unto the Lord a new song, and his praise from the end of the earth, ye that go down to the sea, and all that is therein; the isles, and the inhabitants thereof. Let the wilderness and the cities thereof lift up their voice, the villages that Kedar doth inhabit: let the inhabitants of the rock sing, let them shout from the top of the mountains. Let them give glory unto the Lord, and declare his praise in the islands." Isaiah xlii, 9–12.

5th. In my walks about Mua to-day, viewing the old scenes, the trees, and *abe,* I here and there fell in with a face which I had seen before, but greatly marked with age. One was Malabo, the *matabuli* of Fatu. I asked him if he was *lotu.* He answered, "My prayers are offered up to the Son of God." I met with Afa, an old *towlaegi,* or "priest," whom I formerly knew, who told me that his light was come, that his system of lies had been abandoned at the time when Tungi *lotued,* and his mind was now going after Christ his Lord. One old chief had not prayed yet, because he did not like to part with so many wives. Another was a thief, and got much in that line, which it was hard to give up. A third was still a sinner of the Gentiles; but he made a great merit of having given up to Jesus all his sons and all his daughters, who were *lotu,* and *would not* be heathens any longer.

There is a difference between the older Christian *colo,* and this which has recently turned to God. The town of Nukualofa is much more clean than this; but, in other respects, the houses, the fences, the plantations, the implements, the furniture, and the clothing are pretty much the same, and will, doubtless, so remain until an educated generation shall arise, who shall renew the face of these isles.

Among the articles given to help our missions were several *gods*, which have not been viewed by any mortal eye for several generations. Most of them were whales' teeth, or parts thereof. One of them has hung up for ages in their god-house, to allow a place for the spirit to perch upon when he happens to visit it. Another was an ivory necklace, wrapped up in native cloth, stuck full of small red feathers. But all were filthy and vile, senseless and useless. Some of the heathen came to see me, who once ranked, they said, among the gods; and they wished to see this extraordinary being. I went to my god-basket, and, taking up some of their idols, said, "These are the things you *worshiped;* but me your fathers threatened to kill. Our God has at last triumphed over your ignorance and superstition, and here are your gods in my basket. Would you like to see them?" said I, advancing quickly towards them: but they fled with precipitancy, and then looked back, confounded and ashamed. Almost every one of those who has not yet bowed the knee to Jesus is free to acknowledge that his gods are lying vanities, and that with us is the true religion; but *then* there is this parting with "the sin which so easily besets them!" This may be called their transition state, which would not be of long duration had not Popery stepped in; and, even now, the masses of the people are most cordially with us, even where the dregs of heathenism and Popery linger out their doomed existence.

This is the last struggle with the powers of darkness; and so rapid are the strides of the gospel, that the issue can be neither distant nor doubtful. O happy Tonga! thy God reigneth! "O Zion, that bringest good tidings, get thee up into the high mountain; O Jerusalem, that bringest good tidings, lift up thy voice with strength; lift it up, be not afraid; say unto the cities of Judah, Behold your God."

It is not unworthy of notice that, on the day that Tungi *lotued,* all the gods that could be found were secured, and are now placed in a Tonga basket, and handed over to me. Of these gods the first in rank and power is Feaki, the fountain-head of all the minor gods. This is a large *whale's tooth,* which has not fallen under the gaze of mortal men from time immemorial. To this idol, or medium of worship, the *inachee* ("the offering of their first-fruits") was presented: and to Feaki was offered, thirteen years ago, the *last child* that was sacrificed in Tonga, at the death of Fatu, Tongi's father. Another sacrifice is now declared; and they who were "far off are made nigh *by the blood of Christ.*" Fatu's people were trying their old method; but he was praying to Jehovah, and in his death there was hope.

The next god in order is Finau-tau-iku, the god who looks after the chiefs, and is their shade at their right hand. To this piece of cloth, interwoven with small red feathers, were also offered human sacrifices. He was an incarnation of the daughter of Tuihatakalaua, and a city of refuge from the power of Tuikanokubolu. Exceedingly much blood has flowed to this shrine; and the blood was the blood of men offered in sacrifice. His priests were men who said they were inspired, and before whom the deluded people bowed with awe and trembling; for their life was in his hands. If he said his anger was kindled against a man, or a family, or a city, the club was his instant avenger, and death devoured whom he denounced. So has it been from ancient times in these "dark places of the earth, full of the habitations of cruelty." But God has prepared his way in the Islands, as King George said to me and to my brethren not long since, when we were conversing on this subject. The late wars were seasonable; for the chiefs and people were bent upon mischief; and, had the gospel come before these wars, in which so many strong men fell, would one missionary only have sufficed as a victim to their love of blood? Surely many must have fallen. In these wars George was the GOLIATH in point of stature and strength, and the DAVID of his people in point of courage and prudence. He was, indeed, a man of war from his youth; and he shed very much blood.

The next idol in my basket is called Fakatoumafi. This, also, is an incarnation of the mighty chief, Halaigaluafi, daughter of Tuihatakalaua. This idol is in the form of a large necklace made of whales' teeth. About the same powers and propensities are claimed for him as for the others. His love of the blood of men shows his connection with the old murderer.

There are several others of these *fahe gehe*, "gods," (or "devils," as they now call them,) in my possession; but a minute description of them would be tedious, and without any material difference from those already portrayed.

Tangaloa and Maui are never represented or approached by a shrine or idol of any kind, so far as I am able to ascertain. The Supreme Being is not altogether a " lost idea " among these people; but the *way* to him they knew not, till Christ, " the way, the truth, and the life," was made known to them by their missionaries, who now see the fruit of their labor, and the fall of the gods of the heathen.

Well might the apostle say that " an idol is nothing in the world." But, vanity and lies as they are known to be by those who have the Bible, and obey its holy precepts; yet the soul of man, without a better hope to cling to, hangs by these idols with the tenacity of an immortal spirit hanging over an abyss unknown, flushed with alternate hope and fear, and in terror of the wrath to come, which is felt to be the reward of conscious guilt. To such a person, leaping in the dark, an idol is a *straw*, laid hold upon by a sinking man. But the infinite mercy of God prepares the vilest of men, by his judgments or his grace, for the light of the gospel and the day of salvation. "For by fire and by sword will the Lord plead with all flesh, and the slain of the Lord shall be many. And I will set a *sign* among them, and I will send those that escape of them unto the nations, to Tarshish, Pul, and Lud, that draw the bow, to Tubal and Javan, to the isles afar off, that have not heard my fame, neither have seen my glory; and they shall declare my glory among the Gentiles."

There is also in my possession, among the heathen relics from Mua, a club belonging to a long line of priests; and its name is *hallah*, or "path." When the chiefs came to inquire of the priest, this sacred club was taken down; the priest was inspired, and delivered his message, which might be in anger, or otherwise, as the case might be; then the club smote the beam, and away went the *fahe gehe*, mounting aloft, or plunging into the deep, as they saw fit. This club, then, is a sacred *fàhe gehe*, or "god," of Tonga. Several others are safely lodged with me, which need no description; for all their qualities are the same as those already mentioned, with mere circumstantial variations. "And the Lord alone shall be exalted in that day. And the idols he shall utterly abolish. And in that day there shall be a Root of Jesse, which shall stand for an Ensign of the people; to it shall the Gentiles seek; and his rest shall be glorious. And it shall come to pass in that day, that the Lord shall set his hand again the second time to recover the remnant of his people, which shall be left, from Assyria, and from Egypt, and from Pathros, and from Cush, and from Elam, and from Shinar, and from Hamath, and from the islands of the sea." "And the loftiness of man shall be bowed down, and the haughtiness of men shall be made low; and the Lord alone shall be exalted in that day."

All the Friendly Islands are now Christian and in communion with us, except a few heathens mixed with a few Papists at Mua and Bea. Homa, also, is for the most part heathen still, and a few neighboring places; but their strength is departed from them—they are not at all respected, and neither loved nor feared by any. Popery is so much like heathenism, in this place, that it is not necessary to distinguish the one

A MISSIONARY SHIP VISITING THE ISLAND OF NIUA FOOU.

from the other. I am told that the Tui Tonga and the priests stipulated that, in adopting the *lotu*, he was to retain his women, dances, fishing on the Sabbath, and such-like things, which are accordingly practiced by the Tui Tonga to this hour. This weak-minded chief and some others *lotu* in the Popish faith rather on political grounds than from any love they have to Popery. They dislike the present sovereign of the land, and show that Popery and sedition are the same.

7th. NUKUALOFA.—I met with Stephen Jiale, one of our local preachers, who was formerly our teacher at Niua-foou; and, while there, was conducting the watch-night service on New-Year's eve. When the midnight hour had arrived and long passed away, according to the position of the moon and stars, Stephen looked at his watch, no doubt with an air of satisfaction, and said that the hand did not yet point to twelve: but the people were sure it was past midnight, and got round Stephen to see this lying watch. Upon inspection, an altercation took place between Stephen and them; they declared that the watch was *dead*, while he maintained that it was *alive*, that is, still going. At last it was agreed to carry on a little longer, when the opening day decided that it was past midnight.

Poor Stephen was one day conducting service at Niua-foou, when a few Americans, from a whaler, were present. Having finished his address to the natives, he said, "Shall we not break a little food among these strangers?" and then proceeded to address them in *English!* On he went, gabbling, "*Sabarasa, sabarasee.*" The natives, perceiving the trick, know him and his family by the name of *Saba-rasa* to this hour: nor is there a person, old or young, in the Friendly Isles, but is quite familiar with *Saba-rasa.* The recoil of this attempt to *show off* will effectually check all future adventures of this kind.

9th, Sunday. A whole day of set rain, with high, cold wind. Nevertheless our congregations were good. The large chapel was nearly full, while I preached to them on "the great white throne," &c. The people listened with solemn reverence, and devout feeling. I was surprised to find that a day so cold and wet did not more seriously diminish the assemblies, especially as cold days are severely felt by the natives, and a little wet spoils their dresses. But a little loss and inconvenience are not sufficient to keep earnest people away from God's house on the Lord's day. Alas! when will this be the case in England, and in the Colonies? What a fine example of punctuality and perseverance in religious worship are these simple South-Sea Islanders, to professors in other lands, who are so much more elevated in the scale of civilization! Is there then an extreme point in civilization, which is unfriendly to vital godliness? Is France godless because it is polite, and thoughtless because it is gay? Does the house for plays disqualify for serious attendance at the house of prayer? Alas! who does not know, that to be *happy* a man must be *solemn;* and that the difference is small between mirth and madness? "I said of laughter, It is mad; and of mirth, What doeth it?" These people are sprightly, but, at the same time, they are religious; not merely in word, but in heart and life. And one part of their cheerful conduct does not contradict and refute another. They constitute one uniform, consistent character; happy, cheerful, and religious men.

10*th.* HIHIFO.—In our passage down this morning, Mr. Daniel and myself passed over several miles of coral beds. Some were two feet under water, others more, and many places quite dry. The coral was of almost all colors and forms: some purple, green, ash-color; some white, red, and blue: some large pieces in the form of a forest-oak, others in the form of a creeping shrub. There was also the brain and the boat coral. Mr. Williams was of opinion, that coral was not wholly the work of an insect; but his views are not, as yet, fully confirmed by observation or experiment. There are, doubtless, around these islands many thousands of acres of coral, of almost every kind and quality: but, excepting its appropriation to purposes of mere fancy ornament, little use has hitherto been made of this beautiful production of the All-wise Creator. When Mr. and Mrs. West, with myself, and some natives, were selecting such portions from the *Ligu* here as we might deem most inviting, the brown children of the isle laughed heartily at our picking up *stones*, as they said, and bearing them away. Indeed one of Mrs. West's domestic girls, Maria, measuring five feet eleven inches high, who was sent out into deep water to make her selection there, after a fit of laughter at our expense, stretched out her arms and swam off into the deep, basking in the very ocean, in which the large porpoises were at the same moment performing their gambols. At her leisure she swam back to the shore unencumbered with coral. It may serve to show the *grade* which these people hold among Adam's children, to observe that, with very few and rare exceptions, they seem not to have the least idea of the loveliness of their trees, shrubs, and flowers. Entomology and geology have no charms for them. Admiration, in their case, has nothing in nature on which to fix its beaming eye. But the grace of God in Christ Jesus will, we may be assured, lay a broad platform of pleasures; and even these basking, bounding sons of nature will open their eyes and see that the God of grace is the God of nature also, and that "his hand hath made all these things," and that "he hath so done his marvelous works that they ought to be had in remembrance of all them that fear him. For the works of God are great, sought out by all them that have pleasure therein."

11*th*. The schools were mustered at Hihifo, after our morning missionary meeting, when our chapel was crowded inside, and the green outside covered with listening people. The majestic trees of banian grandeur that cover the *malai*, and shaded the schools, as they advanced with a song and took their seats, gave an air of dignity and solemnity to the scene, where thousands were assembled to exhibit what they had learned of numerals and of Scripture truth. Things so varied in interest, and imposing in their effect, may well set at naught the powers of description, and leave the mind under the storm of feeling which it is impossible to repress. There was not time to hear their rehearsal of the catechism; but all were pleased, and even delighted. Tungi was there from Mua: there was Tuivakano from Nugunugu, and Jephthah Ata, the chief of this place, with most of the chiefs, and young and old people, from all parts of the western end of the island. I saw nothing to find fault with, but much to admire and be grateful for, in these regions. Mr. West has a field here for all his energies, and his prospect is full of rich promise.

In the evening they contributed their thank-offering to the Missionary Society: shells, corals, clubs, cloth, and mats; worth perhaps, when sold in London, about thirty pounds.

13th. I sent for Tata, at Homa, nine miles off, who was sent with Futukava, as hostage for my safety when I came first to Tonga. Tata was then and is now a priest after the fashion of the heathen. After I had preached to him a long and earnest discourse, he said, "All is true, and I am in my heart a *lotu* man: my difficulty in avowing my belief is, first, the state of my family, who are very wicked, especially my children; and my chief Vaea is in the dark: but when my way is open, which it soon will be, I shall *lotu*, if not at Homa, yet at Hihifo or Nukualofa." He said his heart was often praying, and he would confess Christ not long hence. He spoke of his admiration of what he saw in New South Wales, when he was there in our vessel twenty-eight years ago, and how often he had spoken of the Christian people with respect and commendation. Homa, where he lives, is the stronghold of heathenism in this land, but its priest does not believe in its truth. A short time, and we may hope to see the utter overthrow of this system of sin and ignorance in the Friendly Islands. Tata was exceedingly kind and respectful to me. Obeying my message to him, he had walked a long journey, and brought me his present of fowls and yams; and spoke of his deep concern about his soul, and his only hope in the true God. When we asked a blessing, he reverently bowed his head and said "Amen;" so that we may number Tata now among the hopeful seekers of salvation in this land. Ata came in while Tata was yet present, and learned from Mr. West the import of our interview; and Mr. West says the subject will be the talk and wonder of all Tonga in a day or two.

Tata told us, moreover, that the people of Homa were every now and then breaking away from their chief, and going where the gospel was preached, that they might become *lotu* persons. I reminded him of the men whom we had formerly known, but who were now dead, having died in the faith, rejoicing in hope of living with the Lord Jesus Christ forever and ever; to which he responded, "It is true, it is good."

Thank God for Tata, who is a man of good understanding, and, I hope, honestly seeking the salvation of his soul. When he fully yields to the Holy Spirit, no doubt many will *lotu* with him.

When Mr. West and I were walking out in the evening, we soon found that Tata's visit to me was in everybody's mouth. A heathen priest doing homage to the servants of God, was no ordinary thing; and his passing through the city was a strange event, until his errand was known to our people. He bears the marks of old age; but did not know how long it was since he had gone to Sydney as my hostage, but seemed delighted when I told him. We parted affectionately, I exhorting, and he promising to do as I wished him. The day of the Lord shall declare the result.

15*th*. NUKUALOFA.—In our way from Hihifo to this place to day, Mr. West and I passed the island of Toketoke, where poor Mrs. Cross was drowned. Her husband and herself were cast ashore on the reef of this little islet, the large canoe having gone to pieces; the sea was then running high. Mr. Cross was holding up his wife, and making his way to the shore; each successive wave, however, made its way over Mrs. Cross, until at last he perceived his wife's head begin to drop down, speech was gone, and presently life was extinct. The sea washed her away, and he made the shore alone. This was indeed a bitter cup. In those days we had not a missionary vessel to bear the servants of God from island to island in the "great South Sea."

While we were at dinner at Mr. Turner's, an earthquake shook the room, and all the articles on the table were in motion; a bamboo over our head, resting on the cocoa-nut beams of the house, waved to and fro, and under our feet there was an oscillatory motion, but not a violent one. Another motion is often felt, like a pulse, or a powerful knocking upwards from beneath the floor. Sometimes persons turn sick, the furniture is thrown down, bottles and earthenware are broken: this makes sad work in the medicine room. Hence it is necessary to place one's stores, &c., on shore pretty much in the same manner as on board ship.

The houses in the Friendly Isles are built on posts, reeded and thatched, in native fashion; but the missionary adds less or more of European taste and improvement;—glass windows, doors, and floors of wood, in some cases; and here and there a room is ceiled with native cloth, as Mr. Webb's and Mr. West's best rooms are ornamented. These houses cost just nothing to the mission fund, as they are built by the natives, and for the most part improved by the missionaries themselves. They are certainly not very durable; but no European house, built of brick or stone, would stand long against the earthquakes on the one hand, and the hurricanes on the other.

The furniture of the mission houses is far enough from being rich, costly, or abundant. We often see the remains of half-a-dozen chairs, some minus a leg, and others without a back. The earthenware made at home, is broken abroad, and there is no market near, so the supply is cut off; and a cocoa-nut shell supplies the place of a basin, and a covered box that of a toilet table. Our missionaries' wives know the way to turn the best side towards London.

Their fare is not English, but for some tastes and habits it is sufficient. They have pork, fowls, and fish, and sometimes eggs. Yams and bread-fruit supply the place of our various vegetables. Beef, mutton, hams, and butter, they have not; and their water is rained from the clouds—so that occasionally they are in danger of falling short. There are several kinds of fruit; but the young natives are sure to come in for the best share thereof. Preserves are kept with great difficulty, after they are once opened. I may add, that the native cooking is often of a most inferior kind.

The dress of the missionaries is of the plainest sort. A straw hat, a calico coat and trowsers, made by his wife, (in some cases,) under-linen, socks, and slippers, comprise his apparel on week-days, and a thin black coat and shoes on the Lord's day. The ladies also and their children dress as a tropical climate compels them; but the old hands, I observe, put on thick clothes, especially towards evening. This, however, is generally of a coarse and antiquated character. Clothes will not last long where the intense heat causes them to be often saturated with perspiration. The form and cut may be generally dated from the period when the party left England.

The king being expected here from Habai, and having sent word that he shall expect Nukualofa to look clean and dignified, all hands are now fully employed in reeding fences, repairing their *abe*, and clearing away grass and rubbish from their roads. All is stir and preparation, as at midsummer eve at home. The coming of the king, and of such a king, (one who lives before his times, and is wiser than the wise men of his day who dwell in these isles,) is quite an event among this people; and, beside this, the king is coming to preside at our missionary meeting, to consult his chiefs about some new laws, and to honor the marriage of a chief lady of Mua, the daughter of Eliza Ann. Her name is Adelaide. The young chief's name is William Kalanivalu; he is coming from Habai with the king. This is a state match; for the parties have not seen each other since they have grown up to maturity. There was another such wedding when I was here three years ago: I then saw their state union, and I now behold their separation, one party living a hundred and eighty miles from the other. Such things occur at home, and are followed by the same miseries. How can it be otherwise, when the marriage is made merely to promote caste? a thing which ought to be destroyed. Eliza Ann is the daughter of the late Fatu, with whom I lived. She was a little girl in my day; but now she is a staid woman, a great chief, and the leader of a class. To her the *lotu* of her brother Tungi and his people is a matter of great delight and thanksgiving to the God of all grace. She is a widow, with several children, of whom Adelaide is the eldest.

16*th*, Sabbath. At dawn of day the bell rang, and the meeting for prayer began. Many were there. But, previously, the city resounded with the family singing and prayer from house to house, till every house had hung out its banner, and raised its hymn of praise to the Lord of the Sabbath. This is publicly confessing Christ. When will England do the same, from prince to peer, and from the navy to the army, and from the rich to the poor, and from end to end of the land? England will do this when it becomes Christian indeed, and in earnest! Meantime, what an awful responsibility must rest on parents and magistrates, and on all ministers of religion, who have influence and do not use it for the honor of Christ, and the maintenance of true religion! How can any family lay claim to the sacred character of *Christian*, without a regular performance of Christian worship in the family? And if Christianity be there, where is the difficulty of observing family worship? There is none, there can be none, except where religion itself is a mere name, without a reality! It is a sad state of society when the mass of the people become ashamed to pray in their own houses together, and in their closets alone. That society must become less or more corrupt, and will sooner or later sin away God's mercies, till ICHABOD be written thereon, and "the glory is departed;" for, certain I am, that as "righteousness *exalteth* a nation," so will sin *hurl* it down. The Lord in his mercy increase the praying Abrahams in my native land! where, I fear, *no family prayer* is the *rule*, and a *praying family* is the *rare exception!* In this matter the Friendly Isles are far in advance of favored England.

At nine o'clock the large congregation assembled, and Mr. Amos conducted the service with spirit and ability; and the people lent a willing ear.

At three they came together again; and at six in the evening I preached to the mission families in English, "and the power of God was present to heal." The natives held a prayer-meeting as usual in the chapel, and concluded the day with family prayer.

17*th*. At early dawn on Monday morning they meet their classes; and this seems to have become a general practice throughout the Islands. Think of about six thousand people meeting in class at the same hour! I know of no inconvenience connected herewith, except that it interferes with the breakfast hour at the mission houses.

Of each wife, as well as of the missionary, may it be said, "She riseth while it is yet dark;" and the first meal ends about seven in the morning, the second about twelve, or a little before, and the third between four and five. This is the case in all ordinary times; but when the mission-vessel is in, rules are laid aside, and random work, in a few instances, is almost unavoidable. Perhaps it may be just as well, now and then, to break the monotony of an island life. This habit of early rising is quite necessary here, as the natives rise early, and the engagements of the day would quite astonish our friends at home; not only those of the men, but those of the ladies as well. The medical department is often very heavy, and this in many cases falls on the wife. Then comes the barter with the long-winded natives, who will, if you permit them, hold you by the button for hour after hour, debating about the value of an article to cost a penny's worth of something: then comes the local preacher about his Sunday's work, and what he met with at an out-island: the fencing comes next: then the purchase of "the Book." I pass down the pathway to the sea, and meet one with a pig, another with yams, a third with oil, a fourth with cocoa-nuts, &c. I ask them, "Where are you going?" Their cheerful reply is, "To buy 'the Book.'" Nothing is so much in request here as the New Testament. Your store may be full of calico and axes; but in the estimation of these natives "the Book," as they uniformly call it, bears away the prize.

The missionary has his village preaching, his translations: disputes are to be settled, errors corrected, and discipline enforced. The swine eat through the fences, and they get abroad, after they have been paid for; the goats are in all sorts of mischief ever and anon; the turkeys and fowls fly over into the garden; the native girl is told to dry the cloth for the nurse, and she puts it into the boiling tea-kettle, just ready for tea,—the broken order having been mistaken, the language being, as yet, but imperfectly acquired.

Such, and ten times more, are the calls upon attention and patience in this land; and if, by any sudden assault, you lose your temper, you are sure to get laughed at in the bargain.

Some *new laws* are desired by the king; but the chiefs hang as a drag upon his wheels. The present system is this:—The king, as supreme, not only rules all the people, but owns all the land in the Tonga Isles; the chiefs hold under him, and the people under the chiefs. When the king wants a thing, he sends to the chief to send it to him. When the chief desires a thing, he sends for it, and the owner gives it up. Hence no man can say that anything he may possess is his own. This state of things most effectually cuts up by the roots all energy and exertion, and each man tries how little he can do; for he says to himself, "Why should I work hard, and another person eat the fruit of my labor?" The chiefs seldom work, but they sometimes command, and often beg: they are the first beggars in the land. The missionaries see this evil, and the king sees it, with here and there a chief. They propose a tax for the king, and another for the chiefs, and the rest to be the property of the man who holds it, who grew it, or who made it. But this is too great a thing to be done at once: the difference between it and the old system is so great as to create considerable hesitancy on the part of the chiefs and all the *idle* ones, of whom there are many. It is not an easy thing to induce a nation suddenly to change its laws and usages. They must be *instructed;* and this will, in the end, act upon them as a tide, bearing them above their former customs. The men now in our institution here see this matter in its true light, one of whom is a judge. They say, "The land we occupy is given for this one object, the institution; the yams we grow are our own, no one can touch them; our boxes are also our own." Others see this; and, as the dawn of a better day for Tonga has begun to appear, the full day will certainly follow: but it requires *time* to elevate and to civilize a barbarous nation. The schoolmaster has followed the gospel preacher; and when the people are more fully *taught*, they will more easily adopt an enlightened system of civil government. Education is the thing wanted; and, whatever else we have or have not, education with all its modern improvements we must have. In this department, our institution here—with twenty-four young men as persons to become teachers, and a hundred and fifty young people as scholars, all under the able and energetic control of Mr. Amos—is already in full operation, and will turn out a large amount of benefits, in various ways, in the dominions of King Tubou. At the breaking-up of the school this morning, Mr. Amos directed, at my suggestion, that the sum for to-morrow would be to multiply the number of their teeth by the number of their fingers. Upon this they said, "Who knows the number of his teeth? And then some of us have had some of our fingers cut off and offered in sacrifice to the devil: must we count them?" All these preliminaries being settled, Jone Faubula rose and said, "I must have two slates, one to write this new sum upon, and the other on which to write my sermon; but, first, I must get away to my own house, to get my teeth counted!" Jone is a fine young man, the son of the King of Lakemba. Mr. Amos and I walked over the school grounds. The middle path is five hundred paces long, and eight feet wide: on each side is a row of pine-apples about eight hundred in all. On either side grow some hundreds of banana-trees, with yams underneath unnumbered.

18*th*. The wind is from the south, which is the cold wind here, and the mission families are trembling with cold, and loading themselves with clothes; while the natives are crowding round the kitchen fires, and shivering with the cold; the thermometer is at 73° before sunrise, and at 90° in the sun. I am delighted with a fresh, cool breeze, which is merely suited to my habit, when very thinly clothed by day, and with a single sheet by night. Such is the difference between one from a temperate climate, and those who are accustomed to the torrid zone. When the wind falls away, or blows from the north, the heat will become intense, and it will be my turn to suffer, and often shall I sigh for the bracing air of New-Zealand.

In my evening walk I was struck with the bounties of nature, and the resources of the natives. They had gathered their evening meal from many a tree and shrub, from the soil, and from the sea. The reefs around their islands had contributed largely of their varied stores of shell-fish and mollusca. They do not feed richly; but they like to do so: only they do not like to take the pains required to produce that kind of food.

I spent five hours with Mr. Amos at his school and institution. About two hundred pupils were present at the school. They repeated the catechism, read the Scriptures, performed their evolutions, wrote, and went through their geography and figures with admirable ability and order. The institution has twenty-four persons in a course of training as teachers, most of whom give good promise as to future usefulness. It was their day for writing their sermons on slates; and, as it must be interesting to the committee to see what they teach, I have selected, out of the twenty that were exhibited, two, exactly as they are in the handwriting of the parties composing them, translated by Mr. Amos.

JOHN FAUBULA'S SERMON.

God is a Spirit: and they that worship him must worship him in spirit and in truth. John iv, 24.

THIS passage of Scripture forms part of a conversation between Jesus and a woman of Samaria. The woman had said, that on the mountain Gerizim was the proper place to worship God; but the Jews thought that Jerusalem was the proper place. But Jesus said to her, "Woman, believe me, the day cometh in which ye shall not bow to the Father in this mountain, or Jerusalem; for God is a Spirit," &c.

Let us attend,

I. *To make known that God is a Spirit.* There are three persons in the Godhead, Father, Son, and Holy Ghost: those three are one God, and that God is a Spirit. A spirit is invisible, and "no man hath seen God at any time." How different from the gods of idolaters! from the things we considered gods while we were in our heathen state! He is an infinite Spirit. We cannot see him, nor is it good for us to make any visible likeness of him.

How sinful, then, is the Popish religion! I have heard that they make an image of an old gray-headed man, and call it God the Father; that they make a likeness of Christ's human body, and call that God the Son; that the representation of a dove is the likeness of the Holy Ghost. But are not these lying pictures? Does not this text say, "God is a Spirit?" and is not a spirit invisible? Then to what shall we compare him? What likeness shall we make of him? Christ clothed his Godhead with *humanity*, but his divinity was always *unseen*. God is invisible to mortal eye. The dove mentioned in Scripture was only the vessel or shrine by which the invisible presence of the Holy Ghost was indicated. Our God is a great, invisible Spirit.

Notice,

II. *To make known that it is lawful and right for us to worship God in all places.* Not in Jerusalem or Gerizim only, but everywhere; for God is everywhere a Spirit. Not only can we bow to God in the chapel, but also in our own houses. When at our proper employment on land, or on the sea, we may bow to God. To whatever place we go, and wherever we dwell, God is there, and we may worship him.

III. *To make known that they who worship God must do so in spirit and in truth.* "In spirit," that is, with our spirits. It is useless to worship God with a deceitful mind. "In truth," in reality of heart. It is profitable worship which is performed with the spirit and in sincerity. We must bow before God "with all our heart, and soul, and mind, and strength." Let us worship with a believing heart: for God is truth. "He is not a man that he should lie, nor the son of man that he should repent." O, worship this great Spirit!

Mr. Amos adds, "This is a faithful translation. Jone Faubula is the son of Tuinayau, king of Lakemba. The account of Popery he obtained from our conversations on that subject in the institution."

SHADRACH MUMUI'S SERMON.

God is a Spirit: and they that worship him must worship him in spirit and in truth. John iv, 24.

THIS is the word of Jesus to the woman of Samaria, of whom he begged water to drink, as she was drawing water at the well of Jacob.

We therefore know for certain the nature of God, in consequence of the spoken word of Jesus. We also know the kind of worship which is right for us to offer to His Majesty on high, and by which we may live. Let us attend to these things:—

I. *To make known the nature of God.*—"God is a Spirit." God is not like our idols which we once worshiped. Nor is he like unto man. He is not enshrined; has no body, no flesh, no blood, no bones; but is a Spirit. The Father, Son, and Holy Ghost, one God, is a Spirit.

1. He is a *great Spirit.* So great is God, that heaven is brim-full of him, and the earth is full to running over with His Majesty. So great is he that he is in every place, in every moment of all time.

2. He is an *uncreated, eternal, invisible Spirit.* He had no beginning: he will never end. He liveth not through the agency of another, nor does he depend on anything, but has being in himself alone. He is the trust, and dependence, and source of life to heaven

and earth. He is the root and core of our salvation and blessedness.

3. God is a *holy Spirit.* There is not the least thing defective or blemished in his divine character. His being is holy, his nature is holy, his works are holy, his government is holy, his love is holy, his salvation is holy, his wrath is holy, yea, glorious is his holiness. (Isaiah vi, 3.) Let us, then, seek to be made holy through faith in Jesus: for holiness is the mark of God's people. God is holy—be ye holy also.

4. He is an *almighty* and *omnipresent Spirit.* All things are his, temporal and spiritual; all heaven and its glory, all earth and its people, are his. He was the Creator of all: therefore he governs the works of his hands, and will reign forever. Not the most diminutive thing can escape his notice, whether it be in the mind of man, or beneath the earth, or in the sea, whether it be open or concealed, whether it be difficult or easy. He alone is one God of power, wisdom, strength, (or ability,) ever present, in all things.

Notice,

II. *The kind of worship Jesus tells us is good to be offered unto God by his people.*—"They who worship him must worship him in spirit and in truth." This worship is not merely the word of the mouth, the hearing of the ear, or the seeing of the eye; nor is it an accustomed attendance upon the public services of religion, or a boast of being religious. It is to be spiritual and true worshipers.

1. It is for me, myself, to worship with my spirit, in the truth of my heart, in the earnestness of my soul, and with all my mind. Let not my mind be diverted, or my affections be divided; but give up all

my powers of body and soul to the Lord, supplicate with thanksgiving, and with the effort of a sincere spirit.

2. God is the author and object of all true worship, and in this good work we shall receive life. There is no man who can worship God of his own mind: he knows not the way to eternal life, neither can he so approach the Father as to save his soul but through the Son. Christ says, "I am the way, the truth, and the life." John xiv, 6. Man is sinful, foolish, and dark-minded; but by faith in the Saviour Jesus he finds the way of true worship to the Great Spirit.

3. Let us be earnest in this worship, that we may receive its benefits to our souls, through trusting in our Mediator. Repent, believe, entreat, in Jesus' name, that your sins may be forgiven, that your mind may be made new, and the Holy Ghost may enter your spirit. He will make light your darkness, make wise your folly, and help your weakness.

Let us be ready to perform this worship *now*, and on all occasions, according to the spoken command of Jesus. Great will be the advantages,—pardon, holiness, renewal, peace, eternal life, all through faith in Jesus.

Well, then, have we begun this true worship or not?

Mr. Amos adds, "Shadrach is the son of Tubou Malohi, a late king of Tonga. He derived no assistance in the composition of this sermon, and I vouch for its being a literal translation."

CHAPTER IV.

A FLEET of double canoes is just come in from Habai and Vavau. The king was on board: and as they came in the night, a shout was given, and the *lali* (native "drum") began to beat. At one o'clock in the morning the city was vocal with a thousand voices, uttering their joy at this arrival. There was no more sleep; all were cleaving wood, killing pigs, roasting yams, and preparing all kinds of food for at least twelve hundred persons just landed, after a tedious voyage, the wind being contrary. We were strongly reminded of the beautiful expression of the prophet: "Rejoice greatly, O daughter of Zion; *shout*, O daughter of Jerusalem: behold, thy King cometh unto thee." Zech. ix, 9.

The young man whose marriage was the occasion of all this, was on board of this fleet; and accordingly, "at midnight there was a cry made, Behold the bridegroom cometh!" *Such a cry* it has never been my lot to hear in this world until now. The shout was the same as they make in war, only in this there was an air of joy and cheerfulness.

Her Majesty's ship "Meander," the Honorable Captain Keppel, anchored off Nukualofa, and did good service to us and to King George. Him they saluted, to the astonishment of the natives. The band also came ashore and played, much to the gratification of all. Captain Keppel conducted himself, and all under his authority, with dignity and the most respectful attention both towards the king and the missionaries; all of whom will long remember him with much satisfaction and gratitude. Captain Keppel, with his chaplain, the Rev. Mr. Thompson, and his friend Mr. Brierley, examined our school, and expressed themselves as well satisfied with what they saw. Mr. Brierley is an artist, and has sketched several scenes here, which may perhaps one day appear in public. His views are taken with admirable skill and fidelity. The captain, at our suggestion, threw up a few rockets in the evening, with which the natives were much delighted. When the first went up a long way, they shouted amain, "See, see, see how it walks the skies!"

21*st.* We dined with the king and missionaries on board the fine frigate "Meander," forty-four guns. On our stepping on board we found Captain Keppel and his officers in all their uniform, ready to receive us, and the marines drawn up on the quarter-deck, presenting arms, as a guard of honor to King George. The band played during the dinner-hour, which was at sunset; and, with the viands, the wines, the servants, the sailors, the dazzling epaulettes, the great guns, and the grandeur of everybody and everything around George was quite astonished; but he carried himself with dignity; and his speech after dinner I shall here insert, as worthy of him and of ourselves.

KING GEORGE'S SPEECH ON BOARD H. M. S. "MEANDER," JUNE 21ST, 1850, ADDRESSED TO THE HONORABLE CAPTAIN KEPPEL, AND TRANSLATED BY MR. AMOS.

"I RETURN you my thanks for your kind visit. It is only thanks which your visit demands. The honor you have put upon me to-day is great. I thank you for these favors. But, what is most a matter of thanksgiving is, that Britannia sent us the gospel, and the missionaries, and the sacred book, that we might live thereby. These we value more than men-of-war, or the visits of Queen Victoria's ships. But we value these visits also.

"It is great love shown to a weak and friendless people, that a wise and powerful nation, such as Britannia, should cast its shadow over us. Under this shade we live.

"We know of the 'confusion' (*fakamaveuveu*) produced in the world by the French and others. We wish not their visit nor friendship. Theirs is (*unga mate*) 'a deadly shade.'

"Your visits have always been friendly visits. Has it not been so from the beginning? I flatter you not. I do not speak thus because I am on board this great ship, or because one of the queen of England's nobles is sitting beside me. I speak in truth. If my departed ancestors could speak here to-day, would they not bear me witness? Ever since of old has not your course of conduct been uniformly gracious? We know it has; and, if every member of my body had a voice, the only word which it would speak would be, *Thanksgiving!* This is the end of my speech to the chief of this ship."

23*d*, Sunday. The congregations were overflowing to-day at all the four services: I preached in the forenoon, and Mr. Amos in the evening. At six o'clock I preached to the few English sailors who reside here; but preaching to men so idle and so dissolute is plowing on a rock. The spirit and tone of the natives are evangelical and affectionate; but these English runaways display neither intellect nor feeling.

24th. I spent the evening with the king and Messrs. West and Amos. George was utterly tired out with the crowds who waited upon him with food, cava, and cloth during the day; but in the evening he was exceedingly open and communicative. We heard him give a detailed account of his title to the crown of all the Friendly Islands. The contrary has been asserted by interested parties among the natives, and by ill-informed parties who have written on the subject.

The following statement has been collected with care from the best authorities, both heathen and Christian:—

All tradition states that the king of Tonga reigned supremely over Tongatabu, Habai, Vavau, and the islands of Niua and Uvea. Vavau and Habai have never been governed separately, except in the case of revolt. The original kings of the land were the Tui-Tongas, as the name imports, the first of whom is said to have come from the sky. But, ages ago, the royal blood became contaminated by the connection of one of their ancestors with his female slaves. When the sons of these low-bred women came into power, they were despised by the people in general, and often assassinated by their attendants.

Kau-ulu-fonua-fekai, the last Tui-Tonga who was king of the land, was so spirit-broken, in consequence of the murder of his father, Takalaua, that, after pursuing the assassins as far as Uvea to no purpose, he returned to Tonga, and resigned his kingdom to his younger brother, Monga-Motua, whom he appointed Tuihatakalaua. He, in return, engaged to support and defend the Tui-Tonga forever. Kau-ulu-fonua-fekai was induced to take this step because his brother was born of a chief woman, and thereby screened from popular insult. The grandson of Monga-Motua, named Gata, succeeded to the throne, with the title of Tui-kanokubolu, which name has distinguished the sovereigns ever since. Then followed in order, 1. Gata; 2. Ata-mata-ila; 3. Mataele-tua-biko; 4. Mataele; 5. Maafu-o-tui-tonga; 6. Tubou-lahi; 7. Tui-hala-fatai; (king when Captain Cook came;) 8. Maea-liuaki; 9. Tubou-mohe-ofo; (a woman;) 10. Maafu-limuloa; 11. Tubou-lahi-jii; 12. Muli-ki-haa-mea; 13. Mumui.

The son of Mumui, Tuku-aho, the fourteenth in succession, next ascended the throne, and was a brave but cruel man: both Mariner and the present queen agree in this statement. The queen adds that, before the present King George became a convert to Christianity, the old men predicted that he would exactly resemble his grandfather, Tuku-aho, in energy of character and fierceness of disposition. But the gospel has changed the lion into a lamb. Tuku-aho was assassinated, out of private revenge, by Tubou-Niua, and not from patriotic views, as stated by Mariner. The death of the king was the signal for a general struggle after power. When Captain Cook landed here, probably in the reign of Tui-hala-fatai, all was peace and harmony, and the islands all beautiful and gay. Wilkes, I am told, contradicts this; but what authority is he against the truthful Cook and all the natives? Since that period wars have desolated the land; and the traveler sees many a ruined city and decayed rampart. The vampire screams over the forsaken tombs; and the moaning winds, as they pass through the lofty *toa* trees, chant the funeral dirge of the slain in battle. But King George says, he believes the wars tended to break the power of the mighty, and prepare the way for the gospel in these islands; that, if warriors had not fallen, perhaps missionaries would have died by their hand.

Ulu-kalala (the Finow of Mariner) was a designing, murderous rebel, who took advantage of the king's death to raise himself from a second-rate chief in Habai to be the first in power there, and also in Vavau. He also embroiled Tonga in a civil war: nor of means was he scrupulous. But Mariner was his admirer; perhaps from the same principles that led him to sympathize with the mutineers on board the "Port-au-Prince." Finow held for a season Habai and Vavau; and Takai strove to get the supreme power in Tonga. In the midst of this confusion, Tubou-malohi, the eldest son, ascended the throne of his murdered father, Tuku-aho. His reign was very brief; for his subjects continually made war upon him. In 1812 he was succeeded by his younger brother, Tubou-toa ("the brave.") He reigned only eight years. From 1820 to 1826 there was no king; but each chief ruled his own fort.

King George's predecessor, Alea-motua, afterwards baptized by the name of Josiah, was his father's uncle. He early embraced Christianity, and was much persecuted; but his end was peace.

Shortly after the conversion of Josiah, George was converted, being then chief of Habai. Then followed the conversion of Finow, chief of Vavau, (the Finow-Fiji of Mariner,) whose baptized name was Zephaniah.

These men met with much opposition from refractory but subordinate chiefs. George first quelled those at Habai, then went, by invitation, and did the same at Vavau and Tonga. He had now acquired fame; and his enemies feared him everywhere. Wilkes throws dirt at George; but the king's garment is unspotted, and would not be exchanged for that of the commodore.

Upon their dying beds Josiah of Tonga, and Zephaniah of Vavau, resigned the land and people to George Tubou, as the lawful heir of Tubou-toa. George was accordingly placed on the throne of his noble ancestors with great ceremony on the 4th of December, 1845.

There are certain chiefs in these islands whose office and business it is to inaugurate the king: these were all present and did the work required at George's inauguration: nor was any objection offered from any quarter whatever. There was another chief, whose baptized name is Shadrach, equally near in his relationship to the former king, and who was named by Tubou as proper to be the king; but the choice of all fell on George Tubou, who cannot, therefore, be justly charged as being a usurper.

Thus, by heritage, by conquest, and by the suffrage of his people, none opposing, George Tubou sits upon the throne of his fathers, and reigns in righteousness over a prosperous and a happy people.

KING GEORGE ADMINISTERING REPROOF.

One of our teachers, named Silas, was some years ago sent to the island of Ono, in Feejee, to instruct the less instructed there; but he quickly showed the spirit of an upstart, and was dismissed by the missionary.

Back he came to Vavau, and informed the people that his land had been taken away by the king, and his office by the missionaries, and they were the bad folks, and he the good man: such were his "Fly-Sheets!" Who does not know that those who transgress are the first to publish their complaints? Soon, however, the king met his chiefs, and this upstart among them. Addressing poor Silas, the sovereign said: "Why do you mention your paltry island here? and who made it yours? Who are you, and who were your fathers? I will tell you who my fathers were;" and he then enumerated them. "These were my ancestors; but who were yours? I will tell you who they were; they were my father's cooks," (a term of reproach.) "Why, then, do you set up your claim to the insignificant islet which you call *yours?* Why did you not put it into a basket, and send it on board the canoe, and take it with you to Feejee? Then we should never have heard any more of you or your islet." By this time Silas was holding down his head, "glad to be hid, and praying to be forgot."

In my evening walk by the sea-side there was much to soothe and to impress a devotional mind. The calm, moonlight night; the gently-waving banana, cocoa, toa, *ovava*, or banian-tree; the islets in the distance; the noiseless waters of the tranquil ocean; the simple native lute, blown through the nose; the fleet of double canoes, nineteen in number, bearing twelve hundred people to our shore: all these contrasted strongly with the lively population singing at family worship, or chanting their various rehearsals of catechism, Scriptures, hymns, and figures, preparatory to the approaching *katuanga*, or "school-feast," at Nukualofa. All around was magical in its tone and aspect. The serene sky, with Venus and Jupiter descending in the west, and Taurus and the Southern Cross, with their brilliant constellations, in the south, beamed forth His glory who set them in the firmament. These, with the glassy deep and forest grandeur, combined with the indications from a thousand tongues that a nation was here rising from barbarism to life, and devotion, and wisdom; for many are already wise unto salvation, and a multitude of them have escaped to Abraham's bosom. As I walked along the shore, I was asked by many, old and young, "Shall we accompany you in your walk?" "No," was the reply; "I am walking thus to assist me to think, to pray, to feel, and to adore." "Praise the Lord from the earth, ye dragons and all deeps; fire, and hail; snow, and vapor; stormy wind fulfilling his word: mountains, and all hills; fruitful trees, and all cedars: beasts, and all cattle; creeping things, and flying fowl: kings of the earth, and all people; princes, and all judges of the earth: both young men, and maidens; old men, and children: let them praise the name of the Lord: for his name alone is excellent; his glory is above the earth and heaven." Psalm cxlviii, 7–13.

25th. To prevent all possibility of mistake, I wrote the king this morning the following note:—

TO KING GEORGE TUBOU.

"I beg to ask, with great respect, whether I understood the matter correctly last night; namely,

"First, That you were determined not to part with any land in your dominions throughout the Friendly Isles?

"Secondly, That though you greatly desire the friendship and alliance of Great Britain, yet you do not intend to be in subjection to any power or State whatever, but to remain, you and your people, a free and independent nation?

"I am, Sir, your obedient and respectful friend,

"Walter Lawry."

THE KING'S ANSWER.

"My mind is, that I will not verily sell any piece of land in this Tonga; for it is small; then, what of it can we sell? and what would be left for ourselves?

"I verily wish to be the friend of Britain; in friendly alliance, with all fellowship; but it is not my mind, nor the mind of my people, that we should be subject to any other people or kingdom in this world. But it is our mind to sit down (that is, remain) an independent nation. I am

"George Tubou."

28*th*. This day we held our school-examination at Nukualofa: a host of the people from Habai and Vavau combining with those of Tonga. The king was present for several hours, with the queen, and young prince George, a fine sharp lad. The examination lasted from dawn of day till dark, and was in all respects highly satisfactory, doing honor to the master who has control over them: indeed, no one seemed more cheered and animated, during the long process, than did Mr. Amos.

I had witnessed such things on many former occasions; but still the sight was too much for my feelings, and I wept over and over again during the rehearsals.

I thought of the struggle going on at home, and of the many difficulties attending our fathers who conduct these missions; and then I looked upon this scene, in which the king, the judges, and the great chiefs of the land were engaged, with the bulk of the population, reading the Scriptures, repeating our catechism, hymns, geography, spelling, figures, and English; and some of them showed considerable knowledge of maps, pointing out the nations, seas, mountains, and rivers. To these were added frequent intervals of devotional exercises. It was delightful. Many thousands were this day present, enjoying the treat, and performing their part in the transactions of the day, contributing of their substance in aid of the mission funds. Was not this enough to *move* and to *dissolve* the heart of any man who believes the Bible? I hope their contributions, made in their deep poverty, in many instances, may realize about £70 towards the cause of missions.

At early dawn I stood on the top of the hill on which our chapel stands; and, from this little hill of Zion, saw every pathway crowded, and men in all directions, on the land, and on the sea, moving in haste towards the place I stood upon. They were advancing by thousands; each school apart, ten in number; all in full dress, ornamented with vines, and flowers sweet-scented, and large libations of cocoa-nut oil, poured on the head and standing clear as dew-drops on their ringlets, of dropping down to the skirts of their garments. O for such a sight as this, I thought, to set before the British eye! Would not this be the lion of all lions in the great metropolis? Hundreds of them were dressed in European clothes, and all were earnest to exhibit what they had learned at school, the old vying with the young, (but generally at a sufficient distance behind them,) and to lay their offering of love upon God's altar.

When the processions moved along the grassy lawn, and emerged from the luxuriant groves of evergreens and shade, and ascended the Chapel Hill, with measured step and slow pace, singing their *song of degrees*, the females taking their part and the men theirs, all joining in full chorus, I thought, What a rebuke do these simple islanders administer, in their zeal for the religion which saves them from the wrath to come, —what a silencing rebuke do they pronounce, with emphatic energy, upon the "fly-sheet" men lately expelled from this Church of God! "Now is salvation, and strength, and the kingdom of our God, and the power of his Christ; for the accuser of our brethren is cast down."

Where all have done well, it may seem partial to select any one in particular; but I cannot help giving a passing notice of commendation in the case of a little girl. Juliana is about twelve years of age, interesting in her manners and of lovely countenance. She is the daughter of Edwin Tabuola, our teacher at Tofoa, three miles away in the country. Her village is very beautifully situated by the side of a salt-water creek, surrounded by woods, in which are innumerable turtle-doves cooing the live-long day, and fragrant shrubs, without number, send forth their sweet perfume through the village. The high road from Tofoa to Nukualofa is one continued grove of cocoa-nut trees, crested with living beauty. Along this grove little Juliana passed and repassed every school-day for two years, with her younger sister by her side, to Mr. Amos's school at this place, being screened from the rays of the sun by the waving plumes of the cocoa-nut trees. This little girl made rapid progress in learning, and has taught every person in her village, both old and young, what she learned at Nukualofa. The result is, that, at the examination to-day, Juliana's school was the next to those conducted in person by Mr. Amos, in every department of knowledge. She was at the head of the ranks when the school entered the chapel, and took her seat beside her father, who, though an excellent man, is much less instructed than his lovely little Juliana.

My belief is that many more will be found exhibiting the force of this school-system, and the energy of the mind that applies it with such happy results.

Mr. Amos has furnished the subjoined account of Timothy Katóa, late a student at the Training Institution, Nukualofa, Tongatabu. I knew Timothy well: too much is not said of him.

OBITUARY NOTICE OF TIMOTHY KATOA.

WHATEVER other advantages the introduction of Christianity into the Friendly Islands may have conferred upon the inhabitants, it is certain that multitudes of precious souls have been thereby reared to a beauteous and never-fading immortality. When Christ shall be "glorified in his saints, and admired in all them that believe," clusters of gems from these isles will deck the diadem of our great Redeemer, and multitudes of Tonguese, "as the voice of many waters," will swell the anthem of his endless praise. Of one Friendly Islander who has lately passed in triumph to the skies we have collected the following notices:—

TIMOTHY KATOA was born of respectable parents in the fortress of Feletoa, Vavau, during the war between Finau and his aunt Toe-umu. At that time these lands were the abodes of cruelty, and his father Feke, with his mother Fuji, like their neighbors, dwelt in the midst of "wars and rumors of wars," while thick darkness enveloped them, and the deadly shade of heathenism added to the gloom.

Soon, however, did "the Day-spring from on high visit" them, and the subject of this brief notice was among the first to come to "the brightness of its rising." While yet a boy, he embraced the outward form of the *lotu* in Nukualofa before the Wesleyan missionaries arrived, having been instructed in the way of salvation by the Tahitian teachers belonging to the London Missionary Society.

He was an intelligent youth, and eagerly sought information; so that it was not long before he learned to *read* his native tongue, being taught by the Rev. Nathaniel Turner. The late Rev. William Cross admitted him into the Christian Church by the rite of baptism. Having obtained the pardon of sin, and a new heart, he tasted and felt that the Lord was gracious; which led him to seek to be useful in winning the souls of his fellow-countrymen to the *lotu*. He was made a class-leader, and always succeeded in getting a large number of members. The Rev. James Watkin received him on trial as a local preacher; and, by superior talent, he soon rose to the head of that class of laborers in this circuit. His intimate knowledge of the peculiar idiom of the Tonga language induced the missionaries to select him as their instructor.

He became a scholar in Mrs. Tucker's school; and afterwards gave evidence of the great benefit he had derived from that lady's valuable instructions. He always spoke of Mrs. Tucker in terms of the highest commendation, and was ever grateful for the trouble she took with him.

But during the war in 1839 his love to God grew cold; the war-spirit entered into his heart, and the Spirit of Christ departed. He did not fall into gross sin, but he lost his sense of forgiveness, and became worldly. So far did he "backslide in heart," that he removed to the heathen fortress of Bea to get tattooed, which is considered a mark of manliness.

One Sabbath, as a good local preacher was returning from his appointment in the country, he turned into the fort of Bea to seek his erring brother. When he saw his former fellow-laborer coming towards him, he burst into tears in the presence of the heathen chiefs, by whom he was greatly caressed. The Christian conversation of this good man was the means of his recovery. He returned to his *lotu* friends; and under a sermon preached by the Rev. John Thomas, on the evils of war, he was convinced of his error, and sought with deep contrition the return of the Holy Spirit to his heart. It pleased the Lover of souls to pardon his delinquency, and restore unto him the joy of his salvation. His deportment was subsequently consistent and praiseworthy. He was for several years the principal local preacher in Nukualofa. He was employed as an assistant in translating the Scriptures, and became endeared by piety, fidelity, and kindness. He was greatly respected by King George, who regularly corresponded with him; and when the king resided here, he was his constant companion. This was not surprising, as Timothy had acquired a good stock of general information, and was highly respectful and dignified in his manners.

Upon the arrival of the "John Wesley" in 1847, he made a favorable impression upon the newly-arrived missionaries, by the gentlemanliness of his appearance, and he readily won their affections by various acts of kindness in a time of great need.

In 1848 he offered to go as a teacher to the heathen parts of the island, and was accordingly appointed to Makanga. He was a great help to the Rev. Matthew Wilson, being a bold antagonist of Popery; and he met with great success.

He was a man of slender frame, and weakly constitution; so that the long walks, and incessant preaching, were too much for him. The chief of Makanga was unkind; he had to live in a house worse than his cook-house, and was often hungry; but, although he left a good house and a large farm at home, his bereaved widow says he never complained of these painful circumstances. He spent nearly the whole of his time in his closet, and in the heathen villages around. His only cry was for the *maonioni haohaoa*, "perfect holiness;" and God who is faithful sanctified him wholly.

In 1849, he was proposed to go as an assistant-missionary to Wallis Island; but the district-meeting appointed that he should spend a year or two in the Training Institution, with special reference to Wallis Island. But how little do we know of the future! God intended him for himself! He took deep interest in the establishment of the Institution at Nukualofa, and was useful in negotiating with the chiefs concerning the land. He was present at the commencement of our course of instruction: but, having an affection in his throat, and showing indications of consumption, —a disease of which immense numbers of the natives die,—he made a voyage to Haabai to consult Dr. Miller, who prescribed for him, but with little effect; he was appointed to die. He attended the Institution as long as he could walk, and devoured knowledge, until his strength failed. He greatly desired to see the model-farm completed; and when he was on the brink of the grave, he came wrapped up with large folds of native cloth, and stood by his brother, whom he had begged to plant his plot of land with yams, bananas, &c. That was the last time poor Timothy was out.

When confined to his bed, his fellow-students regularly visited him; and many were the seasons of consolation they enjoyed together. He regretted that he could not remove his house to the school-premises, but *he* was soon removed to the mansions of eternal blessedness. My kind superintendent, the Rev. William Webb, visited him frequently; and our late brother was greatly comforted on those occasions. The night before he died, I visited him, and was glad to find all right for eternity. He said, "I rejoice that I can speak to you before I remove hence. My sins are forgiven. Christ sits in my heart. I fear not to die; yet I wish to live to be useful. This is the year in which the *lotu* begins to grow in Tonga, and I wish to live that I may see it spread. But this is my appointed time: for God has chosen me to die. I am very happy. God has made my love to be perfect. I am dying fast." Such was his dying testimony. I saw him no more. The next day, December 13th, 1849, he gently passed into the unseen world. The teachers of the Institution "carried him to his burial, and made great lamentation over him." We shall meet again when the Lord shall come in the clouds of heaven. "And so shall we be ever with the Lord."

July 3d. The wedding took place, for which such large preparations had been made. William is the son of the Tui-Tonga, or is so reputed; for the Tui-Tonga lives at large, and has no wife, but multitudes of women. Adelaide is the granddaughter of Fatu, under whose shield I lived aforetime. Their age is not known with certainty, but they may be safely set down at *seventeen.* Adelaide is a fine girl, with long floating hair, and her stature is of the full size. She measures five feet ten inches high, and I am quite sure she would weigh two hundred pounds; but it so happens that there are no weights in Tonga sufficient to weigh her.

This is a State-match, and the parties have not seen each other since they were children. They came to be married at our chapel, not together, but one party from his friend's residence, and the other from hers. They did not sit together in the house of God, nor go away together; but each went away as they came, without any procession or form whatever, but dressed gorgeously; the female was so large with the mats wrapped round her, that it required three women to support her during the service. At the service the chapel was not merely crowded, but thousands sat outside while Mr. Daniel preached. The conduct of all was solemn and proper.

The friends of each party had provided for the occasion, and, though I cannot pretend to be exact in my inventory, the things provided may be set down at,—native cloth, ten cart-loads; fish, cooked, five hundred, generally large; pigs, roasted and living, one hundred and fifty; yams, ten cart-loads; beside bread-fruit, banana, talau, and ma. But these things were so long before they were served out, that the multitude were all day without food, or nearly so.

Upon the whole I cannot say much in favor of this stupid marriage: it may be oriental, but it is not rational. It did not originate in mutual affection, but in State-policy, or rather in family pride. Such unions generally end in the separation of the parties, who never were united in heart. From one grade they fall to another, until sin, when it is finished, bringeth forth death. Besides, the external pomp and extravagance tends to impoverish, unsettle, and vitiate, and is utterly unworthy of *lotu* people.

4th. I measured the length of the king's canoe, ninety feet long, and the sail is ninety feet high, by sixty feet wide at the top. They sail very fast and near the wind, carrying about one hundred men; but they cannot stand a heavy gale and a high sea.

5th. The king is holding his court, and they have now fully agreed upon a code of laws, which are to be published forthwith. They are not all that we could wish them to be—and this I told the king and chiefs; remarking especially on the mode of paying the judges out of the fines levied on the offenders, which is sure to corrupt the seat of justice—but the king's apology was, "We must do things little by little." Upon the whole, however, this movement is a grand step towards the civilization of the entire nation, comprehending nearly two hundred islands. This ought to have been done several years ago, and there is no good reason why it has been so long delayed. No doubt, however, now rests upon any mind, that much good will result from this first attempt at legislation by a written code. The statute-book is to be printed at our mission press.

These laws were first published by our brethren at Tahiti; and have generally been commended as simple, wise, and just, a pattern of Christian legislation. They were, however, originally drawn up in Sydney, by one of our local preachers, (since deeply fallen,) at that time in high repute among all who knew him. This fact I learned from his own mouth many years ago.

6*th.* In my walk this morning with Mr. Daniel at the Mua, we fell in with a banian-tree by the sea-side of very large dimensions. The branches were solid timber; but the stock was composed of various parts, joined here and separate there, so that the light occasionally came through, and the entire stock had the appearance of net-work, but with all the strength of solid wood, and probably much stronger. Our measurement was not very exact, as the tide was occupying one side, and the longest branches extended over the water, where we could not get; but we did our best, and the result was that the trunk of this *ovava*, or banian-tree, was fifty-seven feet round, and the branches two hundred and forty feet. The roots show themselves above ground, forming seats, on which we sat, and their extent might be traced just as far as the branches. These majestic trees are very common in the Friendly Isles, and under their ample shade the chiefs are used to drink their *cava*. They tend greatly to aggrandize the forest, where they stand unrivaled; and were they and other trees cultivated as they might be, and the soil properly cleared and dressed, these green islands might be made ten times more beautiful and more productive than they are at present; a paradise regained! But it is not easy to induce a people, especially when they are sunk in barbarism, to change their national customs.

Tungi is a fine young chief, and rules the whole of this end of Tonga, and has lately become *lotu*, that is, a praying man, who believes the Bible. He is very fond of salt, and of salt meat; and, sufficiently often, begs the missionary to give him a piece of salt pork for his dinner. He knows that we consider it degrading to beg, and he knows that at the *ligo*, at the back of the island, there is plenty of salt, white on the reefs, and he has pigs on every side: but still, though the means of gratifying his appetite are quite within his reach, who ever heard of his eating salt pork, unless he had first begged a piece from the missionary? If you remonstrate with him, he will readily say, "I know it is wrong; but we are an ignorant people, and this is our way." That is, they never help themselves, while others will work for them.

At the giving out of medicine this morning, a woman asked for some arrow-root, which grows here in great abundance; and some of which Mrs. Daniel had bought of them, then washed and dried it, so that it will keep. The party was refused, on the ground that arrow-root was produced in Tonga, and the natives well knew how to make it clean and preserve it. The woman said, "But I have none, and my husband is ill: will you not have love to me, and give me some, now that sickness has overtaken me?" If the article had been given, that family would *trust* that the same kind act would be repeated, and their neighbors would do the same; and so their improvement would be retarded by giving to them, at a time when it was very difficult to withhold, what they desired.

This is only one of a thousand cases daily passing before the mission family, whose patience is tried to the uttermost, especially here, where they are just beginning to rise out of heathenism. As to servants, these people have no notion of any such thing. One here and there will come into your house, and out of love, as they say, will do a little for you, until you offend them, and then they show their independence by an abrupt departure.

They can subsist upon very little, and prefer idleness and poverty to labor and plenty. Their wants will gradually increase, and with them perhaps their industry.

7*th.* I preached at Mua in the morning, and found it good to be among a people daily coming over from heathenism to our religion. About seventeen bowed the knee to Jesus for the first time on the last two

Sabbaths. King George preached here on Sunday week, and many were his solemn and astonished hearers; for the king has not been here since this city revolted from his authority, and war was threatened. Submission has rendered the carnage of Mua no longer necessary: but, on the contrary, the people and their prince bow down together at the footstool of the Prince of Peace, and I trust that happy day has now arrived when they shall learn war no more. They certainly are now entering on the way, and the only way, which is open to them into the civilized world. Many of them, we feel assured, will obtain a new heart, and a right spirit, and, with these, all the train of elevating blessings, which can prepare man for eternity, and shed a lustre on his nature and his character before he quits his present abode.

8*th*. Mr. Daniel and I walked over the old grave-yards, devil-houses, and *malies*, and the sites of the *hufanga*, or "cities of refuge," which existed when I arrived here in 1822.

The *malies* are still existing, so far as the noble *ovava*, and other forest trees, are concerned. The large *malie* where the *inachee*, or "feast of the first-fruits," used to be held is still adorned by rows of the wide-spreading banian, each measuring from twenty to thirty feet in girth. Their shade forbids the growth of underwood as in other localities. There they nod, with many a shivered limb and riven branch, but with their own self-renewing power of twisted vines winding round them, and, after many years of climbing, at last becoming part of the tree: thus they are succored by a thousand auxiliaries. These monarchs of the wood remain, and tell the tale of ancient men and other times; and may perhaps overshadow Christian rites and enlightened worship in days to come—for their owners are now Christian men.

The devil-houses are not only without a shrine, or a priest, or a worshiper, (almost,) but of the buildings also nothing is left, in most cases, except the posts of iron-wood. In the majority of instances, even these are fallen down; and, with the houses, the kingdom of Satan is tottering.

As to the *hufanga*, or "cities of refuge," so like the Jewish refuge in all particulars, the fences are fallen down, the god-houses are all gone, and no one flees thither for refuge; because heathenism has lost its spell upon the native mind. It is remarkable that at such a juncture, when the ancient superstition was being starved out, the idolatry of Rome is brought in, and, under a Christian name, is offered to this people. By the people in general it is spurned with contempt; but still there are some who are politically opposed to the king: and do not the priests know well how to make their use of this feeling? Then there are backsliders from the Church of the Bible, who turn to the idol called Mary! and thus have their revenge on those who exercised discipline upon them. These also make the pope their refuge: but the days of this refuge also are numbered.

The last human victim sacrificed to the devil, about fourteen years ago, was killed and offered within a few yards of where I am now writing. This spot may therefore be said to be the tomb of heathen superstition in the Friendly Islands. The young chief Tungi intends to erect his new dwelling-house, and a large and spacious new chapel for our worship, just on this spot where idolatry went out; while Rome, in the distance, but still within sight, acts as his foil.

The tombs of ancient kings and mighty warriors are found here, and some of them are surrounded by cut stones of large dimensions. I measured some, and found them fifteen feet by fifteen feet, and fifteen inches thick. Various traditions exist as to whence they came; but no one knows. This kind of stone is not found here, so far as I can ascertain; and to bring them from any distant part would require great skill and power. I think they are from the weather side of the island.

The natives here have too many burial-grounds, and Mr. Daniel will endeavor by all proper means to establish one general place of sepulture.

The Tui-Tonga has one prepared by the priests in this neighborhood, which is called by the natives *Loma*, (that is, Rome,) a name by no means unsuitable, as this Tui-Tonga is known to be the last of his order, and cannot be succeeded in his title, his functions having long since ceased. So also must it be with doomed Rome, the city upon seven hills, mystic "Babylon the great, the mother of harlots and abominations of the earth. And in her was found the blood of prophets, and of saints, and of all that were slain upon the earth. For her sins have reached unto heaven, and God hath remembered her iniquities. Alas, alas that great city Babylon, that mighty city! for in one hour is thy judgment come." The tomb of this cunningly-devised system, which has devoured so many people and nations and tongues, shall be found in the lake of fire which burneth forever and ever. This is the second death. The name of this great apostasy shall be blotted out, or remembered only to be abhorred.

9th. Futukava came to see me, and afterwards Kavalolo, who used to be familiar with us in olden time. They say, that all the people in Tonga know very well that the *lotu* is true; but some few do not embrace Christianity, merely because they love a life of sin and folly. Our struggle at the Mua is not now with heathenism, but with the "man of sin," in the form of Popish superstition: and the issue is not doubtful; for Christ will defend his truth, and those who resist him he is able to cast down.

10th. We were engaged this morning in selecting a proper aspect for the new chapel and school-house, to be erected by the natives of Mua. Mr. Daniel and I were at a loss which way to turn amid this lovely grove of venerable and majestic trees. May God's house rise and prosper in this place!

11th. I went out this morning, to gather from the *capsicum* bushes, which abound here, a supply of cayenne pepper, with the intention of trying whether it would serve as a substitute for common pepper, of which one of the mission families is quite destitute. On my way I met with a large lobster; they are somewhat numerous on the coasts of this island. The lobster was intended for our use, the man who found it being a teacher among us. The cayenne having been secured in sufficient quantity, I went among these natural groves, whose balmy odor and fragrant perfume, added to their overawing grandeur, afford the passenger so much delight on his journey. I was in search of a lofty nutmeg-tree, which used to stand in this locality: I did not happen to light upon it, but found a large orange-tree, loaded with fruit, which the natives say was planted by my own hands. I ate thereof, "and the fruit was good." But if the juicy orange afforded me gratification, after the lapse of so many years, how much greater will be the joy of beholding redeemed souls, who have found their way to their Saviour through our instrumentality, and, after having brought forth much fruit; by his grace, have entered into the joy of their Lord! With a faltering voice, and a full heart, may one then utter the language of the apostle: "For what is our hope, or joy, or crown of rejoicing? Are not ye in the presence of our Lord Jesus Christ at his coming?"

I preached this afternoon (Wednesday) in the chapel; and, with Mr. Daniel, met the local preachers, in all about forty; every one of whom had on a shirt at least, and some few had long coats, or flannel shirts *outside* the other. I was surprised at the solemn attention which was paid to the word of God, and hope that some of the seed will be found to have fallen on good ground, and bear fruit that shall remain.

Preaching the gospel in the great congregation is *one* way of reaching this people. But neither the heathens nor the Papists will come to our worship; and therefore the missionary must preach the word *from house to house*, that by all means he may save some. Mr. Daniel's zeal is very commendable in this particular, and he possesses that quality of a Christian bishop named by the apostle, "apt to teach."

12*th*. It is of importance that our missionaries and their wives should leave home with some knowledge of almost everything that has to be done in the common affairs of life. Moving about, as I am obliged to do, from place to place and family to family, I hear much about the best way to get through the world. Our brethren mind the great business of saving souls, and building up the Church of Christ; but still, they *must* help themselves, or go without the necessaries of life. One hears his wife say, "Our children have not a shoe that they can wear; those sent are too small." "Well, my dear," says the husband, "*you* will have to contrive something, for my hands are quite full." The wife went to work, and produced a pair of shoes, such as they were, and all was well. Another reported that the baking-dishes were all broken: "What can be done now?" "The best you can," was the reply of the busy man, and off he went to his pursuits; but the wife, not at all discouraged, got a sheet of tin-casing from an old box; found a block of wood, larger than a brick; hammered the sheet of tin round the block, leaving the top open, and there was a tin baking-dish! not indeed such as nobles have, but such as are to be had in Tonga.

The men should know how to use tools, and should have various tools to use. The house requires a floor of wood; the books want a case that will preserve them from devouring insects; the iron pot (just come out) has a small hole in the side, and must have a little solder; for the native who purchased it has brought it back, and now it must be thrown away, or mended. The men can saw the timber, but they cannot sharpen the saw—it must be done for them. Two chief women are waiting outside for a ball of cotton, a couple of needles, and some instruction how to cut

MISSIONARY RESIDENCE AT NUKUALOFA.

out the sleeve of a pinafore. Julius asks the way to make a bed, secretly hoping that you will make it for him. The king wants glass for his windows, and who shall put it in? One has a cough, another a curved spine; one has bad eyes, and another a sore throat. Many are the ails and aches of this people, and they only expect you to cure them all!

As our object is not only to evangelize, but also to civilize, our people, every encouragement is given to the poor natives in their attempts to imitate us in all reasonable matters; but who does not perceive that a large demand is thereby made upon the time and patience, as well as upon the knowledge and industry, of the mission family? They must know something about almost everything; how to work in wood, iron, leather, calico, and medicine, and in twenty other things: and all must see how very desirable it is that previous instruction should be given in all such matters before the parties leave home, and that the material to work with should be furnished as part of their outfit.

CHAPTER V.

13*th*. NUKUALOFA.—Seven of the Haabai and Vavau double canoes sailed to-day, and were met by a north-east wind and driven back. All the old hands, and the careful observers of wind and weather in the tropics, say, that of late years the established course of nature has been much changed. The trade-winds have altered their direction, and very little certainty attaches to the strength of the winds, or the point whence they shall come, as in former times. Captain Buck is quite of this opinion, after many years' experience and observation in the South Seas. The winds do not steadily and uniformly blow from the south-east and east as aforetime. Whether this opinion will be confirmed by subsequent observations or not, I am clearly convinced that sometimes there is a pretty large degree of *cold* in the tropics; for, on Tuesday last, when I was at Mua, and the south wind blew high, so great was the degree of cold that we were obliged to have a fire in the room, where there was no chimney, but the fire was in an iron vessel, and the smoke found its way out through the thatch of the house. One evening the wind was so high that we feared to have any fire, and *then* I sat and read with my hat and boat-cloak on, and could but just bear the fanning breeze, as it passed through the slender, hollow, and airy mission house. But in twenty-four hours, the wind shifting to the north, and the rain coming down, the thermometer rose from 58° to 87°, and the atmosphere was quite oppressive. Allowances, however, must be made for those who have been for some time in the torrid zone.

Mr. Amos informs me, that King George has placed his son under his (Mr. Amos's) care, and he is to sit at his table, learn English, (if possible, which I do not think it is,) and in all respects to be subjected to the discipline of the school. George is a fine boy about six years of age, full of energy and life. His reigning father is, in my opinion, decidedly the first man of his race, especially for thoughtful propriety of conduct, and for dignity and energy of character. The king is also deeply pious, and on Sunday last he occupied the pulpit here, greatly to the delight and edification of the crowded congregation. After the sermon, he called upon one from a distant isle to engage in prayer. This man prayed so delightfully and affectingly, that many inquired who and whence he was; while some thought that the king knew his praying men better than many sovereigns in Europe, some of whom would have a better knowledge of the most popular opera singers.

The French have sent some of the sons of the Tahitian chiefs to be educated in France; their fathers stipulating that their sons shall be brought up Protestants. Whoever lives, will see how far this has been done. But George says, " My son shall be trained up in Christian knowledge, and shall go no farther off than this school of Mr. Amos, or, at most, not farther than the school for the preachers' children, and the children of our friends, in New-Zealand." It is impossible to say what may issue from this resolution of King George to give his son a Christian education. This son, being the only one, is morally sure of one day ruling the Friendly Islands. It may be due to ourselves to say, that we have done our best to convince King George of the paramount importance of such a step as he has now taken.

I measured the following persons, and found their height to be as follows:—King George, six feet four inches; Joseph Tonga, a teacher, six feet four inches; Samson Latu, local preacher and teacher, six feet five and a half inches.

Joseph Tonga is the king's right-hand man in time of war, and has slain a great many men; he is now, however, a man of peace.

The "John Wesley" is returned from the out-islands, and reports that Mr. Webb was unable to land at Niua-tobu-tabu, by reason of the violent wind and high sea, but all was rather cheering there. The people were recovering after the famine, which had been occasioned by a hurricane. At Niua-fo-ou all seemed very prosperous. Mr. Webb has baptized ninety-five persons, and found twelve hundred and twelve persons on the island, the whole of whom are praying people. Three new teachers are left there; but, if possible, so large a number of praying people should be shepherded by a missionary. At Uvea, they are still at war; and the Popish party, being the most numerous, and headed by their bishops and priests, will no doubt destroy our praying people, unless God should in his mercy interpose for them!

We have been trying our hand at designing and forming a national flag for the king, which he may hoist on all proper occasions, and thus assert his national character. It has occurred to us, that a fit emblem of the past history of Tonga might be a club and a bow and arrow, showing the warlike character of its people: for its present Christian state, we select the emblem of a dove with an olive branch: and for the natural state of Tonga, and the bounty of Divine Providence, we fix upon the cocoa-nut-tree, as affording so many and various articles, for meat, and drink, and building, and furniture. But devising state flags has formed no part of our early experience; nor should we meddle with it now, only that the king has learned from the captain of the "Meander" that he ought to hoist his flag, and then ships of war would salute the same. The king has come to us and said, "I will fix the flag-staff in the ground, and you will please to prepare the flag."

14*th*. The Sabbath-day was very cheering: overflowing congregations, and the most solemn devotional attention. At their prayer-meetings there went up a very great cry from earnest people to their God and Saviour.

15*th*. We are now preparing to leave Tonga for Feejee, having nearly finished our work in the Friendly Islands. If I never see them again, I shall pass to my final account with the deep and settled conviction that we have succeeded here, by God's favor, in establishing a new and evangelical order of things; that the wicked man has forsaken his way, and the unrighteous man his thoughts; and that the new order of things now in full operation, such as preaching the gospel, translating the Holy Scriptures, and educating the people, will result in their gradual elevation from the lowest grade of barbarism to the comforts and security of civilized life; and that their present happy condition is owing to their having received the gospel of the blessed God, preached to them by the Wesleyan missionaries. These devoted men are now in full work, and cordially united among themselves, of one heart, and of one judgment, efficiently laboring together in the Lord's vineyard with bright prospects before them. May I sit down with them and the Tonga people at the marriage-supper on the great day!

16*th*. We attended the funeral of William Feejeeoi, son of the late king, aged about twenty years. He was a fine young man, and had joined Mr. Amos's school, where he was making rapid progress. His death was rather sudden, and was brought on by his former profligacy: but he had changed his way of life, begun to meet in class, and died calling upon the Saviour for mercy. His funeral was attended by the king and all the great chiefs of the land. I should think that a thousand persons were present while the service was being read. The whole scene contrasted strongly with the first funeral which I witnessed here twenty-eight years ago. At that time, the multitude that attended was great; they cried aloud, and cut themselves from head to foot, till the stream of blood that flowed from their wounds was incredible. But *now* all was silent weeping. The body, wrapt in fine mats, was placed in the vault made of cut stone, with a stone for a cover, and all buried in sand. The bereaved mother held by the corpse till the last; but when it was removed by the chiefs who officiated on the occasion, she did not make any noise, but sat on the earth and silently wept. What power short of a *felt Christianity* could produce such a change in the funeral rites of a nation in the lapse of eight-and-twenty years? The difference is to be attributed to the bringing in of a better hope. The Scriptures have shed a light over the valley of the shadow of death; and the light of truth and love, finding its way into the soul of man, exalts, subdues and refines it.

The following letters are from our young people in the Nukualofa school. I proposed that they should write to me, that I might be able to show their handwriting. This was quite new to them, and they went behind the pillars of the school-room, and peeped round to see if I was looking at them. In a few minutes one got up, then another, and soon all were on their feet with the writing, which, to our utter astonishment, was the same in every instance:—

"O Mr. Lawry, we thank you for coming to see us, and to help in the work of the Lord."

As this was not the thing which I desired, because it did not draw them out sufficiently, I proposed to each a subject on which to write; and this drew from them the following interesting remarks, translated by Mr. Amos:—

QUESTION. *What are the things you wish to inquire about?*

ANSWER. This writing is to make known and discourse upon the meaning of the things that I wish to ask about.

The thing that I attend to is, I wish to know for a certainty what is the way of the working of the Lord, [in the heart, I suppose.] In these last days, I hear the sermons, and begin to find the value of the gospel of Christ, and I want you to show me what I am to do that my spirit may escape and live.

Many are my thanks that I have grown up in this gospel age. I am BOADICEA NIUFOOU.

(Aged thirteen years.)

QUESTION. *What are the evils to which young girls are exposed in Tonga?*

ANSWER. The things from which evil springs in the assembling together of girls is their foolish conversation; their speaking evil of each other; their differing with each other; their lying conversation; their sitting together and defaming the character of others; slandering girls, women, men, teachers, gentlemen, and chiefs. This is their evil thing.

Then if girls get together, and one thinks in her mind an evil thing, they are all of one mind directly to do that evil thing. If one desires to lie, they all begin to tell lies to each other. If one has a mind to pilfer or steal, all become thieves with her. Thus it was in former times. And now, if one who is not a thief goes to keep company with one who steals, she begins to thieve at once, and they join in one to go about and rob. Girls here are in this way, that if one thinks a lie, the others go and report it as true, and much lying arises therefrom. It is therefore not good for girls to gad about, or group together; but it is right for them to stay at home with their own parents and do their proper work; to seek in the Sacred Book; to repent and believe in His [Christ's] death; to love him, and turn to do his will. I am CHRISTIANA FINAU.

(Aged fourteen years.)

QUESTION. *What do you know about the fall and redemption of man?*

ANSWER. O Mr. Lawry, I will discourse a little to you concerning what I know of this matter. The world fell through the sin of the first man [and woman,] by their disobedience to God in eating of the fruit of the tree of which God commanded them not to eat.

Thus sprang the fall of man, from life to the death of sin. But, through the death of Jesus, these last generations of men [meaning, since the gospel came to Tonga] have escaped from death to life; and, in these latter days, I verily, verily give thanks that I know Jesus died to be my Redeemer. I write this writing with fear; because I touch His (Christ's) work with polluted hands, and with hands that are not clean. I am

ANN FANUA.
(Aged fourteen years.)

QUESTION. *What do you learn in this school?*

ANSWER. O Mr. Lawry, I write to you to make known the works we do in this school. These—read the Sacred Book, spell, learn catechism, learn to write, repeat our geography, and read the maps, repeat the arithmetical tables, and cipher, read English books: these are some of the things we learn here in the school with Mr. Amos; and I am trying that I may receive this work fully. But I cannot do so of myself, nor can any man give it me; I must be taught by the Lord alone.

O Mr. Lawry, I also write to you to make known my love to all school-children in all lands. I am

RACHEL HIFO.
(Aged fourteen years.)

QUESTION. *Why did you leave the heathens and become a Christian?*

ANSWER. This is to make known the things which I hated in the doings of my people while I was yet a heathen. These—burning their bodies with fire, cursing, bruising their faces and breaking their heads with their fists and clubs, killing each other; and many other different things which the heathen people did.

This is to make known the spring of my becoming religious. I heard the conversation of the *lotu* [Christian] people, who said that heathenism was bad; but I said, "The *lotu* [that is, Christianity] is a lie." I then heard of the weightiness and solemnity of religion, and I was then verily greatly afraid of God; but, when I found [or knew] religion, I was assured that the worship of God was indeed true. I am

MARY ATU-HA-I-HAKAU.
(Aged fifteen years.)

QUESTION. *What was the former condition of Tonga as compared with its present happy state?*

ANSWER. O Mr. Lawry, the way in which the chiefs and people acted formerly in Tonga, was to have night-dances and obscene games, and filthy songs; to make war, and murder each other, and stir up divisions and tumults. This sprang from their ignorance and darkened minds. They also worshiped false gods. Great was the pain and sorrow inflicted upon the people by their chiefs. They used to give the female children of their people to be prostituted by old men and strangers, and went about to destroy and carry off the property of the common people.

But, after a long time, the missionaries came with the gospel to this Tonga; and the chiefs became Christians at once, and some of the people. Then, after a while, there was a great turning to religion of many people; and in these present days good is growing in Tonga; for Britannia has sent us many missionaries to preach, and great benefits are springing therefrom. Another good is, the coming of Mr. Amos to instruct the people, that they may be wise.

I am JOHN MOHULAMU.
(Assistant teacher, aged seventeen.)

The QUESTION proposed was, *Why do you wish to go to England?*

The following is the ANSWER. The meaning of my desire to go to Britannia is, that I wish to get wisdom. This is the root of it. If you say that there is learning here, I answer, It is true; but I know for certain in my mind that I shall not be wise quickly here, on account of our Tonga habits. It is, therefore, my mind to go, and be separated from Tonga fashion, that I may seek alone the work of the Lord.

I know that instruction is difficult to be obtained, and that great is the price of it in your country; but I trust to you. I wish to be useful in the Lord's work; and I am greatly and verily anxious about that which appears to my mind; so that I hate Tonga fashion, and I wish to seek the right way—that which is becoming the gospel of Christ.

That is why I desire to go; for, if I stay, it will be long before I lose my Tonga habits. This is my mind. Mr. Lawry, have mercy upon me, and let me go. Mr. Lawry, I earnestly supplicate that you and I go together! I am

METHUSELAH FIFITA.

(Assistant teacher, aged seventeen.)

QUESTION. *What benefits have you received from the gospel?*

ANSWER. In the time of the gospel I have seen new things, and have received riches in these latter days of my life. One thing is, the missionaries, who teach and warn and direct me in the path which leads to life. Another thing is, that Christ has redeemed me from my enemy, Satan, that I might receive forgiveness of sins through his blood. One more thing I have received, which is a hope of eternal life, if I overcome these [earthly] things. Another thing is, that I have unceasing rejoicing; for I know that my father and friends are gone to heaven through this religion. [She is the daughter of Shadrach Veehala, whose Memoir is published in the Wesleyan Methodist Magazine for 1840.] Thus is the testimony of Paul's writing true, who says, "Joy springs from religion." ["Rejoice evermore," &c.] These are the things I have received; but "I stretch out toward the things which are yet invisible." ["I press toward the mark," &c.] Mr. Lawry, I give thanks, and again I repeat my thanks, that you have come to Tonga to assist the work [of God.] O that your visit may be useful! May the gospel fly to the residue of the places that are yet heathen! I am

Susannah Veehala.

(Assistant teacher, aged twenty-two years.)

Question. *What have you to thank God for?*

Answer. O Mr. Lawry, that for which I give thanks to the Lord is, that, while I was yet little, I felt religion, and desired to be religious, and I embraced religion. I soon became wise to read the Book; and from that I learned what was good and what was evil. I then wished to meet in class at once, and did so. I grew up to be large about the time of Mr. Tucker; and I am thankful that I knew that missionary. I learned from them both temporal and spiritual wisdom. At that time I got married, and knew well the love of God in me. I well-nigh became a backslider in the time of Mr. Thomas; but my first-born was taken from me, and then my mother died after, which led me again to find forgiveness of sins. This was just as Mr. Amos came here; and many were my thanksgivings when I knew that he was a man come to teach us; and that I was called to the work of the Lord at this time, I am giving thanks. I am

AMELIA MONGA.
(Assistant teacher, aged twenty-five.)

I have also received from the king a letter, which I shall place among these papers; and one from Shadrach, whom Tubou, before his inauguration to the throne, proposed to be king instead of himself. Shadrach is now the supreme judge of Tonga, an eloquent preacher, and probably the most learned man in the king's dominions. I have also received a letter from Jone Soakai, whose father I knew well: his name was Oheela, a man of good sense, who, from my first landing, showed an acute mind, favorable to the *lotu.* He was wrecked near Feejee, and swam in the ocean, with a shark attacking him, three days and nights; and from this deliverance, he told me, he was sure that the great God cared for him. His son, John Soakai, is a lad about seventeen years old, and an assistant teacher in our institution at Nukualofa.

KING GEORGE'S LETTER.

NUKUALOFA, *July* 16*th*, 1850.

O MR. LAWRY,—I write to you to make known my mind concerning the things you were inquiring about.

The good which I have received through the Christian religion is, that I know the truth of the gospel, and its preciousness and value to my soul. I have received the forgiveness of my sins, and am justified by the blood of Christ. God has adopted me as his son, and made my soul anew. I have a hope beyond death, because of Christ.

The benefits of this religion to Tonga are, that it has brought peace to our land. Its present settled and happy condition we all attribute to religion's influence. All the chiefs and people acknowledge this. This *lotu* leaves every one in his proper sphere. A chief is a chief still. A gentleman is a gentleman still. A common person is a common person still. So it was not formerly, [on account of rebellion and conspiracy.] `Our former state was only evil. Our land was verily bad; very different from the blessedness and goodness of these days.

I am very, very pleased in my mind with Mr. Amos's institution; and my will is that these schools of Mr. Amos's teaching shall ever abide in this land, and be handed down for [the benefit of] our seed after us. I *fakamonua* ["move the gift to my forehead, in token of reverent thanksgiving"] the love of Britannia to me and my kingdom, inasmuch as they have given up their children to bring the glad tidings to the Tonga Islands.

I wish that many copies of the Sacred Book may be printed in England, that they may be brought for our people to read; by which they will know the truth of this religion, and be preserved from the Popish religion, which prowls about to scatter the people who are ignorant of the Scriptures. I desire that these missionaries may remain perpetually in this land. This is my will. If there should ever happen a time when the Lord would remove the missionaries from the Friendly Isles, it would be a painful dispensation to us.

O that the Lord would at once grant that long may be your life, Mr. Lawry! that you may again come to this land! for beneficial is your visit: and if there is anything which we would wish repeated, it is your visit. I am

George Tubou.

SHADRACH'S LETTER.

Nukualofa, *July 15th*, 1850.

O Mr. Lawry,—The first thing I make known to you is, that I know assuredly the value and benefit of religion to my soul, to my family, and to the people of my country. We know that we were originally heathens, serving idols, and subject to the influence of devils. We were encompassed by sorrow, and misery, and death, and thick darkness, and blindness of mind. But suddenly the missionaries appeared with the word of God, and we heard their voice discoursing upon the words of life: and the Spirit worked with their words to enlighten and instruct; and the word was like the sun in the firmament; so that day appeared in our hearts, which were darkness before. Then I gazed at it, as I do on the meridian splendor, with my mind; and I found out that of a surety my heart was the den and cave of evil; that I was certainly myself a sinner, an enemy of God, hanging by a slender thread over everlasting damnation, through the wrath of Jehovah. And I was in consternation and terror, and I trembled; and then, like the man in the prison at Philippi, I said thus: "How shall I be saved from the curse of my sins? for they are very great." We soon found, by the guidance of God's word, and the direction of the missionaries, the path that a sinner may tread that he may find salvation. And we went in that path to Jehovah, through repentance and faith in Jesus, and found in it, through that Jesus, the forgiveness of our sins and the graces of the spiritual life; namely, peace with God, the hope of glory, and of that assembly which shall never break up, where we shall join the foremost ranks among the hosts of heaven. But who can tell the extent of the benefit we have known and received in our hearts through the love of God? I know the tested value of this religion; for it has brought us out of darkness into light, from folly to wisdom, from bondage to liberty, from the devil to Jesus, from death to life, from hell and eternal pain to glory in heaven and unceasing pleasures. The inheritance we lost is restored in Jesus. The core of all goodness I have found in religion, and that is the love of God. This love was possessed by the apostles, and is enjoyed by the fathers of our Church in Britannia; therefore the gospel reached this land, and we are saved by it. The love we have received [from him] begets love in us to His Majesty and his people, and also pity for the heathen and for all sinners. My soul, give thou thanks to Jesus for his great love, through which I and my friends live!

2. Another thing is, that I know that my friends who have died in the faith of Jesus are gone to heaven, and are enjoying ever-increasing blessedness in the presence of the Lord. I expect to meet them again, and rejoice together with them, and join the

song of the redeemed in Jesus. I know of a surety it will be so, from the testimony of some who died holy in the name of the Lord, and who said, "We rejoice in anticipation of our death; for the Lord is with us; and we hope that the pain and warfare of this life are nearly at an end on earth, and that we shall enter at once into eternal life." I certainly know that it is ordained, fixed to be thus, in the word of God. Thus saith Paul, "I am in a strait betwixt two, having a desire to depart, and to be with Christ; which is far better," Phil. i, 23: and it is settled that we shall rejoice together, that we shall see each other, and know and be known. We have this hope from the Holy Scriptures, from the testimony of our departed friends; and the Spirit beareth witness in our minds that this is a righteous hope.

3. Another thing is, My mind possesses in it love to the gospel. The root of my love to it is my knowledge of it as the *word of God;* thus saith my family also. The gospel is our father, our mother, and our beloved friend; for it has brought to us news of rejoicing [" glad tidings of great joy," &c.] of a Redeemer, who is Jesus, that we might escape from the horrible destruction of spiritual death. And is it not the work of parents to tell their children how they may live? and that is what the gospel has done for us. It is true that this redemption was made known to Adam, and the patriarchs, and the prophets; but what era in the patriarchal or Jewish economies was equal to the era of the gospel? O its brightness! its light! How clear, lucid, cloudless, and unspotted! How it shines! The gospel is a cloudless sun! In it we find comprehended the doctrines of Jesus, the

works he performed, and what he suffered. There fell upon him the guilty load of our sins, that we might be delivered from them. Yes, the gospel is our true friend. It forewarns us of approaching danger, and reveals the hidden mystery of our future destiny to us,—the things that will effect our ruin, that we may forsake them; and it tells us the way to act uprightly, that we may live thereby. It is therefore exceedingly proper and becoming, that the people on earth should receive the gospel, and search in it, and act according to it: for it directs us in the path which leadeth unto life eternal. ["This is a faithful saying," &c.] Who would not love the gospel? He who loves not the gospel chooses death. And who wishes to meet death so awful? We wish to have the gospel and those who explain it: for it is inestimable riches to our souls.

4. Another thing is, My mind concerning Tonga. I think it will become good and great after the manner of civilization. I do not expect it suddenly in the present generation; for we are the remnants of heathen people. The utmost of the good they will obtain will be religion to save their souls. But civilization, fashion, and different kinds of knowledge, I see even some approaching toward them at this time; but dark are the minds of many. I expect that civilization will grow, if the mind of the king is disposed to it as well as his people. Their minds are a little enlightened on the subject, and will lead them to try and go before the people, and draw them on towards it. But do not startle them at once; rather give them a few bits of civilization, and persevere in the doing of that, training their minds as a bent twig,

until they are accustomed to it; then proceed a step higher, and introduce a few other things, leading their minds on in it, acting upon one plan, and letting one thing succeed another; and thus proceed forwards, setting right the mind at first until it is erect, and then all things will be easy perhaps.

But that from which my mind expects the most is, the instruction given in the Native Training Institution. [Shadrach has attended for two years.] If we teach the youths, and young girls, and children, when they become wise and know the things which are good and worthy of man to do, who will then turn again to look at ignorance with pleasure and joy? Who will turn from wisdom to folly? Who, having found good, will come back and embrace evil? That can never be!

This is the way of my thoughts concerning Tonga, that it will ultimately receive the habits of civilization, and adopt them. I believe my thoughts: for is not this the way of all the world? One man becomes wise quickly, but the masses are slow to learn. Men do not march all abreast toward wisdom. One people is soon civilized by circumstances; but another people proceeds softly thitherward, and finally arrives at civilization. Thus, then, is my mind, that though Tonga is a difficult case, yet it is not incurable, but will be civilized eventually.

5. Another thing is, We verily give thanks to your fathers in the ministry in Britannia, and to the Church there, for the great love of God, which they possess, from which has sprung their great love to heathen people, who were consciously, and without a *Deliverer*, hastening to the misery awaiting this fallen

world. We see the evidences of their love in the united efforts of rich and poor, male and female, old and young, who give their time, their property, their life, and their *children*, to carry the gospel to the ends of the earth. And the gospel has thus come to Tonga, and I and many people are saved. Who, then, will not rejoice, and give thanks to our fathers in the ministry in Britannia, and to our missionaries here? Where is the sick man who would not give thanks to and remunerate the physician, who freely offered him a medicine that he knew would be efficacious in curing his disease? Who would turn aside his head, unwilling to drink it? Would the physician not urge him to drink it, because he knew it would save the man? and if his stomach cast off the salutary draught, would he not apply it again till the man was recovered? And then, how would not the patient rejoice, and offer abundant thanksgivings! Well, apply this to us Tonga people.

We had a deep-seated, spiritual malady: it was about the region of the heart, and affected our spiritual vitality to that degree that we had well-nigh died the second death. But skillful physicians came, —I mean the missionaries from Britannia,—and they brought with them a remedy for our disease of soul,— I mean the gospel of Jesus. They knew that, if we drank the medicine, we should recover of our sickness. They exhibited the remedy, and we drank in the healing words [" the balmy sound drinks in," &c.] and lived. Who, then, among us does not give thanks? Who will not assist this good work that is being done? We verily offer our great thanks to our fathers in England for their love, and desire to do what we can in supporting this salvation-work. You have sent us your missionaries, and they are successful, for multitudes are saved.

6. Another thing is, The Training Institution established in Nukualofa. I say thus, that it will become the greatest, and rank the first, among good works. Great is the benefit of it. It seems to be the cause of the increase, strength, and stability of our good work here. It invests our cause in these islands with an honorable character. It spreads its shadow over our mission, and is highly important. It shakes the minds of the people [from their slumber]. It is marching onwards ; for, ever since the commencement of the Institution, it is as though the minds of the people were brought nearer [to religion]. They are made to know that wisdom is good ; and, ever since, the minds of the people are moved to this good thing. We think if this Institution be established permanently in Tonga, great indeed will be the good results. Have love to us, and let the thing continue its blessings to our people.

7. Another thing is, We have an earnest desire and ardent wish that you would be quick in bringing to us great stores of the Holy Scriptures from Britannia ; for our mind is that our land may be filled with the word of God, that it may teach us and guide our souls into the way of life. Mr. Lawry, have love to us, and bring quantities of the Scriptures, that Tonga may be full of the word of God. We desire that every one may have a portion of the Sacred Book throughout the Islands. We shall not then trust to fables, but shall know from it the true religion. What, if the Scriptures and the missionaries be few ?

O Mr. Lawry and our fathers in Great Britain, we earnestly supplicate, *Have love to us!* HAVE LOVE TO US!! Send us the New Testament, that it may cause us to grow and be established in religion, that it may correct our ways, that we may walk straight in the path of endless life. We love the Holy Book; for it is our riches, our light, and our teacher; therefore, love us, and send us many books. Numbers have embraced the Christian religion here through reading the word of God; and should each one of the people get a copy of the Scriptures, it would then be impossible for them to turn to Popery, and the work of the Papists would be labor in vain.

8. Another thing is, O Mr. Lawry! I verily give you thanks for your love in coming to visit us, to put right our work, and guide us in some matters. It is becoming of you: for you are appointed an overseer, [bishop,] and many have been your years in this world: you are accustomed to voyage, and are wise in different things, and know various instrumentalities by which good will grow, and evil be retarded. We have painful love [deep sympathy] toward you, for we see you to be a man in years; but we behold your great love to us in Jesus's name. We see you enduring cold, and heat, and wet, and rain, and wind, and waves, and disturbed sleep in the night through the rocking and trembling of the ship, in the midst of the sea, upon the great depths:—and all this to come to see us; it is your love and desire to see us correct and walking in the gospel ways. Well done! Our utmost, utmost love to you, Mr. Lawry, our beloved father in the gospel!

9. Another thing is, I will tell you my mind con-

cerning the [Catholic] priests. My thoughts and opinion of them are what my mind says, and that is, that they are the priests of the devil, and no better. Their minds are as deceitful as the surface of the ocean, which seems smooth and level to the eye; but if one steps on it, he sinks engulfed in the depths below. Theirs is a lying humility, and their words are like oil, which cause fools and dark-minded persons to suppose all is right, and thus many sink into the depths [of their hypocrisy]. Then we exclaim, *Alas! assassination!* [of the soul] *alas for the victims!* O that the Lord would do something to prevent the coming of these leaders astray of souls! these curses to our people! these curses to our land! My mind concerning them is, that they are deceitful men, enemies of the holy religion, and of everything that is holy. I think that they are more sinful in the sight of God, than our heathen neighbors.

10. Another thing is, The work of the Popish religion in the world, and their manner of worship, which they call the worship of God, forsooth, is exactly like our former heathen vanities. It is wholly like our devil-worship. This is not a secret, but the thing is known. Behold their error! They do not put faith in the Bible, nor do they act according to the word of God, or teach it to their people. Nor do they direct their people to seek the pardon of their sins from Jesus Christ; but they tell the sinner to go to the priest, and he forgives them their sins. They also trust to Jesuses made of metal! and worship [the Virgin] Mary and the departed saints. When I see them bow to images and worship dead saints, I say to myself, "Is this the worship of God?"

No; but it is heathenism, and no more! The things which God has forbidden to be worshiped, they serve. The root of their cause is lying and deceit. I say, then, that those who support devilism and sin are the soldiers of Satan, visible to all the world, and are the enemies of Jesus, and [of the best interests] of all the people. I do not speak slanderously of them; but we know that such is the way of their doings. If a king decree laws for his people, and any of his people cast away his laws and not obey them, are they not the king's enemies? Thus does Popery! Jehovah has set up his laws for the world to obey, and are not those laws in the Bible—that same Book which Popery has discarded and falsified? Why have they set at naught God's word, and exalted the word of man above it? Do they suppose every man true, and God a liar? Is God more foolish than the wisdom of men? They may call it the religion of God; but it is evidently the religion of heathenism and of the devil.

11. Another thing is, That in the Popish religion, when it comes to a land, that land is thrown into commotion. The reason is, perhaps, that they come with a bad name. It is true that disorder and disturbance comes otherwise into the world: but it generally arises from something temporal, visible, as evil-doing; or about property, or land, or man disagreeing with man; but the confusion that springs from Popery is that which affects the welfare of the soul. I know, when they first came to Tonga, they began to stir up the people to hate the true religion; and said that our New Testament was not true, thereby giving the lie to the word of God. They have also tried to

frighten us with lies, by telling of men-of-war that would come and make war upon us. There spring from their operations divisions, and tumults, and wars, as at Uvea, where they have made war upon and beaten the people who do as the word of God directs, desiring to kill the true religion out of the land and out of the hearts of men. Popery is an enemy to all spiritual religion. Bad fruit grows upon Popery; and it is not surprising, for a bad tree bears bad fruit. [" An evil tree," &c.]

We say now, that it [Popery] is the hinderance of spirituality of religion, and the abettor of "spiritual wickedness in high places;" and it goes prowling over the face of the earth. But we strongly think that their work will not dive deep [take deep root:] for thus saith Jesus, "Every plant which my heavenly Father hath not planted, shall be rooted up." May the Lord ordain something to destroy this monster evil!

I conclude with this word, My love to you, indeed, Mr. Lawry. I am SHADRACH MUMUI.

JOHN SOAKAI'S LETTER ON KING GEORGE'S GOVERNMENT.

NUKUALOFA, *July* 15*th*, 1850.

O MR. LAWRY,—I thank the Lord indeed that you have come to visit the work of the Lord, and the missionaries, and us the brethren in Tonga.

King George is the king of Tonga,—and this is a discourse upon the policy of his government.

In the era that he first became king of this nation, he began at once to rule in wisdom and love to his people. This wisdom and love to the people were visible in his assembling all the governors, and saying thus to them, "My mind is that war shall be illegal, forbidden; that is, that it shall cease as long as I live; that the land shall have peace; that no one shall create disturbance, or beget war. Let us swear to each other that the land shall not see evil, but be at peace!" *This was the origin of peace in this land.*

Again: He governs powerfully on behalf of religion. This is seen in his preaching the word of God to his subjects, in preventing anarchy and confusion, in succoring the villages which have received the gospel, and in sending his subjects as spiritual helpers [teachers] to other nations, as Feejee and Samoa. *This is the origin of the good state of the churches in Tonga.*

Again: He has appointed judges in the land to judge the evil-doers and wicked, and to prevent insurrection in the kingdom. *This is the origin of the orderly and settled state of things.* The chiefs, missionaries, and people also, have great peace through this.

Again: He governs in loving humility, after Christian fashion. *This is the origin of the chiefs' and people's love to him.* They are meek towards him, and wish him long life.

Again: If he know a governor who does wrong to the people, he removes him from his office, and appoints another in his stead. *This is the origin of the revival of religion in that place;* and greatly is the people's comfort augmented by this removal of bad governors.

Again: He governs with great prudence towards

the heathens; hence they love him. *This is the origin of their doing many things which he commands to be done.* I am JOHN SOAKAI.

(Assistant teacher.)

This evening I have had a host of chiefs at the mission-house, from the king downward,—Tungi, Atta, Tuivakano, Abraham, Junia, John Faubula, and who not? There is in these men a shrewdness, a cordiality, and energy, mixed with Christian simplicity and kindness, that renders it impossible not to blend with them in Christian affection and sympathy. They are certainly a loveable class of fellow-travelers to a bright immŏrtality.

17*th.* We are all busy to-day in preparing for our voyage to Feejee: the brethren finishing their letters, the captain filling up his water-casks, and Methuselah taking his yams, mats, and native cloth on board. Joel also is shipping his whales' teeth and other riches, as presents from the king to the Feejee chiefs. Joel is charged with the important message that all the Tonga people are to come away from Feejee, where they have been misbehaving, or the king will cast them off and let them be governed by the man-eating chiefs of Feejee. At the king's request, we take this ambassador and his people with us, not expecting to be above two or three days on the voyage, and Joel being one of our best friends, and a local preacher at Habai.

FEEJEE ISLANDS.

CHAPTER VI.

July 20th, 1850. We came to an anchor at Oneata, Feejee, having passed the Island of Ongea at noon, and seen a vessel on the reef without masts, but no one was on board: and though we were very near, the surge on the reef did not allow of our landing to ascertain the name and state of the wreck.

21*st.* Sabbath. We lay at anchor all day in a gale of wind, within the outer reef, but two miles from the island of Oneata. No communications with the shore, partly in consequence of the wind and sea being so high.

I preached in the morning from, "Where sin hath abounded, grace did much more abound;" a refreshing season to all present. In the evening I spoke closely to the conscience, "I beseech you, brethren, suffer the word of exhortation." How truly grateful are the ordinances of the Lord! "My words, they are spirit, and they are life."

Joel preached, in his native tongue, to the natives on board, who behaved with admirable consistency in all things; so much so, that not one of our seamen would hear a whisper against these natives. So much homage does the dignifying principle of Christianity command from its observers!

The Feejee natives ashore do not stir to-day: it is the sacred day, and all men are commanded to rest and to keep the Sabbath of the Lord. Alas! when shall we see the ordinances of the Lord honored and observed in the civilized world? Not until the religion of Christ has taken a firmer hold upon the intelligence, the hearts, and the consciences of the population, great and small, high and low.

The French priests are reported to me as preaching to these people, that their country is the land for *sports*, and these, they say, are performed on the Sabbath day! Such teaching in any country may have the sanction of law, and may be the established religion; but it cannot save souls, nor have the approval of Christ, nor the sanction of his Holy Book. Alas! why have we so few men among this people, where the word of the Lord has free course, runs, and is glorified? Richard Baxter's ambition was to be in such a place as Feejee, turning a nation "from darkness to light, and from the power of Satan to God." Here is full scope for all the energies of mind and body. A missionary has simply to plunge into pagan superstitions and cruelties, and there cry out, "Arise, shine; for thy light is come!" The heathen will hear with amazement, and many will turn unto the Lord. Their teacher is not met by *exclusives*, whose main object is to save the people from his influence; but as to the great salvation, when did they acquaint themselves therewith? Here the ground is clear, and the people wait for God's law.

There is here no struggle about the decrees of the Most High; but it is taken for truth, that he willeth all men to be saved. Neither is there heard, throughout these many isles, the voice of apostolical-succession men, forbidding to speak in the name of Jesus: our missionaries have spoken, and do speak, and will continue to speak in this name; and multitudes believe and are saved. A Popish priest here and there mutters his protest; but, unheeding, the men of God go on in their great work, unfettered, without any of those obstacles which ancient laws and semi-Popish customs place in their way. Onward they go, preaching "Christ crucified" to the barbarians, who find this "gospel to be the power of God unto salvation," and they exult in this grace wherein they stand, and "rejoice in hope of the glory of God." No doubt the enemy will sow his tares; but when the truth of God, as recorded in the Holy Scriptures, has taken firm hold of the intellect and feelings of a people,

"The enemy his tares may sow,
But Christ shall shortly root them up."

Surely never was there a clearer opening for gospel ministers to open their commission and make full proof of their ministry, than that which now presents itself among the pagans of these seas. Here are multitudes of immortal minds already prepared by the providence of God, and the wolves from Rome are hovering about. There are no remains of Popery, as in England, to meet the man of God at every turn, to bind him in some cases, and to frustrate his aims in others. There are no Romanizing teachers here with a moral malaria issuing from their mouth, and poisoning many, diverting them from the simple truths of the Bible, to the mystics follies of the school-men, and the superstitious noddings of our Papal fathers, and especially of such men as Laud. In these merely pagan islands, we are freed from home superstitions, and, with the Bible in our hands, and God's grace in our hearts, we hold up the pure light of truth, and the blind receive their sight; we exhibit the love of Christ, and the dry bones in the valley shake, stand upright, and, by the Holy Spirit's influence, become an army of living men! Here they are, in the Friendly Isles and in Feejee, numbered by hundreds and by thousands; but where in Europe can we find such a field for a Christian minister to exercise his talents and his graces? And yet there are young ministers at home who earnestly cling to their own home, and refuse the honor, the scope, and the open doors of usefulness presented to them in the mission-fields. Surely such young men are neither in the succession of the apostles, nor of the venerable and ever-moving John Wesley. They seem to forget, and do not see "another angel fly in the midst of heaven, having the everlasting gospel to preach unto them that dwell on the earth, and to every nation, and kindred, and tongue, and people."

The commission of the Christian minister runs thus: "Go ye therefore, and teach all nations, baptizing them in the name of the Father, and of the Son, and of the Holy Ghost: teaching them to observe all things whatsoever I have commanded you: and lo, I am with you alway, even unto the end of the world." There is no special exemption: if we are needed abroad, abroad we must go, or disobey the Lord and Master. I cannot see what *right* any man has to say, "I enter the Christian ministry under the express stipulation not to go abroad." Whence did he derive his commission? Surely not from the Lord Jesus Christ.

Nor are these young ministers rightly informed on

the subject of their strong aversion against going far from home. A pretty intimate acquaintance with several districts in the South Seas enables me to draw comparisons; and men happier and more perfectly content than our missionaries abroad, I have never known in any place or country. As for myself, it would be transportation in the penal sense, for me to be obliged to leave the mission work, and live in the smoke and contamination of the more densely populated parts of England. The only objects worthy of being aimed at are, first, to secure the great salvation for one's self; and, secondly, to sow good seed, and cultivate well the field which the Lord hath assigned to us, doing our utmost every day to make an impression in favor of Christ and his religion—saving souls from death, and training them for God and his eternal kingdom: and this great work, I think, may in general be best performed in our mission stations. As to *home*, "what is our life? it is even a vapor that appeareth a little time, and then vanisheth away." If we stay at home, will our friends live always? Is our living at home essential to happiness? By no means. Living *as* God would have us, and *where* he would have us, is our business and interest: so thought the prophets and apostles, and so our fathers thought and acted. Is not every man upon earth just as safe and happy as God makes him, and not otherwise? And cannot God both keep and bless us when we are doing his will and his work assigned to us? Does he not say, "Lo, I am with you alway?"

Where is our faith in Christ, whose care of us will be equal to our needs, as complete and regular as the solar system, of which he is the Maker and Ruler, whose tender mercy abideth forever? And hath he not said, "Verily I say unto you, that ye which have followed me in the regeneration, when the Son of man shall sit on the throne of his glory, ye also shall sit upon twelve thrones, judging the twelve tribes of Israel?" "And every one that hath forsaken houses, or brethren, or sisters, or father, or mother, or wife, or children, or lands, for my name's sake, shall receive a hundred fold, and shall inherit everlasting life." Therefore let every one that believeth these words not be frightened, nor be much discouraged because of the way: Christ our way is gone before us. And our Lord's promise is fully sustained and experimentally proved by some, if not by all, whom I have known: They who have forsaken all, shall receive a hundred fold, beside the rich and bright hereafter. I very much question if there be a class of men anywhere, whose portion and enjoyments, taken all for all, excel and overtop those of Christian missionaries. In these islands we converse often upon this topic; and all agree that they are happy, having no time to be gloomy; always busy, doing a great work, working for a good Master, and in a good cause; surrounded with the bounties of nature, and many a cheerful scene, and interesting event; seeing new sights, hearing new things, breathing fresh air; and, above all, observing the springing field which the Lord hath blessed; witnessing the effect of the gospel on the pagan convert, and especially in his dying hour, when the opening heavens around him shine. For our children God provides, and for ourselves there is enough and to spare, while we walk uprightly. So that I should be very sorry to see any man or woman in our foreign stations who did not feel a deep and settled conviction that they were honored and exalted by their appointment, and that the best return they could make would be a more complete consecration of all their energies to the Saviour, that at the close of life they might hear him say, "Well done, good and faithful servant." And who among the servants of our Lord and Master would object to live such a life, and die such a triumphant death?

22*d*. We went ashore to-day in a high sea and a high wind; but the poor people of Oneata were afraid of us at first, lest we might prove to be some of their own chiefs either from Lakemba or Bau, come to demand all their little food and property. This at present is their system—for all property to belong to their chiefs; but Christianity will one day correct this sad abuse of authority.

23*d*. We weighed anchor and sailed for Lakemba. So poor a place I have never visited as Oneata appears to be. The island is a mere speck, and by no means rich, having only very few people on it, and they are greatly dispirited by the harsh rule of foreign chiefs. A couple of Tahitian teachers once lived at Oneata.

24*th*. We landed at Lakemba, and found the Rev. R. B. Lyth, Mrs. Lyth, and their children, with Mr. and Mrs. Malvern and their children, all well, and sitting on the beach waiting our arrival as we rolled in among the breakers in the ship's whale-boat. Most cordial was our meeting, and the natives crowded round us, as if their desire to *see* could never be satisfied. The flies and musquitoes also seemed glad to see us, for we were covered all over with them, and not a few of them let me *feel* that they were there.

I was surprised to see the very marked improvement in the dress and general appearance of the people, as well as of the neighborhood around.

25th. The high wind drove our brig to sea; and unhappily there is no anchorage at this island, which makes it very trying for the master and crew of the "John Wesley."

On our passage hither we passed the island of Ongea, where we saw a fine vessel wrecked upon the reef; and on our arrival here we found that her name was the "Lady Howden," just come from California, where the state of things is extremely bad, according to the account given by Mr. Plunkett, a passenger. They left San Francisco on the 7th of April, 1850; and, at three o'clock in the morning of the 22d of May, struck on the weather reef of Ongea. The man at the wheel cried out, "Breakers ahead;" the helm was at once put "hard a-lee," when her keel slightly touched the ground, the wind blowing fresh from the N.E. The command was given to "brace the yards;" but, before the men could obey, the vessel struck heavily upon the reef, carrying away the rudder, and dislocating the shoulder of the helmsman. All command of the vessel was now lost: she rolled about among the merciless waves, until the white foam lifted her upon its crest, and placed her high upon the reef, with a crash that brought terror to every heart. "We now," says Mr. Plunkett, "looked at each other in mute despair; a momentary silence reigned unbroken, save by the roar of the breakers and the dismal sighing of the wind. The sea making continued breaches over her, and threatening to sweep the decks fore and aft, the crew, after a brief consultation, destroyed all the spirits on board, and then took to the boats. They knew they were in Feejee, and dreaded the jaws of the cannibals among whom they were wrecked, but there was no choice; so they pulled towards shore, from which they were distant about seven miles. After crossing other reefs, and getting nearly filled, they approached so near the shore as to enable them to see the natives. They approached," says Mr. Plunkett, "and made signs; but we could not understand them. For a while we lay on our oars, for the purpose of discussing how we should act: some were for seeking a passage out to sea, and shaping their course for the Isle of Pines, nine hundred miles distant: others were for urging our way through the reefs towards the shore; I was of this number, for I preferred the *natives* to the *billows;* and in this, at last, all concurred. We hoisted our ensign and gave it a cheer; upon which the natives launched a canoe and came off, giving us a hearty *shake hands.* We were astonished; and having landed, the moon shone forth and the bay was tranquil. We once more trod the green-sward, and my heart beat quick. Being met by several natives, they conducted us to a hut, where an ample supper of yams and cocoanuts was provided. Before retiring, they had prayers in their native language; and, as they sang their evening hymn, I felt a calm devotion, to which, I regret to say, I had long been a stranger. I need not say I was agreeably surprised to find, that, instead of being among cannibals, I was in the midst of devout Wesleyans. O what gratitude I felt towards those brave soldiers of the cross, who came into these distant lands to teach the will of God to this benighted people! Well and faithfully have they labored, and we derive the benefit of those labors. No longer were the diabolical orgies of the heathen priests tolerated. The wail of victims no longer fell upon the ear; the solitude was undisturbed by sounds of midnight massacre. All here was peace, piety, and religion!"

In a few days the party reached the house of the Rev. Messrs. Lyth and Malvern, where they received that kind treatment which will not soon be forgotten by these shipwrecked voyagers. The "Bramble" from Sydney came in, and all hands escaped in her. The wreck was sold by auction, and bought by Lieutenant Pollard, who presented the same to the mission; but whether anything will become available from this sad shipwreck remains to be seen.

Mr. Plunkett is very loud in his praise of our missionaries, although he was, I believe, brought up in the Roman Catholic religion in Ireland. I understand he is an attorney at Sydney. The master's name was Chalk; and some parties on board say, that much blame attaches to him, as it was moonlight, and full time was afforded to discover the reef and keep clear of it; and, moreover, that he had ample notice thereof. The wrecked vessel on the reef of Ongea is distant from Lakemba about fifty miles.

When I was at Hihifo in the Island of Tonga, there was a great stir about so many of those people going away to Feejee, where they generally act as the English in Paris—cast off restraint and live as they list. A canoe just then starting had very few persons on board but Papists and pagans; our good people having been generally restrained by their pastor, Mr. West. It was, however, agreed that two local preachers should go in the canoe, one of them called Samuel and the other Levi. The canoe started; but soon met with bad weather and a contrary wind, the sea being greatly agitated, and the people sadly perplexed. One advised this, and another that, when one of the local preachers said, "My mind is this,—You see how the elements are against us, and are we not set one against another? Here is a Papist and there a heathen: what can be done better than for us all to become one, by falling down and embracing the one religion—namely, that of God's book?" To this all agreed, and immediately fell down and made prayer, which the two good men conducted with earnestness and propriety; and, to their astonishment, while they were at prayer, the clouds broke away, the wind sprang up fair, and all went on cheeringly with this canoe. They did not, however, depart from their solemn compact; but, having done their work here in Feejee, in a very few days, have sailed again for Tonga, so anxious were they to tell the news of their wonderful preservation through prayer, and the conversion of all the Papists and pagans as the consequence! To a people so little informed as yet, it may be expected that God will sometimes show his favor by outward and temporal blessings. So it was especially in the early days of the Jews, whose conquests in the land of Canaan were viewed both by themselves and by their enemies as so many interpositions from the Almighty. I should further remark, that when this canoe hastened away from Feejee, with glad hearts on board, to tell the glad tidings, she was accompanied by another, chiefly of the Popish party, and especially the chief of the canoe; but the latter canoe is returned through bad weather and contrary winds, while the other is gone on her way.

26th. I paid a visit to the king of Lakemba, who has embraced Christianity since I was last here. His religion, however, is only in word, and not in power, so far. He is by far the heaviest man I have seen, being more than six feet high, wide shoulders, stout limbs, and is withal most astonishingly *fat.* At present he only attends the public worship, and bows the knee to Jesus; but does not put away his many wives: "for," says he, "I cannot afford to do so; these women are the main source of my wealth." The priest tells him, if he will join them, he may keep his wives; but our brethren tell him, that his many wives are not at all necessary on account of wealth; and as they are not sanctioned by Christ, he must give them up, or die the second death. The priests ply their crafty arts; and the gospel has to make its way, in the case of this king, and in a multitude of other cases, in opposition to heathen darkness and prejudice on the one hand, and against Papal indulgence, the indulgence of any and every sin, on the other. What a scourge and curse to man, and what an insult to Christ, is Popery! And what an offense to the Lord and Master must it be, for Protestant England to vote her money to train and multiply the priests, who, if they can, will subjugate all power to themselves! Dominion over the human mind is the object of the priest; and the extinction of the light, by closing the word of God, is the grand means of effecting their object. But who can tell how many *ends* the providence of God may be at this moment accomplishing by the "man of sin?" Perhaps Popery may, without intending it, act upon us as a spur to education and to the wide-spread circulation of the Holy Scriptures. These are now our duties in Tonga and Feejee, and second only to preaching the gospel.

I was struck, when leaving the shores of Tonga, off Nukualofa, with the superlative beauty of the small fishes, about two inches long, playing about the coral reefs. King George was standing on his canoe, observing our embarkation, and bidding us farewell; the coral itself was glowing in various forms and colors; but these lovely little fishes were slowly gliding from one coral-tree to another, some of a dark-blue, others of a greenish-blue, some red, and others orange color; but all these colors were of the most dazzling brilliancy. The same scene on about the same scale was observed yesterday at our reef off this island, (Lakemba,) with the addition of two very large turtles floating in the blue deep sea, at a small distance from the reef.

27th. There is peril to navigation, but still there is beauty, in these coral walls, built almost perpendicularly at a small distance from an island. Take, for instance, the harbor of Ongea: one side is the island, and, supposing its form to be that of the half-moon, the reef strikes off in a circular form from one of the horns, and sweeps round a distance of more than twenty miles, joining the other horn; leaving a tranquil sheet of water within, about twenty fathoms deep, where a frigate might go through the evolutions of a cruise. Upon the reef or breakwater the roll of the ocean breaks with a fearful roar, and showing its milk-white crest, as a strikingly-interesting object to those who are safe within, and a warning not to approach too near to those who are navigating the open ocean. It is probable that lamelliform coral is generally based upon the rocks beneath, and seldom so deep as twenty fathoms, as the coral-building zöophytes are not found efficient at a greater depth.

No doubt there are several causes at work throughout this vast coralline sea, producing their corresponding alterations in the reefs and islands of the ocean. The action of fire in the form of pulsive and oscillating earthquakes, leads to upheavings at one time, and subsidence at another. But to aqueous, probably more than to igneous, causes may be attributed the singular formation, through the vital agency of the coral-building *polypi* in these intertropical seas.

Some of the reefs in Feejee extend fifty miles at least, besides the fringing or detached reefs less or more plentifully scattered up and down among the islands, and beyond them. In New Caledonia there is a reef extending at least one hundred and fifty miles, and almost unbroken the whole distance. Flinders says, the Great Barrier Reef to the N. E. of Australia extends nearly a thousand miles in length, and from thirty to seventy miles from the shore. "There is," says Darwin, "a simplicity in the barrier-like beach, the margin of green bushes and tall cocoa-nuts, the solid flat of coral rock, strewed here and there with great fragments, and the line of furious breakers, all rounding away towards either hand. The ocean throwing its waters over the broad reef appears an invincible, all-powerful enemy; yet we see it resisted and even conquered by means which, at first, seem most weak and inefficient."

It is not that the ocean spares the rock of coral; the great fragments scattered over the reefs, and accumulated on the beach, where the tall cocoa-nut springs, plainly bespeak the unrelenting power of the waves. Nor are there any periods of repose granted. The long swell caused by the trade-wind, blowing so long in one direction over a wide area, never ceases to rage. It is impossible to behold these waves without feeling a conviction that an island, though built of the hardest rock, let it be porphyry, granite, or quartz, would ultimately yield and be demolished by such irresistible forces. Yet these low, insignificant islets stand and are victorious; for here another power as antagonist to the former takes part in the contest. The organic forces separate the atoms of carbonate of lime one by one from the foaming breakers, and unite them into a symmetrical structure. Let the hurricane tear up its thousand huge fragments; yet what will this tell against the accumulated labor of myriads of architects at work night and day, month after month? Thus do we see the soft gelatinous body of a polypus, through the agency of the vital laws, conquering the great mechanical power of the waves of the ocean, which neither the art of man, nor the inanimate works of nature, could successfully resist.

28*th*, Sunday. The early service commenced with the rising sun, and the public preaching at nine o'clock. After the first hymn had been sung, the people fell on their knees, and uttered such piercing cries as I have not often heard; the voice of the minister could scarcely be heard for some time. The crowd of serious worshipers was very great; and many a dark

GRAVE OF REV. W. CROSS, SOMOSOMO, BESIDE A HEATHEN TEMPLE.

Feejeean face was lighted up with the joy that at once subdues and cheers the inmost soul of the true Christian man. Tuinayau, the king of Lakemba, was present. He is now a *lotu* man, and has family prayer; but, so far, his Christianity is little more than nominal. However, as faith cometh by hearing, and Christ is pleased to see a man waiting for him, though it be only by the highway side, we may hope to see, in the case of this king, first the blade, then the ear, and then the full corn in the ear; fruit brought forth unto perfection. The Tonga people residing here used to be, in many instances, mere scape-grace people; but the case is very different now. They are generally an orderly and respectable class, fearing God, and walking uprightly.

Joel is come from Tonga, as an officer of the government, to say, that those who wish to go back and be the subjects of King George, must at once arise and go; and the rest will be no longer acknowledged by George, but will, in future, be subject only to the chiefs of Feejee. This stroke of policy, on the part of the king of Tonga, will greatly assist our missions, by preventing men of a rambling turn from breaking away from under all authority, both in the state and in the Church of Christ.

Mr. Lyth informs me of a war which raged between Somosomo and Natawa a few months since. Tuihilahila, the king of Somosomo, invited his antagonists, who were foolish enough to leave their fort and meet him in open field, where several of them fell down slain in battle, and about forty of them were roasted and eaten; but the principal chief was taken alive, killed, and roasted. He had been the intimate friend of Tuihilahila aforetime; and, when the baked body was set before him, the king soliloquized over his victim thus: "Thou hast been my brother: had I fallen into thy hands, should I not have been eaten forthwith? And dost thou think of an escape? No, verily." This said, Tuihilahila proceeded to feed upon the heart, the tongue, and the liver of his victim.

The entire population of the fine district of Natawa is now either destroyed or scattered; so none remain to cultivate the soil. The gospel, which is the great peace-maker, as well as the great civilizer, has been rejected at Somosomo.

29th. Looking down this morning in front of Mr. Lyth's house, I observed a crowd of boys busily at work near the chapel, preparatory to a forthcoming school-examination, for which they are making all kinds of preparation; and, among the rest, clearing and putting in order their play-ground. I asked Methuselah if he thought the Tonga boys could be induced to work so willingly and briskly. He shook his head in token of his doubt.

To civilize a barbarous people, they must, necessarily, be instructed. There are two ways of doing this,—colonization and missions. A colony of polished adventurers will generally, if not always, swamp a race of barbarians. This seems to have been the case with the aboriginal Greeks, under the denominations of Pelasgi, Aones, Hyantes, Leleges, &c., who were savages, dwelling in caverns, and eating human flesh. The Titans colonized Attica; and, no doubt, the weaker natives were subdued by them: the refined and copious language of Greece is most likely not the language spoken by the savage, but by the more polished invaders from the east. Ignorance is almost sure to fade away in the presence of wisdom and the arts of civilization, but the gospel seems to be the great and most rapid civilizer of barbarous men. It throws a class of new principles into the mind; teaching truth to the liar, cleanliness to the filthy, purity to the unclean, and industry to the idle. And God's law is written in the heart; a power is also imparted that men may do his commandments. The slave is set free by the New Testament, and oppression is melted down, till the tyrant himself becomes no longer an oppressor, but learns to love his neighbor as himself.

As the gospel corrects the morals of any people, so it awakens a thirst for knowledge and improvement. The people want better houses, better canoes, better clothes; they also want books; and all these new wants must lead to new and increased efforts to obtain what they desire: they cease to lie down all the day long, and, by increased labor, their wants are met and their character improved.

With an increase of knowledge will grow up better laws and government; as is the case in Tonga, and will be the case here, where the people are much more under the power of fear, and the grinding tyranny of their chiefs, than they are in the Friendly Islands.

It is truly gratifying to witness the difference which has taken place, since I was here three years ago, in the clothing of this people. *Then* all was offensive and disgusting; men and women of all classes going about in a state only just removed from nudity, and the sons and daughters of great chiefs absolutely naked, and ashamed to meet any one in the pathway, as they well might be! *Now* all is changed; and all persons, from the king downwards, have a good piece of native cloth wrapped round their waist, or a piece of calico. Yesterday I witnessed the crowds of natives passing to and from the chapel; but not one exception did I see: all were clothed sufficiently for their taste and circumstances in nice, clean, and generally *white* garments. Their singing, too, is greatly improved; some of our tunes were sung very sweetly, but not, of course, so powerfully as in Tonga. Perhaps Divine Providence may overrule the coming here, from time to time, of the Tonga people to build canoes. The Tonga men are far the best carpenters, and the greater voyagers; but in Feejee only is found good timber for ship-building. Many irregularities and sins have come out of these visits; but I hope to see the day when the evil shall be avoided, the good retained.

In Tonga, when the wind blows from the south, and the weather is cold, the chiefs spread a banana-leaf on their floor, and kindle a small fire. But, for the purpose of obtaining light, they generally burn a piece of wood, that gives out a clear flame; and, in the king's dwelling, I have seen cocoa-nut oil burning in a cocoa-nut shell laid on the floor, and the king contriving to read by its low and inconvenient light.

It was no better in Homer's time among the Greeks. The palaces of princes were lighted by odoriferous wood; they likewise used torches of pine and resinous wood. In Feejee, as well as in Tonga, they usually burn the dead fibre of the fruit-stem of the cocoa-nut.

The Greek had his olive oil, and these islanders have the cocoa-nut oil; but neither cared much for its use, as a light-giving medium, till civilization had considerably advanced.

The double canoe of these islands resembles the ancient vessels of Athens and Sparta about the time of the Trojan war: in both cases they had no keel, one mast only, carried about eighty or a hundred men each, and were uniformly drawn ashore when the vessel was in port. In both cases, also, the ships of Bœotia, and those of the South Seas, lowered their masts upon deck at the close of the voyage. And who shall say that these fine people, with their Christian Scriptures and their Christian schools, may not, at an early period, outstrip the classic nations in the knowledge which only is worth having, and which may be possessed by any man whose life is a vapor, but whose abiding home is with his fathers, the prophets and apostles; Jesus Christ himself being his exceeding great reward? George Tubou, of Tonga, being a wise, powerful, and Christian king, will, we may confidently hope, give a mighty impulse, by wise government and Christian example, to the upward progress of the people who feel his influence.

There are few things connected with the steady and rapid propagation of the gospel among these islands, of more importance than the appointment of native teachers—truly regenerated men, who are able to teach others in the things which they themselves have learned from the Holy Scriptures, as explained by the missionaries, and sealed home upon their hearts and consciences by the Holy Spirit.

These useful agents generally know much more of

the science of saving truth than the people of their charge; and they know well the way of their own people,—their modes of thinking, their exposure to error, their weak points, and the best way to propose to them the gospel of Christ. They are usually faithful shepherds over the flock committed to their care; and the Romish emissary, who may come after they have taken the oversight, will find them generally very difficult to deal with. They hold up their New Testament, and say, "Here is God's word. Is what you teach about the Virgin Mary here? Where is it? Your ways are from beneath, they are from *man;* but our way is from *God.* Shall I read you the proof?" By this time the poor fellow has more than he came for, and sheers off confounded by the word of God in the hands of a converted barbarian.

CHAPTER VII.

At Moala the people are awful cannibals, and full of all kinds of sin, corruption, and Satan. Two men, whose hearts God had touched, rose up in the love-feast and fully offered themselves as teachers willing to go to Moala. The offer being accepted, they set sail, but met with contrary winds, and hovered about, waiting for a change. The people of Moala saw them, and prepared to cut them off, of which the teachers knew nothing; but in the night the wind changed to the right direction, and in they went. When the morning light came, Paul and Philemon (for so they were called) were in the midst of the heathens, who, being unable to account for their being there, changed their minds, and concluded that their gods had sent them. This was their "entering in" at Moala, where we have now one chief and several of his people who *lotu*. It is true, the beginning is small, but the Day-spring has risen, and the Sun of righteousness will as surely appear in due time.

Mr. Malvern has been over to see them, and was quite a curiosity among the savages, who felt him, and told him he was handsome. At present there is a conflict on this island between truth and error; for

> Satan trembles at his loss,
> And hates the doctrine of the cross.

The Lakemba circuit has twenty-four islands within its circumference, on twenty-two of which we have native teachers, and some who *lotu*. Two islands are still heathen; but even these are crying out for teachers, and glad should we be to have it in our power to send some proper, well-qualified men to these openings, and trust that Divine Providence will send us a supply; "for the harvest truly is plenteous, but the laborers are few."

The case is the same at Tonga: every man has his hands full, and more would be employed if they could be found; this state of things is every way Scriptural, and shows the work to be of God. Let no one, how-ever, suppose that there is no danger in the case of Paul and Philemon: they are living on the graves of the slain; and every day brings threats from the heathen that they shall die next. But they refuse to move, telling the people they are not afraid to die in the cause of their Lord and Master; and if they please to kill them, the Lord must give them leave, and then their murderers will have to meet them before the judgment-seat of Christ: every word of which strikes terror into the poor defenseless pagan's heart. So far these eminently pious men are saved from the jaws of unbelievers; and the hope is, that God will honor them, and continue to preserve them.

Totoya is another fine island, where the gospel has been planted by a native teacher, sent there by the missionaries; one of whom, Mr. Malvern, has made a voyage of four hundred miles, and visited these out-stations. He tells me that Joel is deeply devoted to God: having been very clear in his own conversion, he sets the gospel scheme before his hearers in a striking light, and they hear him with the greatest respect and interest. During the last year, Joel has enrolled sixty persons as meeting in class, and eighty who attend the school, beside almost the whole population who hear the word of God from his mouth.

His own house, built by his own directions, is a pattern of neatness and good taste: while the chapel which the people have raised is the best in this group. Here is the result of a native agency properly superintended by good Mr. Lyth, and his zealous colleague; which demonstrates that God's hand is eminently with his servants. In twelve months, two hundred souls have *lotued*, chiefly through this teacher's instrumentality; and many of these are new creatures in Christ Jesus, and others are earnestly seeking this great salvation.

The island of Cicia, or Thethea, is another of those places full of the habitations of cruelty. Till the native teachers landed there, no white man dared to venture there; and one who accidentally drifted lately to this savage isle was murdered forthwith, and probably eaten. With the exception of one visit each from two of our missionaries, the natives only have sowed the seed, and planted this part of the Lord's vineyard; where we have a Church comprehending a hundred and twelve members, a school of seventy children, and about four hundred regular hearers. The entire population has embraced Christianity; and many of them walk in the light of the Lord, and in the comforts of the Holy Ghost. They have built themselves two good chapels; and being full of life and energy among themselves, they are also zealous for the spread of true religion.

The same process goes on in the interior and distant towns of the large islands; in the majority of cases the converted natives are our pioneers and forerunners in this great work of evangelizing the pagans of their own race, for which they possess many obvious advantages over the missionary, whose oversight, however, they constantly need, and mostly have.

Thus it pleaseth God to work: the missionary plants the tree of life; many are saved in the use of the ordinances of the Lord; the power of Christ rests upon them that believe, and they are willing to go anywhere, carrying with them this gospel of the blessed God. The cry of distant places, like that of Macedonia, is heard by the missionary; and he sends forth the agents whom the Lord hath prepared to his hand, and it happens to them, as to those who were scattered abroad throughout the regions of Judea and Samaria, who went everywhere preaching the word. Such was the order of God and Church order in those days. "Now they which were scattered abroad upon the persecution that arose about Stephen, traveled as far as Phenice, and Cyprus, and Antioch, preaching the word to none but unto the Jews only. And some of them were men of Cyprus and Cyrene, which when they were come to Antioch, spake unto the Grecians, preaching the Lord Jesus. And the hand of the Lord was with them: and a great number believed, and turned unto the Lord."

So the Scriptures teach; and so our Churches do, and have done from the beginning. But I know a colonial bishop, who found our system of local preachers grafted and interwoven into "the Church," and he strove to put it down; but the natives refused to be silenced, and his lordship must wait till they die off before "the Church" can be purged of this part of our Scriptural Methodism.

31*st*. The British Conference begins to-day: may wisdom, peace, and love be there; and may our brethren at home abound in prosperity, that these ends of the earth may be partakers of the benefit! A body of more holy, wise, impartial, or upright men I have never seen, nor expect to see, under the sun.

This morning I measured one of our local preachers, who is chaplain to the king; and he measures six feet five inches and a half, without shoes. He is a man of a fine spirit, and is called Jeremiah. He is of Tonga parents, but born in Feejee; where God has found work for him to do, nor does he withhold his servants' reward.

There is not much idle bread eaten in Feejee. Mr. Lyth has the sick to attend, besides his mission affairs. Mrs. Lyth has her family and the barter going on. Mr. Malvern has his native school and his mission work. Mrs. Malvern has the children of the two families every alternate week, and also her family engagements. There is no time to be dull in the mission work.

I attended the school here conducted by Mr. Malvern, and consisting of about one hundred children. At Tonga I saw the schools in an advanced state, while here we are only just beginning; but the beginning is very hopeful. There is great difference in the material we have to work with. In Tonga the children sit with all the sober dignity of judges on the bench: whereas the raw and lively children of Feejee, without discipline of any kind, just wild from the sea-shore and the bush, are like so many Merry-Andrews: and in the school, while Mr. Malvern was doing his best to hold their attention to the matter in hand, their restless activity and sportive nimbleness reminded me of an inclosure of monkeys in Regent's Park, one of which siezes another's ear, a third holding by the tail of the second monkey; one might safely defy stupor in such a situation. But wait a little, and order will arise out of disorder: and, for this rapid current in the native mind, the hand that educates has scooped a channel, and will guide the energies which now display the wild luxuriance of their native forests, until beauty and grandeur shall grace the scene. Christianity, and her handmaid, useful knowledge, will soon impart a new character to society.

The children learn with great rapidity, especially by heart. Even before they have learned to read they can repeat our catechism, or passages of Scripture, chapter after chapter, hymns, and figures. To teach them to read, will, of course, be one of the objects of their instruction; nor will they be slow to learn.

August 1st. I learned to-day, that, a short time ago, some females ate part of a fish that was *tabu* to all but chiefs, the fish being delicious food. A multitude of women were ordered to be judged by the old pagan priest who lived here at the time: a severe punishment was fully expected; and not only on those who had offended, but on the *lotu* women as well. The missionaries raised their voice against this cruel injustice being carried on under the sanction of the king. He was cunning enough to meet the exigency of the case, and sent for the two Popish priests, and our two missionaries, that one party might neutralize the other. They met in his presence, when he said very large things; and, among the rest, that he was the greatest sovereign in this world. "What!" said Mr. Malvern, "greater than Queen Victoria?" "Yes," said one of his courtiers, "we know, Tuinayau, that you are a great king, and these," pointing to the priests and missionaries, "these are your animals!" The missionaries and priests had but little altercation on this occasion; but our brethren laid heavily on the king, and did not entirely forget the priests. The result was, that the women escaped; and the king has been heard to say, that that was the beginning of his light and *lotu*.

Here, then, is a king so *wise* and so *humble* as to believe himself to be the greatest monarch upon earth, though unable to read a letter in the alphabet; and his imperial city may contain three hundred souls, and is surrounded by a ditch or moat surmounted by a fence of reeds! This great city of Tuinayau is abundantly interspersed with stagnant water and mud-pools, teeming with stinging insects and miasmata. It stands at the foot of high hills; and a small flat occupies the space between the village and the sea, on which trees and esculent roots are growing. But the high land is valueless, or nearly so. The royal palace is a large house without partition, door, or window; a large iron pot is seen hanging over a large fire, screened from a tropical sun by a roof of thatch. King Eglon feeds on the fat of the land when it has passed the process of the iron pot. I regret that his weight cannot be exactly ascertained; but we are, no doubt, within bounds when we judge this stout, tall, and fat prince at three hundred and twenty pounds. He has some twelve wives, who, in reality, are his kept slaves. When Kau, who is ambassador from Bau, was asked if this king was a cannibal, he replied, "I do not know; but the men whom I have eaten, others assisting, are in number forty-five." Kau is a praying and hopeful man; but he trembles at the review of his past life; his tall and bony frame seems, when he is speaking of his enormous sins, to be hair-hung over the bottomless pit; a tremulous quiver tells the tale of emotion within.

Tuinayau has embraced Christianity; and, if he sincerely and humbly seeks divine mercy, casting away all his sin, *he* will find the Saviour. His entire empire may extend over some eight or ten islands, and comprehend about three thousand souls. I set down the main outlines of this small ruler, for the purpose of showing that the circumstances of our missionaries here have been sufficiently trying. Nothing could sustain them for so many years but the hope of saving sinners from the error of their ways, of bringing many souls to glory, and hiding a multitude of sins. "Servants of God, well done!" and let all the glory be ascribed to the Divine Master.

Kau, the ambassador, has just brought me two arm-bones of the chiefs whom he ate on Viti Lavu, near Bau: their names he also gives,—THOLA-MANU-LAVU, and THOLA-NGEO-'MBO-EMBA. They were reputed mighty warriors, and fell in the open field by the club of Kau or his friends. The bones are the small bones from the wrist to the elbow.

Kau has begun to pray and weep before the Lord, and gives me these bones that others may see what a sinner he has been, and with the hope that many will pray for him, the chief sinner in Viti (Feejee). So he says and feels.

How rich are the provisions of that gospel by which such awful cannibals are recovered from their fall, and restored to the favor and image of the holy, blessed God! What a triumph has Christ won over sin, Satan, and fallen man in these islands of Feejee! Surely, "where sin abounded, grace did much more abound;" and "He *must reign* till he hath put all enemies under his feet."

Zephaniah is a good man living with Mr. Lyth; but, in former days, he was a great cannibal, and, though the Lord has forgiven him, he cannot forgive himself. I observe that at family-worship poor Zephaniah is pretty generally weeping and sobbing; and not unfrequently his emotions border on convulsions; and so it is with others in this land. They feel ashamed, amazed, and confounded at their depth of sin and wickedness; and who can wonder at this?

3*d*. My birthday, fifty-seven. How quickly is life ebbing away! My fathers are gone;

> "And I am to the margin come,
> And I expect to die."

I have done but little and suffered less in my Master's employment; boasting is indeed excluded. I might easily discourage myself, and thereby weaken my hands in the conflict; but let me rather cherish gratitude for all God's mercies to me during my past life, and resolve to live nearer to Christ for the future.

> "See there my Lord upon the tree;
> I hear, I feel, he died for me."

By God's mercy, I am in good health, and pursuing my proper work among these brethren and their devoted families. I write this in the house of my kind friends Mr. and Mrs. Lyth, at Lakemba, in Feejee, where we are all busy in God's work, sending to the sea-side clubs, mats, &c., for sale in London, to help the missions.

The cocoa-nut tree is one of the finest objects in nature. Its stem is tall and slender, without a branch; and at the top are seen from ten to two hundred cocoa-nuts, each as large as a man's head; over these are the graceful plumes, with their deep green gloss, and beautiful fronds of the nodding leaves. Nothing can exceed the graceful majesty of these inter-tropical fruit-trees, except the various useful purposes to which the tree, the leaf, and the nut, are applied by the natives.

1. The STEM is used for,—

Bridges, posts, beams, rafters, paling, ramparts, loop-holes, walking-sticks, water-butts, bags, (the upper cuticle,) sieves in use for arrow-root.

2. The COCOA-NUT is used for,—

Milk, a delicious drink; milk from the scraped nut, used for various kinds of food; jelly, *kora*, pulp, nut, oil, excellent and various food for man, beast, and fowl.

Shell.—Vessels to drink out of, water-pitchers, lamps, funnels, fuel, *panga* (for a game.)

Fibre.—Sinnet, various cordage, bed-stuffing, thread for combs, scrubbing-brushes, girdle, (ornamental,) whisk, (for flies,) medicines, various and useful.

3. The LEAF is used for,—

Thatch for houses, lining for houses, *takapau*, (mats,) baskets, (fancy and plain,) fans, *palalafa*, (for sham fights,) combs, (very various,) bedding, (white fibre,) *tafi*, (brooms,) *kubatse*, (used in printing,) *mama*, (candles,) screen for bed-room, waiter's tray.

Here are no less than forty-three uses of which we know something; and the natives know of others to which they can apply this single instance of the bounty of the God of nature. For house and clothes, for food and medicine, the cocoa-nut tree is their sheet-anchor, as well as their ornament and amusement, who dwell in the torrid zone. But there is another tree,—it is "the tree of life, which bare twelve manner of fruits, and yielded her fruit every month: and the leaves of the tree were for the healing of the nations." Sublime emblem of Christ the Restorer! the Fountain of all bliss and glory, ever present with his saints; containing in himself every bounty of every kind, and that forever and ever! "His people shall be all righteous;" "and there shall be no more curse."

Hail, exalted Lord, going forth from conquering to conquer! Thy enemies shall lick the dust, and gnaw their tongues with pain; for thou shalt turn the way of the wicked upside down. Thy servants who sowed the good seed are esteemed mean and feeble things of naught; but thou wilt say to such, "Blessed are they that do his commandments, that they may have right to the tree of life, and may enter in through the gates into the city."

4th, Sunday. The times of devotion were sunrise, nine o'clock, two o'clock, and six. The afternoon service was a love-feast, at which the attendance was good, and the people spoke freely; and almost in every case they declared that the grace of God had brought them salvation. They had passed through the pangs of repentance, and come to the conclusion, "We must go to Jesus, let us go at once;" and in the majority of cases the Lord had cut short the work in righteousness, and fulfilled his own word, "This is the day of salvation;" "He that believeth shall be saved." Generally it appeared, that the applicants laid down their burden at the Saviour's feet, and went away "full of peace and joy through believing."

Forty-eight persons spoke, and at the close of the service some were in distress, and others in raptures of joy. All fell down on their faces, and raised such a cry as made the valley ring again; but the weeping and crying out gently subsided, and the love-feast ended in subdued and reverential love.

My good brother Lyth has, at my request, made notes of what was said in the love-feast, and, since the above was written, has handed me the following brief account:—

LAKEMBA, *Sunday, August 4th,* 1850.—At the love-feast held in Bethel chapel, there were forty-eight persons who spoke of the goodness of God to their souls, amongst whom were a goodly number of girls belonging to the mission school. These have lately turned to the Lord, have sought and found peace with God through our Lord Jesus Christ, and are rejoicing in God their Saviour. Their testimony to-day was chiefly to this effect:—Most who spoke clearly testified, that, though once enemies, they are now reconciled to God through the death of his Son, and have been made partakers of the Holy Ghost. The following are some of the statements made:—

Jeremiah Kienga said, that the work of God has been made very clear to his mind; the eyes of his soul have been opened, and the love of God made clear to him, during the past year. He is now saved through the death of Christ. "If my life was to end just now, I should be with God."

David Palu:—"My original state was bad; but I can now rejoice in the cross of Christ, the source of life. I praise God who has made me his. I am in his presence, and desire to die in his service."

Matthias Waitaiki:—"I am a sinner. I *lotued* formerly to no purpose. I understood not what religion was; but, since my residence in another island, my mind has been enlightened. I formerly pursued sinful pleasures; but now the Lord strengthens me to do all things, and I wish to live and die in the work of the Lord."

Cornelius Musuka:—"I know that Christ died for my sins. I wish to follow his will, and end my life in his service. Before the missionaries came from Britain, we knew not—but now, through them, we know—the way of salvation."

Peter Koroi Randinimbau:—"I know I am a sinner. We are a people divided asunder: some are alive, some are in hell. We know the worth of Christ: he has called us from the grave and from hell. I am accepted of God through Jesus."

Manoah Tuu:—"I make known my joy not in my own wisdom, but in the Lord, because I know his great love. I was a wretched sinner; but the love of God was swift. I expected death, but now have life, trusting in Christ. My flesh suffers pain, but it warns me to prepare; and I am not afraid, but rejoice, having a ground for hope. I glory in the cross of Christ."

Kanakana:—"My heart rejoices in Christ. He has saved my soul. I trust in Christ for salvation, that I may escape."

Joel Mafileo, a Tongan chief:—"I see the work of the Lord. We thought the work of the Lord in Feejee was difficult; but I now see it. I first saw it in Oneata, and now I see it in Lakemba. I see the power of God; the people believe in the Lord. Feejee wants laborers. I give myself to the Lord to be my guide, that I may be where he pleases: this is my mind. I do not choose for myself. I see that God is at work in Feejee."

Adelaide Korosovou:—"I praise God this afternoon. Sweet to my heart is the word of the holy Spirit, his cry in my heart. I am at peace with God, through the blood of Christ. I trust not in myself, but in Christ."

Takelo:—"I have been a great sinner; but rejoice in the Lord, who has died for me; and I desire to work for him."

Loata Biu:—"Joy springs up in my soul every day, because of the life I have through Christ, by whom I am reconciled to God. None was bad like me, but I am now reconciled to God through Christ."

Moses Naulu:—"From my beginning I was a sinner. I rejoice that I have discovered this; at first I was a mere professor; but I heard a sermon on prayer, and then went into the bush to pray, and the Lord turned me. I desire to trust in Christ: in him only I can have life."

Nathaniel Koroi Vuki:—"I was a bad man: twice I came from M'Bau to persecute the Christians. But great is the love of God that has saved me. I was a mere professing Christian four years, I praise the Lord. I was a man-killer; but the Lord has turned me and loved me. It is right I should be sent to work for the Lord in some land, because of having been so great a sinner."

Zephaniah Kuawa:—"I would fain have salvation. I flee to Jesus. I cannot count my sins; but Jesus saves me."

Charlotte Lewamanu:—"I was a very bad woman; was enslaved by a white man, and committed many bad actions. But I have fled to Jesus, to him only. I am reconciled to God through Jesus, and trust in Jesus.

I pray night and day to God, and beseech him to do with me as he pleases."

Raingase (a female who stood weeping some moments):—"I was an enemy of God, but have lately found the mercy of God. I give myself to him to do as he will with me."

Caroline Lauji:—"I rejoice in the Lord and in the great things I see. I trust in Christ. I expected hell, but know he has done great things for me. Praise God, I have peace through Christ the Lord."

Mary Magdalene Veisei:—"I know that Christ died for me, and it is right that I should love him."

Paul M'Biu:—"I was ignorant of the love of God, but now know it. I was a great sinner, but now have life through the cross of Christ."

Adelaide Mafi, a Tongan class-leader:—"I make known not my goodness, but the Lord's love. I know the Lord works in my heart, and I rejoice on account of the kingdom of Jesus within. Great was my trouble; but I found peace and life in him. I do not wish to go to Tonga, but to do the Lord's work in Feejee."

Nathaniel Nainima:—"I delight in nothing else but the religion of Jesus Christ."

Grace Rawa:—"I do not stand up in my own strength: it is God who strengthens me. I thank God, because he has prevented the bad things in my heart. There is one thing that lies heavy on my mind: my children have gone to the Popish religion. I pray God to help me to do what I can to make them turn back."

Sivoki (a young lady chief):—"I praise Jesus, I

know his love. The Holy Spirit is with me. I praise Jesus."

Enea Sau:—"I know I am reconciled to God through Christ Jesus."

Josiah Langi:—"Religion is sweet. Formerly my ways were sinful; but sweet has been the word preached and the death of Jesus. I stand up to declare the power of God in my soul."

Enoch Wanka-ng-gele:—"I *lotued* some time ago, but *lotued* to no purpose. I then began to feel myself a sinner, and trembled on account of it. I then thought of my friends sitting in darkness, and prayed night and day that they might *lotu;* and now the good news has come, that a hundred of them have *lotued:* my heart is very glad because of this."

Mary Usavere:—"I do not stand up to tell of my bad doings, but to testify of the great love of God and the power of the Holy Ghost in me a sinner. The love of God is sweet to my soul. Wherever I go, Christ goes with me. If any one speaks evil of me, the Holy Ghost tells me not to listen. I am employed in the work of God; but I do not trust to that. I cleave only to Christ."

Daniel Havea, a Tongan local preacher:—"I praise Father, Son, and Holy Ghost. My soul rejoices on account of the work of Christ in the souls of the people. My soul looks to Jesus: I still work for him. Some of our friends are gone. My heart is warm. I could not sit without telling you how greatly I rejoice in the work of the Lord."

5th. We have received intelligence from a distant

island, that one hundred persons have taken the profession of Christianity. Goro is its name. Thakumbau was long since solicited to allow a native teacher to go there, but he refused. About twelve months ago he gave way; and, at the earnest request of many people there, a teacher was sent. Goro may contain some ten or twelve hundred people; of whom we hear that one hundred have cordially received Christianity, through the teaching principally of a native man who went there with Christ in his heart and the New Testament in his hand, proclaiming as he best could "the whole counsel of God." The result is, that a great many have cast away their idols and heathenish practices, submitting themselves to the doctrine and precepts of Christ. They will now want to read, and will search the Scriptures for themselves. This is the way in which God has chosen to work in the islands of Feejee.

6th. It appears that Batinamu, the principal heathen chief of Bua, where Mr. Williams lives, had formed a plan for taking Mrs. Williams to himself, murdering Mr. Williams, and sharing out their property among his people who were to assist him in this wicked plot. Up to this time he had been on friendly terms with our missionary. But the character of this murderous wretch is best seen in his *professed* and in his *real purpose.* His people were collected and the army in motion towards Mathuata, where he intended to cut off his enemy, Ritova; and then return, and cut in pieces our missionary and his people at Bua. On his march, however, he turned into a town, where he had a concubine, and tarried there while the people prepared him some food. It had happened, however, that his enemy had sent a whale's tooth to this very town, and hired them to kill Batinamu when a favorable opportunity should offer. That time was now come, and the chief, having eaten his food, prepared to go; but the barbarous people, who knew nothing of his design upon the mission family, rose and showed signs of hostility, and Batinamu, now seeing the trap into which he had fallen, begged for his life, and made large promises: but all was useless. They murdered him while he was trying to get over the fence. His body was cooked and eaten. Our friends knew not the extent of their danger till it was over.

How can any one scruple to acknowledge, that the finger of God was here? A train of providential interpositions like this may well command our admiration, and devout thanksgiving.

When our friends were unconscious of what was passing, the Eye that sleeps not, and the restraining Guardian Hand that guides all events, were there; and pity and love were saying, in tones of majesty, "Touch not mine anointed, and do my prophets no harm."

One of the persons who had eaten part of Batinamu, had traveled with some of his friends beyond Nandi, into the dominions of Tui-Wainunu; who learned from the man himself what he had done, and the king fell on him there and then; the man was killed and thirteen others, all of whom were eaten. But God had taken care of his servants; and as they were secure from danger, the chain was removed, and the lions were free.

7th. The teachers meet to-day. One has come thirty miles by sea; he has charge of three of the windward islands, where he oversees the teachers and their work. Being a clever carpenter, he has built a double canoe, and fearlessly navigates the great South Sea. Everything prospers under his hand: for he is a choice spirit, devoted to his work, and his name is Moses.

These honored men are chiefly supported by the people to whom they minister; but a trifle must be allowed them for books, cotton shirts, and a few other inexpensive articles.

The priests of the pope, on finding that one of their people has cast his brass chain and cross into the sea, have applied to the king to pay for the same; to which the king made this answer: "If the man found your religion to be false, and cast away your trinket as a lying, worthless thing, when he was in a storm at sea, what have I to do with it? Do not I also believe, that your *lotu* system of worship is a lie?" Such waspish, mean, and contemptible men as these poor French priests, I have not met with before at any time or place. By the natives they are held in derision as false and feeble in the extreme.

I am utterly ashamed to place on paper an account of their paltry, shuffling, and dishonorable conduct.

CHAPTER VIII.

LOVE-FEAST AT NASAUKALAU, HELD AUGUST 8TH, 1850, BY MR. MALVERN.

BARNABAS:—"Before I *lotued*, my great besetment was pride. All I cared about and attended to was, to think a great deal of myself, and to appear like a chief, although I was only a poor man. I went with my father to chop a drum out of a tree, that I might bring it to the town, and beat it, and make a great noise, and seem to be some great one. But I began to attend the *lotu*, and to think upon my ways: I then saw how foolish and bad my doings had been. I heard the report of the Saviour, of his coming from heaven to earth on our account. I heard of his wonderful doings, his death, and his rising again from the dead. I then said, Surely this is a strong God. I was led to seek religion, and I found it; and I now know that I am saved and happy. I know that I am reconciled to God through Christ."

Caleb:—"I came from Tonga to Feejee, but did not know what the *lotu* meant. I was a long time in Feejee in the dark, and did not know what the *lotu* meant, only I thought it a useless thing. When I heard Mr. Watsford preach, I then awoke out of my sleep; and just then the Holy Spirit entered into my mind. I then saw that my sins had been very great against God and very abominable. I thought about my sins, and pondered over their filthiness very much; and very much I was cast down. I was sick with pain in my mind. But when I heard of Christ my Saviour, my heart was warmed and encouraged. I heard in the preaching, that I was to go and pray earnestly to God through Christ; that I was to put my trust in him for salvation. I went and prayed, and found mercy. I know now that I am reconciled to God through Christ. I am very happy every day."

Naphtali said:—"When I was a heathen, my mind was very dark; I knew nothing of the *lotu;* nothing of the way to escape hell and get to heaven. I and my companions set sail on the Sunday for a neighboring island, but we had not gone far before one of our yards broke. We returned to the land, and went and made an offering, and set sail again; the *lotu* people advised us not to be obstinate against God and break his Sabbath. But I said, 'Let us go only.' Before long our canoe struck against a rock and was disabled, so that we were nearly lost. We were seen, by the people of a large canoe, rocking about in the sea, sinking, and no help; they came, picked us up, and brought us again to land. I then said to my companions, 'Perhaps the *lotu* is true:' and we at once resolved, and went, and embraced Christianity. I heard and paid much attention to the preaching. The darkness of my mind was taken away by the light of the gospel. I repented truly of my sins, and sought and obtained the Holy Spirit, in answer to earnest and persevering prayer, to tell me, in my mind, that I was reconciled to God for the sake of Jesus Christ. I know now that I am reconciled, and am very, very happy every day."

Josiah said:—"The *lotu* was a long time in Lakemba. I heard the report of it. The Holy Spirit told me, in my mind, that there was only one God, one of whose names was JEHOVAH, and another name was CHRIST JESUS. But I did not regard it; I did not believe it. I *lotued*, however; but not with any benefit until I heard Matthew (the native teacher) preach from, 'Awake thou that sleepest,' &c. The thought then came into my mind, 'What is the use of my *lotu* in this way?' When I was a heathen I thought that there was not anything that I did badly; but now I awoke, and saw and felt that my sins had been very many and great against God. My mind was very much pained on account of my sins. I then prayed and tried to get saved. I prayed very much in secret, in the name of Christ, and obtained the Holy Spirit to tell me in my heart that I was reconciled to God. I now know and feel every day that I am saved and happy."

Lavinia said:—"I went to Oneata; and one day, when we were reading our books together, God began to work powerfully upon our minds. The Holy Spirit fell upon us; and so strongly did he work there that our souls greatly trembled. I then repented truly of my sins. I know now what is meant by the atonement of Christ. I have trusted in him, and have found salvation. I know at this time that he saves me. I have no desire to follow my own mind in anything, nor do I deslre the things of the world. I give up my body and soul to be his only, unto the end of my life."

Isaac Kalou said:—"I was *lotu* before, but turned back to heathenism again. I *lotued* again, and thought then I was a saved man, merely on account of my embracing Christianity. But I went to hear the preaching, and heard, 'Except a man be born again,' &c. I went away from the house of God, and said, 'My mind is just now turned round by hearing this word. When I renounced heathenism and *lotued* only, I thought I was all right; but I just now know the meaning of what I have heard; and if I am not born again, I shall not enter into the kingdom of heaven.' Great fear then sprang up in my mind. My soul was so troubled and pained on account of my sins, that it was like the pain of a spear through my body. The working of the Holy Spirit was very great in me. I prayed very much in a secret place that I might obtain mercy, and my prayer was heard. I know now that Christ saves me."

Matthew (a teacher) said:—"There was a time when I knew nothing of the *lotu*, or of God. I was admitted with a friend into a love-feast by Mr. Webb; and while I was there, the power of the Holy Spirit came upon me, and upon my friend also. My mind was pained very greatly by sin. When I heard of Christ, my soul became hot within me. I then asked Mr. Webb what I must do, that I might be saved. He said, 'Go and pray in secret, and persevere in prayer to God through Christ, to have mercy upon you and save you.' And while I was doing this, peace sprang up in my heart, and I knew that I was reconciled through Christ; and I know now in my mind that he saves me. When I felt what Christ had done for me, I very much desired to do what I could to please him; and asked advice from the missionaries, who told me to follow the word of God, and not fail to go anywhere as soon as my way was opened by the Lord and his Church. I said, 'If it be right for me to go to a distant land, I wish to follow only what is right.' The missionary told me I must go to Feejee; and when I made up my mind to do so, the Holy Spirit filled me with peace and joy. I came to Feejee only to proclaim Christ and his salvation to the people here. This is all I came for; my mind is to do the will of Christ only. I give myself to him unto the end of my life."

August 8th. I kept a sharp look-out last night; not being certain, from the juxtaposition of the two planets, but Venus might obscure Jupiter's disk in their descent in the western sky. But it turned out, that, though Venus was not more than half of a degree, according to our line of vision, from the path of Jupiter as it passed on in its orbit, yet the distance was quite sufficient to deprive us of the hoped-for transit. These planets shine out with transcendent brilliance in the blue, clear sky of the tropics. The constellations in the southern hemisphere are very rich and beautiful, at all seasons of the year; but when Orion and his companions are also above our horizon, the scene is one of glory and magnificence. All these are named and numbered by Him "who hath appointed the ordinances of heaven."

Mr. Lyth has related to me the following fact:—

A chief at this place who had long lived in heathenism and was going to remove, became concerned about his soul, and desired our people, who were at the time in a very lively and good state, to meet at his house and pray for him, that he might be saved. They did so meet, and prayed for the old man; and while they were so engaged, they were thickly sprinkled with a shower of dry earth: this they attributed to the devil, who was unwilling to part with another of his slaves. They had no doubt of the diabolical agent in this matter; but still they informed Mr. Lyth of what was going on, who told them that he did not understand the cause of the earth being showered down upon them in the way stated, but that prayer was their only course. The messenger, having showed Mr. Lyth the small particles of earth upon his hair and clothes, returned to the house, and in true native style proclaimed that they were *to fight it out!* So they renewed their praying, and shortly the fall of earth upon the praying people ceased, and they were in no doubt but Satan was vanquished and had retired. Mr. Lyth says, there can be no doubt whatever of the shower of earth on the people in the house; there was none outside, and the earth went up by one of the posts. Those who bore testimony were unquestionable, and, in every sense, credible witnesses. The old chief, whose official name was Doulakemba, there and then became a *lotu* man, and soon after removed to the island of Mango, where he lately died, professing Christianity.

"The great day" will declare who were right,—*the natives*, who, to a man, affirm that they saw this earth flying about, and resting upon the praying people, and upon the old chief Doulakemba, and that there was no wind or other agent from without to produce this effect; for no person was present but the praying people: or *the minute philosophers*, who laugh at such idle and superstitious nonsense, and attribute the whole to natural causes.

It may be admitted that Satan is sometimes belied; but do all those who object, believe in the personal existence of Satan? Do they believe the Scriptures? If not, the dispute must be carried on on very different grounds; but if they do believe the word of God, they will find but little difficulty in concluding that Satan has much to do with such people as those in Feejee; and that he who tortured the person from whom Christ had commanded him to depart, would only act like himself by taking the course ascribed to him in the case of Doulakemba.

I know from personal observation that the people of Tonga, Samoa, New-Caledonia, New-Hebrides, Tahiti, and Feejee, believe in the existence of separate spirits, and especially of evil angels. They all speak very positively on this subject, and quote facts to prove that now and then the spirit enters into men, and speaks of future events, which always come round and prove true. Do all these nations and people, differing in almost everything else, especially in language, agree upon this point for any other reason than because it is a fact? And does the Supreme Being still afford a measure of the prophetic spirit to rest on one here and there, for the purpose of keeping up the idea of himself and of a spiritual world in the minds of these men, until the gospel light shall arise and shine upon them?

Since I wrote the above I have visited the house where the natives say the dust was thrown. Several persons who were there at the time, stated to Messrs. Lyth and Malvern, and myself, that they saw the earth go up by the post, and that when any one was engaged in prayer this fine earth was dashed in their face. "In mine it was dashed," said one; "And in mine," said another: and with the sprinkling earth there was, they say, a sharp hissing noise. The old man was the last to *lotu* in their village; and the evil spirit was obliged, though unwilling, to quit the place, there being no place left for him. No matter who the man was that began to pray, his eyes, and sometimes his mouth, were soon filled with small fine earth. They all made search to find out if there was any wicked person concealed, and were all fully assured that no natural cause produced the effects which they experienced. They therefore concluded, that the cause was not only an *evil* one, but also *supernatural.*

No doubt the old serpent is extremely exasperated at our invasion of his dominions here, where his reign has been so long unmolested. The intense malignity of this fiend, with those in his train, would soon destroy Christ's agents in the mission field, were it not that their Master is their keeper, and the infernal legion is chained up.

> "Lo! to faith's enlighten'd sight,
> All the mountain flames with light;
> Hell is nigh, but God is nigher,
> Circling us with hosts of fire."

10*th.* This tropical weather seems now settled; the wind generally east by south, and the quicksilver at 80°. Being early in spring, answering to the beginning of February at home, the fruits are not yet ripe. The pine-apple, bread-fruit, and banana, are growing large, but not fit for use. The insects, and especially the mosquitoes, sting sharply, and with acrid venom; these insignificant little creatures are the white people's plague, and the natives' annoyance.

All here is stirring preparation for the forthcoming school-examination, and the distant islands are sending in their *church contributions.*

Daniel brought thirty-four bowls, or *gomate,* last night, from the newly-*lotued* island of Kambara; and this morning, Barzillai, another teacher, has come in from the island of Vulanga, with a dozen good mats, as the contribution from his people towards the support and spread of the gospel. This is only the beginning of a system, which must go on and be encouraged. I observed with pleasure that some articles sent in were payment for the New Testament, which is in great request here, as well as in the Tonga district. Nothing seems so much prized among those who can read, as a copy of the Scriptures, printed at our mission press here; and many are anxious to learn to read, that they may "look into the perfect law of liberty."

We sometimes speak of the cost of the gospel: but what did the devil-worship of this people cost them? Take a writer's ink-horn and walk through Feejee, and report what you see. The list will be *imperfect,* but it is written in blood:—

A man without a finger, offered in sacrifice; another without any fingers, all gone to Satan: a woman without her ears; another without her nose: a man with one arm, the other offered to the god or to the chief: two other men, one without a toe and the other without an arm: a female without legs, being cut off by order of a chief; another without unburnt skin; a man tied down at mid-day with his eyes spread open under the direct rays of the sun, until they were burned out of his head! These and other mutilations of the human body you shall see; but estimate, if you can, the bodies of the eaten and the slain! The carnage of Feejee is fearful to hear of and frightful to behold. Such was the price of their heathenism: but the day of emancipation is come, and there is great joy in these islands.

11*th*. At the morning service fourteen persons were baptized by Mr. Malvern, assisted by myself; all of whom, we believe, give evidence of a true Scriptural Christianity, both by the spirit which they manifest, and the fruits which they bear. A deep solemnity rested on the whole congregation during the service. Some of them were amongst the most hopeful young chiefs in the land, especially Savogae, now named Fanny Maria, a truly pious girl, of high descent.

12*th*. This is a wasting climate; I observed that yesterday Mr. Lyth was obliged to change twice, being saturated with perspiration, though he had only walked each time two miles out and home, and the weather was quite the ordinary temperature. Such a state of things, one would suppose, could never consist with the continuance of good health for a long season, and hence all the mission families maintain that the excellent Mr. Hunt was a victim prematurely to the heat and toils of this climate, and to his efforts, both physical and mental, for the good of Feejee.

As God is graciously raising up well-qualified teachers, just enough to meet the present necessity, some of them fit for taking charge of a town or a small island, and others further advanced and fit to take the oversight of two or three of these, and to marry and baptize, if need require; I hope the wasting toils of our missionaries may be spared a little: the seed is here, and native hands will assist to spread it.

13*th.* We held our school-examination at Lakemba. Two hundred and fifty children were present from various parts of the island, with a host of people, the king and chiefs being at their head. The young people marched, sang, rehearsed the Scriptures and the catechism, and showed other attainments much to the satisfaction of all present. They also laid down their offerings of war-weapons and vestments, shells and curiosities of many kinds, which may one day assist the funds of the society on the opposite side of the world. The Tonguese also took part in the transactions of the day, and by their graceful forms, comely features, and tasteful dress, added dignity to the scene. The superior civilization of these charming people may be rendered, by God's providence, subservient to the more rapid advancement of the active and interesting people of Feejee.

It is impossible to witness the passing events of this day without feeling that great changes must result from them, both of a social and moral character, to the entire mass of this population.

The following composition, written by one of our teachers called Jeremiah, (six feet five inches and a half high,) was sung on the occasion as the people marched in procession towards the chapel, where the king and chiefs were sitting. The words "We'll follow the Lord," were sung in full chorus at the end of every few lines.

VERSES.

The religion of Jesus has come to our land;
The missionaries have brought it.
Repent ye, and let it be done quickly.
The Light of life has risen upon us,
The Light of the world.
Christ, the Redeemer from the curse,
The Redeemer from the curse of the world,
Jesus, who alone is our Lord,
Has given to us his servants,
That the glad tidings of salvation may be told.
The Bible alone is of any use to us:
It points continually to eternal life.
Repent ye, and repent quickly,
While our day of grace continues,
Because of the death which is not far distant,
And will push us to the tomb.

CHORUS.

We 'll follow, we 'll follow the Lord.

The king came with one of his chiefs after the business of the day was concluded, and sat with us at the house of Mr. Lyth. Being asked what he thought of the crowd, and of the rehearsals of Scripture and catechism, he said, "All my people are filled with fear" (a strong Oriental way of expressing astonishment). "We must have another such meeting at once; for all the people are full of desire."

He added, "Formerly we were too much afraid to hold such large assemblies; for one man who owed another a grudge would lift his club and kill him: this would often lead to a general quarrel. If one had a comely daughter present, she would be looked at, laid hold on and carried away in the general stir and confusion: so that parents were afraid to let their children go out on such occasions. But," said the king, "these are the days of the Saviour, the times of peace and of harmony: the light is now come, and we must learn to be wise; for the days of our folly have been many."

The external advantages of true Christianity are so strong and vivid as to give rise to such a testimony from this man, who, I fear, knows nothing yet of real and heart religion.

At the same time there is in these schools, especially among those natives where they are new, such a cordiality and charm of brotherly feeling, as well as intellectual pleasure, that it can be little less in their estimation than a mighty moral revolution of social order and of the relation of man to man. They are permitted to blend by the peaceful Saviour; and they who devoured one another aforetime, are now brought into the state of brotherly love, kindled by the Lord and Master.

14*th.* As the following letter from the captain of a man-of-war to the powerful chief Thakombau is very creditable to that officer, I have pleasure in transcribing it:—

As a proof of the good feeling entertained by the queen and government of Great Britain towards Feejee, I have sent one of her majesty's vessels to Nukulau, with the nine men who last year accompanied Mr. Fitzgerald to New-Caledonia to fish for beche-de-mer, but who were driven out of that country by the people to whom it belonged, and were afterwards brought to Sydney in a very sickly condition. Having been as carefully attended to and as kindly treated as if they had been our countrymen, they are now sent back to their homes.

I am very sorry that these men were ever employed by an Englishman upon an expedition which, I have been told, was conducted from the first with violence towards the people of another country for the sake of gain.

The queen's government disapproves highly of such conduct on the part of her subjects, as it is opposed to the principles of humanity and good-will towards all men, which as Christians they ought to practice, and in this case has been the cause of the death of several persons on both sides. I hope you will in future exert your authority to prevent your people from going upon such expeditions; from which no good can come, and in which they are sure to be the sufferers.

I am also sorry to hear that the men of Solevu have been threatening violence to Mr. Hazlewood and the mission premises at Nandi. You will no doubt remember, that you promised me last year to do all in your power to prevent this happening again; and I therefore hope that you will acquaint these people that such conduct towards British subjects who conduct themselves well, cannot be permitted. I should be very sorry to be obliged to use the power, which you well know we possess, against any persons in Feejee; and my doing so would certainly have the effect of weakening your power and authority, which, so long as it is properly exercised, I should rather wish to strengthen.

I write this to you because I am sure that your mind has before this become impressed with the conviction of the folly and impolicy of the old heathenish practices of violence and bloodshed, which I hope are fast wearing out in Feejee. And I assure you, that nothing would give me, as your well-wisher, greater pleasure, than to hear that you had openly renounced them, and, following the advice of your true friend Mr. Calvert and the other missionaries, had adopted the Christian religion with a full conviction of its truth.

Until then it must be expected that your name, which I should never desire to hear without respect, will be occasionally mentioned in connection with deeds of horror, which, as I have often told you before, cannot be ever alluded to by a civilized people without disgust, and which it is impossible that a chief of so generous a character, and of such intelligence as yourself, can ever approve.

Trusting that it will not be long before you will take the only steps which can make you a truly great chief over a happy and attached people, I remain

Your sincere friend, JOHN E. ERSKINE.

Her Britannic Majesty's Ship Havannah,
SYDNEY, NEW SOUTH WALES. *May* 19*th*, 1850.

15*th*. The district meeting began at Lakemba. All the brethren who were present, appeared in good health and spirits, and greatly encouraged in their work; which has spread so swiftly and so far, that, notwithstanding the native agency so largely employed, we need for Feejee, instead of six missionaries, (the present number,) at the very least sixteen, beside two more for Rotumah.

The Scriptures and the native agency are brought

to bear with admirable effect in Feejee; but still a work so widely spread must have the eye of a superintendent, or we cannot expect the unguided native efforts to be always directed aright; the helm must always be in a skillful hand, or the object will not be attained.

We also greatly need two properly trained schoolmasters for this mission; and fine indeed will be their prospects when they arrive in this interesting mission-field.

18*th*, Lord's-day. We had this morning a heavy fall of rain and a crowded chapel; and the power of God was present to heal.

Mr. Malvern was admitted by imposition of hands into full connection with his brethren, having passed his four years of probation with entire satisfaction to all present. He is a very useful missionary in Feejee, and is blessed with a useful wife.

After the evening preaching, we had the Lord's supper, in which the mission families joined; it was a deeply impressive time;—a few persons from England, who left their all, and followed the Saviour to this small speck in the ocean, engaged in changing the manners and morals of a nation, and preparing to appear before the Judge to give an account of their stewardship! The ladies wept and wiped away their tears; the missionaries sang aloud of help hitherto; and all were resolved and renewed for the future.

19*th*. The chief Waytasau, whose authority in this place is next to the king's, and who is a *lotu* man, came into our house, and was persuaded to be married. So he cast away about sixteen wives, and was married to one, but not without a great deal of haggling and hesitation. It is said that the king threw every obstacle in his way, which I can easily believe.

About this great chief, Waytasau, all are agreed on one subject; namely, that he never did a noble or generous action. He told us we should now have to support him! Nor would he hear of being married without wedding-robes being given both to himself and his intended wife; to which Mr. and Mrs. Lyth were obliged to add a book and a dinner to himself. And this poor mean-spirited man is the first chief after the king, in the island of Lakemba, and a *lotu* man of the nominal kind. But he has a grown-up daughter, Fanny Savogi, who was baptized a fortnight ago, and who promises fair to become a person of intelligence, piety, and great usefulness, being a chief of the first rank, and educated in our school here. It is to the hopeful youth that we must look for the elevation of Feejee in the scale of social comfort and civilization.

20*th*. Our district meeting ended, as it had proceeded, full of peace and brotherly love. Several of the brethren feel their infirmities, and have written to the committee for permission to remove, should protracted affliction require such a step. It is also agreed to request and even urge the committee to send out by the "John Wesley,"

1. Three missionaries, to fill up the places of those who, if necessary, shall remove.

2. Two trained schoolmasters, one for Vewa and the other for Lakemba.

Besides these, several native assistant missionaries are now received, and six others received on trial.

I am persuaded that God will carry on his work in these Islands very much through the agency of missionaries at the head, and native teachers, as the acting agents, thickly sprinkled over the whole country.

NOTE FROM THE FEEJEE DISTRICT MEETING.

LAKEMBA, *August 20th*, 1850.

REV. AND DEAR SIR,—We feel bound to give thanks to God for your present friendly visit to this mission, and for your kind attendance at our district meeting; and, now that it is closed, we cannot but express to yourself the grateful sense we feel for your labors, prayers, and services in the great cause.

We rejoice in having been favored with your presence at our district meeting, and heartily thank you for the fatherly help and counsel so judiciously afforded, as need required, from time to time.

We anticipate much good to result to this mission from your expected visit to the father-land; and we can without reserve confide the affairs of our district to your hands.

May it please our heavenly Father to guide and strengthen you in promoting the good cause, and crown all your efforts and counsels for his glory with a blessing,—is the prayer of

Your much obliged and most affectionate brethren,

R. B. LYTH, *Chairman.*
J. CALVERT, *Secretary.*
THOMAS WILLIAMS.
JOHN MALVERN.
WILLIAM MOORE.

To the Rev. W. LAWRY, *General Superintendent, &c.*

21st. We held our first missionary meeting at Lakemba, beginning at nine o'clock and ending at half-past eleven. The king and chiefs were present. It rained in torrents, but ceased in time for our meeting. The crowd was great, and the interest truly intense. Many cried aloud; and all were very intent to hear. Three of the native teachers spoke; and one of them offered himself entirely for the work. In one of the neighboring islands we have had an offer of a chief and his double canoe to be devoted out and out to the mission work. These things come forth in the ordinary course of events; but the finger of God is in the whole.

The contribution has been made this afternoon, the king bearing his roll of mats and cloth upon his own back, and the long procession following him with a hymn, "We'll follow the Turanga."

Their subscriptions were made up of cloth, mats, spears, clubs, shells, and bowls. Probably about four hundred persons presented their offering; and the value in London would perhaps be not less than £50.

All the people bowed down as they entered the chapel, and chanted the Lord's prayer.

Some of the most notorious murderers and cannibals were there, with the blood upon their skirts; and they roared out as they approached us near the pulpit. They trembled, and were convulsed exceedingly, making the whole neighborhood echo with their wailings. When men of this class become subdued by the gospel, and rank among its supporters, what need have we to fear for the cause we have embarked in? God is now magnified in Feejee.

23d. We passed down before the wind from Lakemba to Vewa, about one hundred and fifty miles: the vessel rolled, and all were sick. During this little trip, Methuselah, a young chief, would not let me rest at Tonga, but he must go and see England; the king spoke for him, and his parents consented to his going. Having, therefore, consulted the brethren, we agreed to let him visit England in the "John Wesley." But, alas for native courage and perseverance! one day of severe sea-sickness fully settled the matter: Methuselah came to me, and, having made lots of apologies, and expressed his very warm affection towards myself, said, his strength was all gone, he was weak and feeble, the difficulties of the voyage he found to be very great, and begged that he might go back to Tonga with Joel, who is here from Habai.

Of all this I am very glad, for the lad would only be a care and burden to me; but it shows how little dependence can be placed, with safety, upon native resolution. *There* is the weak point of this people: they cannot or will not persevere against difficulties with a firm resolution to overcome them; but, when the hour of trial is come, they cease their efforts, and give up all. This fine young chief will now, of course, return to his fatherland, where he will meet with the taunts of his former associates.

24*th*. VEWA.—I am now at the mission-house; but its former occupant is gone. The vigorous and energetic JOHN HUNT is not here, but is passed over before us. A tropical sun; exposure to heat, when in the full power of its blazing forth; working hard in the garden and on the house; sleeping at Bau in wet clothes and in a draught:—these brought on dysentery and death. Alas! the trees of Vewa seem to me to utter a wail over my brother's early removal. There is his grave at the rear of the chapel! He went down with a smile, and shall rise with a shout.

25*th*, Sunday. We had public worship to-day at the usual hours; and the congregations were very good. Only a few of the old faces were present; and among them, Elijah Varani, my old friend, whom I am happy to see fixed and established upon "the sure foundation;" he has also begun to preach, and I hope the Lord will make him extensively useful.

26*th*. My host and hostess, Mr. and Mrs. Calvert, full of kindness and intelligence, talk of sending their daughter Ann by the "John Wesley" to Auckland school; which is a great comfort to them, though the parting with this their third child is felt to be a sharp trial. But the cup of a missionary *in this life* is often mixed with bitterness.

27*th*. I had a visit to-day from Thakumbau, sometimes called, but incorrectly, the King of Feejee. He is naturally black enough; but he had besmeared his face with black coloring matter, and looked like what he was,—a cruel, murderous savage, who kills and eats men, women, and children. Mr. Calvert, who never misses an opportunity of letting in light upon him, communicated his own views and mine upon the *lotu;* and the black chief evaded what was said with considerable cunning; but he contrived to get his head into every room and his hand into every dish. He has no charms for me, after a visit to the superior chiefs of Tonga, who, compared with this naked and cannibal warrior, are high in the scale of civilization. It may, however, be set down to his credit, that he lately fed Tuihilahila with pigs instead of men, as was the custom aforetime. His becoming a Christian is the only way open to him to escape the dark infamy which lies before him.

28*th*. We were passing from Ovalau to Nandi among the reefs, with a very light wind, taking home Mr. and Mrs. Moore to Nandi, and Mr. Williams to Bua; but in the evening, while gliding along in sixteen fathoms of water, the mate sang out from the bowsprit end, "Luff up quickly! a rock right ahead!" All was done that men and activity could do; but on the vessel went, and got fast upon the coral rock. There we were hard and fast upon the rock: this is the fourth time; but, though we knew it would delay us, and add to the fatigues of a very hot day, yet no danger threatened us; for we were in sight of Mr. Moore's station, with hardly any wind, and the water perfectly smooth, and it was dead low water, so that every moment would improve our circumstances. Captain Buck sent out a cable or hawser astern, and, dropping his anchor there, hove away upon this purchase; when off went the "John Wesley," and soon after came to an anchor in Nandi Bay.

29*th*. The rocks are so numerous about here as to make it a most undesirable place for a vessel of above twenty tons to visit, and more especially as they are all *sunken* rocks, about from eight to ten feet under water, and therefore invisible in cloudy weather. Moreover, this locality is remarkable for its wet or showery character, when nothing under water can be seen from the mast-head. This place, therefore, as a port, is left-handed and dangerous, the prevailing wind blowing dead on the shore. When shall we have a good survey of Feejee? How could small ships-of-war be better employed? It might be more agreeable to be snug in harbor, but neither so honorable, nor so useful.

30*th.* We landed Mr. and Mrs. Moore last night, and went ashore at six this morning to see their station, and bid them farewell. Their house, built of wood and floored, has four rooms and a verandah, with a goodly number of kind-hearted natives living about them on the sea-shore, with every prospect of extensive usefulness, which is somewhat interrupted by the never-ending little wars of the tribes in the neighborhood. Two of these tribes have been fighting for several months; and, so far, there is no result, nor any hope of a termination. One man, on one side, had a bullet which passed through him, but is fast recovering; on the other side, one man had a spear in his flesh, but nothing fatal. The two great evils of Feejee are, the tyranny of the chiefs oppressing the poor people, and these continual conflicts between the tribes. However, as the gospel advances, (and advance it must and will,) the Prince of Peace will say, "Thou shalt love thy neighbor as thyself," and "war shall cease unto the ends of the earth."

CHAPTER IX.

We came to-day, before the trade-wind, from Nandi to Bua, about forty or fifty miles, and found Mrs. Williams well, with their four children, though still trembling from two violent shakes of an earthquake, which took place here while we were at sea, in deep blue water, on Thursday night. We felt nothing of the motion; but all on board complained of the very oppressive state of the atmosphere, charged, no doubt, to a high degree with electricity. Mrs. Williams was quite alarmed at the violent rocking, and called out to her native girls, who were in another part of the house; and they, in turn, called out to her: the house, the bed, and all things seemed cracking and tottering. Her thought was, that the natives were breaking into the house, and that all was now confusion. This shows the quarter whence her fears most generally proceed; and no wonder, seeing there are so many heathen tribes at war in this large island, and some of them close at hand; while I had her husband with me on board the "John Wesley," returning from the district meeting.

The missionaries of Feejee and their wives, if they prove faithful, are destined to occupy no ordinary station of glory and honor in the next world, where every man shall be rewarded according to his works, his suffering for the sake of Christ, and his continuance in well-doing; having in this world nobly and intrepidly sustained the conflict in the high places of the field, and in the forefront of the hottest battle.

31*st.* Bartimeus, one of our domestics here, was

introduced to me to-day. He is from Ono; and when Mr. Waterhouse was there, with Mr. Calvert and others, it was quickly noised abroad over this small *lotu* island, that the sacred men were come, who had power to baptize, marry, &c. "Come now," said they, "you who wish to be married, this is the time." So there was a general rising of the people: the men who wished to have wives, or who thought they might wish in that direction hereafter, were running up and down, a hundred in a crowd, asking, "Will you have me?" "No!" was the common reply. Among those who wished to provide for the future was Bartimeus, who, having offered here and there, and meeting only with repulses, at last made an offer to a female far advanced in years, and unhappily was accepted. After their marriage, the old lady told him that she thought he might be of use to her in planting and procuring her food, and on that account she had married him. Poor Bartimeus was chagrined; but there was no remedy. Time rolled on, and he proceeded with his work, but the old lady lived upon another island; and he used to ask if it would be right to pray for her death, and was told it would not be right so to pray; although she was not "a help-meet for him," yet she was his wife.

We have now, however, brought him the news of his wife's death, upon which he remarks, "This is well: but I will never venture upon another; for I see confusion in two-thirds of the cases before me."

Admitting this to be his experience, is there anything in it at which we may be surprised? He began that matter without thought, without affection, and of course without the proper adaptation as ordained by God and placed within the reach of men! How much of this do we see in all countries, and in all grades of society!

Sept. 1*st*, Sabbath. BUA.—Mr. Williams has by far the best chapel that I have seen in the two districts. It is clean, strong, and tastefully laid out and finished, reminding me of one of our cathedrals at home, ornamented to the very ridge pole, and built not only in the best style, but of the best material in the land, and completed by those who use it; and it is free from debt. The worship was solemn and cheerful, intelligent and feeling. About two hundred persons were present.

2*d*. At a small distance from the chapel is the dwelling-house of Mr. and Mrs. Williams, standing by the side of a navigable stream, in a lovely grove of bread-fruit, cocoas, and bananas, with a very rich alluvial soil of several miles' extent, producing fine crops of *tarro*, yams, and other articles of food. The mission-house, as well as the chapel, has about it an air of comfort and finish, which may be decisive of the builder being an amateur architect. The direct and proper work of the missionary has not been neglected while the buildings have been in progress. The spiritual temple has reared its head aloft contemporaneously with the chapel and the mission house.

Yandrana had only some half-a-dozen Christians in it, Mr. Williams says, when he was in that vicinage; but one of our teachers, named Samson, used to visit the place as often as he could, and assisted the *lotu* few in their family-worship; for all who *lotu* pray in their own house and family. It happened one morning when Samson was at Yandrana, and when the *lotu* people, for the sake of convenience, came together for prayer, that one of the party overslept himself, and was not present when the worship was performed; but he came soon after, and urged Samson to go over his devotions again, saying, that he could not yet pray himself, it was so great and sacred a thing: "But," said Wauka, "I know my place and my work; it is to say, AMEN! for I can do this heartily!" O how many places need Wauka there to say heartily, AMEN, in the congregation! Ezekiel and his wife, teachers of some standing, have gone forth to their station this morning. He is the man whom we met on this coast three years ago, having a pulpit on his canoe; and, about a year since, he and his were coming down the coast from Nandi in a small canoe, when Boli-na-vavi had sent a party to bring him a man roasted on the occasion of his completing a double canoe. The party saw Ezekiel and his wife off the coast, and pursued them as their prize, uttering the foulest language and preparing to spear them; but, by God's blessing, Ezekiel got off from these cannibals uninjured, and is still strong to labor in his Master's vineyard. This is Feejeean work! Even to-day he has to pass by some persons of whose disposition towards him and his people there is no doubt; and therefore he is gone with a spear in one hand and the New Testament in the other, having also a friend or two with him.

"The kingdom of God cometh not by observation." There is in this little settlement an old man called Delli, living in the deep darkness of heathenism. He never comes near the chapel, but Mr. Williams has been useful to him in times of sickness; and, in return, the old man never works on the Lord's day, and has sent to the heathen village on the opposite side of the river, desiring them not to work on the Sabbath, out of respect to the man who administers medicine to them. And not long since this man had part of a roasted human body sent to him as a repast; but he sent it back untouched, saying, "The days are passed away when such things were done; we have ceased from such customs on this side the river." Thus silently and indirectly is the light breaking in upon the darkness of this gross and degraded people.

This morning, as Mr. Williams and I were walking in front of his house, an elderly man, called Job, passed us. "There," said Mr. Williams, "goes the last of his tribe; he received Christianity some time since, and earnestly entreated his people to do the same; but they delayed and resisted until Job left them and came here to live for the sake of Christ's ordinances. Another people fell on Job's friends, killed and roasted some, and all who could escape did, until their memorial has ceased to exist, except in the case of Job and two or three others, who, fleeing to Dama, embraced the *lotu* there." Such is the present state of things here, that one sees only two ways before any man; namely, *lotu* and live, or, resist the light and perish! This is the day of decision in Feejee!

4th. The words of the Tonga language are more monosyllabic than those of Feejee; but in both it takes longer space to print the New Testament than in English, owing somewhat, perhaps, to the repetition of the syllable in many common words; such as, *voora voora*, "earth;" *valla valla tha*, "sin;" *vena vena vanaka*, "praise." Not that either of these languages is by any means destitute of energy and nervousness. Some of our missionaries in both districts declare their conviction, that for strength and point their language is not inferior to the English. But their poetry seems deeply impoverished in both languages, as compared with Wesley's Hymns in English; a circumstance this which need surprise no one, as the same hymns in French or German would be sadly deteriorated by their change of clothing. Translation, too, is found to be more difficult than original composition.

5th. Yesterday we went up the river in a double canoe; and in a few minutes after we moved off the bank before Mr. Williams's house, we passed by the yam-plantation of one of our Christian people. It was recently a sacred grove, where heathen worship used to be performed; but the good man, whether prudently or otherwise I need not say, cut down the trees and planted his garden. This matter created great excitement among the heathens; they, however, did not proceed to *blows*, but contented themselves with *predictions* as to what would certainly befall this man, who thus despised their gods and their faith. The result was, that he had a good crop of yams, and the predictions pass for idle tales!

As we glided up the river with the flowing tide, we had a fine view of the lofty mountains of the interior, some of which are fine pointed conical forms of great altitude. On either side of the river stood the graceful and sweet-scented pandanus, with the fruitful cocoa-nut trees. The scenery of these well-watered and very productive inter-tropical islands must be seen in order to be at all conceived of justly and fully.

At another reach of this river, about half a mile from the mission-house, we passed the oven where men are cooked for human food. Several bodies have been baked there since Mr. Williams was stationed here, on my last visit three years ago; but all these gross practices of heathenism are driven back and withered before a triumphant and ever-advancing Christianity.

When and wheresoever the Prince of Peace is proclaimed, the power of sin is arrested, and the reign of death and demons ended. The pagan savage, who believes not at first, is awe-struck at the majesty of Christ's truth, as exhibited in its faithful and holy ministers and confessors. It appears from the statements of Mr. Williams, that infanticide still prevails to a fearful extent in Feejee. Not long since, one of his Church-members committed murder in the case of her infant. The husband asked of which sex it was; and, being told it was a girl, "Kill it," was his command forthwith. The nose of the infant was held between the fingers, and the mouth stopped; and soon the babe was a corpse. Of course, the party was expelled from Christian communion; but Mr. Williams thinks these besotted people did not fully know that their old and undisputed custom was a moral evil. One of the teachers was lately sent off to a distant heathen village to preach the gospel; and Mr. Williams supplied him with a sermon on infanticide, which the native delivered on the following Sabbath, having first raised their expectation of something uncommon, so that the crowd of hearers was great, to whom he delivered his message; after hearing which, the poor people seemed thankful to him, and said, he had opened their eyes, for they did not before see any evil in killing little babes. And, revolting as the thought may be, still it may turn out in their case, as in Paul's, that in this matter they "had lived in all good conscience before God,"—only the learned Pharisee destroyed *Christian men,* and the poor pagan Feejeean only killed *infants.* Here, however, are opposite agents to be saved by the same remedy: the same gospel that converted the bigoted and bloodthirsty Jew, will come home to the bosom of the cannibal; and both will meet at the feet of Christ, claiming to be the chief of sinners, and showing the gospel to be the power of God unto salvation.

Peter, the chief of Bua, on the opposite side of the river, has called on us; unto whom I have delivered a strong exhortation, through Mr. Williams, that he put away his false gods and false morals, and embrace Christ forthwith; which he seems more than half inclined to do. Our duty now is demonstrably clear; we must declare the whole counsel of God to all who will hear.

6*th.* In our walk last evening among the houses, gardens, plantations, and groves of this people, Mr. Williams drew my attention to a well-cultivated yam and tarrow garden, and to the clean and cheerful-looking cottage which stood in the midst of it. "Here," said he, "lives Nathaniel, one of our early converts at this place. Some years ago Joshua, who was at Sydney and elsewhere with the late Mr. Waterhouse, came here to teach the people; and, walking among them at the usual time of preparing their evening meal, he said to this poor heathen man, 'What are you doing here?' 'Preparing food for the gods,' was the answer. 'There is but one God,' said Joshua; and 'the earth is the Lord's and the fullness thereof, the world and they that dwell therein. If I were hungry, I would not tell thee: for the beasts of the earth are mine, and the cattle upon a thousand hills.' Here the light broke in upon the mind of Nathaniel, and 'the word of the Lord was perfect, converting the soul.'" In consequence of this change in the man, all things around him seem to smile, and the "trees of the wood" which he then providentially set in the ground for food, such as the banana and bread-fruit,—these "trees of the wood clap their hands;" enriching and adorning the joyful and beautiful home of this industrious and praying servant of the Lord.

In that locality are some few heathen houses, looking grim, cheerless, and dirty; barren and without anything attractive; for the heathen are idle, warlike, and barbarous, without hope for the future or any amount of comfort for the present.

I often remark among this interesting, but barbarous, people, that to them, as well as to ourselves, there are no words so forcible as "the words which the Holy Ghost useth." They fasten like a nail in a sure place, and strike a chord which is "music in the sinner's ear; 't is life and health and peace." Happy man whom God sends to preach this word! A messenger is just come in from the back of this island and the coast of Mathuata, to report from Ezekiel our teacher, that a town in his neighborhood had been fallen upon at noon-day and utterly destroyed. He reports forty men, and at least as many women and children, killed on the spot. As many as they could they ate on the spot, and the rest remained unburied; the houses and fences being all burned to ashes. This little war has long been going on, one or two falling now, and eight or ten at another time. And there are at this moment, on this one island, some ten or dozen such wars in progress. Killing, eating, "wasting, and destruction, are in all their ways." The very same is the case on the Kauvandra and Ba coasts. By these local broils and fights, the crops are neglected, men destroyed, intercourse cut off, schools interrupted, and the gospel greatly hindered. The name of the burned town is Nangaku. It may not be easy to perceive the design of Divine Providence herein; but it looks as though the disturbing light had come among this people: some obey its call and come to Christ, while others resist and fall by the hands of each other. This is the day of *decision* in Feejee.

Mr. Williams is about sending off a teacher to an island that drove away the Christians some time since: he determines to try them again. Moses is going to preach the gospel to them; and a chief who has great authority there, is going to preach the law. His name is Luke: and he says they cannot now believe and be saved, after having done so wickedly. "See," says he, "your chiefs are all dead, and you are all doomed." But they laugh and reply, "We shall dance and sing, eat and sleep; and when we can, we will fight, and see what will come." This is their condition—"natural brute beasts, made to be destroyed." When they were going to attack the Christians, an old man of our Church learned from them their errand, and said, "Why do you go so far?

Here is a Christian. I am he. Kill me, if you thirst for blood; I am ready now." But their commission did not include him. The progress of the battle now going on in Feejee, between the old murderer and his conqueror and Lord, is waxing hot, and hastening to its close. It is light opposed to darkness, truth against error, sin against holiness, and Christ opposed to Satan. "But the Lamb shall overcome them."

It is not for us to say how much suffering there may be on the part of our native confessors; but, be it less or more, the conflict is begun, and the victory will surely determine in favor of fidelity, and through the blood of the Lamb.

7th. Mr. Williams has amused me not a little, by narrating the impressions of a shrewd man called George, living at Nukunuku, in Lakemba, when he saw the first European vessel, and went on board of her, probably not less than fifty years ago; he was then a boy, but his impression was the general impression of all who saw the two-masted *wanka,* or "ship."

On their approach to this wonderful floating house, they all concluded that it was the production of gods, and used only by gods: but, on their boarding the vessel, they were struck with perfect astonishment at everything they saw; except that they concluded beyond all doubt that the men whom they saw were *all fools,* because they could not speak (Feejee), only chattering like birds or animals. They also told the people ashore, that the strange men on board were not, like themselves, all of one color; but some were black, some red, some white, but hardly any two were alike in this particular. Their simple mistake arose from confounding their clothes with their skin. These poor Feejee Indians never used clothes, and had no conception of such a thing. The blue jacket, the red shirt, and the white frock, were so many blue, red, and white men. Indeed, I remember when I landed in Tonga, some of the country natives seriously asked Singleton if my clothes grew upon me, as they saw the wool growing on the sheep's back. As to the masts of this wonderful vessel, they made no doubt of their being two cocoa-nut trees, which had grown on the *wanga*, and that the wind had blown their tops off.

A man with a respectable amount of what is imaginative and ludicrous, if inclined to indulge his natural taste, might unquestionably find sufficient scope and material here for the utmost gratification of his wishes; but scenes of solemn tragedy claim the first place in the page of a Feejeean journalist.

One of our Tongan teachers, and a youth from Ono, were at Vanua Mblavu, holding forth the word of life. They were by the sea-side, when a party of armed natives rushed down upon them, and fired a shot through the Ono youth, and then pierced him with a spear, so that he died. The Tongan teacher said, "Why do you take one only? will you not take my life also?" "No," they replied, "you are from Tonga, but he is of Feejee; and what right had he to profess Christianity?"

Soon after this, a strong Christian chief, with several large canoes full of men, went to settle this matter with the men of Vanua Mblavu; a host of whom took the profession of Christianity, to save their lives.

After these things were calmed down, Tuihilahila, the chief of Somosomo, paid them a visit, and compelled them to abandon the *lotu;* which, it seems, they readily did, and still remain thorough-paced heathens, respected by no party.

9th. I met with an Albino to-day, born of black Feejeean parents; none of the family were white besides this young man Racivo. His skin hung loose about him, and seemed more the color of a white man when dead; and was, moreover, thickly freckled where most exposed to the sun. His head and beard were white and frizzled; his eye-brows also were white; but his eyes were a light-blue, and his countenance rather agreeable, and very much resembling the Albino race which I have seen in other lands. His habits are industrious, and he is hard-working; but his appearance, at first sight at least, is revolting. He has much white woolly hair, covering, with some indistinctness, his whole body. Mr. Williams gave him his dinner; and I exhorted him to hear the gospel, pray to the Lord for mercy, and then learn to read the word of God; to which he did not make any objection, nor signify any assent. The black natives are rather partial to him; but he has not a wife, and is obliged to work hard for his food.

11th. We held our *solavu,* or school-feast, here. The gathering of our people for many miles round was excellent, and their progress in learning very satisfactory; their learning was sound, and their rehearsals chiefly confined to the Scriptures. Many of the heathen were present and cheerfully contributed, with the Christians, of their substance; but *they* did not give their weapons of war, not having done with them yet. They, however, gave their mats and beds; but Racivo, the Albino, gave his spear. The chief articles presented to the mission-fund were:—11 war-clubs; 38 spears; 14 walking-sticks; 83 mats, or beds; 200 pieces of sandal-wood; 24 ladies' dresses, or *ligu;* 27 hand-clubs for throwing; 12 musquito curtains; 2 bales of sinnet; 1 basket of shells; 3 fish-hooks; 1 native flute, blown through the nose!

When the gospel shall have turned these people from darkness to light, and from the power of Satan to God, the war-weapons will very soon disappear in Feejee, and be found perhaps only in the halls of our friends in England. Their native dresses also will give way before the calico and prints of Manchester. This effect already shows itself around the mission stations in every place.

It was very gratifying to see with what attention and interest the people in general, not excepting the heathen, listened to the Holy Scriptures, while they were being recited, hour after hour, in the charming temple of God at Bua.

Our chief here is a fine spirit, and likely to be a great blessing to his people and to the surrounding villages. When Mr. Williams asked Hezekiah, for so he is called, whether he was willing to become a teacher of Christianity to the heathen, especially on the Lord's day, when his services were needed, he wept, and could not answer for a time; but when he was somewhat recovered, his reply was, "Is there anything that I would keep back from Jesus?" Hezekiah is therefore one of our useful local preachers. In this way does Jehovah spread his truth and mercy among the people. Such men can go where we could not, and they will be heard where we should not be heard. "I have redeemed them, and they shall increase as they have increased, and I will sow them among the people; and they shall remember me in far countries." Again the prophet saith, "And I will have mercy upon her that had not obtained mercy; and I will say to them which were not my people, Thou art my people; and they shall say, Thou art my God."

Here are the seeds of a Christian church planted by Mr. Williams in the deep wilds of Feejee, and God will cause them to grow. Twenty-five adults and fifteen youths repeated what they had learned, and the day will long be remembered as a great *solavu* day in Feejee. God bless our brother and sister Williams at Bua!

12th. We sailed early this morning from Bua for Vewa,—a small distance, but very difficult from reefs, sunken rocks, and, in our case, from contrary winds and a high head sea; so that we were four days in making the passage, looking at the refugee villages on the lofty peaks of Nythumbothumbo, and the Nandi coast, where the wretched natives who have been worsted in war, have fled for their lives, and exist, one knows not how, often among the clouds, and in peril, if they descend for food, water, or fuel.

15th. VEWA.—I learn that since we left this place, about fifty natives have fled from their homes at Varatta, where they were invaded by the Bau chiefs; but who permitted them to come to Vewa, the island of *lotu* people, where their lives are secure, by the consent of the Bau rulers. Such homage do these chiefs now begin to pay to our missionaries, and to our religion! These refugees have, on their arrival here, taken upon themselves the profession of Christianity, as was no doubt intended by their masters at Bau! How strange that, in their case, war prepared the way for the Prince of Peace! and, at the request of Mr. Calvert and our friend Elijah Varani, Thakumbau not only allowed them to live, but also desired that they might forthwith *lotu!* Surely the hand of Jehovah was in this singular event. When will this powerful chief bow his knee to the Saviour?

The king of Lavuga, in the island of Ovalau, has also just become a *lotu* man, with many of his people; and is now entreating Mr. Calvert for more teachers. Here is another open door which we must immediately enter in the name of our Master who has gone before us, and made our way plain.

16*th.* We are just preparing for sea, and taking away Mr. Millard and his wife for New South Wales, whence they came. I know not what to say in the case of this (in many points) respectable young man, who, having offered himself for the *general* work, was sent to Feejee with his own full consent. Since his arrival here, there has been nothing amiss with his moral character; but still he has not been happy, and has told us by word and deed that he shall not feel at home in Feejee, and desires to get away from a scene which he dislikes, and where there is no prospect of *his* being useful.

Our brethren on the spot say, that Feejee *needs* and *must have* men of English nerve and training, rather than persons of less moral resolution.

17*th.* During one of the storms of last year, a

canoe belonging to Nandi was lost, having on board a teacher and several Christians: these were swallowed up in the raging waves, except one lad named Zaccheus, who swam ashore and landed near a heathen town, called Nasavusavu. The people found him, and as the custom is in Feejee towards persons shipwrecked, they prepared the oven to cook the lad. But while the many were engaged in this preparation, one man, a heathen, who knew the boy, stole away unobserved and hid the *lotu* boy in the long grass. He then went into the town to use what influence he had with the people to spare the life of young Zaccheus; who lay secure for the moment, but fully expecting to be roasted and eaten; which no doubt would have been the case, but the men of the town could not see him; their prize had vanished. So the heathen man's request was granted, and the boy allowed to live: he entered the town accordingly. Some time after these things, a report reached the missionary at Nandi, that some dozen of the people of the town had embraced Christianity; a teacher was sent thither forthwith, and the twelve persons with many others, were further instructed in the things of the Lord. Here is the beginning of a Christian Church, founded by a doomed, but rescued, Feejee boy, who was faithful to his Lord and Master; a true successor of apostolic men, who, in any age or place, have done what they could for Jesus Christ! The lady chief of this town, since the arrival of the teacher, has also embraced Christianity, and is zealously engaged in the spread of the gospel among her people.

Nor is this all; for the word has sounded forth

into the regions beyond; and another town, named Mata-ni-ka-viki, has, upon hearing of these things, received the truth, and is now under Christian instruction.

Thus can He who ruled the storm and calmed the raging sea in the days of his incarnation, still control the elements, taking some of his servants to himself, and raising up others, and very unlikely instruments, to carry on his work. "This is the Lord's doing, and it is marvelous in our eyes." "His ways are not our ways." We are to watch the hand of God; not to faint in our minds, nor to repine, saying, "Is the Lord among us or not?" "In all thy ways acknowledge him, and he shall direct thy paths." May I ever ask, "Lord, what wouldest thou have me to do?" This is my privilege by sea and by land, in affliction or prosperity. God is here, and permits me to consult him, to ask favors, to come near to him, to partake of his strength and holiness, yea, to be made a partaker of the divine nature, to have the same mind which was in Christ Jesus! How astonishing is this! "Cry out and shout, thou inhabitant of Zion: for great is the Holy One of Israel in the midst of thee!"

To-day we held our missionary meeting at Vewa: all our people were present, and gave as follows:—100 mats, 103 spears, 83 clubs, 23 baskets, 19 earthenware pots, 6 baskets of sponge, 2 bows and arrows, 1 large wig, 3 pounds of tortoise-shell, cash £12. This was the second thing of the kind this year, and shows that this people are hearty in the cause in which we are embarked. The white men and their families did themselves great credit on this occasion. Sources will most assuredly open, by the providence of God, for carrying on Christian missions, in quarters where we had not ventured to hope for any supplies. The ability is with men of all lands, and the love of the Saviour will draw it forth.

18th. At Ba two villages had long been at war, but at length the heads of these contending parties accidentally met, and by them a peace was agreed upon. A great feast was fixed on to take place in ten days; one party supplying fish from the ocean, and the other yams from their plantations. At the time proposed those whose part it was to supply the fish, appeared on the ground, and placed their fish in order, when an ambuscade sprang upon them, and murdered twenty-three unarmed men! and, instead of waiting till their ovens were hot, and baking the bodies, having first made an offering to the gods, they fell to, cutting off slices, and roasting small portions for immediate use, before the bodies, as a whole, could be got ready. All these were eaten on the spot, and that very recently, notwithstanding one of our teachers was living near this locality.

A great chief said not long since, when asked to bury some dead bodies, "Look at that oven, and look at his stomach:" (the king of Somosomo, who was sitting by:) "these are the graves where we shall bury all the bodies that fall into our hands." Do not the chiefs of Feejee *love* human flesh? What animal is equal for food, in their estimation, to the human animal?

20th. We weighed anchor at Nakurutumbu, where our work is not so cheeringly prosperous as in some other places. We passed along the coast of Ragi Ragi, and in sight of the Kauvandra mountains; but the gospel makes little way among so many "little wars."

As we passed by Ragi Ragi, the teacher on the spot told us that one of the towns, close at hand, was lately burned, and not less than one hundred persons slain by the invaders, who ate what they could on the ground, and the rest lie there unburied, their bones bleaching in the sun: the murderers lived too far down the coast to allow of the bodies being taken away. Alas! when will the old murderer be satiated with Feejee flesh? Or rather, when will the religion of Christ deprive him of victims, and bind him in chains?

21*st.* We dropped anchor in the bay of Vete-row-row, the western part of Great Feejee, and, except Rewa, by far the finest part that I have seen in this group. As a whole, Feejee may be said to be unavailable land for purposes of cultivation; but here and there a rich spot may be found, by the side of a fine river, where the soil, being alluvial, is deep, and covered with fertility suitable to the torrid zone. Most of Feejee, however, is composed of precipitous mountains and inaccessible hills, nude and barren enough, and exposed, moreover, to the vertical sun without a covering.

Our missionary influence is but little felt in this vicinity. As we lay at anchor in this bay, we could see probably not so few as twenty towns; all heathen, and all cannibal inhabitants. However, "the kingdom of God is come nigh unto them."

A few miles off lay the rather lofty island of Malolo, at the end of a range of islands, forming the western barrier of Feejee, and known as "the A-sowa group." This island was the scene of a bloody catastrophe, which was brought on by the natives, and inflicted by the American exploring ships under the command of Commodore Wilkes.

The natives had killed two white men belonging to the squadron; one of whom, I believe, was an officer. The Americans demanded satisfaction, and gave sufficient time; but, instead of the least effort in that direction, the natives fortified, and prepared for war. Possibly they did this in their great ignorance; but the unequal war did not linger; the town and fortifications were quickly battered down, and frightful was the slaughter! The report of the natives is that from seventy to eighty natives were killed, and as many more wounded and maimed!

No doubt exists as to who was first in this wrong. The natives were first in transgression. The blood of two American citizens cried from the ground against the men of Malolo. The only question unsettled seems to be *the extent of punishment inflicted.* The Americans represented a great nation; far advanced in knowledge and great in power. Might not a consideration of these facts have been fairly expected, by civilized Europe, to act as a *screen* for the barbarians from such terrible vengeance? (so the natives call it.) This great example of civilized power over that of a barbarous people, has not had the effect of putting a stop to the murder of white men in Feejee, which, one is willing to think, might have been the hope of the Americans. But murders have rather increased than diminished since the Malolo catastrophe.

CONCLUSION.

HAVING now visited the islands in both districts, and observed the operations of the missionaries in all the departments of the work in which they are engaged, it remains only for me to suggest such improvements in carrying on this great work, as may have occurred to me from time to time.

I. THE AGENCIES to be in future employed, should be

1. Missionaries from home, of the very best mettle, bodily and mentally, with wives as well fitted for this special work as themselves. They should be persons of sound and hardy constitutions, deeply convinced of their call to this work; willing to live anyhow, and to die anywhere, but never dreaming of leaving the South Sea, until the Lord, who called them into his mission vineyard, shall as clearly show them the way out of it, and as fully approve of their going away, as he did of their entering into this great work. These must be men and women who leave all, and follow their Master whithersoever he goeth. Such persons will be always at home; always happy and useful.

2. Native assistant missionaries, who with sound judgments, and sufficient standing in the work as teachers, may be placed over two or three others in the remote islands; being occasionally visited by the missionary as opportunity shall offer. These may baptize and marry.

3. Teachers, whom God has raised up both in the Friendly Islands and Feejee; men of excellent quali-

ties, deep in their piety, and apt to teach; but in most cases they would be greatly benefited by spending a year or two in the Training Institution. This class of men already numbers several martyrs, and a goodly list of confessors, whom God has signally honored, and no doubt will continue to honor. Their knowledge of native habits and language, and their being natives of the inter-tropical climate, point them out as being the agents designed by the Lord for sowing the seed of the word in their native isles. And these agents will be comparatively inexpensive.

II. Educational operations. Our great object in evangelizing and then elevating these natives into a state of civilization, cannot be attained without educating the youth of both sexes; and the education must, if possible, be general. Not less than four well-trained schoolmasters should be at once sent out for the tropical islands, and a fifth for New-Zealand. The power of the gospel has been felt in our older stations, and prejudice is broken down. It is not likely, then, that we shall get any further with the old people; they will die off, and many will enter into life. But the young are most anxious for instruction; and those who have it, as at Lakemba, spend their days and nights in acquiring learning, and their progress is astonishing.

Two masters will be sufficient for the whole of Feejee; and in a few years these will have trained a supply for the requirements of the entire group. And these again will teach others also; and thus we shall "go up and possess the land, for we are well able," maugre Satan, the pope, and antichrist in all his forms.

In this way the gospel will have converted the sinner to a saint, while education will have raised the barbarian into circles of useful knowledge and habits of peaceful industry.

III. FINANCIAL AFFAIRS. It will not be expected, at this early period, that the South Sea missions should have become self-supporting; but much more may be done by the natives, in the way of contributions, than has hitherto been accomplished, or perhaps attempted. Nor is it certain that putting off the time when they should be solicited to give, will answer any valuable end. All my observations go to the opposite conclusion; namely, that as soon as a few people in any place begin to *lotu*, they should be called upon to contribute towards the support of the gospel. Did they not give largely to their heathen gods? not merely a little *property*, but fingers, arms, and legs? Yea, and not in a few cases only, *life itself* was offered at the shrine of an idol.

Nor is this all. Their being asked to contribute towards sending abroad the word of God, would greatly please them, and do them good. They would enter into the matter in due form, and with great ceremony. A day must be fixed for the offering; all necessary preparations are made. They go to their heathen friends for help; and they will and do help them, as I saw at Bua, and heard of elsewhere. The day of offering is a great day with them; they recite what they have learned out of the Scriptures, the catechism, and the hymn-book. They invite their heathen neighbors, who hear these recitals. All are dressed clean and well; and a feast closes the day. When they are asked on the day following, what they think of yesterday, their answer will be, in true Oriental style, "Yesterday was the only day ever seen in this land."

It is much easier to begin early, when their hearts have just begun to open to the Lord, than it is to introduce the subject some years after, when they will be sure to find excuses. New-Zealand may be taken in proof of this. A spoiled professor will be certainly selfish, conceited, and self-willed. Train the plant which the Lord hath planted; and let the training be as early as the plant will bear.

But what have these poor creatures to give? The best answer to this may be found in the hold of the "John Wesley," as the produce of our Tonga *catuanga*, and of the *solavu* of Feejee: here are the givings of the islands to the mission fund; and they are most ready to give such things as they have; some one thing, and some another:—

COCOA-NUT OIL: of this many tuns annually may be obtained, when we have tanks in the brig to hold the same.

SHELLS, many and beautiful on the extensive reefs of these islands.

ARROW-ROOT may be obtained to some considerable extent, both in Tonga and Feejee.

CLUBS and SPEARS cast away to the moles and bats, where the gospel ends their wars.

SANDAL-WOOD: if at all valued, this may be obtained pretty largely.

Beside the above, there are a multitude of articles to be obtained: only let the people know that we can turn them to account, and we shall get sponge, *ligu*, "dresses," pearls, and mats, with bowls, as many as we can desire. But oil and arrow-root will probably be the best.

IV. THE "JOHN WESLEY," in my opinion, should not be required to navigate so much among the dangers of Feejee. A minute and accurate survey of this group is a great desideratum. Two fine brigs, the "Lady Howden" and the "Fanny," lie there on the reefs at this hour, both total wrecks. The "John Wesley" might have made the third vessel on the rocks, but for the unceasing pains and vigilance of Captain Buck, and the care of Divine Providence always over us for good, and in answer to many prayers.

In many cases it is found impossible to make the distance we wish to go in one day; and, if you are out in the night among the reefs, currents, and sunken rocks, what is to become of the vessel? The dangers on every side, *by day*, and with a breeze, are quite enough to try ordinary nerves; but *by night* they are really frightful, and should never be encountered.

The sunken rocks are from four to twelve feet below the surface of the water, and very numerous, upon which there is no breaker, the water being smooth among the reefs; a good look-out from the mast-head is the only security. But if the weather be cloudy, or the sun low and a-head, nothing can be seen, and on you go, bumping upon the hidden danger.

KING GEORGE.

APPENDIX.

The mission to the Friendly Islands, which had been suspended by the departure of Mr. Lawry from Tonga, in November, 1823, was resumed, by the appointment of the Rev. John Thomas, who sailed from England in the month of April, 1825, and arrived in Tonga on the 28th of June, 1826, accompanied by Mrs. Thomas, and Mr. and Mrs. Hutchinson. Mr. and Mrs. Thomas still survive, and are frequently mentioned with honor by Mr. Lawry in the preceding journal.

At that time Mr. Thomas gives it as his conviction, that the character of the natives had not improved since their murder of the missionaries of the London Missionary Society in 1797: he appears to have considered it very doubtful whether the mission would succeed in Tonga; and that if it failed in Tonga, there was no probability of success on any of the other islands of that or the neighboring groups. These were his views after a residence of ten months on the island; so remote at that time appeared the glorious results which he has lived to witness.

Mr. Thomas and Mr. Hutchinson resided with Chief Ata, at Hihifo, who received them with kindness, and made fair promises that he would protect them, and allow them liberty to teach and preach. They soon found that he was no better than Mr. Lawry's chief, Fatu, at the Mua, whom they had avoided because of the reports of his conduct which had reached them. The cupidity and violence of Ata frequently placed their lives in jeopardy. Under such inauspicious circumstances it became a question with them, whether they ought to remain at Tonga or to remove to some station of brighter prospect; but, unwilling to quit the post of duty, however hazardous or toilsome, they still lingered on the island, in hope of events occurring to justify their continued residence, and to encourage the expectation of final success.

A few weeks after their arrival, Ata attended public worship; but it soon became manifest that his views were selfish and sordid. He conducted himself with so much violence as to justify their apprehension, that he intended no less than murder, and the entire destruction of the mission, which was prevented by the courageous intercession of another chief. Two months afterwards Ata assembled his subjects, severely reprimanded the few poor men who attended the instructions of the missionaries, and commanded them to leave the district. He attempted to justify his conduct by saying, that the missionaries were a bad people, who were using their endeavors *to pray them to death.* The chief's wife also took away the few women whom Mrs. Hutchinson had begun to teach; and the people were forbidden to sell the missionaries any food.

The first dawn of encouragement beamed on the mission on the 4th of February, 1827, when a number of persons from Nukualofa, a place twelve miles distant from Hihifo, attended public worship. Two Tahitian teachers connected with the London Missionary Society, on their way to Feejee, had resided with Tubou, the chief of Nukualofa. Under their influence and instruction Tubou gave up the Tonga gods, destroyed the spirit-house, and erected a place for Christian worship, in which he and his people assembled to listen to divine truth in the Tahitian language, which, however, was very imperfectly understood. The number of persons who, together with Tubou, their chief, professed to worship Jehovah at Nukualofa, was two hundred and forty.

Thus was the London Missionary Society permitted the honor of commencing that great work which has resulted in the settled Christianity of the Friendly Islands, and of the neighboring groups. Their first missionaries, as they were called, were ten mechanics, who were landed at Hihifo, Tongatabu, from the ship "Duff," Captain Wilson, in the year 1797. Their labors appear to have had no good effect, being counteracted by the counsels and example of three ungodly sailors who resided on the island. At length a war broke out; the neutrality of the missionaries was disregarded, and three of them, together with an American seaman, were barbarously clubbed. One of the survivors, awful to relate, apostatized to paganism. The rest continued faithful; until, utterly destitute of all the comforts of life, and with no prospect of usefulness on the island, they thankfully accepted the offer of a passage to New South Wales, and left their mission in the year 1800. It has been seen, that two native missionaries from the Society's more successful mission at Tahiti, on their way to Feejee, were at Tonga in 1826, when the Wesleyan missionaries arrived on the island to resume the mission commenced by Mr. Lawry in 1822; and that, moved by their teaching and conduct, Tubou and his people at Nukualofa had embraced the profession of Christianity. Subsequently to this period, the Wesleyan missionaries exclusively have labored in the Friendly and Feejee Islands. "One soweth, and another reapeth:" "Other men have labored, and we have entered into their labors." The London Missionary Society, who willingly left this part of the field to another society, have had the comfort of knowing that their successors have been neither unfaithful nor unsuccessful; and, in their turn, they have received an advantage,—for the Wesleyan Missionary Society retired from the good prospects they had in the Navigators' Islands in 1839, that the London Missionary Society might have uninterrupted scope for the very efficient mission they proposed to establish there.

Tubou was severely tried in his profession of Christianity: the heathen chiefs used their utmost endeavors, by persuasions and threats, to shake his constancy; and at length, other means failing, they promised to consecrate him *Tui Kanokubolu,* that is, "King of Kanokubolu," provided he would engage to abandon Christianity. This is the highest honor a Tonga chief can attain. Though Tubou was proof against threats, he could not withstand this temptation to honor; he therefore consented to leave off praying to Jehovah for the present, but allowed the inferior chiefs and common people to do as they pleased.

In 1827 two missionaries went to reside at Nukualofa, the Rev. Nathaniel Turner and the Rev. William Cross;* and soon after commenced the great work which has issued in the prevalence of a profession of Christianity throughout the Friendly Islands. Tubou was baptized on the 10th of January, 1830, by the name of Josiah; his queen, Mary, had been previously baptized, as well as many of his subjects; the congregation, on the day of his baptism, amounted to about six hundred persons. Tubou, or Josiah Tubou, as he was called after his baptism, died in November, 1845.

At the same time Josiah Tubou was king in Tonga, Taufaahau, now George, was king of Haabai, and Feenau,

* Memoir of the Rev. William Cross, by the Rev. John Hunt. A most interesting and admirable book—not merely containing memorials of the life of an eminent Christian and highly-honored and successful missionary; but also embodying, to some extent, the rich stores of thought and experience treasured up in the capacious and devout mind of the lamented author. In reading it one hardly knows which to admire most, the character of the excellent man who is the subject of the memoir, the strange facts he witnessed, the wonderful success which God gave him and his fellow-laborers, or the piety and ability, combined with the utmost simplicity and earnestness, exhibited in the compilation of the book, the author, meantime, struggling with all the trials and inconveniences of a mission in a savage land, and among a nation of cannibals. What a lesson on the sufficiency of divine grace! To God be all the glory! See note C, page 494.

of Vavau. Feenau died before Josiah Tubou; George then became king of Vavau as well as of Haabai; after the death of Josiah Tubou, George was inaugurated *Tui Kanokubolu*, and now reigns over the three groups of Tonga, Haabai, and Vavau, or the whole of the Friendly Islands.

In 1835 the mission was extended to the Feejee Islands. For the early and eventful history of the Feejee mission, we refer to Mr. Hunt's Memoir of the Rev. William Cross, mentioned above.

A translation of the Scriptures into the language of the Friendly Islands has long been in progress. An edition of four thousand copies of the entire New Testament has lately been issued from the mission-press at Vavau. This precious boon to the native Christians had been preceded by the publication of many thousand copies of various portions of the Old and New Testaments, and of many thousand tracts, catechisms, and hymn-books.

A translation of the New Testament into the Feejee language has also been effected. A copy of this very valuable work was brought to this country by the widow of the late Rev. John Hunt; and, having been first presented to the committee of the Wesleyan Missionary Society, was by them forwarded to the committee of the British and Foreign Bible Society; who, on the 5th of November last, voted three hundred pounds from their funds to the Wesleyan Missionary Society, towards the expense which had been incurred by the society in accomplishing this first complete edition of the New Testament in the language used by the inhabitants of the Feejee Islands. A translation of the Old Testament into the same language is in a forward state.

The present state of the mission is detailed in the preceding journal; and we only add a tabular view, compiled from the most recent reports, of the statistics of those missions to the Wesleyan Missionary Society.

TABULAR VIEW OF THE FRIENDLY-ISLANDS DISTRICT.

	CENTRAL OR PRINCIPAL STATIONS OR CIRCUITS.						
	Tonga.	Habai.	Vavau.	Niuatobu-Tabu.	Niua-Foou.	Uvea.	Total.
Chapels	26	21	33	7	9	..	96
Other Preaching Places	..	..	..	..	..	3	3
Missionaries and Assistant Missionaries	4	2	4	..	..	..	10
Paid Agents:—Catechists, &c.	2	..	..	1	5	1	9
Unpaid Agents:—							
Day-school Teachers	366	277	290	○	○	○	933
Local Preachers	90	160	175	28	34	2	489
Full and accredited Church Members	1830	2184	2170	393	539	86	7202
On trial for Membership	47	35	..	..	..	..	82
Day-schools	58	58	62	○	○	○	178
Day-scholars of both Sexes	2813	2188	2425	○	○	○	7426
Attendants on public Worship, including Members and Scholars	2500	2500	3000	400	700	100	9200

○ No Returns.

TABULAR VIEW OF THE FEEJEE-ISLANDS DISTRICT.

	CENTRAL OR PRINCIPAL STATIONS OR CIRCUITS.				
	Lakemba	Viwa.	Bua.	Nandy.	Total.
Chapels	28	4	3	2	37
Other Preaching Places	10	6	3	4	23
Missionaries and Assistant Missionaries	3	3	1	2	9
Paid Agents:—Catechists, &c.	15	14	4	5	38
Unpaid Agents:—					
Day-school Teachers	75	20	6	16	117
Local Preachers	60	4	2	2	68
Full and accredited Church Members	1160	166	157	230	1713
On trial for Membership	48	31	25	19	123
Day-Schools	35	7	3	4	49
Day-scholars of both Sexes	1060	490	150	260	1960
Attendants on public Worship, including Members and Scholars	2500	698	280	350	3828

The appended description of the Friendly Islands and of the Feejee Islands has been compiled with great care. The accurate and ample information thus presented will be found to add greatly to the value of this book, and will repay an attentive perusal.

THE FRIENDLY ISLANDS.

The Friendly or Tonga Islands are situated in the Pacific, between 18° and 23° south latitude, and 173° and 176° west longitude. They consist of three separate groups, which are said to contain more than one hundred and fifty islands. Fifteen of them rise to a considerable height, thirty-five are moderately elevated, and the rest are low.

The most southern group, the Tongatabu Islands, were discovered by Tasman in 1643. Tonga, the largest of them, is about twenty miles long and twelve wide in its broadest part. The highest part of Tonga, the little Mount of Nukualofa, on which the chapel stands, rises about sixty feet above the sea; the surface of the island generally is only a few feet above the level of the ocean.

The central group, called the Haabai Islands, is composed of a considerable number of small islands. The most populous of them is Lefuka, about eight or nine miles long and four broad. These islands are very fertile. Some of them are very low, but others are of a considerable height, especially Tofua and Kao; the former has an active volcano, which occasionally pours forth streams of lava; the middle of the island is a large sheet of water; and, for a great distance round the mouth of the crater, the surface is torn to pieces by the eruptions which have taken place. Kao is a conical island eight hundred or a thousand feet above the sea: it stands néar Tofua, a little to the north. Tradition says, it was thrown out by the gods from the middle of Tofua, where the sheet of water now is. There are few inhabitants, and but little food, on these two islands.

The most northern group is formed by the Vavau Islands, which are somewhat larger and higher than the Haabai Islands. The island of Vavau, which is a fine island, is about thirty-six miles in circumference: its surface is uneven, and, on the northern side, rises to a considerable elevation.

Funua-lai is a high volcanic island, about ten miles in circumference; until the year 1846 it was covered with verdure, and abounded with fruit-trees. Now, however, it is a huge mass of lava and burnt sand; reduced from a fine cone to a ghastly heap of scoria and black powder, without one leaf or blade of grass of any kind: all things that had life have been utterly destroyed. Of the approach of this terrific calamity the inhabitants had distinct warnings by violent earthquakes, which preceded the eruption; they therefore left the island, and went to Vavau. The terrible eruption soon afterwards happened, which reduced Funua-lai to a smoking ruin, and presented a scene awfully grand The bursting forth of crater after crater was seen in all directions; and the sea, to a great distance, was discolored by the floods of lava poured forth. The flames illuminated the atmosphere at Vavau, distant thirty-five miles; and the noise was distinctly heard, during three successive days, at Niua Foou, distant one hundred and thirty miles! Dust and vitrified matter were discharged to such a distance, that their withering effects on vegetation were experienced thirty-five miles off, at Vavau, where the damage was very considerable, both to the trees, and the crops generally.*

The climate of the Friendly Islands is humid, and the heat rather oppressive, rising frequently to 98° in the shade. Much rain falls periodically. The trade-winds are not constant, and westerly winds occasionally blow in every season, which, from their variable character, have obtained

* The most northern of the Friendly Islands is Amargure or Gardner Island, in latitude 17° 57′; and the most southern is Pylstaart, in latitude 22° 26′.

from the natives the name of "foolish winds." Any variable winds the natives call *matayo vale*, or "foolish winds." Very heavy dews fall at night; the transitions from heat to cold are sudden and great, and the nights are often so chilly as to make blankets necessary. Hurricanes are frequent, scarcely a season passing without some occurrence of the kind. The months of February and March are those in which they occur; but they have also taken place in November and December. The storms begin at the north-west, thence veer to the eastward, and end in the south-east. The wind continues to increase until it becomes a hurricane; and is frequently observed to change almost immediately from one point to its opposite. In the same group of islands, trees have fallen during one gale, some to the south and others to the north. Earthquakes are also frequent.*

These islands are remarkable for their fertility, and the variety of their vegetable productions. Eooa is so fruitful, as to be designated "the granary of Tongataboo." The island of Tongataboo, which is nearly a dead level, with the exception of a few hillocks, thirty or forty feet high, has a rich and fertile vegetable mold, which is not composed of sand, as in other coral islands.

The Friendly Islands abound in those fruits indigenous to tropical climates: as the cocoa-nut, the bread-fruit, the banana, the pine-apple, the orange, the citron, the lime, the custard-apple, &c.; melons and pumpkins are also very plentiful, and of excellent quality. The bays and shores all teem with various kinds of fish.

* If the missionaries on the Friendly and Feejee Islands were furnished with a few instruments, and kept a register of natural phenomena, it would tend to the promotion of science, and might also interest learned men in these missions. A scientific voyager, who recently visited these islands, relates, that he found the missionaries wholly unprovided with any such instruments. The absence of them is deplored by none more than by the missionaries themselves. If possessed, they would not only interest scientific men, but benefit the natives.

The natives of the Friendly Islands, in habits, customs, looks, and general appearance, greatly resemble those of the Samoan or Navigators' Islands. They are a little lighter in color than the Samoans, and the young children are almost white. They were formerly left, both males and females, to run about in a state of nature, with their hair shaved close, except a small curly lock over each ear. But this is not now the case. The youngest Christian child has a covering of *fetaki* or white *tapa* about the loins, unless occasionally in the house. This practice is also prevalent among the Samoans. Indeed, the similarity in the appearance of the children of the two groups is such, that they might be mistaken for each other. The Samoans seem to have derived many things from Tonga, particularly their *tapa* covering from the waist downwards, called *siapo.* The two races also agree in having no covering for the head; and the females resemble each other. Wilkes says, "A larger proportion of fine-looking people is seldom to be seen in any portion of the globe." Their countenances are generally of the Asiatic cast; they are tall, and well made, and their muscles are well developed. The women are equally remarkable for their personal beauty.

The population of the Friendly Islands is estimated by missionaries at about fifty thousand.

Their political constitution is despotism, supported by an hereditary aristocracy. In one view, however, the government may be considered as a kind of family compact; for the persons holding titles and offices address one another by the names of father, son, uncle, and grandfather, without any reference whatever to their real degrees of relationship.

Their manner of investing the monarch with kingly dignity is as follows:—The chiefs of the various islands assemble on the occasion; and the ceremony takes place at a *kava** meeting. Two chiefs, who are called fathers, sit,

* *Kava* is an infusion of the root of a species of the pepper plant (*Piper Mythisticum.*) Among these islanders, there is no religious rite

the one on the king's right hand, and the other on his left. Their office is to relieve the king, and to act on his account. The other chiefs sit on either side, forming a large circle; and the bulk of the people in front. Before the *kava* is served out, the chief on the king's right hand opens the business of the meeting, by stating the object for which they have assembled. The different chiefs, and the king also, speak in turn. When the king's *cava* is poured into the dish, he is saluted by the chief on his right hand with the title expressive of his office or dignity, *Tui Kanokubolu;* that is, "King of Kanokubolu."

The ranks of society are, king, chiefs, matabooles, tooas, and tamaioeikis, or slaves. There are some individuals connected with the heathen priesthood, who are considered superior in rank to the kings, and to whom the kings do homage. The *Tamaha* (see page 33) was considered to have descended from the gods. The Rev. Charles Tucker says, "I have a god, a whale's tooth, which she sent me; she called it her *Kui,* that is, 'grandfather,' or 'grandmother,' for the same term is used for both. I have seen King George and his brother carrying her to and from the chapel in her palanquin, as though they were her children or servants. She was looked upon as a sacred person, having had much to do with the gods. Josiah Tubou, the late *Tui Kanokubolu,* paid her homage, and gave her the precedence at the *kava*-ring. Probably the name will die with the old lady. There are two other persons belonging to the sacred race who are considered superior in rank to the *Tui Kanokubolu;* they, however, are but little known, being still heathen. They are the *Tui Tonga-tagata* and the *Tui Tonga-fefine,* or, literally, the 'Man King of Tonga,' and the 'Woman King of Tonga.' I expect when they die the title will become extinct or obsolete."

of which the ceremony of drinking *kava* does not form a part; and almost every matter to be settled is done at a *kava*-meeting. Great order and formality are observed on these occasions.

The mataboolcs rank next to the chiefs, and are a sort of honorable attendants on them,—their companions, counselors, and advisers. They see that the orders and wishes of their chiefs are duly executed, and may not improperly be called their ministers. They are always looked up to as men of experience and superior information. The sons and brothers of matabooles assist at public ceremonies, under the direction of the matabooles. The matabooles attend to the good order of society, and look to the morals of the younger chiefs, who are apt to run into excesses, and oppress the lower orders. They are much respected by all classes. Tooas are the commonalty, or the bulk of the people.

The present king of these islands is an exemplary Christian, and a preacher of the gospel. The inhabitants are in a transition-state. A new order of things is springing up. Club-arbitration, which formerly prevailed, has been laid aside; a code of laws is being framed, governors are appointed to the different groups, and courts of justice instituted.

Regarding the origin of the people of Tonga, they have the following tradition:—At a time when the islands of Tonga were already existing, but not yet peopled with intelligent beings, some of the minor gods of Bulotu,* being desirous to see the new world which had been fished up, put to sea, about two hundred in number, male and female, in a large canoe, and arrived at the island of Tonga. They were so well pleased with the place, that they determined to remain there; and accordingly broke up their canoe to make small ones of it; but in a few days, two or three of them died. This phenomenon alarmed all the rest; for decay and death was what their notion of their own immortality did not lead them to expect. About this time, one

* Bulotu is the place of residence of certain of their gods and shades of the dead. It is similar to Hades of the Greeks, but not situated under the earth.

of them felt himself strangely affected, and by this he knew that one of the superior gods was coming from Bulotu to inspire him. In a little time he was actually inspired, and was told that the chief gods had decreed, that as they had come to Tonga, had breathed its air, and fed upon its produce, they should become mortal, and people the world with mortal beings, and all about them should be *maha mahaki;* that is, "subject to decay and death." Upon this, they were all exceedingly grieved, and were sorry they had broken up their canoe; but they made another, and some of them put to sea with the hope of regaining the island of Bulotu; in which endeavor if they succeeded, they were to return and bring their companions. They looked, however, in vain for the land of the gods, and were obliged to return, sorely afflicted, to Tonga.

There are four principal gods in the mythology of the Friendly Islands; namely, Maui, Hikuleo, Tangaloa, and Hea-moana-uli-uli. They are brothers.

1. Maui.—Maui is said to have drawn up the islands out of the sea with a hook and line. Those he did not tread down continue to be mountainous. The first he drew up he named Ata, which is referred to Pylstaart; the next was Tonga, with all its group of islands; then Lofanga, and the other Haabai islands; and last, the Vavau group. After he had finished his work, he fixed his residence at Tonga. To Maui is also ascribed the origin of that most useful tree called *toa*, the iron-wood, which in time reached the sky, and enabled the god called Etumatubua to descend.

Maui had two sons; the eldest called Maui Atalonga, and the younger Kijikiji. Kijikiji obtained fire from the earth, and taught them to cook their food, which they found was good; and from that day, food has been cooked, which before was eaten raw. In order to preserve the fire, Kijikiji commanded it to go into certain trees, whence it is now obtained by friction. They further say, that during the time old Maui was on the earth, the only light was like that of the moon, and that neither day nor night existed; that Maui resides under the earth, and bears it on his shoulders. His nodding, when disposed to sleep, produces the earthquake; when this occurs, the people stamp the ground, and vociferate, to awake the god, lest he should nod so violently as to upset the island into the sea.

2. Hikuleo.—Hikuleo is the god of spirits, and is the younger brother of Maui. He lives in Bulotu, which he governs. *Hiku* means "tail," and *leo* means "to watch." This name was given him because, when his body goes about, his tail stays at home and watches. He is a saucy god, and takes away the people to Bulotu. To prevent his destroying all the inhabitants of the world, he is kept in check by two of his brothers; a strong thread is fastened around him, one end of which is held by Maui, under the earth, and the other by Tangaloa, in the sky. In his cave he holds his feasts, and lives with his wives, by whom he has many children. He has absolute power over all, and all are forced to go to him. He is a being without love or goodness. To him the spirits of the chiefs and matabooles go, become his servants, and are forced to do his will, and to serve him for what purpose he pleases. He even uses them, it is said, to make fences of, or to form bars for his gates. They entertain the idea, that the house of this deity, and all things in it, are made of human spirits, where they continue to serve without end. They never pray to Hikuleo, except when some sacrilege has been committed on the offerings they make him; and on this occasion they offer a human sacrifice. They also invoke this deity when the *Tui Tonga*, "King of Tonga," is sick; and it depends on the reigning *Tui Kanokubolu*, whether or not a human sacrifice is offered. None but gods are ever permitted to come from Bulotu. This god has his spirit-temple, where all their valuable offerings to the gods are deposited.

3. Tangaloa.—Tangaloa resides in the sky. He sends

forth the thunder and lightning; and when a thunder-storm occurs, it is supposed that he is killing a chief. Tangaloa is the god of carpenters, whose business is the most honorable employment in the Friendly Islands. He is supposed to be the god of all foreigners, whom he has taught to construct such beautiful vessels. Captain Cook and others were supposed to have come from the sky, sent by Tangaloa. The heathen will sometimes use this plea for not worshiping the God of foreigners: "You serve Tangaloa, the younger saucy brother; we serve Hikuleo, the elder: why should we leave the elder to serve the younger brother?"

4. HEA-MOANA-ULI-ULI.—He governs the sea, and is worshiped under the form of the sea-serpent. The fish are all under his control. Fishermen apply to him for success in their undertakings.*

The Friendly Islanders regard Bulotu as the place of departed spirits. It is the abode of the god Hikuleo. There are several *Bulotus*, and the spirit of the deceased is admitted to that for which he is prepared by his conduct in this world. In one of the *Bulotus* they eat the pink yam; but in all there are plenty of yams and plenty of wives. Here also is the *Vaiola*.

Vaiola, or "water of life."—This is near the residence of Hikuleo in *Bulotu*. Its properties are those of restoring the dead to life, causing the dumb to speak, the lame to walk, the blind to see, &c.: in fact, it cures all diseases. It restores youth to the aged, and causes those who bathe in it to be immortal.

Akaulea, "speaking-tree."—This tree is near the house of Hikuleo in *Bulotu*. It performs a similar office to that

* For many of these particulars we are indebted to Mrs. Tucker, the wife of the Rev. C. Tucker, late of Tonga; Mr. Tucker, also, has furnished valuable information. The Rev. George Kevern has likewise favored us with several hints and corrections, which are here thankfully acknowledged.—EDIT.

of the king's speaker at a *kava*-ring. It receives the commands of the god. Thus, when the god wishes for some one from this world, he tells the tree his mind; the tree sends a canoe, death does his office upon the person, and the invisible canoe bears him off to *Bulotu*.

Is the following a confused account of the Saviour's birth?—At Tonumea, the most southerly of the Haabai Islands, there is a rock, which tradition says was formerly a female. While yet a virgin she was found to be with child. Her friends were astonished, and asked her how it was. She said she had committed no sin, but she was with child by the sun. As the child (a boy) grew up, he was naughty; they accordingly sent him in a canoe to go and *live* with his father the sun in the sky.

Their higher gods do not consider lying, theft, adultery, murder, &c., as crimes, but as things of this world, which are left for the inferior gods to deal with, and do not concern their more elevated natures. The only crime against the higher gods is sacrilege committed on their temples, or an improper use of the offerings.

The Friendly Islanders believe that all evil is inflicted by certain gods, called *Otua Bauu;* that is, "mischievous gods."

There seems to be a considerable difference among the natives of the different clusters of the South-Sea Islands respecting the future existence of the soul. Whilst the Tonguese doctrine limits immortality to chiefs, matabooles, and, at furthest, to mooas, the Feejees extend it to all mankind, to all brute animals, to all vegetables, and even to stones and mineral substances. (See page 474.)

The human soul, after its separation from the body, is termed an *otua;* that is, a "spirit;" and is believed to exist in the shape of the body, to have the same propensities as during life, but corrected by a more enlightened understanding; by which it readily distinguishes good from evil, truth from falsehood, right from wrong. It possesses the same attributes as the original gods, but in a minor degree; and has its dwelling forever in the happy regions of Bulotu; holding the same rank in regard to other souls as during this life. It has also the power of returning to Tonga to inspire priests,* relations, and others, or to appear in dreams to those it wishes to admonish; and, sometimes, to manifest itself to the external eye, in the form of a ghost or apparition. But this power of re-appearance at Tonga only belongs to the souls of chiefs, not of inferior persons. The souls of inferior persons are not supposed to have a conscious existence hereafter.

According to the Tonguese, there is no state of future punishment: all rewards for virtue are bestowed, and punishments for vice inflicted, in this world.

The practice of circumcision was found prevalent in the Friendly Islands, as in other parts of Polynesia; they perform the rite at fourteen years of age.

Old persons of both sexes are highly reverenced on account of their age and experience, insomuch that it constitutes an important branch of moral and religious duty to reverence the gods, the chiefs, and aged persons. It is said, there is hardly an instance, in these islands, of old age being wantonly insulted.

Women have very considerable respect shown them, according to their rank: if the mother was a chief, the daughter will occupy her rank, whoever the father may be. Women are considered as contributing much to the comforts and domestic happiness of the other sex; and as they are the weaker of the two, it is thought unmanly not to show them attention and kind regard. They are, therefore, not subjected to hard labor, or any very menial work.

The women occupy themselves, particularly those of noble rank, in making a variety of articles, chiefly ornamental. But these employments are viewed as accomplish-

* The Friendly Islanders' doctrine regarding inspiration is the same as that of the Feejeeans. See p. 472.

ments, not as professions. Some of the higher classes of women, however, make these not only an amusement, but a sort of trade, without prejudice to their rank. Though the highest accomplishments cannot add to a woman's rank, they do somewhat to the estimation in which she may be held; for such things, when well done, are esteemed honorable in a woman of dignity.

The adoption of children is universally practiced by the Friendly Islanders.

It is a custom in these islands, for women to become what they call mothers to children, or grown-up young persons, who are not their own, for the purpose of providing them, or seeing that they are provided, with all the conveniences of life. And this is often done, although their own natural mothers be living, and residing near the spot. Mariner tells us, that Mafi Habai, one of the wives of the king, was his foster-mother, by appointment of her husband. To this person he was greatly indebted for a considerable portion of his intimate knowledge of the language and customs of Tonga. She took very great pains in teaching him the correct pronunciation; and frequently laughed him out of such habits and customs, in dress, manners, and conversation, as were not strictly according to the Tonga fashion, or not considered sufficiently polished and becoming a noble. In all respects, and on every occasion, she conducted herself towards him with the greatest natural affection, modesty, and propriety. She was a woman of excellent understanding, personal beauty, and amiable manners.

When Captain Cook visited these islands, habits of war, it is said, were little known to the natives. The only quarrels in which they had at that time been engaged were among the inhabitants of the Feejee Islands. Having been in the habit of visiting those islands for sandal-wood, &c., they occasionally assisted one or other of the warlike parties. The bows and arrows which before that period had been in use among the people of Tonga, were of a weaker kind, and fitted rather for sport than war,—for shooting rats, birds, &c. From the fierce and warlike people of the Feejee Islands, however, they soon learned to construct bows and arrows of a much more martial and formidable nature; and soon became acquainted with a better form of spear, and a superior method of holding and throwing that missile. They also imitated the Feejeeans, by degrees, in the practice of painting their faces, and using a peculiar dress in time of war, giving them a fierce appearance, calculated to strike with terror the minds of their enemies. So great, indeed, was the change that passed on the character of the *Friendly* Islanders of Cook, that it was observed of them, that "*war-councils*, making speeches, and drinking *kava*, may be called the business of their lives." This, however, is not now the case. The gospel has taught them the duty and the value of peace. It may now be said, there have been no wars in Tonga since 1840, when Captain Croker, of H. M. S. "Favorite," was unfortunately killed by the heathen warriors at the Bea fortress. (See Waterhouse's Journal, Wesleyan Missionary Notices for February, 1844, p. 470.)

The intercourse between the Feejee and Friendly Islands has, of late years, much increased. The inhabitants of the latter are more inclined to leave their home, than those of the former. And when a Friendly Islander has once visited the Feejee group, and returned safely, he is looked upon as a traveler. In Tonga, they consider the Feejee Islanders as more polished than themselves, and view their opinions with much respect. This is not only observable in their conversation, but they show it by adopting their manners and customs, and by the attention and deference they pay to the opinions of those who have visited or belong to that group. The Friendly Islanders build their canoes in Feejee: they did not learn navigation from Feejeeans; but from the situation of their islands, being more exposed to a rough ocean, they have probably become better and more adventurous navigators. They are of a superior and enterprising spirit in affairs of navigation, which may be said to constitute a feature of their national character. Their superiority in this respect was so great, when Mariner was among them, that no native of Feejee would venture to Tonga, except in a canoe manned with Tonga people; nor return to his own islands, unless under the same guidance and protection. This is still the case. This intercourse is kept up more particularly with the eastern islands of Feejee. When Captain Cook was at this group, little was known respecting the Feejee Islands. Thirty years afterwards, when Mariner resided on the Tonga Islands, the intercourse had increased, and information respecting Feejee became more accurate; and since that period it has been very considerably augmented. The prevailing winds are in favor of the intercourse on the side of the Friendly Islanders, which may, in some measure, account for it; and although it is a practice of cannibal Feejee to cook and eat any persons who may be wrecked on their coasts, yet the flattering accounts those who have returned have given of their reception, may in some degree account for the desire they always evince to pay the Feejee group a visit. In a very few years hence, through the intercourse that will be brought about by the missionaries, probably, there will be as much passing to and fro between them, as there is now among the several islands of either group, which will greatly tend to advance the civilization of both.

The Friendly Islanders, generally, are an idle people. They engage in labor with great reluctance; and when prevailed upon to perform any work, it is very difficult to satisfy their exorbitant expectations. To this remark it must be acknowledged there are very many honorable exceptions. Their progress in civilization has, however, as yet, been but small. This is not so much their fault, as the natural result of their situation and circumstances. In order to form a correct estimate on this point, it is important to bear in mind, that civilization, according to the ideas of a European, is so connected with extensive commerce, vast manufactures, and wonderful machines of various kinds, that with these only it is imagined civilization can exist. Europeans are in this, however, totally deceived. In a country, such as that presented by these islands, where nature almost spontaneously produces every requisite, what need is there (might not the inhabitants argue?) of building ships, and undertaking perilous voyages, to bring those things which we do not require, and to exchange our superior productions for the inferior or useless ones of other countries? Or, why spend our strength in manufacturing those things of which we feel not the want, and know not, till taught, the use? Thus, we see that the development of civilization is essentially various in different situations. That which marks refinement in the coldness of Europe, may be a useless encumbrance, an uncomfortable appendage in the Friendly Islands. A great means, however, of stimulating the industry of these islanders, and of the inhabitants of the South Seas generally, and promoting civilization among them, would be the opening up a channel of commerce with the Pacific by way of the Isthmus of Panama, as has been contemplated. Without some such direct communication with America and Europe, the capabilities of the rich and productive soils of Polynesia must remain undeveloped.

The first attempt to introduce Christianity into the Friendly Islands, was made in the year 1797, when Captain Wilson, of the "Duff," left ten mechanics at Hihifo, a town on Tongataboo, in the capacity of missionaries. After having resided together for some time, they separated for the purpose of being more extensively useful. Their labors, however, proved unsuccessful. The chief, under whose protection they resided, was murdered by his own brother, and the island involved in a sanguinary and desolating war.

Three of them were murdered by the natives. The others were obliged to take refuge among the rocks and dens of the island. They were plundered of their property, stripped of their wearing apparel, and subjected to various kinds of insult. When the strife terminated, the missionaries endeavored to support themselves by hard labor. The natives, however, having stolen everything they possessed, it was with great difficulty they succeeded in constructing a forge. When this was accomplished, the thievish inhabitants brought the articles they had stolen, in order to have them manufactured into some other form that pleased them better. In 1800, an English ship arrived among the islands, the captain of which offered the distressed missionaries a passage to New South Wales; and they, being utterly destitute, and having but little prospect of usefulness among the natives, gladly accepted the proposal. Thus, the mission, for a time, was abandoned.

The Rev. Walter Lawry, of the Wesleyan Missionary Society, arrived at Tongataboo in August, 1822: he was kindly received by the people, and, for a time, well treated. Like his predecessors, however, he experienced but little encouragement. The natives viewed him as the harbinger of soldiers, who would shortly come to kill them and seize their island; and consequently treated him with suspicion. He was ultimately obliged to remove to the colony of New South Wales, in the end of 1823, on account of domestic circumstances. In 1825, the Rev. Messrs. John Thomas, and John Hutchinson, of the same society, were appointed to Tongataboo. They arrived in June, 1826, and fixed their residence at Hihifo; where they erected a substantial dwelling-house, and commenced the study of the language and instruction of the people. They also met with great opposition, and but little success.

The Rev. Nathaniel Turner, the Rev. William Cross, and Mr. Weiss, also of the Wesleyan Society, arrived at Tongataboo, in the year 1827, and found at Nukualofu, one of the chief towns in the island, two Christian teachers, Tahitians, who had been some time employed, in that locality, preaching to the people in the Tahitian language. They had erected a chapel, and two hundred and forty persons attended their teaching.

The preceding Journal contains interesting notices of several islands not included in the number of the Friendly Islands; as, Uvea, or Wallis Island, situated in latitude 13° 24′ south, longitude 176° 9′ east. This, instead of being a single island, as might be expected from its name, consists of nine separate islands, varying in circuit from one to ten miles, inclosed by one extensive reef. The land is in general high.

Another of these remote islands is Niua Foou, situated in about 15° south latitude, and which is of a very remarkable character. It is chiefly composed of blocks of lava, is about fifteen miles in circumference, and hollow in the middle. Its form resembles the brim of a hat, the centre being the crater of an extinct volcano. Some of the old people yet remember the last great eruption. A body of brackish water occupies this immense cavity, which is about three miles across, unfathomable, it is said, but seems to have no communication with the sea. This deep-bedded, unruffled lake contains none of the finny tribes, but has on its bosom three small islets covered with trees, and forms a striking and beautiful contrast with the troubled ocean, whose roaring billows continually lash the vitrified, iron-bound coast of the rim on which the people reside. On this most unique island there are about eight hundred inhabitants, distinguished for simplicity of character, and their ready and thankful reception of the messengers of gospel truth. They have two chiefs, one of whom is designated *tui*, (king,) and the other *tui Niua*; (king of Niua;) both of them are Christians and class-leaders. (*See Waterhouse's Journal, Wesleyan Missionary Notices, March*, 1844, p. 486.)

THE FEEJEE ISLANDS.

The Feejee group is situated about three hundred and sixty miles north-west of the Friendly Islands, between the latitudes of 15° 30′ and 19° 30′ south, and the longitudes of 177° east and 178° west. It comprises one hundred and fifty-four islands, about one hundred of which are inhabited. The remaining islands are occasionally resorted to by the natives for the purpose of fishing, and taking *biche de mer*. There are also numerous reefs and shoals. Two are large islands, stretching north-east and south-west, nearly throughout the whole extent of the group; and are supposed to be each about three hundred miles in circumference.

So beautiful is their aspect on approaching them, that it is with difficulty one can bring his mind to a realizing sense of the well-known fact, that they are inhabited by a savage, ferocious, and treacherous race of cannibals. Each island has its own peculiar beauty; but the eye rests with most satisfaction on Ovalau, which has more of the appearance of civilization than the others: it is also the highest, most broken, and most picturesque. This island is eight miles in length, north and south, and seven in breadth, east and west. The valleys extend only a short distance into the interior; they are, however, exceedingly fertile, with a deep and rich soil, and are well cultivated.

Several islands in the group exhibit signs of craters; although the only place where there are any visible indications of volcanic heat, is Savusavu, on Vanua Levu, where there are hot springs. The peaks, however, are generally basaltic cones or needles, some of which rise to the height of several thousand feet, and no running stream of lava has been discovered on any of the islands. It may, consequently, be inferred that the date of the formation of these islands is more remote than that of the other groups of Polynesia. Volcanic conglomerate, tufa, and compact and scoriaceous basalts are found, of every texture and color, and in all states of decomposition. When decomposed, they afford a rich soil, which, clothed with a luxuriant foliage, covers the islands to their very tops, clinging to every point where it is possible for a plant to take root. This rich vegetation gives a degree of beauty to the aspect of the whole group that is scarcely surpassed in any part of the world.

The Feejee group is composed of seven districts, and is under as many principal chiefs; namely, Mbau, Rewa, Verata, Muthuata, Somosomo, Natasiri, and Mbua. All the minor chiefs on the different islands are more or less connected or subject to one of these: and as the one party or the other prevails in their wars, they change masters. War is the constant occupation of the natives, and engrosses all their time and thoughts. The introduction of fire-arms brought about a great change of power. This happened in the year 1809. A brig was wrecked on the reef off Nairai, which had both guns and powder on board. The crew, in order to preserve their lives, showed the natives the use of (to them) the new instrument. The crew joined the Mbau people, instructed them in the use of the musket, and assisted them in their wars.

The people are divided into a number of tribes, independent of, and often hostile to, each other. In each tribe, great and marked distinctions of rank exist. The classes which are readily distinguished are as follows:—1. Kings; 2. Chiefs; 3. Warriors; 4. *Matanivanua*, literally, "Eyes of the land:" they are the king's messengers; 5. Slaves (*kaisi.*) The last have nominally little influence; in this group, however, as in other countries, the mere force of numbers is sufficient to counterbalance or overcome the force of the prescriptive rights of the higher and less numerous classes. This has been the case at Mbau, where the people, at no distant period, rose against and drove out their kings.

The climate of the different sides of the islands may, as in all the Polynesian islands, be distinguished as wet or dry, the weather side being subject to showers, while to the leeward it is remarkably dry, and droughts are of long continuance. The difference in temperature is, however, small; on comparing a meteorological journal kept on the west side of Viti Levu with one kept at Levuka, in the island of Ovalau, it was found that at the same hours they stood within two degrees of each other. The appearance of vegetation shows this difference of climate more strongly than the thermometer; for, on the lee side, the islands have a barren and burnt appearance, while the weather sides exhibit a luxuriant tropical vegetation.

The winds from April to November prevail from the east-north-east to the south-east, at times blowing a strong trade wind. From November to April northerly winds are often experienced, and in the months of February and March heavy gales are frequent. They usually begin at the north-east, and pass round to the north-north-west, from which quarters they blow with most violence; then, turning to the westward, they moderate.

Earthquakes are not unfrequent: they generally occur in the month of February. Several shocks are often felt in a single night.

By observing the plants whose flowers succeed each other, the natives are guided in their agricultural occupations. The scarlet flowers of the *Erythrina Indica* mark the season of planting; and the natives, it is said, encourage the growth of this plant near the towns, for the purpose of pointing out the proper time for this important operation in agriculture. The labors of agriculture and the phenomena of vegetation serve as the foundation of their calendar, and furnish names to some of the months, or the portions into which they divide the year. Of these they reckon eleven. The first, which corresponds nearly to January, they call "Reeds blossom;" the second, "Build yam-houses;" the third, "Yams ripe;" the fifth, "Digging yams;" the sixth, "Weeding month;" the seventh, "Digging ground and planting." The month of June is known and established by the flowering of a vine that is found on the shore, *tom-bebe.*

Next to war, agriculture is the most general occupation of this people. To this they pay much attention, and have a great number of esculent fruits and roots which they cultivate, in addition to many spontaneous products of the soil.

Of the bread-fruit tree, they have nine different kinds, distinguished by fruits of different sizes and shapes, and the figure of their leaves. The general height of the bread-fruit trees is fifty feet, and some of the leaves are two feet in length. The varieties of the fruit in season follow each other throughout the year. March and April, however, are the months in which it is found in the greatest perfection.

They have five or six varieties of the banana. Of the plantain, there are three varieties cultivated to a great extent in Vanua Levu. The wild species of Tahiti and Samoa, called by the natives *fae,* is here cultivated, displaying its rich orange-colored fruit, densely set on large spikes; but is not found wild.

Of the cocoa-nut tree, there are at least two varieties, distinguished by the brown and red color of the nuts. The two varieties of the tree are much the same in appearance, and frequently grow to the height of seventy or eighty feet. It does not thrive higher than six hundred feet above the sea. All those above that height have a sickly appearance; and the lower it grows, even where its roots are washed by the salt water, the more prolific and flourishing it appears.

The papaw apple, (*Careca papaya,*) called *walete,* is in great abundance, but is not prized by the natives.

The *ivi,* (*Inocarpus edulis,*) called the Tahiti chestnut, produces a large nut that is eaten by the natives, and is the principal food of the mountaineers.

Shaddocks are in great abundance. Both the red and white kinds are indigenous.

The same bitter orange is found here as at the Samoan group. The trees grow to the height of forty feet. The lemon and sweet orange were introduced from Tahiti by Mr. Vanderford about the year 1823, and are called by the natives the "white man's orange."

There are several other fruits; as the *taruvou*, which is about the size of a plum; the *ndawa*, which is about the size of a hen's egg, flattened at both ends; it has a glutinous, honey-like taste, and is much esteemed both by the natives and whites. They have also a number of fruits which are only used in times of scarcity.

Pumpkins, cucumbers, cape gooseberry, guava, pine-apples, water-melons, and large red capsicums, are in abundance.

The chief proportion, however, of the food of the natives is derived from yams, of which they have five or six varieties. The season when they begin to plant their yams is pointed out by the blossoming of the Malay apple. This happens about the beginning of August. The yams are about six or eight months in coming to perfection, and the yam-digging season is in April or May. In some places the yam attains a very large size, as in Somosomo, where they have been seen four or five feet in length, and very farinaceous. In all parts of the group they are found in great plenty, and have already become an article of export; cargoes of them have been taken to Sydney with profit.

They have a great variety of roots, as *ivia*, which is peculiar to the island of Rewa. The people of this island, from possessing this root, it is said, never fear a famine. *Taro* is grown in vast quantities on the margin of streams. Arrowroot also is found in great abundance in a wild state. Sugar is somewhat cultivated by the Feejeeans. It grows wild in all parts of the islands. Tobacco is cultivated in large quantities, and smoked with avidity. They are exceedingly pleased with a gift of it; however small, it is always thankfully received. This is the prevailing taste throughout Polynesia; and the farther west, the more the natives seem to be addicted to its use. The cotton-tree grows to the height of fifteen feet, and produces a fine white cotton.

The soil of the islands consists of a deep loam, of a yellowish color, with a large proportion of decayed vegetable matter: combined as this is with a fine climate and abundance of water, it is no wonder that all the native plants, as well as those which have been introduced, should grow with luxuriance and be prolific. The reader will be enabled to form some idea of the rapidity of vegetation on these islands from the following:—Of turnips, radish, and mustard-seed, after being sown twenty-four hours, the cotyledon leaves appear above the surface. Melons, cucumbers, and pumpkins, spring up in three days; beans and peas make their appearance in four. In four weeks from the time of planting, radishes and lettuce are fit for use; and, in five weeks, marrowfat peas.

The climate of the Feejee Islands is well adapted to all the various tribes of tropical plants, and to not a few of those of the temperate zone; for many of the islands are of a mountainous character, and numerous localities present themselves adapted to the growth of the latter.

These islands were once covered with vegetation from the coral reefs to the top of their highest peaks; but below the elevation of one thousand feet on the leeward side of the large islands, the original vegetation has been, for the most part, destroyed by the fires which the natives use to clear their planting-grounds. The forest above that elevation, having escaped its ravages, forms umbrageous masses, when the underwood and herbaceous part of the vegetation disappear. As the ridges and summits are approached, the trees become more spare, giving an opportunity to the numerous species of ferns to receive both light and air. These are found in great quantities and varieties, both terrestrial and parasitical, intermingled with various forms of epiphytical orchideæ, and many mosses, with which the trees are decked.

The plants that strike the eye of a stranger visiting these islands, are those immediately above the high-water mark; namely, *Hibiscus tiliaceus, Barringtonia, Hermandia sonora, Erythrina Indica,* with rich yellow flowers; *Xylocarpus,* which has a large and very attractive-looking yellow fruit; a species of *Ixona* and a *Volkameria,* both with fragrant blossoms. The mangrove, (*tiri* of the natives,) which pushes its vegetation even into the salt water, and covers large tracts of coral reefs and muddy creeks, gives a beautiful appearance to the low and swampy ground. This plant not only thrives in salt water, but the young plants are found pushing themselves towards the sea, springing from chinks and cracks of the coral. They are frequently overflowed three or four feet at high water, but they nevertheless hold their place; and when they gain sufficient height, they again send forth their aerial roots, which, descending, soon give the parent stem sufficient support to withstand all the efforts of the surf to displace them.

The list of plants which have been collected in these islands, amounts to about six hundred and fifty species; and there is reason to conclude that many more remain to be discovered. This, however, cannot happen until the natives become more civilized, and there shall be more safety in wandering into the regions, which is now attended with much danger. Sandal-wood was formerly found in one part of Viti Levu; for the sake of which, the island was much resorted to by American vessels, &c. The supply is now, however, entirely exhausted; and the tree, it is said, comes to perfection in none of the other islands.

The population of these islands has been estimated at

300,000. This computation, however, proceeds upon the supposition that the interior of the islands is thickly inhabited, which seems very doubtful. There are circumstances which appear to warrant the supposition that the number of the population does not much exceed 200,000.

The Feejeans are generally above the middle height, and exhibit a great variety of figure. The chiefs are tall, well-made, and muscular; while the lower orders manifest a meagerness arising from laborious service and scanty nourishment. Their complexion, in general, is between that of the black and copper-colored races, although instances of both extremes are to be met with, indicating a descent from two different stocks. They are inferior to the natives of Tonga in beauty of person.

In the Tonguese there is a native grace, combined with fine forms, and an expression and carriage as if educated; whilst there is an air of power and independence in the Feejeeans, that makes them claim attention. They at once strike one as peculiar, and, unlike other Polynesian natives, they have a great deal of activity both of mind and body, which may be ascribed, in some measure, to their constant wars, and the necessity of their being continually on the alert, to prevent surprise. They are much more intelligent than those of other parts of Polynesia, and express themselves with great clearness and force. They excel the inhabitants of Tonga in ingenuity, as appears from their clubs and spears, which are carved in a very masterly manner, very neatly formed, and exceedingly ponderous; cloth beautifully checkered; variegated mats; earthen pots; wicker-work baskets, and other articles; all of which have a cast of superiority in the execution.

The faces of the greater number are long, with a large mouth, good and well-set teeth, and a well-formed nose. Instances, however, are by no means rare of narrow and high foreheads, flat noses, and thick lips, with a broad short chin; still, they have nothing about them of the negro type.

Their eyes are generally fine, being black and penetrating. The expression of their countenances is usually restless and watchful; they are observing and quick in their movements. Their hair is somewhat curly, and rather disposed to be woolly. Their whole external character, viewed generally, is fierce and warlike, rather than brave and noble. The natives of the different islands are of various sizes: some have their forms more fully developed than others. Those who have Tonga blood are designated the *Tonga-viti*, and are decidedly the best-looking of the natives. These are more numerous among the eastern islands than elsewhere, showing the effects of the intercourse.

They take great pains to spread out the hair into a mop-like form. The chiefs, in particular, pay much attention to the dressing of their hair; and for this purpose all of them have barbers, whose sole occupation is the care of their masters' heads. The duty of these functionaries is held to be of so sacred a nature, that their hands are *tabooed* (prohibited) all other employment. To dress the head of a chief occupies several hours; and the hair is made to spread out from the head on every side, often to a distance of eight inches. They are very careful not to crush these grand wigs. When they lie down they have wooden pillows to rest their heads on; these pillows are made of blocks hollowed out to hold the neck, so that the head hangs over, and their wigs are not injured. The beard, which is also carefully nursed, often reaches the breast; and when a Feejeean has these important parts of his person well dressed, he exhibits a degree of conceit that is not a little amusing.

The Feejeeans are extremely changeable in their disposition. They are fond of joking, indulge in laughter, and will at one moment appear to give themselves up to merriment, from which they in an instant pass to demon-like anger, which they evince by looks which cannot be misunderstood by those who are the objects of it. Their anger seldom finds vent in words, but has the character of sullenness. A chief, when offended, seldom speaks a word, but puts sticks in the ground, to keep the cause of his anger constantly in his recollection. By this the objects of it understand that it is time to appease him by propitiatory offerings, if they would avoid the bad consequences. When these have been tendered to the satisfaction of the offended dignitary, he pulls up the sticks as a signal that he is pacified.

The Feejeeans are described by one who had an excellent opportunity of observing their character, as addicted to stealing, treacherous in the extreme, and, with all their ferocity, cowards. The most universal trait of their character, is their inclination to lying. They tell a falsehood in preference, when the truth would better answer their purpose; and, in conversing with them, the truth can only be obtained by cautioning them not to talk like a Feejee man; or, in other words, not to tell any lies.

Covetousness is probably one of the strongest features of the Feejeean character, and is the incentive to many crimes. It has, however, been said, that a white man may travel with safety from one end of an island to the other, provided he has nothing about him to excite their desire of acquisition. This may be true; but it is impossible to say that even the most valueless article of our manufactures might not be coveted by them. With all this risk of being put to death, hospitable reception and entertainment in their houses is almost certain; and while in them, perfect security may be relied on.

The Feejeeans build the frames of their houses of the bread-fruit tree, and fill them in with reeds, whilst they cover the roof with a thatch of the wild sugar-cane. They are usually oblong in shape, and from twenty to twenty-five feet in length by fifteen in breadth. They have for the most part, two doors, and a fire-place in the centre, composed of a few stones. The sleeping-place is generally screened off, and raised about a foot above the other part of the floor. The furniture consists of a few boxes, mats, several large clay jars, and many drinking-vessels; the manufacture of pottery being extensively carried on by them.

Their domestic comforts appear much inferior to those of the Tonguese. They do not oil themselves; and to this may be ascribed the coarseness and harshness of their skin, which differs greatly from that of the Tonga people.

Their cannibal propensity is well known. They do not attempt to disguise it. The eating of human flesh is not confined to cases of sacrifice for religious purposes, but is practiced by them from habit and taste. There can be no question that, although it may have originated as a sacred rite, it is continued in the Feejee group for the mere pleasure of eating human flesh as food. Their fondness for it appears from the custom they have of sending portions of it to their friends at a distance, as an acceptable present; and the gift is eaten, even if decomposition has begun before it is received. So highly do they esteem this food, that the greatest praise they can bestow on a delicacy is to say, "It is as tender as a dead man." The bodies of enemies slain in battle are always eaten. David Whippy told Commander Wilkes that, on one occasion, he had seen upwards of twenty men cooked; and several of the white residents stated that they had seen bodies brought from such a distance as to be green from putrescence, and to have the flesh dropping from the bones, which were, notwithstanding, eaten with greediness and apparent pleasure. War, however, does not furnish enough to satisfy their appetites; stratagem and violence are resorted to for obtaining it. The cannibal propensity is not limited to enemies or persons of a different tribe, but they will banquet on the flesh of their dearest friends; and it is even related, that, in times of scarcity, families will make an exchange of children for this horrid purpose. The flesh of women is preferred to that of men; and they consider the flesh of the arm above the elbow, and of the thigh, as the choicest parts. The women are not allowed to eat it openly; but it is said that the wives of chiefs partake of it in private. It is also forbidden to the *kai-si*, or common people, unless there be a great quantity; but they have an opportunity of picking the bones. As a further instance of these cannibal propensities, and to show that the sacrifice of human life to gratify their passions and appetites, is of almost daily occurrence, a feast frequently takes place among the chiefs, to which each is required to bring a pig. On these occasions, Tanoa, king of Mbau, from pride and ostentation, always furnishes a human body. A whale's tooth is about the price they put on a human life, even when the party slain is a person of rank. This is viewed by the relatives of the victim as a sufficient compensation. It is therefore not to be expected, that a people who set so little value on the lives of their own countrymen, should much regard those of foreigners. Hence the necessity, while holding intercourse with them, to be continually guarded against their murderous designs, which they are always meditating for the sake of the property about the person, or to obtain the body for food. Several instances are related of crews of vessels visiting the islands having been put to death.

They are, moreover, a people extremely addicted to war. It is a Feejee maxim, that war and strife are the noble employments of men, and ease and pleasure worthy to be courted only by the weak and effeminate.

These islanders are also bold navigators, and make somewhat distant voyages; but, being unacquainted with the use of the compass, they are sometimes in danger of missing the place of their destination. They steer by the stars, and, when these are obscured, by the direction of the wind, which in tropical climates is pretty constant; when the wind changes, however, which sometimes happens, when it is their only guide, they steer a course very different from that which they intended, and are exposed to considerable dangers.

The religion of the Feejeeans, and the practices which are founded upon it, differ materially from those of the lighter-colored Polynesian people. The tradition given of the various races is singular, and not very flattering to themselves. All are said to have been born of one pair of first parents. The Feejeean was first born, but acted wickedly, and was black; he therefore received but little clothing. Tonga was next born; he acted less wickedly, was whiter, and had more clothes given him. White men, or *papalangis*, came last; they acted well, were white, and had plenty of clothes.

They have a tradition of a great flood or deluge, which they call *wailava-lavu*. Their account of it is as follows:—After the islands had been peopled by the first man and woman, a great rain took place, by which they were finally submerged; but before the highest places were covered by the waters, two large double canoes made their appearance; in one of these was Rokova, the god of carpenters, in the other Rokola, his head-workman, who picked up some of the people, and kept them on board until the waters had subsided, after which they were again landed on the island. The persons thus saved, *eight* in number, were landed at Mbenga, where the highest of their gods is said to have made his first appearance. By virtue of this tradition, the chiefs of Mbenga take rank before all others, and have always acted a conspicuous part among the Feejeeans. They style themselves *Ngali-duva-ki-langi*, that is, "Subject to Heaven alone."

The pantheon of the Feejee group contains many deities. "Many of the natives," says Mr. Hunt, in his Memoirs of Cross, "believe in the existence of a deity called Ovē, who is considered the maker of all men, and is supposed to reside in the heavens, some say in the moon. He is not worshiped, to my knowledge, by any of the Feejeans. Though he is the supposed creator of all men, yet different parts of the group ascribe their origin to other gods. A certain female deity is said to have created the Vewa people; and yet, if a child is born malformed, it is attributed to an oversight of Ovē." The god most generally known next to Ovē is Ndengei. He is worshiped in the form of a large serpent, alleged to dwell in a district under the authority of Mbau, which is called Nakauvandra, and is situated near the western end of Viti-Levu. To this deity they believe that the spirit goes immediately after death, for purification, or to receive sentence.

All spirits, however, are not believed to be permitted to reach the judgment-seat of Ndengei; for, upon the road, it is supposed that an enormous giant, armed with a large ax, stands constantly on the watch. With this weapon he endeavors to wound all who attempt to pass him. Those who are wounded dare not present themselves to Ndengei, and are obliged to wander about in the mountains. Whether the spirit be wounded or not, depends not upon the conduct in life, but they ascribe an escape from a blow wholly to good luck.

Besides the entire form of a serpent, Ndengei is sometimes represented as having only the head and half the body of the figure of that reptile, while the remaining portion of his form is a stone, significant of eternal duration.

No one pretends to know the origin of Ndengei; but many assert that he has been seen by mortals. He is reported to have appeared under the form of a man, dressed in *masi*, (white tapa,) after the fashion of the natives, on the beach, near Ragi-ragi. Hence he proceeded to Mbenga, where, although it did not please him, on account of its rocky shores, he made himself manifest, and thence went to Kandavu. Not liking the latter place, he went to Rewa, where he took up his abode. Here he was joined by another powerful god, called Warua, to whom, after a time, he consented to resign this locality, on the consideration of receiving the choicest parts of all kinds of food, as the heads of the turtle and pig, which are still held sacred.

Under this agreement he determined to proceed to Verata, where he has resided ever since, and by him Verata is believed to have been rendered impregnable.

Next in rank in their mythology, stand the two sons of Ndengei, Tokairambe and Tui Lakemba. These act as mediators between their father and inferior spirits. They are said to be stationed in the form of men at the door of their father's cabin, where they receive, and transmit to him, the prayers and supplications of departed souls.

The grandchildren of Ndengei are third in rank. They are innumerable, and each has a peculiar duty to perform, of which the most usual is that of presiding over islands and districts.

A fourth class is supposed to be composed of more distant relations of Ndengei. These preside over separate tribes, by whose priests they are consulted. They have no jurisdiction beyond their own tribe, and possess no power but what is deputed to them by superior deities.

Besides these benignant beings, the Feejeeans believe in malicious and mischievous gods. These reside in their hades, which they call *bulu*, (underneath the world.) Here reigns a cruel tyrant, with grim aspect, whom they name Lothia. Samuialo (destroyer of souls) is his colleague, and sits on the brink of a huge fiery cavern, into which he precipitates departed spirits.

These notions, although the most prevalent, are not universal. The god of Muthuata is called Radinadena. He is considered as the son of Ndengei. Here also Rokova, the god of carpenters, is held in honor; and they worship likewise Rokavoua, the god of fishermen.

The people of Lakemba believe that departed souls proceed to Namukaliwu, a place in the vicinity of the sea. Here they for a time follow the same employments as when in this life; after which they die again, and go to *bulu*, where they meet Samuialo. This deity is empowered to seize and hurl into the fiery gulf all those whom he dislikes,

On Kandavu they admit of no god appointed to receive departed souls, but suppose that these go down into the sea, where they are examined by the great spirit, who retains those he likes, and sends back the others to their native island, to dwell among their friends. Another belief is, that the departed spirit goes before the god Taseta, who, as it approaches, darts a spear at it. If the spirit exhibits any signs of fear, it incurs the displeasure of the god; but if it advances with courage, it is received with favor.

In Vanua-Levu, it is believed that the souls of their deceased friends go to Dimba-dimba, a point of land which forms Mbau Bay. Here they are supposed to pass down into the sea, where they are taken into two canoes by Rokavoua and Rokova, and ferried across into the dominions of Ndengei. When it blows hard, and there are storms of thunder and rain, the natives say that the canoes are getting ready.

Some few of the natives worship an evil spirit, whom they call *Roko-batin-dua*, "the one-toothed lord." He is represented under the form of a man, having wings instead of arms, and is provided with claws to seize his victims. His tooth is described as being large enough to reach above the top of his head. It is alleged he flies through the air, emitting sparks of fire. He is said to roast in fire all the wicked who appertain to him. Those who do not worship him call him Kalou-kana, or Kalou-du.

At Rewa, it is believed that the spirits first repair to the residence of Ndengei, who allots some of them to the devils for food, and sends the rest away to Nukulau, a small island off Rewa, where they remain until an appointed day, after which they are doomed to annihilation. The judgments thus passed by Ndengei seemed to be ascribed rather to his caprice, than to any desert of the departed soul.

Among other forms of superstition regarding spirits is that of their wandering about the villages in various shapes, and making themselves visible or invisible at pleasure. They believe there are particular places to which the spirits resort; and in passing these, they are accustomed to make propitiatory offerings of food or cloth. This form of superstition is the cause of an aversion to go abroad at night, and particularly when it is very dark.

It is also a general belief that the spirit of a celebrated chief may, after death, enter into some young man of the tribe, and animate him to deeds of valor. Persons thus distinguished are looked upon as highly favored; they, in consequence, receive great respect, and their opinions are treated with much consideration; besides which, they have many personal privileges.

The deities we have named are served by priests, called *mbete,* who are worshiped in buildings denominated *mbure,* or "spirit-houses." Of such buildings each town has, at least, one, and often several, which serve also for entertaining strangers, as well as for holding councils and other public meetings. In these *mbures* images are found; but, although much esteemed as ornaments, and held sacred, are not worshiped as idols. They are only produced on great occasions, such as festivals, &c.

The *mbete,* or priests, have great influence over the people, who consult them on all occasions, but are generally found in concert with the chiefs, thus forming a union of power which rules the islands. Each chief has his *mbete,* who attends him wherever he goes. The people are grossly superstitious, and there are few of their occupations in which the *mbete* is not more or less concerned. He is held sacred within his own district, being considered as the representative of the *kalou,* or "spirit."

The office of *mbete* is usually hereditary; but in some cases may be considered as self-chosen. Thus, when a priest dies without male heirs, some one who is ambitious to succeed him will strive for the succession. To accomplish this end, he will cunningly assume a mysterious air, speaking incoherently, and pretending that coming events have been revealed to him by the *kalou*, whom he claims to have seen and talked with. If he should have made a prediction in relation to a subject in which the people take an anxious interest, and with which the event happens to correspond, the belief that his pretensions are well-founded is adopted. Before he is acknowledged *mbete*, however, he is made to undergo a further trial, and is required to show publicly that the *kalou* is entering into him. The proof of this is considered to lie in certain shiverings, which appear to be involuntary, and in the performance of which none but an expert juggler could succeed.

On such occasions, the chiefs and people seat themselves in a semicircle; and when all is prepared, the principal chief, if the occasion be a great one, presents a whale's tooth. The priest receives this in his hand, and contemplates it steadily, with downcast eyes, remaining perfectly quiet for some time. In a few minutes distortions begin to be visible in his face, indicating, as they suppose, that the god is entering into his body. His limbs next show a violent muscular action, which increases until his whole frame becomes convulsed, and trembles as if under the influence of an ague-fit; his eye-balls roll, and are distended; the blood seems rushing with violence to and from his head; tears start from his eyes; his breast heaves, his lips grow livid, and his utterance confused. In short, his whole appearance is that of a maniac. Finally, a profuse perspiration streams from every pore, by which he is relieved, and the symptoms gradually abate. After this, he again sinks into an attitude of quiet, gazing about him from side to side, until, suddenly striking the ground with a club, he thus announces that the god has departed from him. Whatever the priest utters while thus excited, is received as a direct response of the gods to the prayers of those who make the offering on the occasion. The provisions of which the offering is composed (a hog, a basket of yams, and bananas) are now shared out, and *kava* prepared. These are eaten and drunk in silence. The priest partakes of the feast, and always eat voraciously, supplying, as it were, the exhaustion he has previously undergone. It is seldom, however, that his muscles resume at once a quiescent state; and they more usually continue to twitch and tremble for some time afterwards.

When the candidate for the office of *mbete* has gone successfully through such a ceremony, and the response he gives as from the god is admitted to be correct, he is considered as qualified to be a priest, and takes possession of the *mbure* (temple.) The individual chosen is always on good terms with the chief, and is but his tool. The purposes of both are accomplished by a good understanding between them. By the dexterity with which the *mbete* effect their juggling performances, they acquire great influence over the common people. When the chiefs are about to go to battle, or engage in any other important enterprise, they desire the priest to let the spirit enter him forthwith, making him at the same time a present. The priest speedily begins to shake and shiver, and ere long communicates the will of the god, which always tallies with the wishes of the chief.

The *mbete* are generally the most shrewd and intelligent members of the community; and the reasons for their intimate union with the chiefs are obvious.

The occasions on which the priests are required to shake, are usually of the following kinds: to implore good crops of yams and taro; on going to battle; for propitious voyages; for rain; for storms, to drive boats and ships ashore, in order that the natives may seize the property they are freighted with; and for the destruction of their enemies.

There is a very considerable difference between the opinions of the natives in the various clusters of the South-Sea Islands respecting the future existence of the soul. Whilst the Tonguese doctrine limits immortality to chiefs, matabooles, and at most to mooas, the Feejee doctrine extends it to all mankind, to all brute animals, to all vegetables, and even to stones and mineral substances. If an animal or a plant die, its soul immediately goes to *Bulu;* if a stone or any other substance is broken, immortality is equally its reward; moreover, artificial bodies have equally good luck with men, and hogs, and yams. If an ax or chisel is worn out or broken, away flies its soul for the service of the gods. If a house is taken down, or in any way destroyed, its immortal part finds a situation in the plains of Bulu. As a confirmation of this doctrine, the Feejee people show a sort of natural well, or deep hole in the ground, at one of their islands, across the bottom of which runs a stream of water, in which, they say, may distinctly be perceived the souls of men and women, beasts and plants, of stones, canoes, and houses, and of all the broken utensils of this frail world, swimming along into the regions of immortality.

The only general fact to be derived from the various opinions in relation to the spirits of the dead, is, that a belief in a future state is universally entertained by the Feejeeans. In some parts of the group, this has taken the following form, which, if not derived from intercourse with the whites, is at least more consistent with revealed truth than any of the notions previously mentioned. Those who hold this opinion say, that all the souls of the departed will remain in their appointed place, until the world is destroyed by fire, and a new one created; that in the latter all things will be renovated, and to it they will again be sent to dwell.

Their belief in a future state, guided by no just notions of religious or moral obligation, is the source of many abhorrent practices; among which are the custom of putting their parents to death when they are advanced in years, suicide, the immolation of wives at the funeral of their husbands, and human sacrifices.

Self-immolation is by no means rare. Wives are often

strangled, or buried alive, at the funeral of their husbands, and generally at their own instance. Cases of this sort have frequently been witnessed by the white residents. The sacrifice is not, however, always voluntary; but when a woman refuses to be strangled, her relations often compel her to submit.

Many of the natives desire their friends to put them to death to escape decrepitude, or immolate themselves with a similar view; and families have such a repugnance to deformed or maimed persons, that those who have met with such misfortunes are almost always destroyed.

When a native, whether man, woman, or child, is sick of a lingering disease, their relatives either wring off their heads, or strangle them.

It is among the most usual occurrences for a father or mother to notify to their children that it is time for them to die, or for a son to give notice to his parents that they are becoming a burden to him. In either case, the relatives and friends are collected, and informed of the fact. A consultation is then held, which generally results in the conclusion that the request is to be complied with; in which case, they fix on a day for the purpose, unless it should be done by the party whose fate is under deliberation. The day is usually chosen at a time when yams or taro are ripe, in order to provide for a great feast, called *mburua*. The fear of disgrace, and the miseries that are entailed on the old and helpless by their friends and relations, induce many to submit to be buried alive. Nothing strikes one more among a crowd of natives, than the absence of the aged.

Formal human sacrifices are frequent among them. The victims are usually taken from a distant tribe; and when not supplied by war or violence, they are at times obtained by negotiation. After being selected for this purpose, they are often kept for a time to be fattened. When about to be sacrificed, they are compelled to sit upon the ground with their feet drawn under their thighs, and their arms placed close before them. In this posture they are bound so tightly, that they cannot stir or move a joint. They are then placed in the usual oven upon hot stones, and covered with leaves and earth, where they are roasted alive. When the body is cooked it is taken from the oven, and the face painted black, as is done by the natives on festal occasions. It is then carried to the *mbure*, where it is offered to the gods, and is afterwards removed to be cut up and distributed to be eaten by the people.

Human sacrifices are a preliminary to almost all their undertakings. When a new *mbure* is built, a party goes out and seizes the first person they meet, whom they sacrifice to the gods; when a large canoe is launched, the first person, man or woman, whom they encounter, is laid hold of and carried home for a feast. Circumcision is practiced; their manner of performing the rite, however, is somewhat different from that of the Tonguese.

The Feejee mode of sending messages (*rongo*) is as follows: A chief, when he wishes to send one, gives the messenger as many reeds as the message is to contain separate subjects. These reeds are of different lengths, in order to distinguish them from each other. When the messenger arrives at his destination, he delivers the reeds successively, and with each of them repeats the purport of the part of the message of which it is the memorial. Such messages are carried and delivered with great accuracy; and the messengers, when questioned on their return, repeat them with great precision.

A reed is also used as the pledge on closing an agreement, and the delivery of it makes it binding. If a chief presents a reed, or sticks one in the ground, it is considered as binding him to the performance of his promise.

A formal declaration of war is made by an officer, resembling in his functions the heralds (*feciales*) of the Romans. Every town has one of these, who is held in much respect. When he repairs to the town of the adverse party, where he is always received with great attention, he carries with him an ava-root, which he presents to the chiefs, saying, "I bid you good-by, it is war." The usual answer is, "It is well, return home." Preparations are then made on both sides.

If one of the parties desires peace, they send an ambassador, who carries a whale's tooth as a token of submission. The victorious party often requires the conquered to yield the right of the soil, in which case the latter bring with them a basket of the earth from their district. The acceptance of this is the token of peace.

They keep their women in great subjection. They are not permitted to enter the *mbure.* Wives, like other property, may be sold at pleasure; and the usual price is a whale's tooth, or a musket. Those who purchase them may do with them as they please, even to knocking them in the head. The girls of the lower classes of a town, or *koro,* are entirely at the disposal of the chief, who may sell or bargain them away as he pleases. The women, in fact, are their beasts of burden, and are everywhere considered as an article of trade.

The island of Ovalau is the principal residence of the white men in the group, some of whom are married to native women, and have large families. Many of the whites on these islands are men of abandoned characters, whose bad example has had a pernicious influence on the natives. A white man, resident some years ago at Somosomo, was known to eat human flesh with as much avidity as any Feejeean cannibal.

The harbors are formed by the reefs; and but for these, there would be very few in the group. The remarkable peculiarity of these coral harbors is, that in gaining them it is but an instant from the time the sea is left, until security is found equal to that of an artificial dock. This is particularly the case with the harbor of Levuka, in Ovalau, which is safe, has good holding-ground, and is easy of access.

Mbau, the metropolis and imperial city of Feejee, is situated on a small island about two miles in circumference. It contains nearly one thousand inhabitants, most of whom are chiefs. The houses are of a very superior description.

According to the statements of the natives, the rivers of the two large islands, Viti-Levu and Vanua-Levu, are of considerable magnitude; by which they can pass in their canoes from one coast to the opposite. That on which Ba is situated is a very fine river, almost as wide as the Thames.

The coasts of the islands abound with excellent fisheries. The *biche-de-mer*, sometimes known as the *sea-slug*, is plentiful. This animal belongs to the genus *holothuria*, and, when prepared, finds a ready sale in the China market, where it is used as an ingredient in rich soups. Of the *biche-de-mer* there are several kinds, some of which are much superior in quality to the others. The most esteemed kinds are found on the reefs, in water from one to two fathoms in depth, where they are caught by diving. It is found in greatest abundance on reefs composed of a mixture of sand and coral. The *biche-de-mer* is rare on the southern side of any of the islands; and the most lucrative fisheries are on the north side, particularly on that of Vanua-Levu. A considerable trade in this article has been carried on by American vessels.

The sperm whales begin to frequent the seas around these islands in the month of July; are most plentiful in August and September; and continue about the reefs and islands four or five months. Such being the case, it seems remarkable that the natives, who value whales' teeth so highly, should have devised no means of taking the animal that yields them. Although daring navigators in other respects they manifest great difficulty in comprehending the mode of capturing whales. Their canoes are not adapted for this object, being easily overturned.

The hot springs in Savu-savu, already alluded to, are five in number, and occupy a basin forty feet in diameter.. The temperature of the water of these springs stands at from 200° to 210° They are used by the natives to boil their food, which is done by putting the *taro* or yams into the spring, and covering them up with leaves and grass. Although the water has scarcely any appearance of boiling before, rapid ebullition ensues. It gurgles up to the height of eight or ten inches, with the same noise as is made by a caldron when on the fire. *Taro*, yams, &c., that are put into it, are well done in about fifteen minutes. The mouths of the springs are from eighteen inches to two feet in diameter, and have apparently been excavated by the natives for their own purposes.

We cannot more appropriately close this description of the Feejee islands, than by the following remarks from Hunt's Memoirs of Cross, a volume to which we have often had to acknowledge our obligations:—

"It will at once occur to the reader, that there are many things in the religious views of the Feejee islanders which are favorable to their understanding Christianity. It is not difficult for them to conceive of the inspiration of the Scriptures. Their own prophets, priests, and poets, &c., are recognized as inspired persons. They may also comprehend the important distinction between an atoning sacrifice and a thank-offering. The absence of gross idolatry, and the acknowledged distinction between gods who were originally such and those who are only the spirits of men, is a knowledge of a spiritual world not without its use. At the same time it must be lamented that their worst crimes are sanctioned, and are continually promoted, by their divinities, who are not only cannibals and adulterers like themselves, but have pleasure in those that are such. Their religion only pertains to the body and the present life. It is amazing how this notion respecting it cleaves to them, even after they have renounced their former deities. You will hear

BOILING SPRINGS OF SAVU-SAVU.

them continually inferring the favor of God to them, from the health and strength of their bodies, notwithstanding they are living in enormous sin. Though they have some idea of a spiritual world, they find it very difficult to conceive of the spirituality of religion, and are very slow in learning that 'the kingdom of God is not meat and drink, but righteousness, peace, and joy in the Holy Ghost.'

"One remark more shall close this digression. It is this: The natives of the South-Sea Islands appear to be a people upon whom the 'mother of harlots' shall operate for the purposes of superstition and error. They would see no absurdity in worshiping the Virgin Mary, or any number of saints: a religion which consists chiefly in external ceremonies would exactly meet their views, and suit their natural taste. Pictures, images, &c., affect them exceedingly. Sacred days, things, persons, &c., would be readily countenanced: in short, a religion, however expensive, that would dispense with the strict morality of the New Testament, is certain of having free course among them. One thing would be difficult; namely, receiving the eucharist according to Romish views. The Feejeeans dare not even eat the shrine of their god: it would, therefore, be difficult to persuade them to eat the god himself. This they would consider the height of impiety.

"Surely the Protestant missionary societies ought to exert themselves to the utmost to take possession of the numerous groups of islands in the Pacific yet destitute of their agents. A great deal remains to be done. Nominal Christians are not unfit subjects for Popery; and many, very many, of the Christians of the South Seas are of this character, numerous groups being destitute of the means of religious instruction. Rome is exerting herself with new and increasing vigor in these parts; and we know not what the Head of the Church may permit as the punishment of our supineness and neglect. Unless we bestir ourselves, the probability is, that we shall have to convert many of the

South-Sea islanders from Popery instead of from heathenism, which is much more difficult and dangerous. The world must be converted to the truth: and who can think of the struggle between truth and Popery without thinking of the Inquisition and its tortures, public and private murders, wholesale butcheries, fire and fagot, together with all the hideous forms of death?

"We have no reason to expect that Popery will change. Babylon will fall; but it will fall as Babylon. She will retain her character to the last, and continue, as opportunity serves, to glut herself with the blood of the saints, until the 'mighty angel' shall proclaim her eternal ruin. The time to rescue ourselves, or rather our successors, from another sanguinary struggle with Popery, is now. Let Protestants, at any rate, do what lies in their power to secure the South Seas, which have evidently been placed in their hands. Where have missions succeeded as they have done here? and yet there are some of the finest groups without a single herald of the cross. I mention New-Guinea, New-Ireland, New-Britain, New-Hebrides, Solomon's Islands, and New-Caledonia.

"The following brief account of the islands mentioned above, is taken from the best sources the writer has met with. The accounts of many of the South-Sea Islands found in the common geographies are not to be depended on, and those in the narratives of voyagers are necessarily very imperfect: it is from the latter source that the following particulars are taken:—

"'New-Guinea, or Papua, is the largest mass of southern continent next to New-Holland. It is from twelve hundred to fourteen hundred miles in length, and varying from one hundred and fifty to two hundred miles in breadth, and is probably one of the finest countries in the world. There is abundance of pine, cocoa-nut trees, and bread-fruit trees. The inhabitants appear to be very rude; and from the circumstance of many of them building their houses on posts in the water, it would appear that they are frequently at war. Like the Feejeeans, they trade in sea-slug, or *biche-de-mer*, and tortoise-shell. But very little is known of the inhabitants, either as it respects their number or character.

"'New-Britain and New-Ireland are a series of groups of islands, beginning near the north-eastern boundary of New-Guinea, and ranging in a circuitous line parallel to New-Holland, and in the direction of New-Zealand. The inhabitants have been supposed to be of two kinds, the Malay and the Negro; but I imagine that visitors have been led into this opinion by the striking difference often to be seen between the chiefs and the common people,—a difference which I believe exists in most of the South-Sea islands. The difference in Feejee is very striking; more so, perhaps, among the female than the male part of the population; but it may be accounted for, without supposing them to be of different races. They have numerous temples, and a regular form of idolatrous worship.

"'Solomon's Islands. They were discovered by Nandana in 1567. The inhabitants appear to be much the same as the Feejeeans; but they are little known. Eighteen islands of considerable size have been named.

"'New-Hebrides are a group to the south of the last-mentioned. The northern islands were discovered by Quiros in 1606, and surveyed by Captain Cook. They have lately become famous by the murder of the missionary Williams, on one of them, named Erromanga. The inhabitants are said to be fierce and energetic, and are supposed to be two hundred thousand in number.

"'New-Caledonia is an island about two hundred and fifty miles long, and forms the southern termination of this great range of archipelago. The soil is very fertile. The inhabitants are reckoned at forty thousand. The manners and customs resemble those of the other islanders, so far as they are known.'"—*Memoir of the Rev. William Cross, by the Rev. John Hunt,* pp. 123–126.

LIST OF MISSIONARIES

APPOINTED TO THE FRIENDLY ISLANDS AND FEEJEE ISLANDS, FROM THE COMMENCEMENT OF THE MISSION.

FRIENDLY ISLANDS MISSION.

Date of Departure from England.

1817. Walter Lawry. Appointed to New South Wales. Proceeded to Tonga, July, 1822. Sailed from Tonga, October 3d, 1823, and arrived at Sydney, New South Wales, November 7th. Returned to England, 1824. Appointed to New-Zealand, 1843. At present General Superintendent of Missions in New-Zealand, and Visitor of the Missions in the Friendly Islands and Feejee Islands.

1821. Nathaniel Turner. Removed from New South Wales to Tonga, 1827. Appointed to Van-Dieman's Land, 1831. At present Missionary in Australia.

1824. John Hobbs. Removed from New-Zealand to the Friendly Islands, 1832. Returned to New-Zealand, 1838. Remains as Missionary in New-Zealand.

1825. April 27th. John Thomas. Returning home, 1850.

John Hutchinson. Removed from New South Wales to Tonga. Returned to New South Wales, 1828. Subsequently retired from the Mission.

1827. March 15th. William Cross. Removed to Feejee, 1835. Died, October 15th, 1842, at Somosomo, Feejee.

1830. Aug. 7th. James Watkin. Appointed to New-Zealand, 1838. At present Missionary in New-Zealand.

Aug. 7th. William Woon. Retired from Tonga, 1833. Remains as Missionary in New-Zealand.

Aug. 7th. Peter Turner. Remains as Missionary in the Friendly Islands.

1832. Oct. 22d. Charles Tucker. Returned to England, 1842. At present Minister in England.

Oct. 22d. David Cargill, M. A. Removed to Feejee, 1835. Visited England, 1841. Re-appointed to Friendly Islands, 1842. Died at Vavau, April 25th, 1843.

1834. Nov. 7th. Stephen Rabone. Remains as Missionary in the Friendly Islands.

1835. Oct. 13th. William A. Brooks. Removed to Van-Dieman's Land, 1840. Returned to England, 1843, and retired from the ministry.

1835. Oct. 13th. MATTHEW WILSON. Remains as Missionary in the Friendly Islands.

Oct. 13th. JOHN SPINNEY. Removed to Feejee, 1839, and from thence to New South Wales, in consequence of failure of health. Died at Sydney, February 10th, 1840.

1836. Oct. 7th. RICHARD BURDSALL LYTH. Removed to Feejee, 1839. Remains as Missionary at Feejee.

1839. Sept. 14th. FRANCIS WILSON. Died, March 4th, 1846, at Vavau, Friendly Isles.

Sept. 14th. GEORGE KEVERN. Returned to England, 1847. At present Minister in England.

Oct. 1st. WILLIAM WEBB. Remains as Missionary in the Friendly Islands.

1843. GEORGE MILLER. Received into the work in the Friendly Islands District. Remains as Missionary in the Friendly Islands.

1845. Oct. 18th. THOMAS WEST. Remains as Missionary in the Friendly Islands.

Oct. 18th. JOEL BATE. Returned to England, 1848, and retired from the ministry.

1846. Nov. 21st. THOMAS ADAMS. Remains as Missionary in the Friendly Islands.

Nov. 21st. GEORGE DANIEL. Remains as Missionary in the Friendly Islands.

Nov. 21st. WALTER J. DAVIS, *Mission-Printer*. Received on trial for the ministry. 1849.

Nov. 21st. RICHARD AMOS, *Training Master*.

1848. [Received into the work in the Friendly Islands District.] BENJAMIN LATUSELU, *Native Assistant Missionary* in the Friendly Islands.

FEEJEE MISSION.

1835 WILLIAM CROSS. Removed from Friendly Islands to Feejee. Died, Oct. 15th, 1842, at Somosomo, Feejee.

DAVID CARGILL, A. M. Returned from Feejee in 1841. Appointed to Friendly Islands, 1842. Died April 25th, 1843, at Vavau, Friendly Islands.

1838. April 21st. JOHN HUNT. Died, October 4th, 1848, at Vewa, Feejee.

April 21st. JAMES CALVERT. Remains as Missionary at Feejee.

April 21st. THOMAS J. JAGGAR. Retired.

1839. Richard B. Lyth. Removed from Friendly Isles to Feejee. Remains as Missionary at Feejee.

John Spinney. Removed to Australia, in consequence of failure of health, 1839. Died, February 10th, 1840, at Sydney.

Sept. 14th. Thomas Williams, 2d. Remains as Missionary at Feejee.

1844. John Watsford. Removed from Australia to Feejee. Remains as Missionary at Feejee.

David Hazlewood. Remains as Missionary at Feejee.

1846. Nov. 21st. John Malvern. Remains as Missionary at Feejee.

Nov. 21st. James Ford. Removed to New-Zealand in consequence of failure of health, 1848.

NOTES.

Note A, pages 86, 169.—*Conversion of Varani.*

The first event of much consequence that occurred in our little world during the past year, was a revival of spiritual religion in the mission families. For some time after our last district-meeting we were unusually dull in spiritual things. There was not so good a feeling in our native meetings as we had felt during the previous year. The Lord, however, was pleased to revive his work in our souls, principally by means of our English class-meetings. In many instances, we have felt much of the presence of God in these means of grace; and have thereby been strengthened for the performance of those duties which the great Head of the Church has called us to perform.

The result of this new baptism of the Spirit of Holiness was soon felt in our congregations, and among the people generally. Such is the connection between holiness and usefulness, and such our obligation to be entirely holy, that we may answer all God's designs with respect to others.

The conversion of Varani was an event we had long

prayed for, and, as you will see from our report, was evidently a work of God. He had long been convinced of the truth of Christianity, but was prevented from making a public profession of it, by his connection with Seru, the chief of Bau. He has long acted as the human butcher of this young chief, who is the Napoleon of Feejee. Varani learned to read during the early part of the year; and, what was of still more importance, he began to pray. Often would he retire into the woods to entreat God to have mercy on his soul. He was, in fact, so fully convinced of his need of a Saviour, that the name of Jesus became very precious to him. If he found, in the course of his reading, a passage which referred to the love of Christ to sinners, he would kiss the book for joy and thankfulness. Two or three Vewa men, who are truly devoted to God, attended to him continually. They frequently spent whole nights in reading, conversation, and prayer. Two of these young men were, at the time, students in our institution, and are both now in circuits. Varani would talk about nothing but religion, either to heathens or Christians. He was obliged to go to war; but it was exceedingly against his will. The Lord protected him in a remarkable manner. On one occasion he was ordered to attempt to set fire to a town, and had to approach very near to effect his purpose. He was perceived by the enemy, and a musket ball passed close to his head. He immediately fell on his knees to thank God for his deliverance, not merely from death, but from hell, which he feared much more than death; and which he fully believed would be his portion, if he died without making a public profession of Christianity. He felt that praying, while he still remained a heathen, would not do, but that he must take up his cross, and follow Christ, as his professed disciple, before he could hope for salvation. This conviction induced him, at length, to inform the chief of Bau that he must become a Christian. The chief, as might be expected, endeavored to dissuade him from taking such a step, at any rate, at present. This, however, only led Varani to exhort the chief to join him. Seru, the chief, knowing the firmness of the man, said no more; and thus gave an unwilling assent to what he evidently disapproved. All that remained was to take the important step, which is always done, if the person is able, by bowing the knee in the house of God at a public service. Providence, even as to the time of taking this step, evidently interposed. I had published, on the Sunday before Good-Friday, that we should observe that day as a *singa tambu*, "sacred day," in honor of the death of our Saviour. Varani heard of this, and determined that this should be the day of his decision. He came early in the morning to inquire when this day would return. I informed him, of course, not till another year. "Then," said he, "I'll become a Christian to-day." A short time after, the bell rang for the morning prayer-meeting, which Varani attended, and at which he publicly, to the great joy of many, bowed before Jehovah's awful throne.

I observed that the time of his embracing Christianity was evidently an interposition of Providence. Had he been an hour later, the Bau chiefs would have suspected him of having embraced Christianity because he was angry, and the whole affair would have had a political aspect, which it was very desirable to avoid. As soon as he returned from the chapel, a messenger came from Bau to inform him that Komaimbole, a chief of Lasakau, had been shot during the previous night. This chief, a man of great rank, had long lived under the protection of Varani, his own people being opposed to him. Finding it impossible to kill him while he remained at Vewa, they pretended to be reconciled to him, in order to persuade him to return to his own town. He went on a visit to them first, intending to remove his family after a while, believing, in part at least, their professions of friendship. One night he was invited to drink *yang-gona* with some other chiefs, and, it is said, was warned not to go. He, however, determined to go, as he had been invited. He had taken his bowl of *yang-gona*, and was sitting down to smoke a Feejeean cigar, when a person from without, employed by the chief who had invited him to his house, shot him in the breast. He fell at once, and his wicked host rose up with a hatchet-club to finish the murder. The father of the fallen chief, though an old man, rose up to intercede for his son; but the monster pushed the poor old man away, and, having dispatched his son, turned round and killed the father. It was all done in a few moments. They insulted the unfortunate chief by cutting his body with knives; after which he and his father were buried. This was a most cruel affair, and a great insult to Varani. If he had heard of it before he had embraced Christianity, probably it might have put him off for some time—at any rate it would have been the occasion of much misrepresentation and wrong feeling. It was very affecting to see the anxiety manifested by the wives of the murdered chief to be strangled. One of them came to Varani, while I was in his house, begging him to dispatch her. She, however, was too late. They were all spared, and are now all professing Christians, and some of them are meeting in class. Varani bore the painful event like a Christian, and has never mentioned it in my hearing in any way that indicates a desire to be revenged on his enemies.

In a day or two he was married to his principal wife, a fine woman. He began at once to meet in class. He is now baptized by the name of Elijah. He is humble, zealous, and conscientious. He is exceedingly diligent in all the means of grace, and not ashamed of confessing Christ before men. He has many enemies, and has need of our prayers and counsel. May God keep him, and make him as successful a servant of the Saviour, as he has been of the arch-murderer!—*Extract of a Letter from the late Rev. John Hunt, dated Vewa, September 12th,* 1845.

Note B, page 210.—*Obituary of the Rev. John Hunt.—Extracted from the Minutes of Conference*, 1849.

"John Hunt. This exemplary Christian missionary was born at Balderton, near Newark, June 13th, 1812. Early in life he had impressive views of the providence of God; but in the eighteenth year of his age he was deeply convinced of sin, trusted fully in Christ for his own personal salvation, and, 'being justified by faith,' had 'peace with God' through him. From the period of his conversion he was eminent for simple and devoted piety, sincerely seeking that the love of God might be perfected in him. He was a man of prayer; and assiduously diligent in searching the Scriptures. When he had acted in the capacity of a local preacher for about four years, he was accepted by the conference as a candidate for our missionary work, and placed as a student in the Wesleyan Theological Institution, at Hoxton; where he remained nearly three years, a pattern of attention, diligence, uniform Christian circumspection, and the kindest regard for his fellow-students. The progress which he made in his studies was great. He went as a missionary to Feejee in the year 1838, and entered upon his extraordinary labors in that distant land at the commencement of the year 1839. For nearly ten years he was indeed instant 'in season, out of season;' crowding the services of a long life within that comparatively short space. He speedily acquired a knowledge of the language. The translation of the New Testament, which has been published in Feejee, and which is pronounced to be a most excellent one, was made almost entirely by him. At the time when his last sickness came upon him, he was occupied in the translation of the Old Testament, which he hoped, if life were spared, to accomplish in five years. He also issued a course of Christian theology in short sermons, which has been of very great use, and of which a much enlarged edition was nearly finished at the time of his decease. To the spiritual work he was devoted with all his heart, and rejoiced in the abundant success which, by the visitations of the Holy Spirit, accompanied the preaching of the truth; of which a most cheering example occurred in a signal revival of religion at Vewa, in 1845. Mr. Hunt was a man of singular intellectual energy; of a piety which breathed the purest spirit of love to God and charity to man; of a patience which accumulated trials and difficulties failed to move; and of a 'calmly-fervent zeal' which, in sickness and in health, in strength and in weakness, was always in pursuit of its one grand object,—the salvation of man. The influence which he possessed over persons of all classes, natives and foreigners, was exceedingly large and beneficial; and his 'memory' among them is 'blessed.' Early in the month of August last he had a severe attack of illness, from which he never recovered. His death admirably corresponded to his life. 'You see a bright prospect before you?' said Mr. Lyth. He replied emphatically, 'I see nothing but Jesus.' On another occasion, Mr. Calvert read the seventeenth chapter of St. John's Gospel, and engaged in prayer. Towards the close, Mr. Hunt began to weep. At length he burst out, and cried, 'Lord, bless Feejee! Save Feejee! Thou knowest my soul loves Feejee. My heart has travailed in pain for Feejee.' Again he said, with great vehemence, 'O, let me pray once more for Feejee! Lord, for Christ's sake, bless Feejee! save Feejee! save thy servants! save thy people! save the heathen in Feejee!' 'How strange,' he said, at another time, 'I cannot realize that I am dying! and yet you all look as if I were. Well; if this be dying, praise the Lord!' Shortly before his death, he cried, 'O for one more baptism!' 'Have you had a fresh manifestation?' asked Mrs. Hunt. 'Yes!' he replied: 'Hallelujah! Praise Jesus!' He then added, 'I do not depend on this,' significantly shaking his head: 'I bless the Lord, I trust in Jesus.' Many expressions which he uttered are recorded by his affectionate colleagues and attendants, all indicating his love to the will of God, his entire trust in his Saviour, his freedom from all disturbance, and his triumphant victory over his last foe. He expired October 4th, 1848, in the thirty-seventh year of his age, and the tenth of his ministry."

NOTE C, page 436.—*Shipwreck of the late Rev. William Cross.*

THE necessity for the employment of a vessel, exclusively for the use of missionaries, so as to be always at their disposal when they remove from one island to another, and the sufferings which were endured by the early missionaries to the Friendly Islands, are so strikingly illustrated by Mr. Cross's narration of his shipwreck, and the death of his wife whilst he was endeavoring to sustain her in his arms, that we cannot forbear adding an extract from it. He says:—

"January 7th, 1832. We left Nukualofa in a large canoe, belonging to Tubou, to proceed to our new station at Vavau. We rose at four in the morning, to prepare for sailing, and proceeded to the canoe between six and seven o'clock. It was an interesting season. Many surrounded us, weeping because of our departure. Having been at Nukualófa more than four years, the people had acquired a strong attachment to us. Two smaller canoes were to accompany us; but as we were detained by the lading of our boat, they sailed about an hour earlier. We put to sea, and for a few hours went forward with a fair and moderate wind, although there was a heavy swell, which increased as the wind became more strong. This occasioned the breaking of the yard, and shortly after of the mast, which happened about noon. The sail was immediately taken down, and another smaller set. By the time these arrangements were completed, we had lost sight of the two canoes. As the evening advanced, the sailors were anxiously looking out for land. Night, however, came on, but no land appeared. The men having toiled hard all day, and provisions being scarce, many of them slept through weariness; and those whose anxiety for the safety of the vessel kept them awake, were unable to manage her; so that we did not get on. We were driven hither and thither till break of day; but no land appeared till about an hour after sunrise. The people fearing the wind might change, and thus prevent us reaching the island before dark, inquired if they might prepare a small mast and yard. I said, 'If you cannot reach the island without working, you must do so, as it is lawful to work on the Sabbath-day to save life.' They immediately began to prepare another sail, and then made towards the land. We arrived about noon, and found it was one of two uninhabited islands called Hunga Tonga, and Hunga Haabai. On approaching the island, we found it impossible to land, on account of the steepness of the rocks and the heavy swell of the sea. After deliberating for some time as to what we should do, it was determined to attempt to return to Tongataboo. In order to lighten the canoe, the mast and part of the yard were thrown into the sea. The wind now became favorable, blowing from the north; and the canoe being lighter, there was less motion. My dear wife and I took a little refreshment, both of us being very faint. I had not taken any food for upwards of thirty hours, and Mrs. Cross had only tasted a little cocoa-nut milk. What added to the weakness of the latter was, that she had been very ill on the previous Saturday. However, the wind being favorable, we made way, and sighted one of the Tonga isles, called Atata, before sunset. This occasioned a general thanksgiving. The people expected soon to reach this island, which was not more than seven miles from Tongataboo, and then to proceed homeward on Monday. By nine o'clock we were not distant more than three or four miles. But as the moon went down, the wind changed, and blew tremendously against us. The people immediately took down the sail, and had scarcely reached their paddles, when the canoe was driven with fearful violence on the reef, and began to break up. Joseph, a native teacher, came to me and said, in the native tongue, 'Mr. Cross, be strong our mind toward God: we are all dead.' We committed ourselves to God, and in a few minutes were washed off the canoe into the sea, and the boat was immediately dashed to pieces. I had my arms round Mrs. Cross, nor did I let her go. The water was six or seven feet in depth. Several times we rose to the surface, but were as often overwhelmed by the surf. I continued to hold my dear wife with my right arm, while my left was employed in catching at poles and broken pieces of the canoe, by which means we had an opportunity of breathing. No word of complaint or fear escaped her lips; but she several times said, 'Lord, have mercy upon us! Lord, deliver us in this our time of need!' I said, 'Look to the Lord, my love; we are both going to heaven together.' A few more seconds, and she spoke no more. I still clasped her with my right arm, was perfectly recollected, and expected in a few moments to be in heaven with her: but the Lord, contrary to my expectation, made a way for my escape.

"A short time after the spirit of Mrs. Cross had fled, I found myself near to some boards, part of the deck of the canoe. My strength was nearly exhausted, but I still held the body of my dear wife. One of our people, a Feejeean, a member of our society in Tongataboo, then discovered me, and, taking me by the hand, kept me close to the boards as they were driven about in the water. I became very weak; but another of our people assisted me to get on the boards. Being unable any longer to take care of the body of Mrs. Cross, I desired Jonathan, the Feejeean, to make it fast to the piece of the wreck upon which they had placed me; which was done. By this time several parts of the canoe were lashed together, forming a raft, and upwards of twenty persons seated thereon. We were then driven about we knew not whither. The general expectation was, from the course of the wind, that if the boards held together, we should be driven to Hihifo, which is about eight miles from the place where we were. In about two hours after the canoe had broken up, to our great joy, we found ourselves drifted to an uninhabited island, called Tokeloke. We might have been driven above or below it; but such was the goodness of God, we were taken against it. It was difficult to land, on account of the sharp rocks that hung over the sea, and the dashing of the waves; but, through divine mercy, all who were on the raft got safe ashore. I shall not soon forget how eagerly the men caught hold of a tree which overhung the sea, to which they tied the raft. Some climbed up, and these assisted others, so that ultimately we were all saved from a watery grave. But the body of my dear wife was not to be found. Being safe on land, the natives with much difficulty kindled a fire, and warmed a cocoa-nut for me. They likewise made a little shed with some branches of the cocoa-nut tree and a mat. Though more than twenty persons landed by means of the raft, this was but a small number out of seventy, which was the number in the canoe. We were much concerned respecting the others, and felt exceedingly glad as one and another was driven to the island, some on boards, others by means of a paddle, and two on a gate which we were taking to Vavau. The fire we had kindled was also of great assistance to them in finding the landing-place. During the night one man reached the shore whose sister had perished. He had but recently made a profession of Christianity, and was ill-prepared to bear such a trial. The poor fellow threw himself upon the ground, and roared as one deranged. Another individual said to me, 'I was much afraid of dying without having worshiped God with all my heart, and I long to get home that I may do so.'

"I now wished much to be at Nukualofa, and consulted the men about it, urging them to attempt to proceed on the raft, as I thought, if I remained another night on the island, I also should die. But the people being all very feeble, and the wind blowing a gale, none were willing to venture with me, fearing we should lose our lives in the attempt. The wind became more moderate about noon: we were afterwards visited by four men in a small canoe from Hihifo. I asked them if they would venture to take me to Nukualofa, promising to reward them well. They consented, and I was soon in the canoe; but such was the agitated state of the sea, that in two or three minutes the boat was overturned. As there was only five feet depth of water, I remained in the sea until the people emptied the canoe, and then got into the canoe again. Had the canoe upset in deep water, in all probability we should have been drowned. It was now agreed that one of the men belonging to the canoe should remain on the island, and the others proceed with me, the boat being safer with only four persons in her. It being low water, they were obliged to put me ashore about four miles from the mission-premises; which distance, though I was in a very enfeebled condition, the Lord enabled me to walk. When I had proceeded about two miles, I was overtaken by a messenger, sent to inform Tubou that the body of Mrs. Cross had been found at Hihifo. As soon as I reached home, a number of men were sent to convey the body, while Mr. Thomas directed the carpenter to make a coffin. After taking some refreshment, I, with a sad heart, retired to rest.

"On Tuesday, January 10th, I was very weak in body; but was able to be present at the funeral. I was considerably bruised, but not so much as others of my companions: and, considering my situation, it is astonishing that I did not suffer more.

"The total loss of life connected with this melancholy event, is fourteen men and five children. The greater part of my books, furniture, and wearing apparel, a number of useful articles, together with a considerable quantity of mission property, are lost. Of my property I think but little; my greatest loss is the partner of my life. We had enjoyed each other's society thirteen years; and though we have always been happy during our union, yet I think we have been increasingly so during the past year. Mrs. Cross had long lived in the enjoyment of the favor of God, and could daily look to him as her reconciled Father through faith in our Lord Jesus Christ. She is now, I doubt not,

'Far from a world of grief and sin,
With God eternally shut in.'"

Hunt's Memoirs of Mr. Cross.

THE END.

BOOKS PUBLISHED BY LANE & SCOTT,

200 Mulberry-street, New-York.

[A discount of 15 per cent. allowed to wholesale purchasers.]

Kidder's Brazil.

Sketches of Residence and Travels in Brazil, embracing Historical and Geographical Notices of the Empire and its several Provinces. With illustrations. By Rev. Daniel P. Kidder, D. D.

12mo., 2 vols., pp. 369, 404. Sheep $1 50

Those who wish to form a correct idea of the actual state of society in the Brazilian empire must read Mr. Kidder's book.—*London Sentinel.*

Destined to be considered as a standard work in the literary communities both of Europe and America.—*Christian Advocate and Journal.*

As a contribution to the literature of our age and country, the work is deserving a cordial reception. It will live longer than its author.—*Methodist Quarterly Review.*

The work is a veritable and valuable history of that important empire, of which, hitherto, but little has been known. The author's skill in description is great. . . . His style is easy, flowing, and perspicuous.—*New-York Commercial Advertiser.*

From these volumes it would not be difficult to select specimens of brilliant descriptions, and some episodes of stirring narrative. We can call to mind no book of travels in which the historical portions are more wisely interspersed so as to satisfy reasonable curiosity, and yet avoid tedious annals. As a whole, the work is worthy of a place among the more elevated productions of our national literature.—*Princeton Review.*

The very best work extant on an empire destined to play no unimportant part in the world's fortunes. The volumes are, as a whole, lively, entertaining, instructive, and truthful.—*London Atlas.*

The research is accurate, and the topics are various, so that the reader will be carried on with a constantly recurring novelty that will never fail to create the greatest interest as he progresses.—*Western Christian Adv.*

The author, with a keen relish for the beautiful in nature, and a chastened, but occasionally playful fancy, has given to his sketches a permanent interest.—*Columbian Magazine.*

Martyrs of Bohemia.

The Martyrs of Bohemia; or, brief Memoirs of John Huss and Jerome of Prague.

18mo., pp. 237. Muslin.................................... $0 25

The following pages depict great men—nature's noblemen—living and acting amid stirring scenes and the conflict of great principles.—*Author's Pref.*

A thrilling record of faithfulness and constancy even in the flames of persecution. No one can read this volume without interest and profit.—*Descriptive Catalogue.*

Medhurst's China.

Medhurst's State and Prospects of China.

18mo., pp. 272. Muslin $0 30

The work . . . . is one of the best which has been written upon the Celestial Empire. . . . The principal facts in reference to China are here stated in a manner which will be interesting to youth.—*Western Christian Advocate.*

The present volume is carefully compiled, and in no other book of the same size will the reader be able to obtain more correct and useful information respecting China.—*Descriptive Catalogue.*

BOOKS PUBLISHED BY LANE & SCOTT,

200 Mulberry-street, New-York.

[A discount of 15 per cent. allowed to wholesale purchasers.]

Women of the Bible.

The Women of the Bible. By CHARLES ADAMS.

12mo., pp. 225. Muslin **$0 40**

Rev. Charles Adams has aimed to write a sober, faithful book, keeping his eye upon recorded facts and incidents, and restraining all undue license of the imagination.—*Christian Advocate and Journal.*

In this book, the author has sought to contemplate woman precisely as the inspired pen has represented her, so far as she has arisen to view in the divine history of God's providential and gracious dispensations to mankind, and so far as that pen may have sketched more didactically her true position and duties.—*Introduction.*

Peeps at Nature.

Peeps at Nature; or, God's Work and Man's Wants. With Illustrations.

18mo., pp. 526. Muslin **$0 60**

It is an interesting production for the tender mind, besides being a beautiful book for a gift. I love such books. They bring the child's mind in sweet and reverent communings with nature's God.—REV. F. G. HIBBARD.

A very fine Sunday-school book. These conversations on natural science contain all the rudiments of natural theology, and yet in a style so clear and so simple, as to captivate the juvenile mind.—*Northern Christian Adv.*

The whole have the same design, to furnish interesting information on natural science to the young.—*London Child's Companion.*

Roland Rand.

Roland Rand; or, God's Poor. By MRS. C. M. EDWARDS. With Illustrations.

18mo., pp. 131. Muslin **$0 20**

We have read it with great profit and delight, and we think that he who can read it without feeling prompted to nobler action, and without moistened eyes, has but little generous emotion or philanthropy.—*Illinois Christian Advocate.*

The design of this narrative is to show the triumph of virtue over vice, and the necessity of active, energetic effort on the part of the disciples of Christ. —*Author's Preface.*

Ancient Egypt.

Ancient Egypt: its Monuments and History.

18mo., pp. 214. Muslin **$0 25**

To the youthful student of sacred history this work will afford a key to many of those beautiful figurative expressions used by inspired writers in the Old Testament. The manners and customs of the ancient Egyptians are ably delineated, and cannot fail to afford profit and instruction. It . . . . will make an agreeable companion during an idle hour, or a leisure moment.—*Christian Advocate and Journal.*

An account of one of the most ancient and interesting countries of the world. It furnishes a topographical description of Egypt, . . . its history, especially as connected with the Scriptures; . . . and illustrations of the Bible, derived from the whole history.—*London Tract Magazine.*

BOOKS PUBLISHED BY LANE & SCOTT,

200 Mulberry-street, New-York.

[A discount of 15 per cent. allowed to wholesale purchasers.]

Merchant's Daughter.

The Merchant's Daughter, and other Narratives. By the Rev. J. T. Barr, Author of "Recollections of a Minister," "Memorials of Mercy," etc.

18mo., pp. 228. Muslin **$0 25**

A series of sketches for the young, illustrating the fatal consequences of sin and the happy effects of true piety even in this life. Extraordinary as some of the incidents related in this volume are, every one of them is a well-authenticated fact. Truth is indeed stranger than fiction. The book proves a valuable addition to that array of good books for the young furnished by the Methodist Book Concern.—*Methodist Quarterly Review.*

These deeply-interesting sketches, the author assures us, are not narratives of imaginary events, but a faithful record of authenticated facts. It forms a most attractive volume.—*Christian Advocate and Journal.*

Here is a new book of thrilling interest. It is from the pen of a Wesleyan minister in England. It contains a series of most affecting narratives of fact, well calculated to arouse the caution of young persons of both sexes, and to admonish them to tread carefully in

"Life's devious way."

It cannot fail to be popular and useful.—*Sunday School Advocate.*

English Country Pictures.

English Country Pictures; or, Drawing without a Pencil. With numerous Engravings. By Old Humphrey.

18mo., pp. 182. Muslin **$0 25**

A series of sketches of home and country scenes in merry England, by a well-known writer.—*Methodist Quarterly Review.*

Here we have twenty-four graphic pictures of English life by "Old Humphrey," drawn in his best style. . . . No recommendation of this work is needed at our hand. The interest of the stories is well sustained, and the moral lessons inculcated important and practical.—*Christian Advocate and Journal.*

Here are pictures of farm-houses, farm-yards, cottages, fields, &c., . . . and other rural scenes . . . . which cannot fail to interest by their descriptions, and do good to the reader by the good advice which is judiciously interwoven.—*London Child's Companion.*

Mines and Mining.

Mines and Mining.

18mo., pp. 212. Muslin **$0 25**

After a general view of mines, the writer proceeds to describe the great mining districts, and the processes of working these artificial excavations, together with the various minerals and metals raised from them, and closes with a chapter on the incidents and perils of mining. It forms a very readable and instructive volume.—*London Visitor.*

This is an excellent book, containing much important scientific information, in a condensed and popular form. In the fullness, extent, and variety of its contents, it more than fulfills the promise of its title. The reader will not only learn from its pages many interesting and useful facts about miners and mining, but may also acquire . . . . a respectable acquaintance with metallurgy and mineralogy.—*Christian Advocate and Journal.*

www.ingramcontent.com/pod-product-compliance
Lightning Source LLC
LaVergne TN
LVHW021321110826
845150LV00003B/634

* 9 7 8 1 4 2 5 5 5 6 7 2 3 *